Briefs and Beyond

ASPEN COURSEBOOK SERIES

Briefs and Beyond

PERSUASIVE LEGAL WRITING

Mary Beth Beazley

Professor of Law
William S. Boyd School of Law
University of Nevada, Las Vegas

Monte Smith

Assistant Clinical Professor of Law
Michael E. Moritz College of Law
The Ohio State University

Wolters Kluwer

Published by Wolters Kluwer in New York.

Wolters Kluwer Legal & Regulatory U.S. serves customers worldwide with CCH, Aspen Publishers, and Kluwer Law International products. (www. WKLegaledu.com)

Cover image: Photograph by Hakinmhan/Shutterstock.com

To contact Customer Service, e-mail customer.service@wolterskluwer.com, call 1-800-234-1660, fax 1-800-901-9075, or mail correspondence to:

Wolters Kluwer
Attn: Order Department
PO Box 990
Frederick, MD 21705

Printed in the United States of America.

1 2 3 4 5 6 7 8 9 0

ISBN 978-1-5438-1391-3

Library of Congress Cataloging-in-Publication Data

Names: Beazley, Mary Beth, 1957- author. | Smith, Monte G., author.
Title: Briefs and beyond : persuasive legal writing / Mary Beth Beazley
    (Professor of Law, William S. Boyd School of Law, University of Nevada,
    Las Vegas), Monte Smith (Assistant Clinical Professor of Law, Michael E.
    Moritz College of Law, The Ohio State University).
Description: New York : Wolters Kluwer, [2021] | Series: Aspen coursebook
    series | Includes index. | Summary: "Law school book for courses on
    persuasive or advanced legal writing"—Provided by publisher.
Identifiers: LCCN 2020053171 (print) | LCCN 2020053172 (ebook) | ISBN
    9781543813913 (paperback) | ISBN 9781543823226 (ebook)
Subjects: LCSH: Legal composition | Legal briefs—United States. | Forensic
    orations—United States.
Classification: LCC KF250 .B383 2021 (print) | LCC KF250 (ebook) | DDC
    808.06/634—dc23
LC record available at https://lccn.loc.gov/2020053171
LC ebook record available at https://lccn.loc.gov/2020053172

About Wolters Kluwer Legal & Regulatory U.S.

Wolters Kluwer Legal & Regulatory U.S. delivers expert content and solutions in the areas of law, corporate compliance, health compliance, reimbursement, and legal education. Its practical solutions help customers successfully navigate the demands of a changing environment to drive their daily activities, enhance decision quality and inspire confident outcomes.

Serving customers worldwide, its legal and regulatory portfolio includes products under the Aspen Publishers, CCH Incorporated, Kluwer Law International, ftwilliam.com and MediRegs names. They are regarded as exceptional and trusted resources for general legal and practice-specific knowledge, compliance and risk management, dynamic workflow solutions, and expert commentary.

To David Rosmarin, Kai Rosmarin, and Charlie O'Hara, who have nearly doubled the size of our family, and increased our love and joy a hundredfold.
Mary Beth

*To Kay Bork, Donita Hill, and Sharon Stone, three extraordinary high school teachers who changed the course of my life by convincing me that working harder felt better than accepting good enough. I was privileged to be a high school student during an era when many of the very brightest and most capable women chose teaching as a profession. These three women could have done **anything**. Their choices may have been narrower than they would be today, but they did not let any limitations stop them from rising high and leaving a legacy that will live on and on. I hope that I do them justice.*
Monte

CHAPTER THREE

THE MOTION MEMO AND PERSUASIVE WRITING AT THE TRIAL LEVEL   33

CHAPTER SIX

USING CASES EFFECTIVELY 141

CHAPTER SEVEN

PERSUASION WITH STATUTES AS AUTHORITY 171

CHAPTER TEN

FORMAL REQUIREMENTS IN APPELLATE BRIEFS AND MOTION MEMOS   235

CHAPTER ELEVEN

ORAL ARGUMENT   297

CHAPTER FOURTEEN

LOGOS, PATHOS, ETHOS, TYPOS: WRITING AND DESIGNING A READER-FRIENDLY DOCUMENT   375

CHAPTER FIFTEEN

EVERYTHING ELSE   403

How to Use the Samples in This Book

1. *The part of the text that is not samples is not written in formal legal writing style, so don't imitate that style when you write briefs and memos.* Legal writing teachers write comments on student papers all the time, and that's the writing style we've used here. We hope it communicates effectively, but we were not trying to sound like lawyers, or even grown-ups, so you shouldn't imitate that style when you are trying to write like a lawyer.

2. *Don't imitate the samples slavishly.* Some samples are bad on purpose, and some are partly good and partly bad. If you ask the question, "Can I imitate this sample?," the answer is the answer you hear all the time in law school: "it depends." As you know, legal readers need different information depending on their role, on the relevant legal issue, and on many other factors. Some techniques are great in a motion brief but not in an appellate brief, and vice versa. Some techniques are great for one client's problem but not for another client's problem; some are appropriate for a federal law legal issue but not for a state law question of fact. So when you are debating whether to imitate a sample, consider whether you are in the same rhetorical situation. And by "rhetorical situation" we mean: why you're writing, who you're writing to, the role you are writing in, and what you're writing about.

3. *Don't rely on the law we cite in the samples.* We based almost all of the samples on realistic legal issues, but we didn't update things to make sure the law was still valid. And when we had to choose between using the law precisely and making the sample a useful sample, we went with making a useful sample. Some of the law is obviously fake; you may see us citing to the fake state of Vanita and the fake regional reporter of "Region East, Second Series," abbreviated "R.E.2d." Even when we cite to seemingly real cases, they—or the law we reference—may be fake or out of date. So if you find yourself addressing a legal issue that one of our samples addresses, don't rely on the sample. If our sample gives you a hint as to the relevant law, wonderful—but do your own research.

Online Appendices are available at **www.wklegaledu.com/ Beazley-PersuasiveLegalWriting**

We would like to recognize and thank the many people who helped us as we worked on this book. We have been working on it, in various iterations, for several years, and the list is long:

Several sets of students at both Ohio State and Boyd Law at UNLV have used versions of the text in classes taught by both of us. They have been patient and have provided helpful feedback. We want to thank them especially.

Six anonymous reviewers of a draft of this book provided enormously helpful suggestions, nearly all of which we have attempted to incorporate or address in this final version. We hope that we would have been as careful and thorough, and we hope that they recognize their contributions.

We acknowledge and are grateful to Professor Sarah Rudolph Cole for her insights and guidance on trends in arbitration briefs as we were writing Chapter 3.

Mary Beth acknowledges her research and teaching assistants at Boyd over the years, including David Chavez, James Puccinelli, Taylor Buono, Hannah Nelson, Rachel Howard, and Allison Hedrick. She is also immensely grateful for the generous research support of Dean Dan Hamilton and the Boyd School of Law at UNLV. Joining the Boyd faculty remains the best decision of her professional life.

Monte acknowledges that Ohio State's Moritz College of Law encouraged his work on this book through a summer research grant. He is grateful for that support.

Where applicable, we have used charts and other materials from another text authored by Mary Beth Beazley: A Practical Guide to Appellate Advocacy (Aspen Coursebook Series), 5th Edition, 2019. Reprinted with permission by Wolters Kluwer. We thank Wolters Kluwer for its permission.

Finally, we both acknowledge Jessica Barmack of The Froebe Group, and Justin Billing of Wolters Kluwer Legal Education, for their patient guidance and gentle prodding throughout this process. The diplomatic corps may be calling.

Briefs and Beyond

CHAPTER ONE

An Introduction to Persuasive Legal Writing

1.1. Most Legal Arguments Are Written Arguments

  1.1.1. Foundations of Formal Rhetoric: Logos, Pathos, Ethos

  1.1.2. Positions of Emphasis

  1.1.3. Narrative Reasoning

1.2. Conclusion

Imagine that you are a law clerk for a federal judge. It's the end of a long day, but before you go home, you have to read the opening briefs on a case that the judge will be hearing next week. She wants to meet with you about the case tomorrow morning, so you have to read the briefs tonight. You take both briefs and flip to their tables of contents, knowing they will give you an overview of the arguments. We've reproduced the first page of each table of contents below, but with nonsense words instead of actual text. We want you to look at just the way the information is laid out on the page. Which one looks more appealing? Which one would you want to read first?

If you're like most people, you would want to read the appellee's brief (on the right) first. The use of white space and the alignment of the text makes the writing easy to read. The dense layout of the appellant's brief is intimidating, and the lack of white space and inconsistent formatting sends the signal that this writer doesn't care much about the reader. The appellee's table of contents sends the message that this brief was written by a thoughtful writer who cares about the reader. Before you begin reading, you are likely to feel more positively about the appellee's argument.

The decisions each of these writers made are *document design* decisions. We won't be talking in detail about document design until Chapter Fourteen, but we want you to learn one of its lessons now: good legal writers understand how their readers feel about reading, and all of the writers' decisions — even seemingly unimportant ones like the format of a table of contents — make their documents easier to read and understand.

1.1. MOST LEGAL ARGUMENTS ARE WRITTEN ARGUMENTS

Many law students first got interested in going to law school when they saw lawyers in movies or on television presenting legal arguments. When talking to judges, juries, or opposing counsel, these lawyers are almost always on their feet, making these arguments seemingly off the top of their heads. You've probably already learned that effective lawyers don't usually argue that way. They spend a lot of time researching and reading about how the law applies to their clients' facts before they present a legal argument.

Most lawyers spend a lot more time arguing on their keyboards than on their feet. They need to think on their feet, of course, for oral arguments, and for mediation and negotiation. But most legal problems need lawyers who can argue in writing. Arguments in writing are more efficient: we read words faster than we hear them. They also allow asynchronous communication, and they're more permanent.

This book is about how to make legal writing persuasive. You've probably already learned how to write objective legal analysis, and that's great. The more you know about objective legal writing, the more you know about persuasive legal writing.

The most important aspect of persuasive legal writing is the legal writing itself, and you've already studied how to make legal writing effective: the accurate identification of legal issues, relevant law, and legally significant facts. It is true that, sometimes, taking a persuasive angle will change the arguments you make in your case. More often, however, both the method and impact of persuasive writing will be more subtle. In fact, the more subtle the method and impact are, the better. As the table of contents example above shows, many decisions that aid persuasion are subtle.

Of course, to accomplish any type of legal writing, you have to be good at both the "legal" part and the "writing" part. You might think of the "legal" part as what you say, and the "writing" part as how you say it. Chapter Two will help with what you say by reviewing research strategies, and Chapter Fourteen will help with how you say it by addressing effective sentence structure and writing techniques.[1] But the main focus of this book is going to be looking at different legal documents through the lens of *persuasion*. Using this lens means we will address what you say in each of the documents we discuss; but we will look even more closely at the "how you say it" part by considering how legal readers read, think, and behave when they interact with legal documents.

You may feel like you know a lot about how people read, since you've been doing it for most of your life. But you've probably done much of that reading in a linear fashion — from beginning to end of whatever document (or section of a document) you were reading — and you've done much of that reading with an open, trusting mind: you wanted to find out what the document had to tell you.

As you may have already realized, legal readers don't always read that way. First, they don't always read in a straight line. They may skip around the document, looking for the information that they want or need (you may do this type of reading as you prepare for casebook courses, especially if your time is limited). Second, they may not always be receptive readers. Instead, legal readers are often skeptical readers. They don't accept the writer's statements at face value, and they grow suspicious (and less likely to agree with the words they've read) if they believe that a writer is concealing information or trying too hard to persuade them of something.

In this book, we'll talk about some of the more effective ways to try to persuade these suspicious readers. Although some techniques

---

1. If foundational grammar and sentence structure are issues in your writing, we recommend consulting either or both of the following: ANNE ENQUIST, LAUREL CURRIE OATES, & JEREMY FRANCIS, JUST WRITING: GRAMMAR, PUNCTUATION, AND STYLE FOR THE LEGAL WRITER (5th ed. 2017) (a fabulous grammar and style book full of legal writing examples); RUTH ANN McKINNEY & KATIE ROSE GUEST PRYAL, CORE GRAMMAR FOR LAWYERS, https://www.coregrammarforlawyers.com (the title explains it perfectly; it's an online self-directed learning tool).

are unique to specific documents, it will help if you learn a little bit about some fundamentals of persuasion before we begin:

(1) Foundations of formal rhetoric
(2) Positions of emphasis
(3) Narrative reasoning.

1.1.1. Foundations of Formal Rhetoric: Logos, Pathos, Ethos

Aristotle's Rhetoric describes three methods of persuasion: *logos, pathos,* and *ethos.* You use *logos,* or logic, to persuade when you support your arguments with effective analysis and when readers can understand how and why the law applies to the facts in the way you describe. You persuade with *pathos,* or emotion, when your words stir sympathy or passion in readers, feelings that help the readers to feel or believe that the result you seek is a just result. Finally, you persuade with *ethos* when your reputation and your current performance give readers confidence that you are a trustworthy person whose arguments can be believed.

Your words can activate pathos if you phrase your writing in a way that emphasizes the sympathetic side of your argument. You activate ethos by representing the law and the facts honestly. You may also activate ethos by your document design, however. As you may have discovered in the table of contents illustration above, readers feel better about and are more likely to accept the content of a document that is both easy to read and inviting.

Effective legal writers make the most of logos, pathos, and ethos by writing honest briefs that highlight sympathetic arguments and by using effective writing and document design techniques that promote reading comprehension.

1.1.2. Positions of Emphasis

Scientists know that readers process information differently, depending on its location on the page or in the document. Whenever there is a break of any kind — at the end of a sentence, a paragraph, or a section of the document — that little shot of white space helps readers to perk up a bit and pay more attention to the information before or after that break. This reality means that attention peaks when readers encounter headings, first and last paragraphs and sections of a document, first and last sentences of paragraphs, and even, to some extent, beginnings and endings of sentences. Conversely, reader attention is likely to sag when readers encounter information farther from that white space: the middles of sentences, paragraphs, and documents.

We also know that when readers encounter a new document, or new information in that document, they search their brains for previous relevant information to help them to interpret the new information. Typically, they consider information in beginning positions of emphasis to determine the right *context* in which to put the information. Legal writing is more persuasive if this context frames the information in a way that creates sympathy for the client's point of view or a lack of sympathy for the opponent's point of view. For example, if you were describing the facts in a brief arguing against significant personal injury damages for pain and suffering after a car accident, you could describe the initial accident in either of two ways:

Non-framing: The defendant ran the stop light and hit the plaintiff's car.

Framing: Although the defendant may have caused damage to the plaintiff's car, the plaintiff did not suffer physical injury, and all damage to her car was reparable.

The non-framing example evokes neutral emotions, or even anti-defendant emotions, while the framing example reassures the reader that both the plaintiff and her car are fine.

1 In a motion memo, for example, the introduction section provides an opportunity for a writer to describe the issues before the court. As its title indicates, the introduction is often read first, and so it is the writer's first (and often best) chance to highlight the strongest arguments in favor of the writer's client and to establish a theme. Broadly stated, the writer has two choices: (1) a generic introduction that merely identifies the nature of the case and the type of motion, or (2) a case-specific introduction that begins the argument by succinctly stating the writer's strongest argument. The two sample introductions that follow illustrate the difference in a trademark infringement case in which the central issue is whether consumers are likely to be confused by competing uses of the word "rush" in a logo.

1 A motion memo is a persuasive document written to convince a court to grant or deny a motion. These documents are sometimes called "motion briefs" or "memoranda of points and authorities." We will discuss motion memos in Chapter Three.

Generic Example
This motion is filed in response to an action by Rita Rush, doing business as Rush Courier Service, alleging a trademark violation under federal law against Armstrong Cycle Manufacturing Enterprise ("ACME"). This memorandum supports ACME's motion to dismiss the complaint pursuant to Rule 12(b)(6) of the Federal Rules of Civil Procedure for failure to state a claim upon which relief can be granted.

The writer has identified the parties, the nature of the case, and the type of motion, but she has lost an opportunity to tell the court why it should rule in the client's favor at a point when the court is likely to be most attentive.

Better Example
This motion is filed in response to an action by Rita Rush, who operates a local courier service. Rush seeks to prevent Armstrong Cycle Manufacturing Enterprise (ACME), an international bicycle manufacturer, from using the common descriptive word "rush" in its logo. ACME asks this Court to dismiss the complaint because confusion cannot result from the two uses of the common descriptive word "rush."

② This text uses the label "phrase-that-pays" for a key word or phrase from a legal standard. Most legal controversies focus on the meaning of language from legal standards, so identifying the phrases-that-pay at issue helps you as a writer. Further, using each phrase-that-pays consistently in your argument helps readers see how the law connects to the facts in your case.

② In this introduction, the writer has also identified the parties, the nature of the case, and the type of motion. More importantly, she has also highlighted the strongest argument in ACME's favor, a phrase-that-pays, and a theme for the argument as a whole. The strongest argument is that "rush" merely describes a feature of the businesses that both parties operate: speed. The phrase-that-pays from the relevant legal standard is "common descriptive word," and the writer uses it twice in the introduction. The theme is skepticism: the writer wants the court to be skeptical about the possibility that consumers could be confused by two businesses in two different industries using a common descriptive word like *rush*. By including these specifics in the introduction, a strong position of emphasis, the writer has effectively framed her argument, giving her readers context for the specific legal points of the argument that will follow.

Physical locations are not the only positions of emphasis. Readers of English place more emphasis on concepts expressed in verbs than on concepts expressed in nouns, for example. This impact occurs because readers understand verbs more quickly than they do nouns. Likewise, information has more impact when expressed in concrete language than in abstract language. Again, the impact occurs because readers spend less time trying to understand concrete language, so they have more time to consider its meaning. For example, "The defendant negligently caused harm to the plaintiff's car" has less impact than "The defendant ignored the red light and slammed into the plaintiff's car."

Thus, whenever possible, persuasive writers frame their arguments effectively and make sure that all positions of emphasis contain information that supports their client's case. Further, they make persuasive choices about how to phrase their arguments and structure their sentences.

1.1.3. Narrative Reasoning

We talked earlier about how legal readers are suspicious readers, sometimes refusing to take your words at face value. That suspicion is a conscious reaction to your words. Readers are also likely, however, to have unconscious reactions when they read. They draw connections, jump to conclusions, and decide why things happened the way they did. They do this (and we do it, too), because it's often an efficient way to think.

If we see someone walk in the door holding a wet umbrella, we conclude that it's raining outside rather than concluding that someone just washed an umbrella. Scientists describe mental "schemas" that we form, based on our experiences and on our knowledge about the experiences of others. These schemas may be based on how people communicate (if my teenager doesn't want to tell me something, I'm guessing it's bad news) or about how people behave (if a coworker avoids me as the deadline for a joint project approaches, she has probably not completed her part of the project).

Scholars use the label "narrative reasoning" to describe the way we leap to conclusions, because when we jump to those conclusions, we are reasoning our way to the end of a story, or "narrative." We look at the details we've been given, and we fill in the blanks, reaching a conclusion that feels correct (and of course, it often is correct). As legal writers, we can exploit narrative reasoning by considering what conclusions we want the reader to reach, and then deciding which details will make the reader more likely to reach those conclusions.

Narrative reasoning is particularly useful in formal fact statements, where argument is not appropriate. For example, in the following fact statement about an anti-discrimination lawsuit, the writer needs to explain that a person was hired in 2003 and filed an anti-discrimination lawsuit in 2019. Here are two ways to convey that information:

Weaker Example
Stevie Wendl filed an anti-discrimination lawsuit against Bank Two in 2019. Wendl has worked for Bank Two since 2003, when she was hired to work in the commercial lending department. . . .

Stronger Example
Stevie Wendl sued Bank Two three months ago, claiming that Bank Two had discriminated against her sixteen years ago when it assigned her to a supervisor position in its commercial lending department.

Both examples are truthful, but the second example exploits narrative reasoning by making the reader think, "Why did Wendl wait sixteen years to complain about the discrimination? Something seems fishy here."

1.2. CONCLUSION

This book will provide many more examples of persuasive writing, but we hope you have noticed two things already. First, effective persuasion is subtle. It does not hit the reader over the head. The best persuasive techniques are invisible to readers. If your readers perceive that you are trying to persuade them, they may resist your arguments.

Second, as we will discuss throughout this book, almost every writing decision presents opportunities for persuasion: the issues you address, the authorities you cite, the words you choose, the way you structure your paragraphs, and the way you design your document. The bottom line is that every encounter with your reader presents an opportunity to persuade. Don't waste any of them.

Review of Research and Analytical Structure

If you have been assigned this textbook for a course, you're probably at least a spring semester 1L who's already learned something about legal research and something about the analytical structure of legal writing. In this chapter, we will review the fundamentals about legal research and analytical structure. Later, in Chapter Five, we will talk about how to use legal research to decide what points to make and how to organize them.

2.1. RESEARCH REVIEW

We know that you're at least somewhat familiar with legal research. You also know something about research in general, because you've been using search engines to do your homework and answer random questions that occur to you. You might not have realized it at the time, but when you conducted those searches, you were being scientific. You formed a hypothesis that feeding those words into the search box would get you the information you wanted, and then you tested that hypothesis by putting the search in and checking the results. Sometimes you found that your question didn't lead you to the information you wanted, so you had to word your question a different way, or maybe a few different ways. Sometimes, you may have realized that you didn't even know enough about your subject to ask the right question, and so you gave up.

Whether you realize it or not, you are relying on *algorithms* when you use search engines to conduct research. The site's programmers figure out how the program is going to use the information you gave it to produce a result. Algorithms are at work in many or most of your apps. For example, if you choose to listen to (or buy) a song on a music app, the app may suggest other songs for you to listen to. If you listened to every suggested song, you would probably love some, like some, and hate some. And we're guessing you wouldn't decide to love a song you hated just because the app suggested you would like it. Likewise, if you're allergic to strawberries, you're not going to buy some just because your grocery-ordering app suggested it. So let that be the first lesson of this chapter: sometimes algorithms just don't understand what you want, or what you need.

You rely on algorithms when you conduct legal research, too. Like a scientist, you use the algorithms to help you test a hypothesis, which is that certain words or phrases will appear in sources that will answer the questions you need to answer. As with other types of research, legal research is more successful if you know enough about your subject to ask the right questions. And, as with all kinds of algorithms, once you get the answers, you need to know enough about what you need and want so that you can figure out what to accept and what to reject.

In this section of the chapter, we will start by discussing how to get background information about the relevant law so that you can search more effectively. Then, we will review fundamentals about the two main techniques for conducting computer research, followed by methods for researching effectively based on a known statute or common law rule. Finally, we'll discuss how to feel confident that you are "done" with your research, or at least the first stage of it.

2.1.1. Getting Background Information to Support More Effective Research

You can always research more effectively if you start with some knowledge about your subject matter. Unfortunately, you might have to do some research to get that knowledge. One good way to measure how much background research you need to do is to draft a research question. We recommend a method, developed by Professors Christopher and Jill Wren,[1] which uses the classic "under-does-when" structure. The amount of information that you put into the "under" clause tells you how much background research you need to complete. As you may know, the generic format of the under-does-when question reads as:

Under relevant law

Does legal status exist

① **When** legally significant facts exist?

For the "under" clause, include what you know about the law. It might be very general ("Under state or federal law . . . ") or very specific ("Under 18 U.S.C. § 1519, the anti-shredding provision of the Sarbanes-Oxley Act . . . "). As you might have guessed, the broader your "under" clause, the more background reading you need to do.

For the "does legal status exist" clause, identify the relevant legal status as specifically as you can. The relevant legal status will often be something about guilt (in a criminal case) or liability (in a civil case), but your research will be more effective if you know enough about the rule to ask a more precise question. Sometimes the legal status might be about meeting or not meeting a certain element of a test, or about being included in the meaning of a key term, or, as we call it, a phrase-that-pays. If you don't know the legal status you are looking for, that is also a signal that you need to do more background research.

The "when" clause is the easiest. You might not know the most legally significant facts at this stage, so just include a general description of the facts that you believe to be relevant. Including these facts will help you to identify analogous cases and other relevant authorities.

Let's suppose your client complains that her daughter's soccer team at the local public high school is not getting the same funding or treatment as the boys' soccer team, even though the girls' team won the state championship. You might presume some sort of sex discrimination cause of action is possible. Of course, both the state and the federal governments have sex discrimination laws, so your research question might look like this:

Under State and/or federal anti-sex-discrimination law

Does a public high school have to provide equal treatment for the girls' and boys' soccer teams

① Note that different phrasings are sometimes appropriate. You might also ask, "Under relevant law, does legal status include legally significant facts?" or "Under relevant law, can a plaintiff establish legal status when legally significant facts exist?"

---

1. This method can be found in their text, The Legal Research Manual: A Game Plan for Legal Research and Analysis (2d ed. 2000).

When the girls' soccer team gets worse treatment than the boys' team, even though it has a better record?

This "under" clause tells you that you need to get some background information on what specific laws govern sex discrimination. The "does" clause tells you that you need to know more about what kinds of causes of action are available for student athletes. You may have heard of Title IX, which mandates equal treatment for males and females in publicly-funded educational settings, but you don't know what causes of action are available under the statute.

The "when" clause may or may not be relevant. If the relevant statutes mandate behavior but do not allow damages, you may be able to require equal treatment. In that case, the way the teams are being treated now is only marginally relevant to the legal research; it will be relevant only to monitor the remedy. On the other hand, if damages are available for current or past unequal treatment, you may need to know more details about how each team has been treated so you can find appropriately relevant authorities.

Once you've assessed your level of ignorance, you can start doing your background reading. You might begin with a non-legal search engine, using language like *lawsuit sports team unequal treatment high school*. It can be helpful to read reports on law firm websites to get a general idea of the kinds of causes of action that are available. Looking on legal databases can also be helpful, but for background reading, you should start in the secondary source databases.

2 As you know, you can order your search results in a few different ways, including by relevance and by date.

2 For example, if you put the terms "sports team public high school unequal treatment" into Westlaw's secondary sources page, you'd get over 100 law review articles. If you filtered by looking for the specific phrase "high school" in those articles, you'd get down to 98 articles. Of course, you don't need to read those 98 articles; in fact, you probably don't even need to read any of them completely. Instead, try reading the titles of the 20 most recent and the 20 most relevant to find those that seem the most on-point for your situation. Then, scan the introductory material in those articles to look for those that are particularly on-point. Unlike case names, the names of law review articles usually signal their relevance.

3 Note that a literature review is not always labeled as such.

3 Law review articles can also be helpful because many articles begin with a "literature review" that discusses how the relevant issues have been addressed in the past. Articles that address statutory issues often begin by discussing how the statute was enacted and how the law developed in ways that are relevant to the issues discussed in the article. Reading the introductory material in a few law review articles—and checking out some of the more relevant authorities cited in those articles—is a great way to get good background information on the issues your client is facing, and on the language that courts use when they talk about those issues.

4 Before we move on, a word about serendipity. As you may know, *serendipity* occurs when you receive a benefit that you were not looking for. In research, serendipity happens when you are focusing your research on A, but see information about B that turns out to be relevant. Looking at a long list of law review titles may help you achieve serendipitous results—you may learn about a cause of action or a focus that you didn't know about. You can find other opportunities for serendipitous learning in digests, indexes, and tables of contents in relevant sources.

As you gain knowledge about your issues, you can move from secondary sources—which are typically not limited to one jurisdiction—to primary sources, which typically are limited to one jurisdiction. It can sometimes be helpful to conduct some of your research in a multi-jurisdictional database so that you can see whether your jurisdiction is part of the mainstream. But for the most part, you should conduct your primary research by focusing on your own jurisdiction. Of course, use database controls to limit your search appropriately. To research a Nevada state law issue, for example, search "Nevada state and federal cases" because federal courts sometimes consider state law issues (e.g., if the lawsuit was filed in federal court under diversity jurisdiction). In contrast, when researching how a federal statute applies in Nevada, focus your research on cases from the United States Supreme Court and the Ninth Circuit (including trial courts within the Ninth Circuit) because Nevada state courts rarely address federal statutes and are never mandatory authority for their meaning.

Of course, you may need to conduct statutory research as well as case law research. Below, we will talk about using *notes of decisions* when doing statutory research. The notes of decisions are short descriptions, or annotations, of cases that have cited or discussed the statute. If a statute has been cited in hundreds or thousands of cases, the annotated code will usually organize the annotations into some sort of index or table of contents. These indexes can be a particularly helpful opportunity for serendipitous learning.

2.1.2. Algorithm Searching and Boolean Searching

Broadly speaking, lawyers typically have two goals when they conduct legal research. First, they want to find authorities that enable them to understand what the relevant rules are and how the relevant legal rules operate in situations that are roughly similar to a client's situation. Second, they want to find authorities that will

4 Monte once assigned his students an ADA problem in which the alleged disability was obesity. The employee could do the job, but the employer perceived him as disabled because he believed that the employee's weight might slow him down. He asked the students to look for helpful law review articles, and one of the first hits was "Do I Look Fat? Perceiving Obesity as a Disability Under the Americans with Disabilities Act." The article cited all of the leading cases and provided several theories for supporting a claim.

allow them to explain or argue how a court would or should apply the law to the facts in a client's particular case.

Algorithms are great for the first goal, but to achieve the second goal, you may need to use Boolean search techniques to give you confidence that your research has uncovered all of the relevant authorities. Regardless of how you conduct your research, you're going to do a better job if you have a general understanding of how these research systems work.

a. Algorithms and You

It's beyond the scope of this book—and our knowledge—to give you a detailed discussion of how algorithms work. In general, algorithms take note of millions of searches and uses of data, and they recognize patterns. A bookseller's algorithm notices that most people who buy a civil procedure textbook also buy a copy of the federal rules of civil procedure, and so it recommends a copy of the federal rules to everyone who buys any civil procedure textbook. A legal research algorithm notices that most people who search the phrase "search incident to arrest" end up clicking on X case, so they put that case at the top of their results list.

The designers of algorithms make dozens of choices that can affect how an algorithm works, and what it recommends.[2] For example, some research algorithms look at words within a phrase like *sex discrimination,* and they first look for sources that use both words together, followed by sources that use the words separately, within a certain defined proximity. Other research algorithms might consider the search first as meaning *sex* or *discrimination* and then *sex* and *discrimination*. One algorithm might prioritize United States Supreme Court decisions, while another might prioritize more recent decisions. When you conduct an algorithm search, the algorithm is in control.

Professor Nevelow Mart's research has shown that the results of algorithm searches vary widely from one database to another. Legal research databases like Westlaw and LexisNexis typically refer to algorithm searching as "natural language searching," which is the kind of searching you typically use on Google and other search engines. If you do an algorithm search of *elements of a Title IX claim* on LexisNexis or Westlaw, for example, or even on Google or Bing,

---

2. To learn more about how research algorithms work, *see* Susan Nevelow Mart, *Results May Vary*, A.B.A. J., Mar. 2018, at 48, available at http://scholar.law.colorado.edu/articles/964/. Professor Nevelow Mart is the Director of the Law Library at the University of Colorado Law School at Boulder.

you will get some hits that look pretty helpful. If you glanced at the first hit that came up when Mary Beth searched this phrase via Bing in 2019, you would have seen that plaintiffs must prove that they had engaged in "protected activity," that the defendant took an "adverse action" against the plaintiffs, and that the adverse action "caused" harm to the plaintiffs.

But when Mary Beth conducted the same search on Westlaw, boxes popped up that indicated that "actual notice" of discrimination is a required element of a Title IX claim for "deliberate indifference." This result was different than the Bing result, so we went back to the attorney website and read more carefully. It turns out that the attorney website was describing the elements for a Title IX claim based on "retaliation," not for claims based on sex-based discrimination per se. So, here's the most obvious lesson of this chapter: one of the most important things to do in legal research is to *read carefully*. If you are too eager to grab some seemingly helpful language from your hit, you may miss crucial information that can make a huge difference in the effectiveness and accuracy of your search, and your research.

Of course, careful reading is one of the most important skills for any lawyer. It becomes more important in legal research, however, because it is very easy for many of us to over-rely on computer algorithms. We don't know why the retaliation information popped up first on Bing. It could be that there are many more retaliation lawsuits filed under Title IX than there are "deliberate indifference" lawsuits. It may be that the attorney running the website specializes in those lawsuits, and paid Bing to have that link pop up first for any Title IX-related search.

What this search experience also shows is that researchers must not only read carefully; they must recognize when they don't have enough knowledge to do in-depth research. If you get contradictory results like the ones in the Title IX search discussed above, it probably means you need to do more background reading about your topic, and about relevant causes of action, so that you can design an effective research strategy.

Exercise 2A

Try doing the same algorithm search via four different search engines, e.g., Google, Bing, LexisNexis, and Westlaw. Studies show that people tend not to go beyond the first 5–10 hits when they do non-legal research, and the same may often be true for legal researchers. Take a look at the first 10 hits in each location. How much overlap is there? What did you learn about how well you understood the issue you were searching? Do you think that searching in multiple locations gives you a better picture of the legal issue?

b. Boolean, or "Terms and Connectors" Researching

As we noted above, algorithm searching of crucial words is a great way to get knowledge or to test your knowledge about a legal issue. But the good legal researcher should also know how to conduct what is known as a "Boolean" search (named after George Boole, the founder of algebraic logic). A Boolean search includes the crucial words, and it also specifies their relationships to each other. The two major commercial databases allow sophisticated Boolean searches. For example, with a Boolean search, you can ask to see all cases that contain words or phrases in the same sentence, in the same paragraph, or in the same document. We hesitate to give detailed guidance on Boolean search methods because the databases frequently update their search functions. In general, you should use the advanced search method, and use the "full text" or "text" box. Ask a law librarian or database rep for guidance on how to conduct effective Boolean searches.

More significantly, Boolean searches allow you to use quotation marks to control which words will be searched as a unit. While algorithm searching can sometimes get you most of the sources that you need, Boolean searching allows you to do narrow, focused searches, to have more control over the search, and to have confidence that you have found all of the relevant sources in a particular category.

As we noted above, Boolean searches are more effective once you know about the language that courts and commentators use when discussing the issues you are researching. One of the best ways to develop search terms is to imagine one or more phrases or sentences that would appear in relevant sources. For a Boolean search, it's also helpful to consider where those relevant phrases or sentences would appear. Of course, once you know the relevant phrases-that-pay, you can search more effectively, which is why having or gaining background knowledge is a vital part of legal research.

To develop an effective Boolean search, you need to know how courts use the relevant language. If you conducted a Boolean search asking for cases with the phrase "sex discrimination," for example, the Boolean search would override the algorithm's decision about searching for *sex* and *discrimination* versus *sex* or *discrimination*: the Boolean search "sex discrimination" mandates that the computer limit its search to sources that have those words in that exact order, in that exact proximity.

Further, when you use Boolean searches, you override the algorithm's methods of guessing what different word forms you might be interested in seeing. As you know from using "Ctrl + F" when you search documents, what you see is what you ask for. If you use a Boolean search to ask for cases about "discrimination," you won't get cases about "discriminatory" behavior, or "biased" behavior. Thus, with Boolean searches, you need to identify the appropriate synonyms, and use appropriate search tools (like * and !) to make sure you get all the relevant word forms.

Of course, that level of control requires greater precision on your part. Novice legal researchers often use root expanders on words imprecisely, or put words into quotation marks when they shouldn't. You should put a phrase into quotation marks only when you are confident that those exact words are extremely likely to appear together in the sources that will be useful to you, and that they will not appear in other combinations.

For example, "sex discrimination" seems like a useful, common phrase, so you might be tempted to use that phrase in quotation marks. In doing your preliminary background reading, however, you would see that courts also use the phrases "sex-based discrimination" "gender-based discrimination," and "discrimination based on sex." Further, descriptions of plaintiff claims include phrases like "the plaintiff claims that the defendant discriminated against her based on her sexual characteristics." In conducting a search, therefore, you will get more hits if you don't put that phrase into quotation marks. Further, you should not use the term *sex* or *discrimination* as is because you might miss cases that used *sexual* or *discriminated*. Algorithm searches often use fuzzy logic to take care of these distinctions, but when doing Boolean searches, you need to exercise more control. You do, however, want to find cases in which the concepts of sex and discrimination are closely linked. You might therefore try a search like the following:

> sex! or gender! /5 discrim!

This search would retrieve more than 10,000 cases, however, which would almost certainly be more than would be helpful. So, let's think about that high school student who is complaining about the girls'

The use of the exclamation point at the end of a term is a "root expander." It tells the computer to look for all words that begin with those letters. The search term *discriminat!* will retrieve *discriminate, discriminatory, discrimination,* and any other words that begin with *discriminat*. Take care when using the root expander. If you use *disc!* as a search term, the computer will also search for words like *discretion*. Likewise, if you use *tax!* when searching for cases about tax, taxation, and taxable income, you will likely retrieve cases about *taxicabs*. This reality means that sometimes you must use more than one term. For example, to get tax cases but avoid taxicab cases, you might have to ask for cases that contain either the word *tax* or any word that begins with *taxa: tax or taxa!*

team being treated worse than the boys' team. You don't want to use "soccer" as a search term, because a case about other kinds of teams would be just as useful. You also know that there are many kinds of teams, but it is typically sports teams or athletic teams that are segregated by sex. By doing background research, you have learned that Title IX is a common legal basis for § 1983 cases based on sex discrimination in educational settings.

5 Did you know that "discrete" and "discreet" are different words? *Discrete* means "separate and distinct," while *discreet* means "careful, circumspect, and guarded."

5 Accordingly, now you try a search that looks for cases that talk about sex discrimination AND talk about high school sports teams. You can use parentheses to separate the discrete parts of your search:

(sex! or gender /s discrim!) & ((sport or athlet! /s team) /p "Title IX")

This search would find cases in which the source talked about sex discrimination AND, at some point in the document, talked in the same paragraph about Title IX and about sports teams or athletic teams.

Exercise 2B

Try the search above in both LexisNexis and Westlaw, and note the differences. Search in a particular circuit to reduce the number of hits. Because LexisNexis does not (currently) allow use of parentheses in its initial advanced search, you might have to structure the search in LexisNexis as follows:

Initial search: sex! or gender /s discrim!

Filter: ((sport or athlet! /s team) /p "Title IX")

Once you have done the search, compare the similarities and differences to the similarities and differences in the searches you did in exercise 2A. Are your results more similar in LexisNexis and Westlaw when doing algorithm searches or when doing Boolean searches?

Exercise 2C

Your client has appealed a federal district court's decision to deny her motion to suppress. You've already done some appellate work, so you know that the most common appellate standards of review are "clearly erroneous" (generally used for findings of fact), "de novo" (generally used for conclusions of law), and "abuse of discretion" (generally used for judges' rulings on evidentiary and procedural matters). You form a hypothesis that either the de novo standard or the abuse of discretion standard applies. From your reading of cases and legal practice books about appellate standards of review, you know that judges sometimes say "the court abused its discretion" and that they sometimes say "applying the abuse of discretion standard, we find that. . . ." On the other hand, when they talk about the de novo standard, they don't use any variations on the words *de novo*, although they sometimes say *plenary review* or *plenary standard* instead. When they discuss motions to suppress, they sometimes refer to *defendant's motion to suppress*, but at other times, they say things like *defendant has moved to suppress the evidence that. . . .*

Construct and conduct one search to test your hypothesis that the de novo standard applies to a review of a decision denying a motion to suppress, and another search to test the abuse of discretion hypothesis. Set the search in the jurisdiction your law school sits in. What do your results show?

You will find more in-depth coverage of appellate standards of review in Chapter Seven.

2.1.3. Researching Effectively Based on a Known Statute or Common Law Rule

Of course, sometimes you will know a little bit more about your client's problem. If your client tells you that she has been charged with violating a particular statute, your path is clear. Likewise, if a plaintiff has filed a cause of action against your client, or if you are appealing a trial court or intermediate appellate decision, you will know a lot about the relevant legal standards. Let's review some of the well-worn paths you can follow when researching issues related to statutory and common law rules.

a. Statutory Research

If your issue is statutory, knowing the statute's number (i.e., its citation) and its common name (if any) can help you in at least two ways. First, both the statute number and name can be useful search terms. Because many statutes have decimal points or hyphens in the statute number, they are often unique terms that help to focus Boolean searches. If the statute at issue could include multiple possible issues, add language

> We use these marks << >> (found above the period and comma on your keyboard) to indicate quotations when we need to distinguish our quotation of material from preexisting quotation marks in the material we are quoting. Using these non-standard symbols as quotation marks can be helpful when you block and copy material as part of your legal research. Of course, be sure to remove these marks, and use standard quotation marks appropriately, before you submit the document to a professor—or a court!

to the search that focuses on facts or phrases-that-pay that are relevant to your client's case, e.g., <<123.45 /p "personal threat">>.

Be aware that on rare occasions, courts use a statute's name without its accompanying citation. For example, the Civil Rights Act of 1964 is formally cited as follows: Title VII of the Civil Rights Act of 1964, 42 U.S.C. §§ 2000e, *et seq.* Often, however, courts will refer to any or all of the statutes codified in Title VII by simply saying "Title VII." They may be particularly likely to do so if they are noting that Title VII does not apply. Since you may want to find cases in which courts have refused to apply the law to a similar set of facts, you should be sure to include the name and number in at least some of your searches.

Second, once you know the citation of any relevant statutes, you can go to the statutory compilation on Westlaw or LexisNexis and study the notes of decisions. As we noted above, just reviewing the table of contents or index to the notes of decisions can help you to pick up valuable information about the statute. For example, if you look up the initial statute in Title IX (20 U.S.C. § 1681), you would see that it has over 1,000 notes of decisions. On Westlaw, those notes come with a table of contents that has over 150 headings, and many of those headings have sub-headings. Simply by reading the table of contents, you can learn not only that there are notes of decisions about high school sports, but also that Title IX actions are frequently brought under § 1983, a valuable detail that will help you to discover relevant causes of action.

In addition to reading what others have said about the statute, be sure to spend some time reading the statute itself. Be sure to read the entire statute; if the statute is part of a larger act (as is the case with, e.g., the ACA, the ADEA, Title IX, and Title VII), be sure to read the table of contents of the act so you can read relevant provisions (ideally, you will read all of the provisions of an act, but with longer acts, that may not be practical). When reading the statute and its relevant neighbors, be on the lookout for four kinds of provisions:

(1) **Definition provisions.** Definitions may be included in the statute itself, in a separate definition provision in the same act, or in a definition provision of a related or generally applicable statute.

(2) **Purpose provisions.** Particularly in recent years, legislatures may include a specific statute that describes the statute's purposes; it frequently appears early in the relevant act. You can use purpose provisions to support your arguments or attack your opponent's arguments.

(3) **Enforcement provisions.** As you have probably already learned, statutes declaring that people or entities should or should not do something are worthless unless they are enforceable. Thus, when reviewing statutory language, look for "penalties" provisions (common in criminal statutes) or "remedies" (more common in civil statutes). Be aware that legislatures may use different language when describing enforcement provisions.

(4) **Provisions delegating regulatory authority.** As you know, the agencies of the executive branches of state and federal governments can promulgate rules that can change the meaning or enforcement of statutes. They can generally only do so, however, if the legislature has explicitly granted them the authority to do so. Look for statutory provisions with titles like "Agency Guidance," "Regulations," or "Rulemaking Authority."

If the phrase-that-pays of your argument comes from the statutory language itself (as opposed to a common law rule), be sure to search for that word or phrase throughout the whole act. If your phrase-that-pays is "personal threat," for example, you would want to see if the legislature used the phrase "personal threat" elsewhere in the act, because its other uses may make evident what the legislature had in mind for that language. Likewise, you should search "personal" and "threat" independently. Doing so might enable you to distinguish the legislature's intent when it used one of the words as opposed to both.

Researching the statute's legislative history may also help you to understand the statute and develop arguments. Although detailed information about finding legislative history is beyond our scope, look for two things in particular. First, if the statute has undergone revision since it has been enacted, you may argue that language that was not changed should be interpreted in line with then-extant authorities. If you need to look at floor debates and other pre-enactment documents, don't start from square one. Courts and other commentators may have done some of the work for you. For example, suppose you are wondering about the legislative history surrounding language about the problem of "refusing to hire" a person under 42 U.S.C. § 2000e-2. The following search could be very fruitful:

"legislative history" /p "title VII" or 2000e-2

Finally, be aware of other similar statutes that you may use to fashion arguments. You may often see references to other similar statutes when you are doing preliminary reading or other research. For example, in a Title VII search, you are likely to see the phrase

"Title VII" mentioned in the same sentence or paragraph with other civil rights statutes like the ADEA, the ADA, and the FMLA. If you are researching state statutes, you may be able to use information in the state code or search an "all states" database to find similar statutes.

If the similar statutes have provisions similar to the one at issue in your case, you can see how relevant courts have interpreted those provisions. If you are making an argument about language in a federal statute that your jurisdiction has not yet interpreted, a court may be willing to follow its own interpretation of that language in a similar statute, or another court's interpretation of the language from the same statute in a case from another jurisdiction. If you are arguing about the meaning of a state statute, a court may be willing to look at decisions from another state if both the statutory language and the legal issue are very similar.

b. How to Research Effectively If You Are Researching a Common Law Issue

Of course, common law rules are almost always going to be relevant to your research. Very often, statutory language will be only the starting point of legal analysis, and much of your focus will be on a rule or test that a court has developed to interpret that language.

By its nature, common law research is not as easily mapped as statutory research. Once you have identified a significant common law rule, however, there are a few paths that are often fruitful. First, of course, you should identify the foundational case or cases that are the source of the rule, and use Shepard's and Keycite to determine how the rule has developed recently.

Boolean searches can also help these common law issue searches. If you find that one or more cases are commonly cited when courts discuss the rule, search in case and law-review databases, using any unusual case names as search terms, coupled with a term-frequency search of language from the phrase-that-pays. In advanced search settings, term-frequency searches let you specify that you want to see only the results that have mentioned your term a certain number of times. This kind of search omits authorities in which the court mentioned a test once, and then never referred to the phrase-that-pays again. Using this method helps you to find sources that contain an in-depth discussion of the relevant issue.

Non-traditional resources can also be useful when searching common law rules. Looking at relevant practice tools, including form jury instructions or complaints, can frequently help you to identify the recognized elements of a common law rule.

6 As with statutes, you should be prepared to review and even cite non-mandatory and non-jurisdictional authorities when appropriate. In a perfect world, you would cite only the court of last resort from your own jurisdiction. You would cite only cases that are addressing the same issue, analyzing the same rule, and focusing on the same cause of action, the same phrase-that-pays, and identical facts. The decision would be a decision on the merits rather than a motion decision or a kickback case, and it would discuss the issue in depth.

But of course, we don't live in a perfect world. You may have to sacrifice one or all of these best-case features to find useful authorities. One word of caution: once you have traveled outside of your jurisdiction, it becomes very important that the authority have as many as possible of the other best-case markers. Courts are willing to look at authorities from other jurisdictions, but they grow more unwilling as the facts and issues under review in those authorities grow more dissimilar.

6 As you might have already observed from the cases you've read in your casebooks, many appellate decisions are appeals of trial court decisions in which the court granted a motion to dismiss or motion for summary judgment. If the court reverses and remands one of those decisions, the court essentially "kicks it back" to the trial court. And so, we call these cases "kickback cases."

2.1.4. How to Feel Confident that You Are "Done" with Your Research

You might never feel 100% confident that you have found every single relevant authority, but there are a few ways to feel confident that you have researched well and thoroughly. First, you should be able to articulate in general how the relevant rules operate. Second, you should know whether your jurisdiction is a "freak"—that is, is your jurisdiction the only one in which a particular type of statute exists, or in which courts find that a particular legal issue reaches a given result? Knowing this information can help you craft or defend against an argument that your jurisdiction should join the mainstream.

Third, you should know specifics about each relevant rule. When was that rule interpreted most recently in any court in your jurisdiction, and particularly in its court of last resort? If your arguments are focused on particular phrases-that-pay, you should also be able to answer that question about those phrases-that-pay. Note, of course, that knowing about these recent interpretations does *not* mean that you have to cite them in your argument. Rather, having found these interpretations enables you to be confident that courts have not recently made significant changes in how they have interpreted the relevant rules.

If your issue is one that has spawned dozens or even hundreds of cases interpreting it, you may feel particularly daunted. If so, you may take comfort in doing what we call "surgical strike" research. First, do a broad search that brings in those hundreds of cases. Then, filter that search with the relevant statute number, if any. Undo that filter and filter with the statute's popular name, if any. Undo that filter and filter the search with the phrase-that-pays. Undo that filter and filter with relevant facts and synonyms for those facts. If your results are still daunting, use combinations of the filters; e.g., filter with the statute number and the facts, and then filter with the phrase-that-pays and the facts, and then with the statute number and the phrase-that-pays. As noted, using this method cannot guarantee 100% completeness, but you can at least feel confident that you have exercised due diligence in your research.

2.2.   REVIEW OF ANALYTICAL STRUCTURE

As we're sure you know by now, legal writing is not like creative writing. Legal readers generally don't like suspense, and they don't like surprises. They have certain expectations about the documents they read, and they get frustrated if they can't find what they're looking for where they expect to find it. In other words, legal writers help their readers when they provide certain information in a certain order.

A great way to figure out what information to provide is by using an analytical formula. Before your first set of exams, you probably learned at least one formula: IRAC, the acronym that helps you remember the information, and the order of information, that many professors like to see in exam answers: Issue-Rule-Application-Conclusion. IRAC is a good building block for legal analysis, but it doesn't always give legal readers everything they need.

7 You may have learned the acronym CREAC, which stands for pretty much the same thing as CREXAC. Mary Beth has been using the CREXAC acronym since before you were born. She left the X in there because she thought it would help her students remember the "EXplanation" part of the formula.

7 When writing briefs and memos, as opposed to exams, your formula needs to be more sophisticated than IRAC. You may have heard of TREAT or IREAC, or CRuPAC. In this book, the formula is called CREXAC, and it stands for Conclusion, Rule, EXplanation, Application, and Connection-conclusion. You can use CREXAC to structure any "unit of discourse" that you use to analyze a legal issue. As George Gopen has noted, a "unit of discourse" is "anything in prose that has a beginning and an end: a phrase, clause, sentence, paragraph, section, [or] subsection."[3] In analytical writing, then, a "CREXAC unit of discourse" refers to a section or subsection in which you use legal analysis to prove the truth or validity of a legal assertion.

---

3. George D. Gopen, *Let the Buyer in the Ordinary Course of Business Beware: Suggestions for Revising the Prose of the Uniform Commercial Code*, 54 U. Chi. L. Rev. 1178, 1185 (1987).

8 CREXAC and similar acronyms are a special kind of formula called a *heuristic* that can guide you to answer vital questions about your analysis, questions that IRAC alone won't answer:

1. What rule governs this issue?
2. What does this rule mean, and/or how has it been applied in appropriately similar situations?
3. How should this rule be applied (or not applied) in this case?
4. What impact does that application have on the court's decision in this case?

9 For each point you need to prove or analyze, you should write a CREXAC unit of discourse, or, as our students sometimes call them, "a CREXAC." Each element of the CREXAC formula is explained more fully below.

2.2.1. State Your Issue as a Conclusion (the First "C" of CREXAC)

In the first "Conclusion" element of the formula, the writer articulates the specific issue that is being addressed or articulates the problem (or part or subpart of the problem) that is being solved in that CREXAC unit of discourse. For example, if you have a client who has a possible negligence claim, you could have at least one CREXAC for each of the four elements of negligence: Duty, breach, causation, and damages. If you were writing a CREXAC for the breach issue in an office memo, you might state the issue objectively:

> **This Court must decide whether O'Hara's behavior constituted a breach of her duty to Fulmer.**

Although this method effectively announces the issue, it is not the best choice in a brief to a court because it is not argumentative. Generally, in persuasive writing, you should make your arguments as if they are the only reasonable resolution to the issues before the court. Therefore, it is often best to state your issues as conclusions:

> **O'Hara breached her duty to Fulmer when she jumped off the high-dive without first looking to see if anyone was in the water below.**

By stating your issue as a conclusion, you begin to focus your reader not only on the issue that you will be addressing in that section of the argument, but also on the result that your analysis of the issue will reveal. It might help you to think of this conclusion as a thesis-conclusion, as opposed to the conclusion at the end of CREXAC, which we call a connection-conclusion.

8 FYI, you pronounce *heuristic* as hyer-ISS-tic, with the emphasis on the second syllable. Mary Beth likes to pronounce it as a sneeze sometimes. . . .

9 As we will discuss in Chapter Five, sometimes the "E" stands for "Evidence" rather than "Explanation." Likewise, sometimes you will provide less detailed analysis (or perhaps none at all) for points that are essential but that do not need to be proved to your reader.

Will My Writing Be Boring If I Use the CREXAC Formula in Each Section?

The CREXAC formula does not provide one rubric that governs the whole argument section. CREXAC provides a rubric that can be used over and over again, any time a writer has some point to explain or prove. The argument section itself will be organized according to the unique issues and sub-issues that the case presents. CREXAC can be used, however, as a formula for your analysis of each significant issue and sub-issue within that argument. Some writers worry that their writing will be boring or overly predictable if they follow a formula like CREXAC in each section of a document. This worry is unfounded for a couple of reasons.

First, CREXAC does not tell you *what to say*. Instead, it recommends a particular *organization* for the information that readers traditionally need when analyzing legal issues. Most legal readers want to know the rule first, then understand the rule's meaning, and then see how it applies to the facts. Most judges want a simple organization; they don't want to have to struggle to find a rule that a writer "creatively" saved for the end of the analysis of a legal issue.

The second reason not to worry is related to the first. CREXAC is only an organizational structure. With no extra effort on your part, each section of your argument will vary from the section before it according to the *substance* of the argument itself and the particular demands of the issue. As we will discuss in Chapter Five, every issue needs a rule, but sometimes the rule is a simple quote from a statute, while at other times it is a common law rule, and at other times it is a cluster of rules that end on the particular rule that governs the narrow legal issue that is the focus of that section of the document. Similarly, the explanation of the rule and application of the rule to the facts will also vary from issue to issue.

Even if CREXAC is not the most perfect organization for the analysis of a particular legal issue or sub-issue, it will probably still be an effective organization. Thus, it is probably most practical for an attorney to assume a CREXAC organization rather than to spend precious time trying to determine what is the "best" structure for analyzing a legal issue.

Further, even if you decide that another organizational method is appropriate, the elements of CREXAC, which track the heuristic questions noted earlier, provide a good checklist. In every section of the argument, the reader will always need to know the issue you're addressing, the rule that governs the issue, what the rule means, how it applies in this case, and how that application connects to your argument.

2.2.2. Provide the Rule (the "R" of CREXAC)

After you have focused the reader's attention on the issue being addressed, you should articulate the rule that governs the issue. First, let's define our terms. A rule essentially says that "if a certain condition exists, then a certain legal status results." For example, in the famous syllogism about whether Socrates is mortal, an if-then statement of the rule might look like this:

> **If you are a human being [certain condition], then you are mortal [legal status].**

You may have taken Torts last semester, and learned the rule for establishing liability in negligence, which could be stated in if-then terms as follows:

> **If you have a duty and breach a duty, and the breach causes injury that results in damages to the person you owed the duty to [certain condition], then you are liable in negligence [legal status].**

However, each part of the negligence rule could also be thought of as a rule. For example, if you were writing a CREXAC on the breach issue, an if-then statement of that rule might look like this:

> **If you fail to exercise ordinary care in performing a duty [certain condition], then you have breached that duty [legal status].**

10 What's more, some sub-rules have further sub-rules. In many states, for example, proving the causation element of negligence requires the plaintiff to prove both legal cause and proximate cause. Thus, each of those sub-issues would have its own rule, which could be expressed in if-then format as follows:

> **If your breach sets in motion a chain of events that results in injury to a person you owed a duty to [certain condition], then you meet the standard for the legal causation part of the causation element [legal status].**

> **If the injury legally caused by your breach was a foreseeable result of your negligent behavior [certain condition], then you meet the standard for the proximate causation part of the causation element of a negligence claim [legal status].**

10 As you may know, various states use various labels for these two items: but-for cause, actual cause, factual cause, etc.

Notice that for some rules, the legal status is sort of a "final result" legal status like guilt or liability. For other rules, however, the legal status might be something like meeting a part of the test, as in the causation examples. Remember that within a CREXAC unit of discourse itself, you will not necessarily use the if-then structure to state your rule; using the if-then structure is just a technique you can use to test rules and to help you identify phrases-that-pay. Identifying the phrase-that-pays helps you with the substance of your analysis because the phrase-that-pays is almost always the condition that the rule requires in order for the legal status to result. For example, writing out the proximate causation rule as an if-then statement might have helped you to realize that "foreseeable result" is the phrase-that-pays for that issue, and that the plaintiff would need to prove that the injury that occurred was a foreseeable result of the breach that occurred.

In the proximate cause unit of discourse, for example, you might state the rule in a brief as follows:

11 Of course, you should use a citation the first time you state a rule, and almost always when you quote or paraphrase language from a source. *R.E.3d* is the abbreviation for our fictional regional reporter; it stands for "Regional East Third." And *Van.* is the abbreviation for our fictional state of Vanita.

11 **Proximate cause exists when the injury caused by the breach was a foreseeable result of the defendant's behavior.** *Smith v. Beazley*, 101 R.E.3d 105, 107 (Van. 2020).

12 One more point before we move on: law students, lawyers, and legal writers may talk about *issues* and *sub-issues*, and *rules* and *sub-rules*, when they need to clarify the relationships between those issues and rules. But please don't get hung up on these "sub" labels. The proximate cause rule we've articulated above is a *rule*, even though it could also be characterized as a sub-sub-rule of the negligence rule. In this text, when we refer to the rule (you might think of it as The Rule), we will usually be referring to the rule, sub-rule, sub-sub-rule, etc., that is the governing principle for that issue; more specifically, it is the *principle that articulates the certain condition that results in the legal status*. While you can expect that your discussion of a legal issue may include many sentences that contain language that could be thought of as *a rule*, be sure that your analysis stays focused on *the* rule that governs the issue.

12 Our students have noticed that many topic sentences and case descriptions contain language that could be thought of as *a* rule—they sometimes call it "rule-ish" language. *See* Chapter Nine for more information on topic sentences, and Chapter Six for more information on case descriptions.

2.2.3. Explain the Rule (the "EX" of CREXAC)

After you have articulated the rule, you must provide your reader with any needed explanation of the rule. Each CREXAC unit of discourse should focus on one phrase-that-pays, and you should use the rule explanation section to explain the phrase-that-pays in appropriate detail. Doing so helps the reader to understand how the rule works. A typical rule explanation describes at least one case in which the court has found that the phrase-that-pays is met, and at least one case in which the court has found that the phrase-that-pays is not met. A rule explanation of the proximate cause argument might look like the following:

> Events are a foreseeable result of careless conduct if they are a predictable consequence of the negligent behavior. *Gray v. Campion*, 101 R.E.2d 115, 132 (Van. 2016). In *Gray*, a defendant driver in a "chain reaction" collision was found to have breached his duty to maintain an assured clear distance between himself and the car ahead. *Id.* The driver argued that it was unforeseeable that the car ahead of him would stop suddenly after beginning to make a left turn. *Id.* The court disagreed, noting that such unexpected behavior is the precise reason behind the assured clear distance requirement, and was thus foreseeable. *Id. See also Keita v. Berry*, 144 R.E.2d 144, 149 (foreseeable that pedestrian would be on median of roadway at night, even though unusual).

13 Harm to another may not be a foreseeable result of a breach if a victim exposes himself to danger through sudden, unpredictable action. *See Mensah v. Cadden*, 85 R.E.2d 240, 245 (Van. 2010). The defendant driver in *Mensah* struck and injured a seven-year-old child who had wrenched himself away from his father's hand and darted into traffic. *Id.* at 242. The driver testified that before stepping on the gas, he had specifically noted that the child was holding his father's hand. *Id.* The court affirmed a finding that the driver had breached no duty, and observed that even if the driver had somehow breached a duty, the child's behavior in pulling himself away from his father and darting into the street was not foreseeable, and so any breach could not have been the proximate cause of the injury. *Id.*

13 The writer uses "may" here, and the citation signal "*see*" because the court did not *hold* that the harm was unforeseeable; it made the statement in dicta.

Chapter Five explains how to decide how much rule explanation is needed and how to write an effective rule summary.

2.2.4. Apply the Rule to the Facts (the "A" of CREXAC)

14 After you have articulated the rule and explained it as needed, it's time to apply the rule to the facts. Just as you touch your skin when you apply lotion to your body, when you apply law to facts, you explain how the law does or does not touch the facts. How do the required elements or factors exist (or not exist) in your case? You should never substitute synonyms for the phrase-that-pays in

14 Although it grates on our ears, some legal writers say "applying the facts to the rule" to mean the same thing.

any section, but particularly not in the application section. Here is a possible rule application for the proximate cause issue in our fictional client's case:

> Ms. O'Hara's breach proximately caused the injury to Mr. Fulmer. At any swimming pool, it is reasonably foreseeable that some swimmers are underwater and not immediately visible at any given time, particularly in the deep water around the diving boards, and particularly just after they have jumped off a high-dive. It is also foreseeable that if someone jumps off a high-dive without looking, she increases the chances that she will land on an underwater swimmer.
>
> Thus, when Ms. O'Hara failed to look carefully before cannonballing off the high-dive, it was foreseeable that there would be other swimmers below her in the water, it was foreseeable that she would land on one of them, and it was foreseeable that landing on the swimmer would cause injury to him. Indeed, this is exactly what happened. When Ms. O'Hara reached the top of the high-dive ladder she shouted, "Look out! Here comes the cannonball!" as she raced to the end of the board and jumped off. Mr. Fulmer was underwater at this moment, after his own leap from the board, and did not hear the shout. He emerged just in time for Ms. O'Hara's cannonball to land directly on the back of his neck, causing severe spinal injury.
>
> **15** Mr. Fulmer did not cause the accident by deciding to spring straight up from the bottom of the pool rather than angling away from the area directly beneath the board, as Ms. O'Hara argues. Mr. Fulmer took the most direct path back to the surface of the water so that he could take a breath. He had no duty to get out of the way as quickly as possible. Ms. O'Hara's argument defies common sense as well as the legal standard. After all, the cliché is "look before you leap," not "look out because someone may be leaping." Just as drivers have a duty to obey the assured-clear distance law so that they can be ready to stop safely at any time, those who use high-dives have a duty to look to make sure the water below them is clear so that they do not hurt someone already in the water.
>
> When someone who jumps off a diving board breaches her duty to look before she leaps, it is foreseeable that her leap may harm another.

15 This writer makes a subtle analogy to one of the cases cited in the rule explanation section. Being able to draw analogies is a vital skill, but being *able* to draw analogies does *not* mean that you must explicitly analogize each case from the explanation section in the application section. As we will discuss in Chapter Five, use analogies and disanalogies only as needed to highlight aspects of your argument that need highlighting. Don't use analogies to beat points into the ground.

Chapter Five goes into more detail on issues that arise in the rule application section, particularly issues relevant to persuasive writing.

2.2.5. Make the Connection (the Second "C" of CREXAC)

The second C in CREXAC stands for "connection-conclusion." We call it that because, after you have applied the rule to the facts, you need to show your reader how the result of the rule application connects to your argument. Sometimes, the connection-conclusion is relatively straightforward and can follow in the same paragraph as rule application, as in this example, which repeats the end of the rule application above:

> When someone who jumps off a diving board breaches her duty to look before she leaps, it is foreseeable that her leap may harm another. Accordingly, Ms. O'Hara's jump proximately caused Mr. Fulmer's injury.

Chapter Five explains situations in which your connection-conclusion may be more detailed.

2.3. CONCLUSION

By following a research protocol, you can make sure that you're starting your research with some foundational knowledge about the relevant law. By looking for particular kinds of statutes, you can avoid missing crucial supplements to the statute at issue. Finally, by making sure you know what you need to know about your issue and its governing authorities, you can have some confidence that your research has been appropriately thorough.

Likewise, using the CREXAC formula ensures that you answer the crucial questions that all readers have about points in controversy: What rule governs this issue? What does the rule mean, or how has it been applied? How might it be applied to this set of facts? What impact does that application have to this argument as a whole? You fulfill your duties as a legal writer by providing the information that your readers expect, in the order in which they expect it.

CHAPTER THREE

The Motion Memo and Persuasive Writing at the Trial Level

If you were to ask a litigator how she spends her time, she would list a number of tasks, but she would be quick to tell you that the bulk of her *writing* time is spent on persuasive writing in the form of briefs and memoranda in support of or in opposition to motions. Many, but not all, of those motions will be dispositive. We'll explain the concept of a *dispositive* motion in a moment. For now, we want you to understand that drafting motion memos is a very significant component of the litigation attorney's job. In many ways, the motion memo is similar to an appellate brief, so you will recognize echoes of what we tell you here when we get to appellate writing. In this chapter, our goal is to familiarize you with the purpose and form of the motion memo and other persuasive documents written to a trial court.

3.1. THE MOTION MEMO

While attorneys sometimes write in-house research memoranda, as you may have done during your first semester of law school, litigation

① As we noted earlier, these documents are also called *trial briefs, motion briefs, memoranda of points and authorities,* and *memoranda in support of or opposition to a motion.*

attorneys write documents to courts much more frequently. Attorneys write ① motion memos to persuade courts to take certain actions or make certain decisions. Motion memos are often similar to research memoranda in format and analytical structure.

A motion memo is usually filed to a trial court. Attorneys write motion memos to argue that a court should *grant* or *deny* a particular *motion*. A motion is a formal request that a court take an action or make a decision relevant to a case before the court. Whenever a party wants the court to take any action in the case other than make a decision on the merits, the party must *move* the court or file a motion. The parties may file a motion to ask the court to postpone the trial date, to limit the kinds of evidence that may be heard in a case, or to decide in favor of one party or the other without a formal trial. Procedural motions, such as motions to extend deadlines, are not normally supported by lengthy motion memos. The more significant the motion, however, the more likely it is that the *moving party* or *movant* will support the motion with a motion memo.

In a motion memo, the attorneys support their arguments by analyzing how the controlling law applies to certain facts (the facts that the plaintiff alleged in the complaint, for a memo in support of a motion to dismiss; the facts as demonstrated by evidence, for a memo in support of a motion for summary judgment; and the facts as they were presented at trial, for a memo in support of a post-trial motion). The movant writes the *Memorandum in Support of the Motion*. The party who did not file the motion, sometimes referred to as the *opponent* or the *non-moving party*, writes the *Memorandum in Opposition to the Motion*. In many instances, the movant then writes the *Reply Memorandum in Further Support of the Motion*. The parties are also referred to by their categorizations as *plaintiff* or *defendant*, as appropriate.

As part of understanding the type of document you are filing, you must know and understand the standards that a court applies to different types of decisions. This chapter discusses how writers can use the appropriate standards in motion memos.

Courts sometimes use the term *standard of review* to describe the standards used to decide some trial-level motions.[1] The term *review* is imprecise in this context, for usually the trial court cannot be said to be *re*-viewing anything; the motion to the trial court typically represents the first time that any court has viewed the legal issue. Unlike appellate standards of review, motion standards do not

---

1. *See, e.g.,* DAVID F. HERR, ROGER S. HAYDOCK & JEFFREY W. STEMPEL, MOTION PRACTICE (4th ed., Aspen 2004), for detailed information on motion practice in litigation. (Hereinafter "Herr, Haydock & Stempel.")

ask a court to apply a particular level of deference to the actions of another decisionmaker. While we will use the term *motion standards* to describe the standards that trial courts apply to various types of motions, you should be aware that the phrase *standard of review* is still in circulation.

2 Many motions govern routine matters, such as requests for extensions of time or for discovery. These motions may require little more than a request for action accompanied by the citation to a statute or rule. Other motions, however, may require formal briefing that is similar to the briefing done for appellate courts. Motion memos may be the sole basis for a decision; trial courts frequently decide motions based on the memos alone, without oral argument.[2] The motion standard is particularly important for motions like the motion to dismiss (i.e., Fed. R. Civ. P. 12(b)(6)) and the motion for summary judgment (i.e., Fed. R. Civ. P. 56).[3] These so-called dispositive motions can "dispose" of a case at least temporarily, and thus present an important opportunity for advocacy.[4] Counsel may use motion practice strategically, to educate the court as to the issues the case presents, or to narrow the factual or legal issues in dispute.[5]

The motion standards for dispositive motions derive from the trial court's competing needs to allow access to the courts on the one hand and to use judicial resources efficiently and prevent frivolous lawsuits on the other. Whatever your purpose in filing a dispositive motion, or any other motion, you will want to know and use the appropriate motion standard. The sections below discuss the motion standards for the most common dispositive motions and address general methods for using motion standards in motion memos.

2 We focus here on dispositive motions, but many types of motions require persuasive writing that can use analytical methods described in Chapter Five. Important examples include motions in limine, in civil cases, and motions to suppress evidence, in criminal ones. Each asks the court to exclude certain evidence from a trial. These motions are not dispositive in the same way as a motion to dismiss is, but a decision on either can profoundly affect a case's outcome. An attorney writing to support or oppose one of these motions should research and use both the legal rules governing the evidence in question and the legal rules related to the relevant motion standards.

---

2. The local rules of many trial courts require counsel to apply to the court for permission to present an oral argument on a motion.

3. Of course, these are not the only kinds of motions that require briefing or that are decided based upon so-called standards of review or motion standards. *See, e.g., Deborah Heart & Lung Ctr. v. Children of the World Found., Ltd.*, 99 F. Supp. 2d 481, 488 (D.N.J. 2000) (describing the standard for a motion for a preliminary injunction).

4. Unlike other motions, dispositive motions may dispose of the case by creating a final appealable order. *See, e.g.,* Herr, Haydock & Stempel, *supra* note 1, at § 4.03 (detailing the differences between motion practice and appellate advocacy).

5. Motions for summary judgment or partial summary judgment may often be used strategically in this way. *See* Herr, Haydock & Stempel, *supra* note 1, at § 16.02 (discussing when to use motions for partial summary judgment).

3.1.1. Motions to Dismiss

A motion to dismiss for failure to state a claim upon which relief can be granted is filed in lieu of answering the complaint, pursuant to Rule 12(b)(6). The motion standard for this motion states, in essence, that the court can dismiss a complaint only if the facts do not allow the plaintiff to establish a claim that will entitle him or her to relief. The court must take the factual allegations in the complaint as true.[6] The "facts" for the purpose of a motion to dismiss are the allegations in the complaint.

For example, Title VII provides that "employers" may not discriminate based on race, sex, or other factors. The statute defines an "employer" as someone who employs more than 15 employees. If a plaintiff filed a Title VII action even though he or she worked for a company with only 10 employees, the company would probably file a motion to dismiss. The court would not analyze whether the allegations of discrimination were valid or invalid. Instead, it would ask, "even if these allegations are true, can this plaintiff recover against this defendant under this statute?" The plaintiff in this example could never recover against this defendant under Title VII because Title VII does not apply to employers with fewer than 15 employees. Accordingly, the court would grant the motion to dismiss.

In general, the motion standard for a motion to dismiss strikes a balance among the needs of plaintiffs, of defendants, and of the judicial system. The plaintiff need not specify every detail of his or her claim, but the complaint must give the defendant fair notice and must contain either direct or indirect allegations as to all of the claim's material elements. Two United States Supreme Court cases have an effect on how motions to dismiss are analyzed.

In 2007, the United States Supreme Court decided *Bell Atlantic v. Twombly*, 550 U.S. 544 (2007). In that case, a somewhat complex antitrust cause of action, the Court arguably made plaintiffs' job more difficult. The Court seemed to require more than mere notice pleading, holding that while "a complaint attacked by a Rule 12(b)(6) motion to dismiss does not need detailed factual allegations . . . a plaintiff's obligation to provide the 'grounds' of his 'entitle[ment] to relief' requires more than labels and conclusions, and a formulaic recitation of the elements of a cause of action will not do." *Id.* at 555 (citations omitted). The Court noted that "[f]actual allegations must be enough to raise a right to relief above the speculative level" but that "the assumption" is "that all the allegations in the complaint

---

6. *See, e.g., Bell Atlantic Corp. v. Twombly*, 550 U.S. 544, 555 (2007).

are true." *Id.* (citations omitted). A complaint must include factual allegations that make its legal allegations not merely "conceivable," but "plausible." *Id.* at 570.

Two years later, the Court decided a post-9/11 anti-discrimination case, *Ashcroft v. Iqbal*, 556 U.S. 662 (2009). The Court reaffirmed its decision in *Twombly* and articulated a standard that it called context-specific and rooted in "judicial experience and common sense":

> [A] court considering a motion to dismiss can choose to begin by identifying pleadings that, because they are no more than conclusions, are not entitled to the assumption of truth. While legal conclusions can provide the framework of a complaint, they must be supported by factual allegations. When there are well-pleaded factual allegations, a court should assume their veracity and then determine whether they plausibly give rise to an entitlement to relief.[7]

Although the Court took care to say that a "plausibility" requirement is "not akin to a probability requirement,"[8] this standard puts an additional burden on plaintiffs, requiring that they craft a "plausible" complaint before undertaking formal discovery.[9]

Accordingly, the careful pleader will be sure to make the complaint's allegations as fact-specific as possible. Admittedly, even after *Twombly* and *Iqbal*, courts will construe the factual allegations as true. If, however, the court can be convinced that the plaintiff cannot establish a set of facts that will entitle him or her to relief, either because the law does not apply to that set of facts or because the set of facts alleged is too speculative, incomplete, or implausible, the court will dismiss the complaint before trial, and often before formal discovery has begun.

3.1.2. Motions for Summary Judgment

The motion standard for a motion for summary judgment is more complicated than the standard for a motion to dismiss. The plain language of Federal Rule of Civil Procedure 56(a) indicates that the motion should be granted when the evidence shows that there is "no genuine issue as to any material fact" *and* "the moving party is entitled to a judgment as a matter of law." In 1986, the United

---

7. *Iqbal*, 556 U.S. at 679 (citation omitted).

8. *Id.* at 678.

9. Edward A. Hartnett, *Taming* Twombly, *Even After* Iqbal, 158 U. PENN. L. REV. 473, 474 (2010).

States Supreme Court decided three summary judgment cases that provided clearer guidelines to the trial courts for when they should grant such motions.[10] The guidelines from these cases provide the motion standard that trial courts apply when considering motions for summary judgment. Many state courts have adopted the same motion standard.

When a party believes that its opponent will be unable to produce evidence in support of an element for which the opponent bears the burden of proof, that party will often file a motion for summary judgment pursuant to Rule 56 of the Federal Rules of Civil Procedure (or, in a state case, a parallel state procedural rule). The purpose for filing such a motion is to obtain a favorable judgment without a trial. In that respect, the motion for summary judgment is similar to the motion to dismiss. One significant difference between the two is timing.

3 *Discovery* occurs after a lawsuit is filed. It allows both sides to discover or develop accurate, relevant evidence. Each side may request that the other side reveal certain information, including names and contact information of those who may have knowledge about the events of the case; parties may also have to "produce" certain documents or digital evidence. As part of discovery, parties may submit interrogatories or requests for admissions to parties; they may also conduct depositions to take testimony from those with knowledge of the case.

3 While a motion to dismiss under Rule 12(b)(6) is usually filed in response to a complaint (in other words, at the beginning of the case), a motion for summary judgment almost always follows the close of discovery. Indeed, a court will usually issue a scheduling order shortly after a case is filed and include a motion for summary judgment deadline that follows the discovery cutoff by some short period of time, often 30 days. The reason for this chronology is that a motion for summary judgment tests the evidence in support of a claim rather than testing the plaintiff's allegations. A party cannot be expected to identify all of its evidence until discovery has closed. The "facts" for the purpose of a motion for summary judgment are pulled from the evidence on record in the case. The complaint's allegations will be treated as "facts" only if they are backed up by appropriate evidence. Accordingly, the motion for summary judgment is timed to permit the opposing party to obtain and organize its evidence before having to respond. The rules governing motions for summary judgment do not prohibit the filing of a motion prior to the close of discovery, but when a party files a motion for summary judgment before the end of discovery, the court will often exercise its authority under Rule 56(d) and extend the response time for the non-moving party until the close of discovery.

When a party files a motion for summary judgment, the motion standard requires it to articulate a basis for judgment in its favor on any claim as to which it seeks judgment. The motion must be

10. *Anderson v. Liberty Lobby, Inc.*, 477 U.S. 242 (1986); *Celotex Corp. v. Catrett*, 477 U.S. 317 (1986); *Matsushita Electrical Industrial Co. v. Zenith Radio Corp.*, 475 U.S. 574 (1986).

"properly supported."[11] Because a motion for summary judgment tests the evidence in support of a claim, the moving party will almost always be the defendant, and the discussion below relates to motions for summary judgments by defendants.

When a defendant files a motion for summary judgment, the defendant need not produce any evidence in support of the motion, in order to "properly support" it. Rather, as the movant, the defendant may simply identify the elements of the claim as to which judgment is sought and argue that the non-moving party, who bears the burden of proof as to those elements, will not be able to produce evidence in support of one or more of them.[12]

In response to a motion for summary judgment, the non-moving party is required to produce evidence, in the form of deposition testimony, affidavits, or documentary or tangible evidence, in support of each element of the claim that is the subject of the motion. The motion standard for a motion for summary judgment indicates that the amount of evidence required to defeat a motion for summary judgment is "more than a mere scintilla."[13] The Supreme Court was not intentionally being obscure when it used the "mere scintilla" language as the standard. Rather, it was reacting to a previous articulation of the motion standard, which indicated that a motion should be denied in the face of a scintilla of evidence. In *Anderson*, the Court raised the bar by requiring something more. Because a scintilla is a minute particle or a speck, the non-moving party must produce more than a speck of evidence, enough that a jury could find in the non-moving party's favor, in order to defeat the motion.[14]

Many complaints allege more than one cause of action, and some may be over-optimistic as to the plaintiff's chances of success on some of these causes of action. The defendant may respond to this type of complaint by using a motion for summary judgment in a couple of different ways. First, a defendant may file a motion for summary judgment that forces the plaintiff to produce sufficient evidence to support the allegations. In other cases, the defendant may file a motion for summary judgment supported by its own evidence as to one or more of the plaintiff's causes of action. A defendant may use this tactic in hopes of forcing a plaintiff to reveal that it has no evidence to support certain allegations, leading the court to grant summary judgment to the defendant as to those allegations.

---

11. *Anderson,* 477 U.S. at 248.
12. *Celotex Corp.,* 477 U.S. at 322.
13. *Anderson,* 477 U.S. at 250.
14. *Celotex Corp.,* 477 U.S. at 322.

You might analogize the adversarial nature of the trial to a poker game. In many motions for summary judgment, defense counsel is saying "I call"—in other words, "show me what evidence you have." In others, when the defendant has evidence that it believes will support its arguments as to one or more elements, a motion for summary judgment says, in essence, "Read 'em and weep"—in other words, "Look at the evidence I have; I bet you don't have enough evidence to match it"—that is, enough evidence to force the court to find in the plaintiff's favor or even call this issue into question.

Thus, when arguing a motion for summary judgment, be sure to research both how your jurisdiction articulates the motion standard for this type of motion and the relevant burdens of proof for the underlying cause(s) of action. Your argument will combine both the motion standard and the law applicable to the specific claims that are the subject of your motion.

3.1.3. Post-Trial Motions

A third type of motion, the post-trial motion, is also potentially dispositive in that the court's decision on such a motion may change the outcome, or disposition, of the case. A *post-trial motion*, as the name suggests, is a motion that a party files after the court has entered judgment in a case. In the federal system, Rules 50(b) and 59 allow parties to seek several forms of relief after the court has entered judgment by filing one or more of the following motions: a motion for judgment as a matter of law (Rule 50(b)), a motion for a new trial (Rule 59(a)), and a motion to alter or amend the judgment (Rule 59(e)). Rules 50(b) and 59 allow 28 days after the entry of judgment for such motions. Nearly every state has similar rules, numbered 50 and 59.

Post-trial motions under Rules 50 and 59 are like motions to dismiss and motions for summary judgment in two important respects. A motion standard applies to each type of post-trial motion, and the organization of a memorandum in support of or in opposition to a post-trial motion is essentially the same as the organization of any other form of dispositive motion.

a. Motions for Judgment as a Matter of Law

The motion for judgment as a matter of law is the simplest of the three post-trial motions to describe because Rule 50(b) supplies the motion standard and identifies the focus of the motion. Rule 50(b) provides that a trial court may enter judgment in favor of a party who has lost on an issue in a jury trial if the court concludes that "a reasonable jury would not have [had] a legally sufficient evidentiary basis to find for the [other] party on that issue." So, a party who moves for judgment as a matter of law after a jury verdict will succeed only by convincing the court that the other party did not present *sufficient evidence* to have permitted the favorable jury verdict. The rule does not permit a motion based on arguments about errors in the law; the focus must be the evidence in support of the jury's verdict. Like a motion for summary judgment, therefore, a motion for judgment as a matter of law will set out the motion standard and the legal rules governing the claim or issue in question and then will apply the motion standard and the legal rules to the evidence that was presented at trial. The parties' memoranda will look very much like memoranda in support of, or in opposition to, a motion for summary judgment, and the individual arguments included in the memoranda will follow the same analytical format (CREXAC or CRAC, for example, for the more controversial arguments).

b. Motions for New Trial and to Alter or Amend the Judgment

4 Post-trial motions under Rule 59 are more complicated because Rule 59 does not supply the applicable motion standards. The rule acknowledges that motion standards exist for motions for a new trial but sends lawyers elsewhere to find those standards. Rule 59(a)(1)(A) states that a court may grant a new trial after a jury verdict "for any reason for which a new trial has heretofore been granted in an action at law in federal court." Rule 59(a)(1)(B) states that a court may grant a new trial after a nonjury trial "for any reason for which rehearing has heretofore been granted in a suit in equity in federal court." Rule 59(e) says nothing about a motion standard for a motion to alter or amend the judgment.

While we cannot tell you every reason for which a new trial has *heretofore been granted*, we can provide guidance about the types of reasons that are the most common bases for new trials and how to identify the appropriate motion standard. Rule 59 uses "heretofore been granted" to mean *reasons for which courts granted new trials before rules of civil procedure existed*. So, while rules of civil procedure have largely replaced common law and equity in most procedural matters, Rule 59 preserves the common law and equitable reasons for new trials. Among the most common reasons for new trials before rules of civil procedure existed were (1) legal errors; (2) newly-discovered evidence; (3) inconsistent verdicts; (4) procedural errors during trial; and (5) misconduct by an attorney, a party, or a witness. If an attorney believes that one of those reasons sup-

4 Lawyers sometimes entitle their motions under Rule 59(b)(1) "motions for reconsideration." While that title does not echo the language of the rule, it accurately describes the action the lawyer wants the court to take. That is, the lawyer is asking the court to reconsider its own earlier decision.

ports a new trial in her case, she should conduct research to determine whether courts in her jurisdiction have cited that reason as a basis for a new trial. If courts have cited that reason, either before or after the adoption of Rule 59, the attorney will study their opinions to determine the motion standard the courts have applied in granting the motion. For example, a lawyer in the Third Circuit who believes that misconduct by an attorney at trial should be the basis for a new trial will learn that the motion standard for a motion for a new trial on that basis is that it must be "reasonably probable that the verdict was prejudicially influenced by" counsel's conduct.[15]

The motion standard for motions to alter or amend judgments is a bit easier to find. Courts have expressed it in various ways, but most versions resemble this one from the Sixth Circuit: a court may not grant a motion to alter or amend a judgment unless the movant clearly establishes a "manifest error of law" or presents "newly-discovered evidence."[16] A lawyer who wonders about the availability of a motion to alter or amend judgment in the case would conduct research to ascertain the motion standard in her jurisdiction. Most often, the *manifest error of law* must be a change in controlling law. The alternative is a legal error by the trial court that is so obvious that the court is moved to correct it after trial. Obviously, the same error could be raised in an appeal, and a court of appeals is much more likely to say that the trial court was wrong than a trial court is to admit that it was wrong. *Newly-discovered evidence* almost always means evidence that the movant did not have and could not have discovered before trial.

You will be happy to learn that the motion standard is the only *new* aspect of the memorandum in support of, or in opposition to, a post-trial motion under Rule 59(e). In other respects, the parties' memoranda will look very similar to memoranda in support of, or in opposition to, other dispositive motions, and the individual arguments included in the memoranda will follow the familiar analytical structure.

3.2. ELEMENTS OF A MOTION MEMO

Motion memos have much in common with the office memoranda or research memoranda that you may have written during your first semester of law school. The office memorandum tries to *predict* how a court will apply the law to the facts. The motion memo, in contrast,

---

15. *Greenleaf v. Garlock, Inc.*, 174 F.3d 352 (3d Cir. 1999).

16. *Roger Miller Music, Inc. v. Sony/ATV Publ'g, LLC*, 477 F.3d 383, 395 (6th Cir. 2007).

tries to *persuade* a court to apply the law to the facts in a particular way. In both documents, the writer must discuss relevant rules and authorities and show how the law can or should apply to the facts of the client's case.

The office memorandum has a formal caption that usually lists the person who requested the memo, the author of the memo, the subject of the memo, and the date of the memo. The caption in a motion memo is laid out differently; it usually identifies the court in which the motion is being filed, the parties to the case, the docket number of the case, and the type of document that is being filed (e.g., "Memorandum in Opposition to Defendant's Motion to Dismiss"). The party who wrote the memo may be identified in an opening paragraph, and/or at the end of the document, in a signature line after the conclusion. This chapter will first explain common formal requirements for motion memos; although many courts don't specify particular formats for these documents, we will describe requirements that would be helpful to include in memos that are supporting or opposing dispositive motions. The discussion will also provide detail as needed for some of the more complex sections.

3.2.1. Formal Requirements

Although fulfilling your memo's formal requirements is a much less intellectually demanding task than writing the argument, it is nonetheless important. Rightly or wrongly, many readers form an impression of your credibility based on whether you conform to the minutiae of court rules. Your willingness to learn and follow rules about document format and filing guidelines tells the court that you are a professional, and that you take court requirements seriously. More significantly, if you fail to follow certain rules, you may suffer sanctions, such as having to fix offending portions of the motion memo, or even having your case dismissed.[17]

Most state and federal courts in the United States are governed by at least two sets of rules. The more significant rules are the rules of procedure that govern all of the courts within a certain jurisdiction, for example, state and federal rules of civil procedure.

Most courts also have so-called "local rules" that may deal with requirements such as filing requirements, page length, certificates

---

17. Judith D. Fischer, *Bareheaded and Barefaced Counsel: Courts React to Unprofessionalism in Lawyers' Papers*, 31 SUFFOLK U.L. REV. 1, 31 et seq. (1997) (this article also contains several examples of courts' reactions to misstatements of law and facts and other failings). *See also* JUDITH D. FISCHER, PLEASING THE COURT: WRITING ETHICAL AND EFFECTIVE BRIEFS (Carolina Academic Press 2005).

of service, service on opposing parties, citations, and the like. Although local rules may seem less significant, you fail to follow them at your peril. In 2002, the Ninth Circuit dismissed an appeal for failure to comply with certain Federal Rules of Appellate Procedure (FRAP) and with circuit rules.[18] The court noted that "[a]n enormous amount of time is wasted when attorneys fail to provide proper briefs and excerpts of record that should have supplied the court with the materials relevant to the appeal. The FRAP and Ninth Circuit rules are not optional suggestions . . . but *rules* that . . . are entitled to respect, and command compliance."[19]

In addition to expecting counsel to follow local rules, some courts expect counsel to be aware of local practices, the customs and behaviors that are unwritten but practiced by experienced local lawyers. Courts that allow electronic filing may prefer to have counsel file an additional hard copy if a document is lengthy. Trial judges may have "standing orders" that lay out rules or guidelines for counsel to follow in all trials in front of that particular judge. Taking the time to read a judge's standing order (often posted on the judge's website) may provide you with valuable information that will save you time and trouble and help you to make a good impression on the court. Whenever you have to file a motion, make sure that you have copies of all of the written rules that apply to documents submitted to that court, and try to find out the local practices and customs by consulting court websites, more experienced colleagues, or both.

This chapter explains the format requirements that are common to motion memos, including memos in support of and in opposition to motions of summary judgment, and it will refer to federal court rules as appropriate. Unless court rules designate otherwise, you can assume that Arabic numerals (1, 2, 3) are appropriate for all pages in a motion memo. Motion practice in the state courts is similar to that in the federal courts, but counsel should be certain to consult the appropriate rules before filing a brief or memo with any court. The annotated sample memo at the end of the chapter illustrates many of these requirements.

a. Caption

A motion memo requires a formal caption that includes the name of the court hearing the case, the parties, their procedural titles, the case's docket number, and the title of the document (e.g., "Memorandum in Support of Defendant Bolitho's Motion to Dismiss").

---

18. *In re O'Brien*, 312 F.3d 1135, 1136 (9th Cir. 2002).
19. *Id.* at 1137 (citation omitted) (emphasis in original).

Note that in some courts, if counsel desires oral argument, it must request oral argument within the caption; it is therefore particularly important to consult local rules in this regard.

b. Introduction

Although motion memos do not typically include a *questions presented* section, the motion memo may include an "introduction" (or "preliminary statement") that uses a short paragraph to lay out the issue(s) before the court. The introduction often appears under a heading just below the caption. In the introduction, an effective attorney will also include a very short summary of the major arguments in the motion memo. This summary is where the attorney attempts to make the most compelling case for either the movant or the non-moving party in a few sentences.

c. Statement of Facts

The statement of facts usually follows the introduction. It will usually include all of the facts to which the argument will refer. If a fact is supported by evidence, the statement of facts will identify the evidence and provide a citation to the exhibit or document in which the evidence is found.

The evidence upon which a party relies must be in the court's record. If a party relies on a piece of evidence that is not part of the record that has already been filed with the court, that party should either attach this evidence as an exhibit to the motion memo or file it simultaneously as a separate document.

You will recall that office memoranda also include statements of facts. The statement of facts in a motion memo is similar in the sense that it should usually include every "fact" to which the analysis that follows refers. The statement of facts in a motion memorandum also accomplishes two purposes that are not relevant in the office memorandum context. First, the statement of facts is the section of the motion memo in which the party identifies all of the favorable facts upon which it relies in support of or in opposition to the motion. Second, the statement of facts in the motion memo is the best opportunity for the attorney to tell a compelling story about the case. Because evidence is the focus of the motion for summary judgment, and the statement of facts is the place where the evidence is identified, the statement of facts is also where a skillful attorney will highlight any strengths in the evidence supporting its own claims (or opposition to claims) or any weaknesses in or absence of evidence in support of its opponent's claims (or its opponent's opposition to claims). A defendant's attorney should exercise great care in the organization and presentation of the evidence and should attempt to create an impression in the court's minds about the futility of the plaintiff's claims in light of the evidence. The plaintiff's attorney, of course, attempts to do the opposite.

There is one other difference between a statement of facts in an office memo and a statement of facts in a motion memo. Nearly every sentence in a motion memo should be followed by a citation to the record, either to the page or the paragraph on or in which the information can be found. Further, citations to the record are so important that when you mention facts of any significance in the argument, you should follow the sentence with a citation to the record as well.

d. Motion Standard

As you read above, the motion standard is the framework within which the court makes its decision. You must tell the court what motion standard applies to your argument. If the standard is controversial, you must include appropriate argument(s) about the standard. If the standard is not controversial, you should refer to it at least within your introductory material and your conclusion. A motion memo in support of a motion to dismiss or a motion for summary judgment will almost always include a separate section setting out the motion standard. For other types of motions for which the standard is very brief, a writer may choose to incorporate the standard in the umbrella section.

Some courts ask writers to place the motion standard in a separate section before the argument, and there may be good reasons for doing so. As you know, many readers—including readers of this book—skip information if they believe it is not important or relevant to them. When it comes to dispositive motions, judges know the motion standards so well that they may skip over paragraphs as soon as they realize the paragraph is laying out a motion standard. Thus, if a motion standard is incorporated into the umbrella section, a skimming judge may also skip over aspects of the umbrella section that are unique to the motion or brief. Accordingly, if the rules allow you to do so (or do not forbid you to do so), you should consider creating a separate section for the motion standard. Of course, even if you create a separate section, you must still address the motion standard as appropriate in the body of your argument.

e. Argument

The argument in a motion memo is the counterpart to the discussion section of an office memorandum. Some trial courts specify that counsel should cite only or primarily to mandatory authority and may ask for copies of any non-mandatory sources. Some courts ask counsel to formally list any relevant authority that goes against counsel's argument. Some courts may allow or ask for an electronic document that includes links to all authorities cited in the brief. Thus, even though the method of written argument may not vary from court to court, you must still consult local rules about the argument itself.

Specific methods of persuasive writing will be discussed in a later chapter. For now, understand that CREXAC applies equally in persuasive and predictive writing. While the goal in a motion memo is to convince the reader that your argument is more correct than your opponent's argument, the framework for the analysis has not changed. Your main goal when writing an argument section should be to conduct effective analytical writing, using the same methods that you would use to write the discussion section of an office memorandum. That is, identify relevant rules, explain what they mean, and apply them to the facts. When writing to persuade, the way you choose which rules to analyze, the ways in which you articulate those rules and explain their significance, and the ways in which you apply them to the facts will vary slightly from how you performed these tasks when you were writing to inform. Of course, your goal should never be to misrepresent what the law is, nor how the law applies to the facts. Rather, your goal should be to identify when reasonable alternatives exist, and to persuade the court that your alternative is the more appropriate application of the relevant rule or that it promotes a preferable policy.

f. Conclusion

At a minimum, your conclusion should tell the court what you want it to do: grant the motion or deny the motion. You will sometimes see flowery language in the conclusion, such as "Counsel for the Plaintiff respectfully requests that the Court deny Defendant's motion for summary judgment." Although this language probably does not hurt counsel, it probably does not help, either. Because the words "respectfully submitted" appear in the signature block, just below the conclusion, there is probably no need to use "respectfully" in the conclusion itself.

Some lawyers write only one sentence as a conclusion, as in this example:

For the foregoing reasons, this Court should grant Defendant's motion to dismiss.

Although many courts will not wish to read a conclusion that is much longer than a paragraph, the conclusion for a motion memo may sometimes be longer than a sentence. As noted above, it is appropriate to connect the motion standard to your conclusion, as in this example:

> **Defendant Paperbook Publishing has only ten employees and thus does not meet the definition of "employer" in Title VII. Accordingly, Plaintiff can establish no set of facts that plausibly gives rise to an entitlement to relief, and this court should grant Defendant's motion to dismiss.**

In any event, be precise when requesting relief: You should *not* ask a court to "uphold," "strike down," or "overrule" the motion; these terms do not describe what courts do with these types of motions. Ask the court either to "grant" or "deny" the motion.

g. Signature

Federal Rule of Civil Procedure 11 requires that at least one attorney "sign" every motion and state the signer's address, email address, and phone number. Many state court rules also require that the signer's attorney include an attorney registration number. If you are filing the motion memo electronically, you may not need to include a "real" signature; you may, however, be required to verify your identity through some means such as your registration in the system. If you must file a document in hard copy, presume that a handwritten signature is required. Whether your signature is manual or electronic, you should include the phrase "Respectfully submitted" before the signature line.

h. Certificate of Service

Most courts require that litigants who serve papers on the court also certify that they have served copies of those documents on opposing counsel. Essentially, the certificate of service is a document accurately describing how one party served another. Usually, counsel for both parties are registered in the court's e-filing system, so service can be accomplished electronically.

i. Appendix

Few courts have rules that require an appendix for every motion. Counsel should consider including in an appendix any information the court may need to refer to while it considers the case, and which the court would otherwise not have easy access to. For example, counsel may include unpublished decisions, copies of documents (or segments of documents) that are at issue, and the like.[20] Note that some court rules may require an appendix in certain circumstances; some trial courts require that counsel attach copies of unpublished decisions or of decisions from courts of another jurisdiction.

3.3. DECIDING WHICH ISSUES TO INCLUDE IN A MOTION TO A TRIAL COURT

The process of deciding which issues to raise and which arguments to make in a motion memo can be complicated. The process begins as the writer identifies all of the possible issues and the arguments in support of the writer's position on each. Rarely will the writer include every issue and every argument in the final version of the document. Instead, the writer will examine the available legal authority and the facts and focus on the issues and arguments that are most likely to be successful. We recommend, in most situations, that a motion memo or brief include fewer strong arguments rather than more weak arguments. To decide which arguments are strongest, the writer must honestly evaluate the facts and the legal support for each. One very important consideration should also guide the writer's choices about which issues and arguments to include: preserving issues for appeal.

An appellate court will rarely consider an issue that a lawyer has raised for the first time on appeal, so every motion memo must include any issue that the writer's client may want to raise to a higher court, even if mandatory authority means that the trial court cannot rule in favor of the client. The act of including an issue because it may be the subject of an appeal is called *preserving* the issue, and, just like preserving fruit requires handling it now so that it will be available in an appropriate form later, preserving an issue for appeal requires careful handling of the issue at one stage of a case so that it will be available in an appropriate form at a later stage.

You may be thinking that the process of identifying the strongest issues at the trial level will automatically result in preserving the best issues for appeal because the strength of each issue is unlikely to change as a case progresses through the courts, and you are partially right. Your careful selection of issues and arguments at the trial stage is a big first step in the process of preserving issues. Many

---

20. *See, e.g.*, Ruggero J. Aldisert, Winning on Appeal 84-89 (rev. 1st ed., Natl. Inst. Trial Advoc. 1996); Carole C. Berry, Effective Appellate Advocacy: Brief Writing and Oral Argument 107 (3d ed., Thomson/West 2003).

of the issues that you have identified as the most compelling at the trial stage are likely to continue to be compelling at the appellate stage, even if you have been unsuccessful in asserting them at the first stage. Some issues that rarely move trial courts are more likely to succeed at the appellate level, however, and a careful writer will identify and preserve those issues so that they will be available if an appeal follows final judgment in the trial court.

5 Trial courts also resolve disputes about what evidence to admit in a trial. Lawyers who believe that a trial court has erred in an evidentiary decision must object when the evidence is excluded or admitted to preserve for appeal the issues related to that decision. Likewise, counsel must object to any other trial court actions *when they occur* to preserve the relevant issue for appeal. For example, to argue on appeal that a client was prejudiced by overlong trial delays, the attorney must object to the trial schedule at a time when the trial court could have changed it.

5 Trial courts most often resolve disputes about facts, and appellate courts most often resolve disputes about law; the respective roles of the courts affect the likelihood that a particular argument will succeed at each level. A lawyer will be careful to raise issues about the facts at the trial level because the lawyer knows that an appellate court is unlikely to change the trial court's decision about the facts. Indeed, as we will discuss below, standards of review dictate that an appellate court must generally find clear error before it can alter a trial court's factual findings. On the other hand, while trial courts make decisions about how the law applies to the facts, a trial court will rarely resolve disputes about what the law is. For example, a lawyer will rarely convince a trial court to ignore mandatory authority on the ground that it is incorrect or unconstitutional. Those decisions are the province of the appellate courts. Still, a lawyer must raise challenges to the law at the trial level to preserve them for appeal. So, the evaluation of issues and arguments at the trial stage must include an analysis of legal issues the lawyer may want to raise at the appellate level, and the lawyer must preserve those issues at the trial level even if the trial court cannot resolve them definitively.

3.4. OTHER TYPES OF BRIEFS SUBMITTED TO TRIAL COURT

We have identified several types of persuasive documents that lawyers write to trial courts. We have not exhausted the category, however, and we will not try to do so. Before we leave the subject, however, we want to tell you something about trial briefs and arbitration briefs.

3.4.1. The Trial Brief

A trial brief is a document that a lawyer submits to a court before a trial begins; it includes the lawyer's position on points of law related to her client's claim and items of evidence that the lawyers may seek to introduce at trial. Rules of civil procedure do not mention trial briefs. Some trial judges include a deadline for the submission of trial briefs in their pretrial orders, but few, if any, judges require parties to submit trial briefs. Unless a court instructs the parties to file trial briefs and prescribes the issues to be addressed, a lawyer may choose to address one, many, or no issues in such a document. Our purposes here are to help you to think about when a trial brief may be a good litigation strategy and what issues you should include if you choose to prepare one. We will also address, very briefly, the format of a trial-brief argument.

6 While a lawyer may choose to submit a trial brief in any case, she will most often choose to do so when the case has *not* been the subject of dispositive motions. Dispositive motions usually serve to inform the trial court about the lawyers' positions on the controversial issues in a case and to identify some or all of the evidence they may seek to introduce at trial. So, when a case has been the subject of dispositive motions before trial, the court will often have decided which rules the court or a jury will apply to the evidence at trial and which evidence the court will admit. A lawyer who has participated in dispositive motion practice may well conclude that a trial brief would not add anything to the court's understanding of the issues. On the other hand, a lawyer in a case that has not been the subject of a dispositive motion may decide that a trial brief would help the court to identify the rules or to consider the admissibility of evidence before the flurry of trial activity begins.

> **6** Even if a case has been the subject of a dispositive motion, a lawyer may choose to submit a trial brief to address issues that were not resolved in the motion process.

A trial brief will most often include the author's position on only potentially controversial points of law and potentially controversial items of evidence. A trial court is much more likely to thoroughly study a trial brief that is limited in content to the truly controversial issues in the case. So, if a lawyer recognizes that several elements of her client's claim are not contested, she will address only contested elements in her trial brief. The same guidance applies to arguments about evidence. A lawyer will not include an argument about the admissibility of every item of evidence she intends to introduce at trial. Rather, she will narrow her focus to those items about which the parties are most likely to disagree.

You may be wondering why a lawyer would submit a trial brief at all, and some information about the decisions a court makes during a trial will help to clear the fog. The purpose of a trial, as you know, is for the court or a jury to decide whether the party with the burden of proof has carried that burden by introducing evidence that meets the evidentiary standard: usually the *preponderance of the evidence* standard in a civil trial and the *beyond a reasonable doubt* standard in a criminal trial. That decision requires an understanding of the law and knowledge of the evidence on the part of the court or the jury.

7 A bench trial is a trial to the judge. In other words, the judge, or bench, decides whether the party with the burden of proof has proved a claim. In a bench trial scenario, a court may instruct the lawyers to submit post-trial briefs, sometimes called *proposed findings of fact and conclusions of law.* A lawyer may include arguments about the applicable law in that document.

7 One purpose of the trial brief, therefore, is to influence the court's or jury's understanding of the law. To determine whether a party has proved a claim, the *finder of fact* must know what the party is legally required to prove; in other words, the finder of fact must understand the law that governs the claim. In a *bench trial* scenario, the finder of fact will be the court. If the lawyers have not submitted trial briefs identifying the applicable law from their points of view, the court will decide what law applies without any help from the lawyers. In a jury trial, the court will instruct the jury about the applicable law. If the lawyers have not submitted trial briefs, the court will prepare the jury instructions without guidance from the lawyers about the applicable law. The court may allow the lawyers to review the jury instructions shortly before the court reads them to the jury, but the time allotted for that review will rarely be sufficient to conduct full-scale research into the governing law in order to support objections to the court's version of the law. So, one important purpose for the trial brief is to advise the court of the lawyer's position on the governing law before the court prepares the jury instructions.

If the law governing an element of a claim is unsettled or controversial in any sense, the lawyer will include arguments about why her version of the law governs the claim or element in question. The lawyer's argument about the governing law may follow a format similar to CREXAC, but the conclusion will be something like "rule x governs plaintiff's claim that defendant breached its duty of care" and not "plaintiff can prove that defendant breached its duty of care." The rule will be something like "rule x governs the duty element of a negligence claim against a nurse practitioner" and not "plaintiff can prove that defendant violated the duty element." The lawyer will dedicate the explanation portion of the argument to persuading the court that x is the governing rule for the duty of a nurse practitioner and the application portion to establishing that rule x should apply to the duty element of plaintiff's claim. A similar format applies to trial-brief arguments about the admissibility of evidence.

A second purpose of a trial brief is to persuade the court that an item of favorable evidence is admissible or that an item of unfavorable evidence is not admissible. If you have observed a trial, you already know that a trial court rules on the admissibility of evidence when it overrules or sustains objections during the course of the trial. If you are like most observers, your head has spun at the speed with which courts make those rulings, often without any argument at all from the lawyers. When the court does allow the lawyers to argue about the admissibility of an item of evidence during the trial, the arguments are usually quite short. A trial brief provides a lawyer an opportunity to set out the best arguments about the admissibility of controversial pieces of evidence and to identify the authority in support of those arguments. The court may even decide the admissibility question before the moment when one of the lawyers would attempt to introduce the evidence. If the court has not ruled before that moment, the lawyer will have the assurance that the court has had the opportunity to consider the arguments about the evidence *and* that the lawyer has preserved issues related to the admissibility of the evidence for appeal.

You may not be asked to prepare a trial brief as a law student, but you will certainly consider submitting trial briefs if you practice as a litigator. We hope that this discussion has enlightened you just a bit about the purposes, content, and argumentative format of a trial brief.

3.4.2. The Arbitration Brief

8 Lawyers engage in dispute resolution processes in addition to litigation, and at least one of those processes often includes persuasive writing. We wade into the murky waters of arbitration briefs only to advise you that such documents exist and to identify the most fundamental differences between the litigation and arbitration processes as they influence the content of persuasive writing in each context.

Arbitration is an alternative to litigation. In almost every instance, parties participate in arbitration instead of litigation because a contract requires them to do so. In other words, the parties chose arbitration as their dispute resolution process when they entered into a contract with each other and not when the dispute arose. The subject matter of the arbitration will almost always be an aspect of the parties' contract that included the arbitration provision.

The arbitration process differs from litigation in many respects. For our purposes, three differences are most important. First, rules of evidence and civil procedure do not apply in arbitration. The applicable rules arise primarily from the parties' contract. Second, the arbitration process is not built on the assumption that lawyers will represent the parties. Parties often represent themselves, and they may be represented by non-lawyers. Third, principles related to precedent do not apply in the arbitration context. Many arbitration decisions are available in online legal research services; however, an arbitrator is not bound by past arbitration decisions or judicial decisions about the same or similar agreements. So, the parties are not obliged to look for those decisions or to identify them to the arbitra-

8 Parties in mediation sometimes submit briefs before a mediation begins. The mediation process is not governed by rules of procedure. Unless the mediator has prescribed the form or content of the document, a mediation brief may include just about anything that a party or its representative wants to put in writing.

tor. Now that you know about those three differences, you may have concluded that persuasive writing has no place in the arbitration process. Not so fast.

Persuasive writing has increasingly become a part of the arbitration process. Historically, parties in arbitration presented their arguments at the opening and closing of the process. They presented their opening arguments orally, but they often presented their closing arguments in writing. Remember that these arguments were not about legal rules but about provisions in the parties' contract. Over time, in certain types of arbitration, parties have come to rely on lawyers to present their arbitration cases and make their arguments. Those lawyers increasingly rely on written arguments before and after trial, and those written arguments have come to resemble trial briefs or post-trial briefs.

Because the forms that persuasive writing may take in the arbitration context are so varied, we cannot begin to address all of them here. We do want you to know that in areas of the arbitration process that are increasingly lawyer-dominated, arbitration briefs have become increasingly common. Their format is often similar to the format of a trial brief; without governing rules of procedure, however, the variations are much wider. Because the concepts of precedent and authority do not apply, lawyers will often not cite previous decisions by arbitrators or courts. When they do cite earlier decisions, they do so only to persuade the arbitrator that a particular outcome would be within the mainstream or outside the mainstream. Lawyers in the arbitration process are more likely to focus their arguments on the correct interpretation of the contract language using common-sense or customary definitions within the relevant industry. They may cite treatises or other support for those interpretations.

We hope that this short description of arbitration briefs has enlightened more than it has confused you. Arbitration often includes persuasive writing, but its content is heavily influenced by the fact that rules of civil procedure and evidence and the principle of precedent do not apply.

3.5. CONCLUSION

Whenever you submit a brief to a trial court, an arbitrator, or a mediator, be sure to consult any existing local rules to verify what you will be expected to submit. Your knowledge of both legal and procedural rules will help you to provide the needed legal analysis.

A sample motion memo follows.

SAMPLE MOTION MEMORANDUM

IN THE UNITED STATES DISTRICT COURT
FOR THE SOUTHERN DISTRICT OF OHIO
WESTERN DIVISION

Stevie Wendl,   :

                Plaintiff,   :

v.   :   Case No. C-1-13-01

Bank Two, N.A.,   :

                Defendant.   :   Judge Beckwith

Memorandum in Support of Defendant's Motion to Dismiss   **9**

                                        Monte Smith   **10**
                                        Moritz & Michaels
                                        55 W. 12th Avenue
                                        Columbus, OH 43210-1391

Introduction

    This motion is filed in response to an action by Plaintiff, Stevie Wendl, alleging sex discrimination in violation of Title VII, 42 U.S.C.A. § 2000e-2, against   **11**
Defendant, Bank Two, N.A. This memorandum supports Defendant's motion to
dismiss pursuant to Rule 12(b)(6) of the Federal Rules of Civil Procedure for

---

9 Here is the name of the document. Note that it names the specific motion, and whether the document is in support of or in opposition to that motion.

10 Most memoranda of this type are attached to the motion itself, and the writer's name appears there. When you are submitting a document that is not attached to a motion (e.g., a Memorandum in Opposition to a Motion), you should include your name and address on the cover page. In a real scenario, you would also include your attorney registration number.

11 Note that because this is a statutory claim, it's important to name the statute. Since this statute also has a "nickname," that is included as well. Most statutes will have some sort of descriptor (e.g., "the Indian Child Welfare Act"), and that descriptor should be included to give the court context.

12 Plaintiff's failure to state a claim upon which relief can be granted. Plaintiff has failed to allege facts in support of two of the essential elements of her claim. Specifically, she has failed to allege that Bank Two treated her differently from any other employee who was in a similar position or under similar supervision. Therefore, she cannot prove discrimination.

13 Statement of Facts[21]

14 Plaintiff, Stevie Wendl, has filed a lawsuit against Bank Two, claiming that it discriminated against her when it terminated her employment as part of a restructuring process in 2012. In early 2003, Bank Two hired Stevie Wendl, Todd North, and Jason South to management positions. Bank Two placed new managers solely on the basis of the qualifications of the applicants. All new managers at Bank Two in 2003 had the same starting salary.

---

21. The facts described in this Statement of Facts are as alleged in Plaintiff's Complaint. By repeating them here, Defendant neither verifies nor contradicts them. This sample brief is full-justified because our publisher has sophisticated kerning software. You should usually left-justify your documents.

12 At the very least, the introduction should specify the particular basis for the motion to dismiss—don't just say 12(b)(6) or whatever rule it is—that's not specific enough. If including details would help create sympathy for your client, you may include a sentence more, but it would rarely be appropriate to provide an introduction that is longer than a 6–7-line paragraph; a 4–5-line paragraph is usually sufficient. Here, including more detail requires the writer to address some of plaintiff's allegations or, more precisely, some of the gaps in plaintiff's allegations.

13 Generally, the writer should cite to the complaint at the end of every sentence in the fact statement. Some defendants prefer not to include citations, perhaps because citations may seem to give credence to the complaint's allegations. If you do not include citations, you should include a disclaimer like the one in this footnote. Whether or not you include citations, you should be careful when discussing allegations of illegal behavior. Writers often use distancing phrases like "the plaintiff claims," or "the plaintiff has alleged" in sentences that discuss the core allegations of illegality.

14 Note that this first sentence provides context for the fact statement, by noting that it is a discrimination suit and describing in general terms the facts that led to the claim. Note also that the writer uses the distancing word "claiming." The plaintiff might provide context by saying, e.g., "Plaintiff Stevie Wendl has sued Bank Two for discriminating against her when it terminated her employment in 2012."

Todd North and Jason South worked in the International Transactions department at Bank Two. The vice president of that department supervised them, set their performance standards, and evaluated their performance annually. Plaintiff worked in the Commercial Lending department where she was supervised by the vice president of the Commercial Lending department for the duration of her tenure at Bank Two. From the time of her hiring until after the termination of her employment, Plaintiff never complained to anyone that her placement in Commercial Lending was an act of discrimination.

Every raise at Bank Two is merit-based as determined by annual performance evaluations. The evaluations focus on five performance categories that Bank Two has identified as imperative to effectively managing in each department. The higher an employee's annual evaluation score is, the higher that employee's annual salary increase will be.

Mr. North and Mr. South received the highest-attainable scores in each of the five categories in their first annual performance evaluations. Plaintiff did not score as well in one category, employee management. Consequently, Mr. North and Mr. South received larger raises than did Plaintiff. On every subsequent annual evaluation, Plaintiff failed to improve her performance in the area of employee management and received the same less-than-perfect score in that area. On the other hand, Mr. North and Mr. South maintained their perfect-scoring performances on subsequent annual evaluations. All three employees' merit-based raises were appropriated accordingly, and, as a result, Mr. North and Mr. South worked their way to higher salaries than did Plaintiff over the course of their employment.

In late 2011, Bank Two announced a management restructuring program as part of a necessary contraction in its workforce. Although terminations were an inevitable part of the restructuring, Bank Two committed to retaining its best-performing and most senior managers. Bank Two based all termination decisions strictly on salary levels; salary is the most accurate indicator of performance and seniority level at Bank Two, as raises are based strictly on performance-based merit. In determining which workers are the best performing of those employed at Bank Two for the same length of time, higher salary is indicative of better performance, and lower salary is indicative of poorer performance.

Bank Two selected Plaintiff for termination because her performance scores and salary were lower than those of other managers. Although Plaintiff's termination was an unfortunate part of the restructuring program, her selection for termination was merely a consequence of the overall workforce contraction scheme. The termination became effective on March 30, 2012.

Plaintiff did not complain of discrimination by Bank Two until after her termination. On April 30, 2012, she filed a charge of discrimination with the Equal Employment Opportunity Commission ("E.E.O.C."). The E.E.O.C. issued her a right-to-sue letter on October 3, 2012. She now brings a Title VII sex discrimination suit against her former employer, Bank Two, nearly ten years after her initial hiring and placement.

Argument

15 **The Court should dismiss Plaintiff's complaint for failure to state a claim upon which relief can be granted because she has failed to allege facts that**

---

15 This memo contains only one major argument, so it is not numbered. If there were two major arguments, they could be numbered as 1 and 2. Note that some writers use a Roman numeral "I" to designate the major argument, even if there is no second argument. While that practice represents poor outlining form, no one has ever lost a case because of it.

are plausible on their face and that would allow her to prove two   **16**
of the four essential elements of the claim of disparate treatment
under Title VII.

Defendant, Bank Two, moves the Court to dismiss Plaintiff's complaint pursu-   **17**

ant to Rule 12(b)(6) of the Federal Rules of Civil Procedure, which allows for the

dismissal of a complaint that fails to state a claim upon which relief can be grant-

ed. Under Rule 8(a)(2) of the Federal Rules of Civil Procedure, a complaint must   **18**

provide "a short and plain statement of the claim showing that the pleader is en-

titled to relief" in order to give the defendant notice of the nature of the claim and

the grounds upon which it stands. *Bell Atlantic Corp. v. Twombly*, 550 U.S. 544, 555

(2007) (quoting *Conley v. Gibson*, 355 U.S. 41, 47 (1957)). Generally, when consid-

ering a Rule 12(b)(6) motion to dismiss, the court must construe the complaint

in the light most favorable to the plaintiff, accept the plaintiff's factual allegations

as true, and draw all reasonable inferences in the plaintiff's favor. *See Erickson v.*

Pardus, 551 U.S. 89, 93 (2007); *Haines v. Kerner*, 404 U.S. 519, 520 (1972).

The Supreme Court recently raised the standard for allegations sufficient to   **19**

survive a motion to dismiss pursuant to Rule 12(b)(6). In order for a claim to

---

16 This language comes directly from the motion standard and is a "phrase that pays" for that standard.

17 The umbrella section begins here. It incorporates the motion standard, as well as other rules that govern everything that follows. It then includes the roadmap for the argument (including the brush-clearing, or "tell" issues).

18 The explanation of the motion standard begins here. The motion standard is the standard a court will apply when considering a particular type of motion, e.g., the Rule 12(b)(6) motion standard, as in this instance.

An alternative to including the motion standard in the umbrella section is including a separate "Motion Standard" section before the "Argument" section.

19 Notice that the writer uses language that makes the motion standard sound more stringent (which, frankly, it is). If you were describing this rule from the plaintiff's perspective, you might use more benign language, e.g., "The Supreme Court recently clarified. . . ."

survive such a motion, it must include "factual allegations [which are] enough to raise a right to relief above the speculative level." *Twombly*, 550 U.S. at 555. The plaintiff may not rely on mere "labels and conclusions" or a "formulaic recitation of the elements of a cause of action." *Id.* Rather, the plaintiff must plead facts that, if accepted as true, "state a claim to relief that is plausible on its face." *Id.* at 570. The Court has clarified that the pleading standard of *Twombly* applies in all civil actions. *Ashcroft v. Iqbal*, 556 U.S. 665, 684 (2009).

20 A court addressing a Rule 12(b)(6) motion to dismiss must, therefore, continue to accept as true all well-pleaded allegations of fact. Twombly, 550 U.S. at 555. It need not, however, "accept as true a legal conclusion couched as a factual allegation.'" Id. (quoting Papasan v. Allain, 478 U.S. 265, 286 (1986)).

21 This Court should dismiss Plaintiff's disparate treatment claim pursuant to Rule 12(b)(6) of the Federal Rules of Civil Procedure because the facts Plaintiff alleges do not state a claim upon which relief can be granted. To establish a *prima facie* case of disparate treatment under Title VII, a plaintiff must allege facts that are plausible on their face and that would allow her to prove that (1) she is a member of a protected class; (2) she was qualified for her job; (3) her employer took an adverse action against her; and (4) she was replaced by someone outside the protected class or treated less favorably than similarly situated non-protected **22** employees. *See McDonnell Douglas Corp. v. Green*, 411 U.S. 782, 802 (1973).

---

20 The explanation of the motion standard ends here. Because it was written by the defendant's lawyer, it has made the bar for surviving a motion to dismiss seem very high.

21 In this paragraph, the writer connects the motion standard to the particular claims in this case.

22 Here the writer lays out the main rule at the root of this case. It's appropriate to cite to authority in the umbrella section of the document.

As a female employee, Plaintiff can prove the first element of the *prima facie* case of disparate treatment. Defendant also acknowledges that Plaintiff was an exemplary employee in many respects and well-qualified for a management position at Bank Two. Indeed, her qualifications were never in question at Bank Two. In order to avoid dismissal, however, Plaintiff must also have identified in her complaint (i) an adverse action that her employer took against her and (ii) a similarly situated male colleague whom Bank Two treated more favorably. She has not alleged facts that are plausible on their face and that would allow her to prove her claim that Bank Two treated her male colleagues more favorably. Rather, she relies upon the bare legal conclusion that Bank Two treated her less favorably than male employees in two employment actions: her initial placement and her eventual termination.

Plaintiff's claim fails for two reasons. First, to the extent that her claim is based on the termination of her employment, it fails because she has not alleged facts that are plausible on their face and that would allow her to prove that Defendant treated a similarly situated male employee more favorably. Second, to the extent her claim is based upon the alleged adverse action of her initial placement in the Commercial Lending department, her claim fails because it is untimely.

23 In this paragraph, the writer "clears the brush" and disposes of tell issues. By admitting that plaintiff meets two of the elements of the *prima facie* case—indeed, the writer praises the plaintiff—defendant seeks to establish credibility with the court so that the court will be more likely to believe defendant's attacks on the other elements of the case.

24 Here the writer provides the roadmap to his two main points. Note that one of his main points is further subdivided. *This* roadmap does NOT signal that further subdivision—the writer does so in the "mini-roadmap" that precedes those subsections.

25 This is an *argumentative* roadmap; the points of the argument are listed as mini-arguments rather than in neutral language.

26

  A. **The Court should dismiss Plaintiff's disparate treatment claim based upon the termination of her employment because she is unable to establish that she is similarly situated in all material respects to any of her retained male colleagues who reported to a different supervisor.**

27

  Plaintiff has not alleged facts that are plausible on their face and that would allow her to prove that Defendant treated her less favorably in the management restructuring than similarly-situated male employees. *See McDonnell Douglas*

28

Corp., 411 U.S. at 802. She has, therefore, failed to state a claim upon which relief can be granted based upon the termination of her employment.

29

  In order to successfully plead a claim for disparate treatment sex discrimination under Title VII, a plaintiff must allege facts that are plausible on their face and that would allow her to prove that her employer treated her less favorably than male employees who were similarly situated in all respects that were material to the employment decision that she challenges. *Ercegovich v. Goodyear Tire & Rubber Co.,* 154 F.3d 344, 352 (6th Cir. 1998); *Mitchell v. Toledo Hosp.,* 964 F.2d 577, 583 (6th Cir. 1992). Where the plaintiff has reported to a supervisor who was not the comparator's supervisor and the supervisor's actions or decisions were a factor in the challenged employment decision, the employee will not be able to prove substantial similarity. *See, e.g., Duncan v. Koch Air, L.L.C.,* No. Civ.A. 3:04CV-72-H, 2005 WL 1353758 at *3 (W.D. Ky. June 2, 2005) (relying on *McMil-*

26 This sub-heading successfully incorporates the phrase-that-pays, "similarly situated in all material respects," and the legally significant facts.

27 Notice that the writer also incorporates the phrases-that-pay from the Rule 12(b)(6) motions standard, "facts that are plausible on their face" and "that would allow her to prove."

28 Pay close attention to how often the writer repeats this phrase-that-pays in one form or another.

29 These two sentences are the R for this unit of discourse. We might refer to them collectively as a "rule cluster." Together, they incorporate every aspect of the rule as it will be explained in the EX that follows.

lan v. Castro, 405 F.3d 405, 413-14 (6th Cir. 2003); *Mitchell v. Toledo Hosp.*, 964 F.2d at 583).

To satisfy the similarly-situated element of the disparate treatment claim, a plaintiff must allege that the identified employee was "nearly identical" to the plaintiff. *Pierce v. Commonwealth*, 40 F.3d 796, 804 (6th Cir. 1994). In determining whether a demotion violated Title VII, the court in *Pierce* looked at non-protected employees and concluded that they were not similarly situated to the plaintiff in all material respects. *Id.* at 801. The plaintiff in *Pierce* had significantly different job duties than the employee he identified as comparable. *Id.* at 802. The court concluded, therefore, that the plaintiff had failed to meet his burden of pleading a Title VII claim. *Id.* at 804.

The Sixth Circuit has upheld this "similarly-situated-in-all-material-respects" standard in more recent cases, most notably *Mazur v. Wal-Mart, Inc.*, No. 06-2485, 2007 WL 2859721 (6th Cir. Oct. 3, 2007). In *Mazur*, the court restricted consideration of employee similarity to those employees who were subject to the same supervisor and held to the same standards, with no differentiating or mitigating circumstances. *Id.* at *5.

In the age discrimination context, courts need not "demand exact correlation;" plaintiffs must, however, establish "relevant similarity," that is, similarity in all material respects. *Ercegovich v. Goodyear Tire & Rubber Co.*, 154 F.3d 344,

30 The EX begins here. The writer has chosen to lead with a case in which the court set the bar for a plaintiff very high ("nearly identical").

31 This phrase signals both the relevant issue (were other employees similarly situated?) and the disposition of that issue (they were not).

32 Here, the writer includes the relevant facts.

33 This "therefore" refers back to the "significantly different job duties" and explains, by implication at least, the court's reasoning for its conclusion that the plaintiff could not meet the standard.

352 (6th Cir. 1998). In *Ercegovich*, the court held that a coordinator in human resources development who was denied an opportunity to relocate during a reorganization was similarly situated to a manager of human resources and a personnel development specialist who were relocated because the differences in their positions were not relevant to the challenged employment action. *Id.*

34 One district court, applying the standards established by the Sixth Circuit, held that a plaintiff whose claim was based on differing applications of the same rule to different employees could not meet the similarly-situated standard. *Duncan*, 2005 WL 1353758 at *3 (citing *McMillan v. Castro*, 405 F.3d at 413-14; *Mitchell v. Toledo Hosp.*, 964 F.2d at 583). The plaintiff in *Duncan* could not establish that her employer discriminatorily applied the same rule differently to two different employees because she could not demonstrate that the same supervisor had interpreted and applied the rule to each of them. *Id.* at *3. Where two different people are interpreting the rule, absent some evidence of coordination, logic does not support a conclusion that discrimination must be the cause of differences in application. *See id.*

35 The *Ercegovich* decision does not suggest a lower similarity standard merely because it applies a "relevant similarity" standard in the age discrimination context. *Ercegovich*, 154 F.3d at 352. The Court in *Ercegovich* carefully confined its rule to the age discrimination context. *Id.* Nearly all of the Sixth Circuit decisions that have followed *Ercegovich*'s "relevant similarity" standard have been age

34 Here, the writer is justifying the inclusion of this non-mandatory authority in the rule explanation by making clear that it is illustrative only.

35 In this section of the rule explanation, the writer incorporates a counterargument to preemptively challenge the anticipated arguments of the plaintiff about how the court should interpret the rule. Effective counterargument should always come after the writer's own position on the same issue.

discrimination actions. *See, e.g., McElroy v. Philips Med. Sys. N. Am., Inc.*, 127 F. App'x 161 (6th Cir. 2005); *Weigel v. Baptist Hosp. of E. Tennessee*, 302 F.3d 367 (6th Cir. 2002); *Grant v. Harcourt Brace Coll. Publ'rs*, No. 98-3829, 1999 WL 717982 (6th Cir. Sept. 9, 1999). In any event, as noted above, the *Ercegovich* standard requires that the identified employee have been similar to the plaintiff in all respects that are relevant to the claim. *Ercegovich*, 154 F.3d at 352. The *Ercegovich* standard is, therefore, not substantially different from the standard applied by the Sixth Circuit in more recent age discrimination cases. *See, e.g., Minadeo v. ICI Paints*, 398 F.3d 751, 764 (6th Cir. 2005) (plaintiff could not establish a *prima facie* case of discrimination because he was not similar in *all respects* to the employees to whom he compared himself). The Sixth Circuit in *Minadeo* concluded that the plaintiff could not establish similarity because the younger employees to whom she compared herself held different positions and were held to different standards. *Id.* The *Ercegovich* standard, to the extent that it is different from the similarly- situated-in-all-material-respects standard, should be applied only in age discrimination cases.

In summary, to survive Defendant's motion to dismiss, Plaintiff's allegations must be plausible on their face and must allow her to prove that the male managers to whom she compares herself were similar to her in all material respects. If a supervisor's actions or decisions form a part of the basis for the Plaintiff's disparate treatment claim, she cannot satisfy the similarity requirement by comparing herself to employees who reported to different supervisors.

36

---

36 Here is the writer's rule summary. In a motion memo, the rule summary is your chance to restate the rule in a way that is very favorable to your position and to provide a roadmap to the application that will follow.

37   Ms. Wendl has failed to allege facts that are plausible on their face and that would allow her to prove the "similarly-situated" element of the disparate treatment claim. Plaintiff has alleged that Mr. North and Mr. South are similarly-situated male co-workers whom Bank Two treated more favorably than it did the Plaintiff when it allowed them to retain their jobs but terminated Plaintiff's position. Plaintiff, North, and South were all similarly-situated in that Bank Two hired all three at the same time. Furthermore, Bank Two evaluated all three of these individuals using the same system for each year of their employment. The three worked at the same management level, reported to their respective departmental vice presidents, and supervised other employees. The similarities end

38   there, however. Plaintiff is not similar to North and South as to the aspects of their employment that are material to her claim.

39   Mr. North and Mr. South worked in the International Transactions department of Bank Two, while Plaintiff worked in the Commercial Lending department. Plaintiff reported to a different supervisor. That different supervisor assigned her

37 Here, the writer begins the rule application by stating, in essence, "phrase-that-pays does not equal client's case." In this instance, as in many motion memos, there are two phrases-that-pay: the motion standard phrase-that-pays (plausible facts that allow the plaintiff to prove an element of the case) and a Title VII phrase-that-pays (similarly situated). Notice that the thesis of this application section mirrors the rule summary, which immediately precedes it.

38 As this application develops, notice that it tracks the development of the rule explanation by applying the aspects of the rule in generally the order in which they were explained.

39 The writer uses several paragraphs to give factual details that establish *why* the phrase-that-pays does not equal the client's case. Many writers are too conclusory in the application, failing to specify the facts that give the reader confidence that the writer's conclusion is correct. Note that motions for summary judgment, unlike motions to dismiss, are often supported by voluminous evidence. In summary judgment motion memos, therefore, the writer should cite to the specific pieces of evidence (and the page, paragraph, and/or line of text referred to) whenever mentioning specific facts.

lower performance evaluation scores, which resulted in her lower salary. Performance evaluation scores and salaries were the critical factors in Bank Two's decision about which managers would be retained and were, therefore, material to the decision. Because Plaintiff's scores and salary were set by a different person, she was, unquestionably, *dissimilar* from North and South in a *material* respect

Plaintiff's responsibilities were also different in another material respect because she supervised a different type of employee than did Mr. North and Mr. South. Further, Mr. North and Mr. South performed more effectively in supervising and retaining their employees than Plaintiff did. Her performance in these areas was a critical factor in her annual evaluation scores and was, therefore, *material* to the termination decision *and* another respect in which Plaintiff was *not similar* to Mr. North and Mr. South.

These material dissimilarities defeat any claim by Plaintiff that Defendant treated similarly situated male managers more favorably in the management restructuring. Plaintiff has not alleged facts that are plausible on their face and that would allow her to prove the "similarly situated" element of the *prima facie* case of disparate treatment under Title VII.

Plaintiff is in the same position as was the employee who could not prove [40] sufficient similarity in *Duncan v. Koch Air*, 2005 WL 1353758. The plaintiff in *Duncan* could not establish that her employer discriminatorily applied the same rule differently to two different employees because she could not demonstrate that the same supervisor had interpreted and applied the rule to each of them. *Id.*

---

[40] Both this analogy and the one after follow this formula: (1) thesis of the comparison, (2) comparable facts from authority case, (3) facts from writer's case, (4) mini-conclusion that supports the A (application) and the second C (connection-conclusion) of the CREXAC unit of discourse.

at *3. The fact that two different vice presidents evaluated the performances of Plaintiff and Mr. North and Mr. South, likewise, precludes her proving that they were similar in all material respects.

Plaintiff Wendl is also like the plaintiff in *Minadeo v. ICI Paints*, who could not establish sufficient similarity because of the differences between her position and the positions of the employees to whom she compared herself. 398 F.3d at 764. Ms. Wendl supervised a different type of employee than did North and South. Her employee management scores were based upon different responsibilities and duties than were the scores of the employees to whom she compares herself. A different supervisor evaluated her performance. The fact that the three employees worked at the same level of management within Bank Two is insufficient to establish the requisite similarity. *See id.*

The Court should dismiss Plaintiff's claim based upon the termination of her employment because the facts as alleged do not state a disparate treatment claim under Title VII upon which relief can be granted. Plaintiff has failed to allege facts that are plausible on their face and that would allow her to prove that Messrs. North and South were similar in all material respects as regards the management restructuring. Even if Plaintiff is able to establish all of the other elements of the *prima facie* case, she has not stated a claim upon which relief may be granted. Accordingly, the Court should dismiss her complaint pursuant to Rule 12(b)(6) of the Federal Rules of Civil Procedure.

---

41 After applying the rule to the facts, the writer concludes that the plaintiff has not alleged plausible facts that will allow her to prove that she was similarly situated to Mr. North and Mr. South. The writer does not end there but connects that point to his overall thesis: that this conclusion alone will allow the court to dismiss the complaint.

B. **The Court should dismiss Plaintiff's claim, to the extent that it is based upon the alleged adverse action of her initial placement, because the claim is untimely and Plaintiff cannot establish a continuing violation.**

42

Plaintiff also claims that her initial placement in the Commercial Lending department of Bank Two was discriminatory. (Complaint ¶ 23). She attempts to rely upon that placement to satisfy the adverse action element of her *prima facie* Title VII disparate treatment claim. She does not allege that she challenged Bank Two's allegedly discriminatory placement of female managers in less favorable positions either at the time of her hiring or when she first suffered allegedly adverse employment conditions as a result of her placement, as required by Title VII. *See* 42 U.S.C. § 2000e-5(e)(1).

Accordingly, allegations about Plaintiff's initial placement in the Commercial Lending department are untimely and therefore insufficient to establish the "adverse action" necessary for a *prima facie* Title VII case for two reasons. First, the action Plaintiff alleges to have violated Title VII occurred nearly eight years ago, and the statutory filing requirement mandates that a charge under this section must be filed within three hundred days after the alleged unlawful employment practice occurred. 42 U.S.C. § 2000e-5(e)(1). Under these facts, this untimeliness can only be remedied if Plaintiff has alleged facts that are plausible on their face and that would allow her to prove a continuing violation. *See E.E.O.C. v. Penton Industrial Publishing Co., Inc.*, 851 F.2d 835, 838 (6th Cir. 1988). Plaintiff's allegations do not satisfy this standard.

43

---

42 This heading encompasses both of the sub-arguments from this section of the motion.

43 Here, the writer provides a mini-roadmap to show the reader how the analysis of this issue is divided into two subparts. Note that the writer cites to authority appropriately.

Plaintiff cannot, therefore, establish an exception to the statutory filing requirement. Accordingly, the Court should dismiss her Title VII claim to the extent that it is based upon her initial placement in the Commercial Lending department.

44

1. Plaintiff's initial placement occurred longer than 300 days ago, so her claim based upon that alleged adverse action is untimely.

45

Plaintiff's claim fails to the extent that it is based upon her initial placement in the Commercial Lending department because she did not file a timely charge of discrimination relating to that placement. Before an aggrieved employee may bring suit under Title VII to challenge alleged discrimination, she must file a charge of discrimination with the Equal Employment Opportunity Commission ("E.E.O.C.") and receive a right-to-sue letter from the E.E.O.C. 42 U.S.C. § 2000e-

46

5(e)(1). Title VII bars recovery for employment discrimination that occurred

47

more than 300 days before the plaintiff filed the E.E.O.C. charge. *Id.; Puckett v. Tennessee Eastman Co.*, 889 F.2d 1481, 1486 (6th Cir. 1989). A plaintiff who

44 This sub-heading succinctly incorporates the rule and the legally significant fact that the action that is the basis for the plaintiff's claim occurred more than 300 days before she filed her complaint. The phrases-that-pay for this subsection are "300 days," "untimely," and "timely."

45 This opening conclusion (or thesis conclusion) neatly incorporates the phrase-that-pays.

46 This sentence is the rule in this subsection. In this instance, a sentence of legal background precedes the rule because context is necessary to an accurate understanding of how the rule operates.

47 The "rule explanation" in this section is quite short because the phrases-that-pay in the rule are very concrete and thus less controversial. Either the suit was filed within 300 days or it was not; either she has alleged an equal pay violation, or she has not. There is no need to provide rule explanation to explain concrete and uncontroversial phrases-that-pay. If plaintiff had filed suit on the 300th day, it might be appropriate to cite cases that clarified whether or not a 300th day filing was appropriate, but no such hair-splitting is needed in this case.

has not received a right-to-sue letter from the E.E.O.C. has not satisfied a condition precedent to bringing suit in federal court under Title VII. *Puckett,* 889 F.2d at 1486. One exception to the prohibition is for claims of unequal pay, which arise each time an employee receives disparate pay. *See* 42 U.S.C. § 2000e-5(e)(3)(A). That exception does not apply to claims outside the unequal pay context. *See id.*

Plaintiff does not allege that she filed a charge of discrimination with the E.E.O.C. on the basis of her initial job assignment or the first performance evaluation in which she received a lower-than-perfect score for employee management. She has not, therefore, asserted a claim under Title VII on the basis of her initial placement upon which relief can be granted. The period of time that has elapsed since her initial placement far exceeds 300 days, so Plaintiff's claim based upon that placement is untimely. Plaintiff cannot now file a charge on the basis of that placement. *See* 42 U.S.C. § 2000e-5(e)(1).

Plaintiff's claim is not saved by the unequal pay exception embodied in § 2000e-5(e)(3)(A) because she has not alleged that it is a claim for equal pay. Moreover, even had Plaintiff alleged that her claim is a claim for equal pay based upon the exception embodied in § 2000e-5(e)(3)(A), she has not satisfied the E.E.O.C. filing requirement and has not received a right-to-sue letter with respect to that claim. So, the claim is untimely, and Plaintiff has not alleged facts that are plausible on their face and that would allow her to prove that she has satisfied the condition precedent to filing a Title VII action on the basis of her initial placement.

48 This relatively short application tracks the rule explanation point-by-point. A reader who is keeping score will have checked every box on the scorecard by the end of the application.

For those reasons, Plaintiff has failed to state a claim on the basis of her initial placement upon which relief can be granted.

49

2. Plaintiff has not identified an action within the 300-day period preceding her E.E.O.C. complaint that is part of a longstanding and demonstrable policy of discrimination, so she cannot establish a continuing violation of Title VII.

50

Plaintiff has failed to allege facts that are plausible on their face and that would allow her to prove that the termination of her employment was part of a continuing violation. The Court should, therefore, dismiss her claim to the extent that it is based upon her conclusory allegation to that effect.

51

The Sixth Circuit has identified exceptions to the 300-day filing requirement, including where an employer has maintained a demonstrable, longstanding policy of discrimination, thus engaging in a *continuing violation*. *E.E.O.C. v. Penton Industrial Publishing Co., Inc.*, 851 F.2d 835, 838 (6th Cir. 1988). To benefit from the continuing violation theory, a Title VII plaintiff must identify a discrete discriminatory action within the 300-day period that is part of a "longstanding and demonstrable policy of discrimination." *Sharp v. Cureton*, 319 F.3d 259, 268 (6th Cir. 2003). The policy must be one of intentional discrimination against the protected class of which the plaintiff is a member. *Id. at 269* (citing *Penton Industrial Publishing*, 851 F.2d at 838).

49 By now, you can probably guess that "longstanding and demonstrable policy of discrimination" and "continuing violation" are the phrases-that-pay in this subsection. This sub-heading incorporates the phrases-that-pay and the legally significant fact that the plaintiff has not identified an action within the 300-day period.

50 This opening conclusion incorporates the phrases-that-pay from the Rule 12(b)(6) standard and a phrase-that-pays from the rule that governs this unit of discourse.

51 These two sentences combine to form the rule for this unit of discourse.

The exception is strictly construed and applies only where the employer has a known policy or rule supporting discrimination. *See, e.g., Alexander v. Local 469, Laborers Int'l Union,* 177 F.3d 394, 408-09 (6th Cir. 1999) (finding a longstanding and demonstrable policy where a union rule contained in by-laws and a union constitution resulted in the "de facto exclusion" of African Americans from union membership). In essence, the plaintiff must establish that the employer's "standing operating procedure" included intentional discrimination against the class of which plaintiff was a member. *Austion v. City of Clarksville,* 244 F. App'x 639, 647 (6th Cir. 2007) (quoting *EEOC v. Penton Indus. Publ'g Co.,* 851 F.2d 835, 838 (6th Cir. 1988)). The court in *Austion* found that the plaintiff failed to meet this standard when his complaint alleged only that his own demotion occurred within the statutory time limit and did not allege any longstanding discriminatory policies at his former place of employment. *Id.*

Accordingly, a plaintiff may rely upon this theory only when she is able to identify a demonstrable and known policy or rule supporting discrimination and a discrete act within the 300-day period in furtherance of that policy. Even if Plaintiff's complaint may allege a discrete act that occurred within the 300-day period, it does not tie that discrete act to the furtherance of a longstanding discriminatory policy at Bank Two.

Plaintiff has alleged that Bank Two engaged in a continuing violation of Title VII by maintaining a longstanding policy of placing female managers in less

52

53

---

52 Notice how brief the two case descriptions in this rule explanation are. The writer has included only the facts that are essential to an understanding of the rule as it is illustrated in the authority case.

53 This rule summary includes the phrase-that-pays.

advantageous positions. She has not, however, alleged that Bank Two took any discrete discriminatory action in furtherance of that policy during the 300 days prior to the filing of her complaint in this action. The only alleged action by Bank Two within that period is the termination of Ms. Wendl's employment. While that action is discrete, Plaintiff has not alleged that it was, in itself, discriminatory. In the absence of allegations that the termination was discriminatorily motivated, Plaintiff cannot rely upon that action as the basis for reviving past actions as the bases for current Title VII claims under a continuing violation theory. Plaintiff's claim based upon her initial placement rests upon conclusions masquerading as allegations and is, therefore, subject to dismissal pursuant to Rule 12(b)(6). *See Twombly*, 550 U.S. at 555.

54 Plaintiff's claim is just like the plaintiff's claim in *Austion*, in which the court found fatal the plaintiff's failure to identify a discrete, discriminatory act that occurred within the limitations period. *See Austion*, 244 F. App'x at 647. The *Austion* court reversed a refusal to dismiss that claim, and this Court should dismiss Plaintiff's claim for the same reason.

55

C. Conclusion

Plaintiff has failed to allege facts that are plausible on their face and that would allow her to prove a claim of disparate treatment sex discrimination in violation of Title VII against Bank Two. She has not alleged facts that would establish one of the essential elements of the *prima facie* case of discrimination on

---

54 The writer uses this analogy to end and support the application and as a brief, punchy conclusion to this subsection.

55 This conclusion section incorporates all of the phrases-that-pay from the argument, the most legally significant facts, and a summary of all of the CREXAC connection-conclusions.

the basis of her termination. Specifically, she has failed to allege that she was treated less favorably than any male employee who was similarly situated in all relevant respects. Accordingly, her claim on the basis of that termination fails, and the Court should dismiss it pursuant to Rule 12(b)(6) of the Federal Rules of Civil Procedure.

Plaintiff's claim also fails to the extent that it is based upon her initial placement in the Commercial Lending department of Bank Two. Her claim on that basis is untimely because she has failed to allege that she filed a charge of discrimination with the E.E.O.C. within 300 days of her initial placement. That failure is not excused under a continuing violation theory in Plaintiff's case because she has failed to allege a discriminatory action within the 300-day period prior to the filing of the complaint. She has not, therefore, alleged a plausible continuing violation. Accordingly, the Court should also dismiss her claim to the extent that it is based on her initial placement.

X

March 8, 2013

Monte Smith
Attorney for Bank Two, N.A.

Certificate of Service

I, Monte Smith, attorney for the Defendant, Bank Two, N.A., certify that I have served upon the Plaintiff a copy of this Memorandum in Support of the

56 Defendant's Motion to Dismiss, by placing a copy in the United States Mail, sufficient postage and addressed as follows: 55 W. 12th Avenue, Columbus, OH 43210.

Monte Smith
Attorney for Bank Two, N.A.

57 March 8, 2013

56 Most courts will also allow electronic service; of course, you must check local rules to verify what types of service are allowed.

57 This is an example of an electronic signature. Again, the court's local rules will specify what types of signatures are allowed.

Rules Governing Appellate Practice

If you're a law student, you've probably spent most of your time in law school reading appellate court decisions. Without getting too deep into the Langdellian tradition,[1] you're doing that because lots of law gets made in those decisions, whether through the development of common law or the interpretation of statutes and constitutions. So if you're going to practice law, it helps you to understand how those courts get those cases, and how court rules and common law rules control the ways in which the courts decide them.

In this chapter, we will provide a brief discussion of the rules that trial lawyers follow to make sure that they preserve legal issues so

---

1. Christopher Columbus Langdell is credited with having changed American legal education in the late-nineteenth century. He proposed studying law through Socratic dialogue, rather than through lectures. He also sought to make the study of law more scientific; just as medical students learned how the human body is made by dissecting cadavers, Langdell proposed that law students should learn how law is made by dissecting court opinions—usually appellate decisions. Lisa Eichhorn, *Writing in the Legal Academy: A Dangerous Supplement?*, 40 Ariz. L. Rev. 105, 109-10 (1998).

the issues can be heard at the appellate level. Then we will explain the different types of appellate courts and the rules that they follow when choosing which cases to decide, and when deciding those cases. Finally, we'll explain the ways that different standards of review interact in appellate courts.

4.1. PRESERVING ISSUES FOR APPEAL

An appellate court will rarely consider an issue that a lawyer has raised for the first time on appeal, so every motion memo and trial brief must include any issue that the writer may want to raise to a higher court. The act of including an issue because it may be the subject of an appeal is called *preserving* the issue, and, just like preserving fruit requires handling it now so that it will be available in an appropriate form later, preserving an issue for appeal requires careful handling of the issue at one stage of a case so that it will be available in an appropriate form at a later stage.

As we noted in Chapter Three, one way to preserve the appropriate issues for appeal is to carefully select issues and arguments at the trial stage. But that's only part of the story. While many issues are significant at both the trial and appellate stages, some issues that rarely move trial courts are more likely to succeed at the appellate level. Accordingly, a trial attorney may argue some issues that will be almost certain losers at the trial stage, for the sole purpose of preserving them for appeal after a final judgment in the trial court.

Trial courts most often resolve disputes about facts, and appellate courts most often resolve disputes about law; these roles affect the likelihood that a particular argument will succeed at each level. A lawyer will be careful to raise issues about the facts at the trial level because the lawyer knows that the trial court is the place where those arguments must be heard; an appellate court is extremely unlikely to change the trial court's decision about the facts. Indeed, as we will discuss below, standards of review dictate that an appellate court must generally find clear error before it can alter a trial court's factual findings. On the other hand, while trial courts make decisions about how the law applies to the facts, a trial court will rarely change existing interpretations of what the law is: thus, a lawyer will rarely convince a trial court to ignore mandatory authority on the ground that it is incorrect or unconstitutional. Those decisions are the province of the appellate courts. Still, a lawyer must [1] raise challenges to the law at the trial level to preserve them for appeal. So, the evaluation of issues and arguments at the trial stage

[1] As noted in Chapter Three, one way that trial attorneys preserve issues is by making objections to procedural decisions at the trial level.

must include an analysis of legal issues the lawyer may want to raise at the appellate level, and the lawyer must preserve those issues at the trial level even if the lawyer knows that the trial court cannot resolve them definitively.

The following example may help to illustrate the distinction between a "trial court issue" and an "appellate court issue." Suppose that you represent a company that is the defendant in a sexual harassment action. The plaintiff claims that a coworker sexually assaulted her, and she wants to hold your client accountable for allowing a sexually hostile work environment. Your client has told you that no one within the company knew about the assaults. The problem for you is that the federal appellate court in your circuit has held that an employer may be liable for damages for sexual harassment even if it had no reason to know that an employee was repeatedly sexually assaulting a coworker. That holding represents mandatory authority in your case. Several other circuits have held that an employer is liable for an employee's action only if the employer knew of the behavior and failed to stop it, and you want to argue that your circuit is wrong about the law. You know that the trial court is very unlikely to say that the circuit court, whose decisions are mandatory authority, is wrong. Still, even though you know you will lose at the trial court level, you must raise the issue there, or the court of appeals will not consider it.

Of course, the circuit court may decide not to change its own interpretation of the law, so you will also be preserving the issue for appeal to the United States Supreme Court by raising it at the trial court and circuit court levels. The bottom line is that even at the trial stage, you must be considering what issues might end up being heard by courts of last resort, and structure your arguments with those issues in mind.

4.2. JURISDICTION OF APPELLATE COURTS

Once you have decided to appeal a decision (or once you have learned that your opponent has appealed a decision that was in your favor), you will need to understand some fundamental principles about the various courts and their powers; this knowledge will help you to make decisions as you prepare your written and oral arguments. Your arguments will be different if you are writing a brief to a trial court as opposed to an appellate court. Even within the appellate system, you may argue differently to an intermediate court of appeals than to a court of last resort.

Intermediate courts of appeals must hear every appeal (with few exceptions)[2] and must follow the decisions of the courts above them. Courts of last resort, on the other hand, usually have some authority to decide which cases they will hear[3] and the authority to make new law.

4.2.1. Jurisdiction in Courts of Last Resort

A "court of last resort" is the highest court in a particular legal system. It is the last court to which a litigant can resort when seeking resolution of a legal issue. In the federal system, the United States Supreme Court is the court of last resort, and the majority of its cases come from the United States Courts of Appeals of the various circuits. In state systems, the highest court of appeals—often called the supreme court—is the court of last resort, and it generally hears cases from that state's intermediate appellate courts. The United States Supreme Court can also hear appeals from state courts of last resort, but only if the issue is a matter of federal law. For example, the Court may hear an appeal from a state court in order to determine whether the court has interpreted one of that state's laws in a way that may have conflicted with the United States Constitution.

Most courts of last resort are not merely courts of error; that is, they do not take cases simply because one party claims that there was an error of law in a lower court decision. If you want to appeal a decision to the United States Supreme Court, you have to file a petition to ask the Court to grant a "writ of certiorari" to the court that issued the opinion you want reviewed. "Certiorari" is a term of Latin origin that means *to be informed of*. When the Court issues a writ of certiorari to a Circuit Court of Appeals, it is essentially informing the court that it will be reviewing its opinion.

But just asking the Court to issue a writ of certiorari does not mean the Court will do so. Rule 10 of the Rules of the Supreme Court of the United States explicitly says that "[a] petition for a writ of certiorari is rarely granted when the asserted error consists of erroneous factual findings or the misapplication of a properly stated rule of law." Instead, a court of last resort takes cases in order to resolve pressing issues, and it may refuse to take cases unless or until it believes that its intervention is necessary. Rule 10, for example, also mentions factors that make it more likely that the United States Supreme Court will grant a petition for a writ of certiorari.

---

2. *See, e.g.,* Tenn. R. App. P. 3; Fed. R. App. P. 3.
3. *See, e.g.,* U.S. Sup. Ct. R. 10 (governing certiorari).

It notes that the Court frequently grants certiorari if it believes that a state court or a lower federal court of appeals is misinterpreting or misapplying the Court's jurisprudence, and that the Court may be more likely to grant certiorari when two or more courts are in conflict over an interpretation of the federal Constitution, or when courts are in conflict over a question of federal law.[4] **2**

2 When the same statute is being interpreted differently in different courts, lawyers and judges often say there's a "split in the circuits" (referring to circuit dispute) or that "the courts are divided" (referring to any courts).

Interestingly, the Court does not always grant certiorari immediately when either of these factors is present. It is not uncommon for the Court to let a conflict simmer for a few years, with different lower courts writing decisions either way. The Court may use this method purposefully, to benefit from the analysis and reasoning of several different lower courts. By allowing several opinions to be written on a subject, the Court can assess the potential and actual impact of several different resolutions and analyses of the same issue.

Perhaps for these reasons, the Court attaches no precedential value to the denial of a petition for a writ of certiorari. That is, a denial of certiorari does *not* indicate that the Court approves of the decision below. Rather, it means only that the Court did not believe, for whatever reason, that it was an issue that was worthy of its review *at that time.*

4.2.2. Jurisdiction in Intermediate Courts of Appeals

The rules are somewhat different in intermediate courts of appeals. Generally, state and federal intermediate courts of appeals will hear any appeal of a final order if the appellant has met specified procedural guidelines.[5] The United States courts of appeals have jurisdiction over appeals from all final decisions of the United States district courts.[6] The courts of appeals also have jurisdiction to hear

---

4. *See generally* U.S. Sup. Ct. R. 10.

5. *See, e.g.,* Ohio R. App. P. tit. II, R. 3; Fed. R. App. P. 3. Appeals of certain criminal appeals may have to meet different standards. Interlocutory appeals are governed by the guidelines in 28 U.S.C. § 1292. *See also In re United States*, 138 S. Ct. 443, 445 (2017) (noting that on remand, the district court may consider whether to certify a ruling for interlocutory appeal under § 1292(b)); *Coopers & Lybrand v. Livesay*, 437 U.S. 463, 475 (1978) (describing court discretion). Of course, states may have different rules as to various kinds of appeals. *E.g., Shearer v. Hafer*, 177 A.3d 850, 861 (Pa. 2018) (quashing an appeal as an "unauthorized interlocutory appeal"); *Commonwealth v. Harris*, 32 A.3d 243, 250 (Pa. 2011) (allowing interlocutory appeals of orders that would reveal privileged information, and noting that "Pennsylvania law permits interlocutory appeals by permission, but under a somewhat different standard than the federal system").

6. 28 U.S.C. § 1291.

appeals from a variety of other judicial and quasi-judicial bodies, including, for example, appeals to enforce or challenge orders of the National Labor Relations Board.[7]

Although most people think of oral arguments when they think of appellate advocacy, federal intermediate courts of appeals often decide cases without oral argument. According to the rules, oral argument is presumed, but a three-judge panel can vote unanimously that oral argument is unnecessary in a given case for any of the following three reasons:

1. The appeal is frivolous.
2. The dispositive issue or issues have been authoritatively decided.
3. The facts and legal arguments are adequately presented in the briefs and record, and the decisional process would not be significantly aided by oral argument.[8]

What this rule means in practice is that a large percentage of cases are assigned to the so-called summary docket, and many of those are decided based on memoranda submitted by law clerks and staff attorneys who have reviewed the party briefs. Federal court statistics indicate that in the year ending December 31, 2017, about 80 percent of the appeals terminated on the merits were decided without oral argument.[9] When cases are on the summary docket, some judges make their decisions based on staff memoranda alone; they may not read the briefs in full at all. With that fact in mind, if you are writing a brief to a federal appellate court, you should presume that oral argument will not be granted, and you should write a brief that can persuade a law clerk as well as a judge.

4.3. APPELLATE STANDARDS OF REVIEW

Whether an appellate court is an intermediate court of appeals or a court of last resort, whether it hears an appeal as of right or as a mat-

---

7. 29 U.S.C. § 160(e), (f).
8. Fed. R. App. P. 34(a)(2).
9. *See Table B-1, U.S. Courts of Appeals—Cases Commenced, Terminated, and Pending, by Circuit and Nature of Proceeding, During the 12-Month Period Ending December 31, 2017 (Excludes Federal Circuit)*, http://www.uscourts.gov/statistics-reports/caseload-statistics-data-tables?tn=&pn=78&t=537&m%5Bval ue%5D%5Bmonth%5D=12&y%5Bvalue%5D%5Byear%5D=2017. *See also* Patricia M. Wald, *19 Tips from 19 Years on the Appellate Bench*, 1 J. App. Prac. & Proc. 7, 9 (1999) (estimating that 60 percent of cases nationwide are decided without oral argument).

ter of discretion, it agrees only to *review* the decision below. Hearing an appeal does not mean that the court will retry the case. Instead of observing the examination and cross-examination of witnesses, hearing opening and closing arguments, and seeing the attorneys present various evidentiary exhibits all over again, the court *reviews* important evidence (whether findings of fact, testimony, or exhibits) and the attorneys' written arguments—in the form of briefs to the court—about the significance of that evidence. During the oral argument on appeal (if any), the court questions the attorneys about the sufficiency of the evidence, the significance of the arguments, or the impact of a holding one way or the other. The court then decides whether to affirm, to reverse, to reverse and remand, or to vacate the decision below.

When reviewing the decision of any lower court, the reviewing court—explicitly or implicitly—applies a certain appellate standard of review to that decision. The *appellate standard of review*[10] is a label that a reviewing court puts on the level of deference it gives to the findings of the court below. The appellate standard of review tells the court how "wrong" the lower court has to be before it will be reversed.

The appellate court decides which appellate standard of review to apply by identifying which aspect of the case is under review: an evidentiary ruling, a finding of fact, a legal ruling, or some other type of decision. Some decisions can be reversed simply if the reviewing court disagrees with the lower court. Others can be reversed only if the reviewing court can identify a serious error on the part of the court below. Generally, courts give high deference to decisions about facts—that is, they are loathe to upset a finding of fact—and low deference to conclusions of law. Because the appellate standard of review can significantly affect the arguments that you make to the court, you should consider this issue early in your research process and decide what standard the court is likely to apply to the decision that you seek to have reversed or hope to have affirmed.

---

10. For the sake of clarity, we use the label *appellate standards of review* to refer to these standards. However, as noted below, many courts use the label *standard of review* to refer to appellate standards of review, motion standards of review, and government action standards of review.

4.3.1. Purpose and Meaning of Appellate Standards of Review

Various public policies support the different appellate standards of review.[11] Appellate courts use a low deference appellate standard of review for decisions about the law because they believe that those who must use the law benefit from uniformity.[12] Low-deference standards give reviewing courts an opportunity to create a consistent body of law, which may be particularly important for issues of constitutional rights.[13] In fact, when a constitutional issue is involved, courts may decide to substitute the low-deference de novo standard for a higher-deference standard that might normally be appropriate for a given issue.[14]

A high-deference appellate standard of review promotes judicial economy and finality of certain types of decisions. A high-deference standard is also based on the premise that the trial court is in the best position to understand evidence. Particularly in the case of witness testimony, a trial court judge or jury has an opportunity that the court of appeals doesn't have. The judge or jury can observe the witnesses' demeanor, tone of voice, and body language, and use its best judgment based on those intangibles when it makes findings of fact.

Although many advocates ignore the standard after articulating it, the appellate standard of review is really the context within which the entire argument rests. Because there is often no controversy about which standard applies, however, some litigators are lulled into complacency on this subject and may miss fertile ground for legal argument.[15]

---

11. For an interesting discussion of the policies behind certain appellate standards of review, *see* Michael R. Bosse, *Standards of Review: The Meaning of Words*, 49 Me. L. Rev. 367, 374-84 (1997), (hereinafter "Bosse").

12. *See, e.g., Cooper Indus., Inc. v. Leatherman Tool Group, Inc.*, 532 U.S. 424, 436 (2001); *Ornelas v. United States*, 517 U.S. 690, 698 (1996); *United States v. Gasca-Ruiz*, 852 F.3d 1167, 1172 (9th Cir.), *cert. denied*, 138 S. Ct. 229 (2017) (noting that "concerns with ensuring uniformity . . . ordinarily weigh in favor of de novo review").

13. *See generally* Bosse, *supra* note 11, at 383, 397.

14. *See, e.g., Cooper Indus., Inc. v. Leatherman Tool Group, Inc.*, 532 U.S. 424, 434 (2001) (Court used de novo standard to review a district court determination of the constitutionality of a punitive damages award).

15. The United States Supreme Court frequently addresses standard of review issues. *See, e.g., McLane Co. v. E.E.O.C.*, 137 S. Ct. 1159, 1170 (2017), *as revised* (Apr. 3, 2017) ("a district court's decision to enforce an EEOC subpoena should be reviewed for abuse of discretion, not de novo"); *Brown v. Plata*, 563 U.S. 493, 517 (2011) (deciding appropriate standard of review of a three-judge

When you are beginning the process of writing an appellate brief, you should devote serious attention to the standard of review early in the research process in order to determine the role it will play in your case. The discussion that follows describes the most significant appellate standards of review, using the labels most commonly used in federal courts. Although, of course, you must rely on research rather than a textbook to provide support for any standard of review argument, state courts often apply standards that are similar to the federal standards.

a. Clearly Erroneous

A clearly erroneous standard applies to findings of facts. Rule 52(a)(6) of the Federal Rules of Civil Procedure provides as follows: "Findings of Fact, whether based on oral or other evidence, must not be set aside unless clearly erroneous, and the reviewing court must give due regard to the trial court's opportunity to judge the witnesses' credibility." This standard reflects the attitude that the fact finder is often in the best position to observe the presentation of the facts. In 2015, a Louisiana judge explained the importance of the clear error standard (called "manifest error" in that court) and explained what kind of evidence might meet that standard:

> Further, when findings are based on determinations regarding the credibility of witnesses, the manifest error-clearly wrong standard demands great deference to the trier of fact's findings; for only the factfinder can be aware of the variations in demeanor and tone of voice that bear so heavily on the listener's understanding and belief in what is said. Where documents or objective evidence so contradict the witness's story, or the story itself is so internally inconsistent or implausible on its face, that a reasonable fact finder would not credit the witness's story, the court of appeal may well find manifest error or clear wrongness even in a finding purportedly based on a credibility determination. However, where such factors are

---

district court opinion deciding legal and factual issues relating to prison over-crowding); *Cooper Indus., Inc.*, 532 U.S. at 434 (finding that de novo review, rather than abuse of discretion, was appropriate standard of review for district court determination of the constitutionality of a punitive damages award); *Ornelas*, 517 U.S. at 699 (holding that determinations of "reasonable suspicion" and "probable cause" should be reviewed de novo by appellate courts). *See generally* Bosse, *supra* note 11, at 374-84 (discussing *Ornelas*), and Kelly Kunsch, *Standard of Review (State and Federal): A Primer*, 18 SEATTLE U. L. REV. 11, 25 (1994).

not present, and a factfinder's finding is based on its decision to credit the testimony of one of two witnesses, that finding can virtually never be manifestly erroneous or clearly wrong.[16]

Courts often note that a court should find clear error only when its review of the record leads to "a definite and firm conviction" that the court has committed a mistake.[17] The clearly erroneous standard is a high hurdle for an advocate to overcome.

b. De Novo

Because most decisions that come before appellate courts are based on questions of law, the most commonly applied standard is the de novo standard. The de novo standard is a low-deference standard—or, more aptly, a no-deference standard—that applies when courts are reviewing the meaning or application of the controlling law. De novo review is sometimes referred to as "unlimited review," "unrestricted review," or "plenary review" (which might be paraphrased as "plenty of review") because it allows the court to give a full, or plenary, review to the findings below. When courts apply the de novo standard, they look at the legal questions as if no one had yet decided them, giving no deference to legal findings made below. When this standard is applied, the reviewing court is willing to substitute its judgment for that of the trial court or the intermediate court of appeals.

Courts apply the de novo standard not only to questions of law, but also, in most (but not all) cases, to mixed questions of law and fact.[18] A mixed question of law and fact is often characterized as a question about whether certain agreed-upon facts meet a legal standard. In *Ornelas v. United States*, for example, the United States Supreme Court decided that de novo was an appropriate appellate standard of review when it reviewed a trial court's determination as to whether a police officer indeed had probable cause based on the undisputed facts.[19]

---

16. *Robinson v. Bd. of Supervisors*, 2015-1707 (La. App. 1 Cir. 11/4/16), 208 So. 3d 511, 517-18, *writ granted sub nom. Robinson v. Bd. of Supervisors*, 2016-2145 (La. 2/3/17), 215 So. 3d 688, *and aff'd as amended sub nom. Robinson v. Bd. of Supervisors*, 2016-2145 (La. 6/29/17), 225 So. 3d 424. (citations omitted).

17. *See, e.g., United States v. U.S. Gypsum Co.*, 333 U.S. 364, 395 (1948); *Brown v. Plata*, 563 U.S. 493, 517 (2011); *J. L. v. Mercer Island Sch. Dist.*, 592 F.3d 938, 949 (9th Cir. 2010).

18. *Brown v. Plata*, 563 U.S. 493, 517 (2011) (applying a deferential standard to a mixed question of law and fact because, in the Court's opinion, "the mix weigh[ed] heavily on the 'fact' side" (citations omitted)).

19. 517 U.S. at 695.

The Court justifies the de novo standard in mixed question situations, as it does when it reviews other questions of law, with the goal of unifying precedent and stabilizing legal principles.[20] In 2018, however, the Supreme Court found that what it characterized as a "mixed question" should be reviewed "for clear error" because the particular issue, unusually, required the court to conduct "primarily . . . factual work."[21]

If the de novo standard applies, the legal findings of the courts below have *no weight* other than their intrinsic validity. Some novice legal writers make the mistake of citing to the decision under review in order to justify a conclusion that they want the appellate court to accept. It is certainly appropriate to argue that the decision below is correct, but you must support that assertion with citations to authorities other than the decision under review, because the reviewing court need not give any deference to that court's legal decisions.

c. Abuse of Discretion

The abuse of discretion standard is typically used to review discretionary decisions such as a judge's procedural rulings during a trial. These decisions might include decisions on nondispositive motions, objections, admissibility of evidence, or general conduct issues.[22] Commentators have noted that language such as "the court may" or "for good cause" are often predictors of an abuse of discretion standard of review.[23] Like the clearly erroneous standard, this standard presumes some expertise on the part of the trial court judge. Some judges see the standard in the same light as the clearly erroneous standard. For example, the United States Court of Appeals for the First Circuit has noted that, as to evidentiary rulings, "[o]nly rarely—and in extraordinarily compelling circumstances—will we, from the vista of a cold appellate record, reverse a district court's on-the-spot judgment concerning the relative weighing of probative value and unfair effect."[24]

---

20. *See generally id.* at 697; *United States v. Arvizu*, 534 U.S. 266, 275 (2002).

21. *U.S. Bank Nat'l Ass'n ex rel. CW Capital Asset Mgmt. LLC v. Vill. at Lakeridge, LLC*, 138 S. Ct. 960, 967 (2018).

22. *See, e.g.*, Kunsch, *supra* note 15, at 34-35.

23. Kunsch, *supra* note 15, at 35 (citing Maurice Rosenberg, *Judicial Discretion of the Trial Court, Viewed from Above*, 22 Syracuse L. Rev. 635, 655 (1971)). *See also In re Terrorist Bombings of U.S. Embassies in E. Afr. v. Odeh*, 552 F.3d 93, 135 (2d Cir. 2008) (noting use of phrase "the court may" in rule of criminal procedure as signal that abuse of discretion is appropriate standard of review).

24. *Freeman v. Package Mach. Co.*, 865 F.2d 1331, 1340 (1st Cir. 1988).

3 On occasion, you may devote a section of your argument to the appropriate standard of review. In that situation, you would seek out court statements like this one, which is in essence a rule for determining whether deference is appropriate.

In 2017, the United States Supreme Court decided that it must use the abuse of discretion standard to review a district court's decision to enforce a subpoena from the Equal Employment Opportunity Commission.[25] In analyzing the issue, the Court noted that when deciding whether a deferential or "searching" review is appropriate, the court must first look to the "history of appellate practice" and then ask whether, "as a matter of the sound administration of justice, one judicial actor is better positioned than another to decide the issue in question."[26] **3**

d. Other Appellate Standards

All federal (and most state) jury findings, which may be hard to separate into distinct questions of law and fact, are usually reviewed under the "substantial evidence" standard per the Seventh Amendment to the United States Constitution, which provides that "no fact tried by a jury shall be otherwise re-examined in any Court of the United States, than according to the rules of the common law." Those "rules of the common law" generally provide that such a finding must have only a "reasonable basis in the law" and have "warrant in the record."[27] Commentators have noted that courts are extremely reluctant to find that there is not "substantial evidence" to support a jury finding.[28]

Review of administrative agency decisions is governed by the Administrative Procedure Act, which provides at 5 U.S.C. § 706 that reviewing courts should "set aside" agency "actions, findings, and conclusions" that are "arbitrary, capricious, an abuse of discretion, or otherwise not in accordance with law." When an agency holds a formal hearing that creates a record, the reviewing court may set aside agency decisions only when they are "unsupported by substantial evidence."[29]

---

25. *McLane Co.*, 137 S. Ct. at 1166-67.

26. *Id.* (citations omitted).

27. *NLRB v. Hearst Publications,* 322 U.S. 111, 131 (1944).

28. Kunsch, *supra* note 15, at 43. *See also United States v. Ellefson*, 419 F.3d 859, 862-63 (8th Cir. 2005) ("We may reverse a jury's verdict only if 'no reasonable jury could have found the accused guilty beyond a reasonable doubt.'") (citation omitted). *See also Vetter v. McAtee*, 850 F.3d 178, 185 (5th Cir. 2017) ("our standard of review with respect to a jury verdict is especially deferential").

29. *See, e.g.,* Kunsch, *supra* note 15, at 40-41; *see also, e.g., Metro-N. Commuter R.R. Co. v. United States Dep't of Labor*, 886 F.3d 97, 106 (2d Cir. 2018). That court defined "substantial evidence" as "more than a scintilla, but less than a preponderance." *Id.* (citation omitted).

4.3.2. Identifying the Appropriate Appellate Standard of Review

Of course, knowing the standards is only the first step. You must then decide which standard or standards apply in your case. Some issues are obviously questions of fact (e.g., Did the defendant hit the victim? Did the officer ask a certain question of the defendant?), while others are obviously questions of law (e.g., Did the court apply the correct legal standard? Did asking that question constitute intimidation?). Mixed questions are more difficult to identify; courts generally identify a mixed question of law and fact as one that is based on how a legal principle applies to established or agreed-upon facts.

Applying one standard over another—for example, a clearly erroneous appellate standard of review rather than a de novo standard—can lead to a vastly different review of the same case. Accordingly, you should study the record below carefully. Identify the decisions, rulings, or findings that are at the crux of your client's case. First, identify who made the ruling. The standard of review depends on whether the decision maker was a judge, a jury, or an administrative body. Second, focus on what kind of decision was made. If it was a ruling on an evidentiary matter, the abuse of discretion standard will probably apply. If it was a finding of fact, the court will apply the clearly erroneous standard. If, as is most likely, it was a decision of law, the court will apply a de novo standard. If you are arguing to a court of last resort, you may look to the intermediate court of appeals decision to see what appellate standard of review that court applied. If a standard is not mentioned in the decision (and the standard is often not mentioned), the court probably applied a de novo standard. Of course, if appropriate, you may decide to argue that the lower court applied the wrong standard of review.[30]

If you are in doubt as to the appropriate standard of review for the legal issue your case presents, do a little focused research. You may find precedent as to the standard of review for the narrow legal issue that exists in your case. In addition to conducting primary research, you may find secondary sources helpful. Many practice manuals are geared to attorneys who practice within the courts of a

---

30. *See generally Cooper Indus., Inc.*, 532 U.S. at 434 (noting that court below erred when applying an abuse of discretion standard rather than the de novo standard); *Ornelas*, 517 U.S. at 698-99 (noting that court below erred when it applied a deferential appellate standard of review). *See also United States v. Benitez Alvarado*, 622 F. App'x 215, 217 (4th Cir. 2015) ("[t]he parties do not agree on the appropriate standard of review").

specific jurisdiction; some of these manuals address appellate standards of review as they apply to particular legal issues.[31]

Although the appellate standard of review is usually not controversial, at times it is at the heart of the appellate decision.[32] If the standard of review in your case is de novo, it will have almost no impact on your argument. You will address the standard of review—either in the introductory section or in a separate, labeled section—and then you will spend the rest of the argument discussing the appropriate legal standards and how the appellate court should apply those standards.

If your case could or should be reviewed under a more deferential standard, however, that standard will have a significant impact on your argument, and you should expect to feature it in your point headings. For example, your heading might say, "the district court abused its discretion when . . ." or "the trial court's finding as to X was clearly erroneous because. . . ." Even if the court you are writing to asks for the standard to be announced in a separate section, it will be a big part of your argument if it is a high-deference standard. For example, if the clearly erroneous standard applies, your argument must identify the particular finding of fact that you assert to be clearly erroneous, and cite to the record. Then, you must show how the evidence indicates that the finding was clearly erroneous, and show how the erroneous finding changed the outcome of the case. Alternatively, if you must assert that the judge did not abuse his or her discretion, you must identify the particular decision the judge allegedly made in error and use appropriate authorities to explain why the judge's decision was appropriate under the governing authorities.

As you must with any legal argument, make appellate standard of review arguments honestly. Do not create an appellate standard of review issue where none exists. If the standard genuinely makes a difference in the case, however, you can and should use it to demonstrate the justice of the result you seek.

---

31. *See, e.g.,* Anderson's Sixth Circuit Federal Practice Manual ch. 7 (Lexis-Nexis Matthew Bender 2017) (updated annually).

32. For an interesting discussion of using policy concerns to drive the discussion of appellate standard of review, *see* Bosse, *supra* note 11, at 374 et seq. If the appropriate appellate standard of review is controversial, you can and should justify your argument with references to policies served by choosing the standard you favor. *See* Section 5.2.2 in this text for guidance on presenting rule-choice arguments.

4.3.3. Format Considerations for Placement of the Standard of Review

During recent years, many courts have begun using their local rules to require briefs to include a separate statement of the appellate standard of review. The Pennsylvania Rules of Appellate Procedure, for example, require that a statement of "both the scope of review and the standard of review" appear in the appellant's brief, "separately and distinctly entitled," between sections containing the "order or other determination in question" and the "[s]tatement of the questions involved."[33] The Federal Rules of Appellate Procedure now require that for each issue, the argument must contain "a concise statement of the applicable standard of review (which may appear in the discussion of the issue or under a separate heading placed before the discussion of the issues)."[34] The Rules of Court for the Kansas Supreme Court require that within the appellant's brief, "[e]ach issue must begin with citation to the appropriate standard of appellate review and a reference to the specific location in the record on appeal where the issue was raised and ruled on."[35] If the local rules do not demand a separate statement, the standard should at least be included in introductory material within the argument. No matter what method is used, you should cite to authority for the standard of review, just as you would for any legal proposition.

In most situations, the statement of the appellate standard of review requires no more than a paragraph. As noted previously, however, if the standard is controversial or if it is otherwise significant to your argument, it should be treated like any other major issue, with appropriate point headings and text used to make the point. This method should be used even if the local rules require a separate, formal statement of the standard.

4.3.4. Avoiding Confusion among the Different Uses of the Term "Standard of Review"

Unfortunately, courts do not always use the term *standard of review* precisely. We have used the phrase *appellate standard of review* to refer to standards that appellate courts apply to their review of

---

33. Pa. R. of App. Proc. 2111(a).

34. Fed. R. App. Proc. 28(a)(8)(B).

35. Kan. Sup. Ct. R. 6.02(a)(5). Of course, the appellee's brief should reflect any disagreement as to the appropriate standard of review. *See, e.g.,* Kan. Sup. Ct. R. 6.03(a)(4) ("Each issue shall begin with citation to the appropriate standard of appellate review; appellee shall either concur in appellant's citation to the standard of appellate review or cite additional authority.").

lower court decisions, and *motion standard* to refer to standards that courts use when deciding particular motions. Courts, however, often use the bare phrase *standard of review*[36] to mean either or both of these things—and to mean other things. Besides its use to refer to appellate standards and motion standards of review, courts commonly use the phrase *standard of review* in at least one other context: to describe the level of scrutiny that a court may use to review the constitutionality of a state statute or other government action.

Understanding how "government action standards of review" work, and how all three uses of the term may be relevant in a single case, can help you to master the concept of standards of review.

a. Government Action Standards of Review

Courts usually use the phrase *standard of review* to describe the standard that a court will use to review the constitutionality of a state statute or other government action. Some actions will be reviewed under a "strict scrutiny" standard, some under a "heightened scrutiny" standard, and others under a "rational basis" standard.[37] Although these phrases all describe *standards* that are used to *review*, they are not the same thing as appellate standards *of* review. Thinking in terms of "deference," which is so crucial to appellate standards of review, may be helpful. When the court is asked to review the constitutionality of a state statute or other government action, it is deciding whether to defer to the decision of a state legislature or other government actor. The government action standard of review tells it how closely to scrutinize the government actor's decision when conducting its review.

All types of courts, from the trial court on up through the United States Supreme Court, may use a strict scrutiny, heightened scrutiny, or rational basis standard to review the constitutionality of a government action.

---

36. As noted above, courts may use the phrase *legal standard* or *pleading standard* to refer to a motion standard of review.

37. *See. e.g., Trustees of Indiana Univ. v. Prosecutor of Marion Cty.*, 289 F. Supp. 3d 905, 932 (S.D. Ind. 2018) (noting that a "rational basis standard of review applies"); *Kolbe v. Hogan*, 849 F.3d 114, 134 (4th Cir.), *cert. denied*, 138 S. Ct. 469 (2017) (considering whether to apply an "intermediate scrutiny standard of review"); *O Centro Espirita Beneficiente Uniao Do Vegetal v. Duke*, 286 F. Supp. 3d 1239, 1266 (D.N.M. 2017) (discussing "strict scrutiny standard of review").

b. Multiple Standards of Review in the Same Case

One way to gain a clearer understanding of different standards of review is to identify which standards are used in which courts and how multiple standards may occur in one case.

Motion standards and government action standards of review can be applied in trial courts, courts of appeals, and courts of last resort. Appellate standards of review can be applied only in courts of appeals and courts of last resort. It is not unusual, in fact, for an appellate court to apply all three types of standards in the same case.[38]

For example, a trial court may grant a motion for summary judgment in a case in which the issue was the constitutionality of a state action. That trial court would have used a motion standard and a government action standard of review. The appellate court reviewing that case must use the appropriate (1) appellate standard of review to analyze whether the trial court properly applied the (2) motion standard and used the correct (3) government action standard of review. Because the appellate standard in that situation would almost certainly be de novo, the appellate court would, in essence, reapply both the motion standard and the government action standard of review as part of its de novo review of the decision below.

Although the use of the same term for three different meanings may be confusing, keep the distinguishing factors in mind:

(1) Trial courts may not use appellate standards of review. *Only courts of appeals and courts of last resort* may use appellate standards of review when they review *lower court decisions*.

(2) *Any* court (trial or appellate) may use a *motion* standard to decide, or to review the validity of a decision on, a *motion*.

(3) *Any* court (trial or appellate) may use a *government action* standard of review to review *actions by governmental entities* or to review the validity of a court's decision about the government action.

Table 4.1 will help you to understand these three different standards.

---

38. *See, e.g., Hughes v. City of Cedar Rapids*, 840 F.3d 987, 996-97 (8th Cir. 2016) (court applied a de novo standard to its review of a decision granting a motion to dismiss; it used rational basis to find that a traffic camera ordinance did not violate equal protection rights); *Windsor v. United States*, 699 F.3d 169, 176, 181 (2d Cir. 2012) (applying de novo standard of review to review a decision granting summary judgment to plaintiff and deciding to apply heightened scrutiny to determine whether taxation statute unconstitutionally denied spousal deduction to surviving spouse of same-sex marriage), *aff'd*, 570 U.S. 744, 775 (2013).

TABLE 4.1

TYPE OF STANDARD OF REVIEW	MOTION STANDARD[39]	GOVERNMENT ACTION STANDARD OF REVIEW	APPELLATE STANDARD OF REVIEW
Type of court that may use this standard:	Trial court Intermediate court of appeals Court of last resort	Trial court Intermediate court of appeals Court of last resort	Intermediate court of appeals Court of last resort
Example(s) of this type of standard:	Whether the facts alleged plausibly give rise to an entitlement to relief	Strict scrutiny Heightened scrutiny Rational basis	De novo Clearly erroneous Abuse of discretion
What the court uses this standard to decide:	Whether it's appropriate to grant or deny a motion	Whether certain government action is constitutional	Whether to affirm, reverse, or vacate a decision of a court below
Whose decision the court is being asked to defer to:	N/A	The decision of a government actor	The decision of a lower court

4.4. CONCLUSION

The type of court that hears your case and the standard of review that the court applies can each make a significant difference in the way that you structure your arguments. Even if the applicable standard is not controversial, you must keep that standard in mind as you conduct your research and write your brief. Be sure to update your research so that you are confident about the standard itself and its judicial gloss. In your brief, be sure to connect the standard explicitly to the legal or factual conclusions that you ask the court to accept. If the standard raises substantive or factual issues, you may well need to address those issues in depth within your argument.

It is likely that most of the appellate cases you argue will be reviewed under a de novo standard. However, do not make this decision on automatic pilot. Carefully consider the record, the issues, and the relevant appellate standards of review so that you can make an informed decision about which standard applies to your case.

---

39. As noted above, courts also use the terms *legal standard* and *pleading standard.*

Developing and Structuring Your Argument

When you took writing courses in college, you may have had a hard time figuring out what to write about. Undergraduate writing teachers spend a lot of time helping their students choose their topics. If you are a lawyer, you will never have that problem again. Your clients, their problems, and the law will provide all the topics that you need. The difficulty arises when you have to take all of that information and present it to somebody else. And, if in your undergrad writing courses you worried about making your essays long enough, now you may well have the opposite problem: how to keep them short enough. You know the result you want, but how do you decide which issues to address and which to ignore, how to organize the issues you do address, and how much detail to provide about each issue?

1 As you know, CREXAC stands for Conclusion-Rule-EXplanation, Application, and Connection-conclusion. You may have used CREAC, TREAT, or some other formula in another course; as we will discuss below, most of these formulas function in much the same way.

1 Fortunately, just as the law provides you with topics, it can also provide you with structure. And also fortunately, the writing formulas you learned in objective legal writing courses are just as viable when you write persuasively. In this chapter, we will identify methods you can use to structure analytical writing in motion memos and appellate briefs. We will also discuss ways that persuasive writers use "CREXAC," an analytical formula that is either identical to or very close to the formula you learned in your objective legal writing course. Finally, we will review variations on CREXAC along with a protocol you can follow to help you decide when it's time to use one of those variations.

5.1. FINDING STRUCTURE

At some stage in your writing process, you find yourself with a stack of authorities (either paper or digital) that you plan to use in support of your client's case. Now, you must make the move from that stack of law to some sort of an outline. Effective legal arguments are usually best organized around issues, rules, and arguments rather than around authority cases. The court's major concern is not whether the cases you have found are analogous to your client's case. Instead, the court wants to know the issues that your case presents, the rules that govern those issues, and how those rules should apply to your case. Of course, you will probably use cases to illustrate or explain the rules that you identify, but the *rules*, rather than the cases, should be the focus of your analysis.

When trying to identify the rules that you want to use to structure your argument, it may help you to think of possible categories of arguments. Since legal arguments are typically based on authority, you may try to develop your arguments based on the categories of authority: case law, constitutions and statutes, regulations, or extra-legal authority. Since these different types of authority may interact within one argument, however, you may wish to think of categories from a different perspective.

If the rules that govern your case are well established and you must argue how those rules apply, you can structure your argument around those established rules.[1] If your case is not governed by well-

---

1. *See, e.g.,* Linda H. Edwards, Legal Writing: Process, Analysis, and Organization chs. 2-6 (5th ed., Aspen 2010); Richard K. Neumann, Jr. & Kristen

established rules, or if you are struggling to discover or articulate the relevant rules, you can use both research and brainstorming techniques to help you discover your structure. Furthermore, remember that some of your rules may be policy-based rules, and that those policy-based rules can help you to structure your argument. Once you have identified the issues, rules, and policies that are relevant to your argument, you can create a working outline.

5.1.1. Using Existing Rules and the "Phrase-That-Pays" to Structure Your Argument ②

If your argument is based in whole or in part on well-established statutory or common law rules, you can structure your argument by looking for each rule's "key terms,"[2] or, as we call them, the "phrases-that-pay." As you know, the phrase-that-pays is the label for the word or phrase that is the focus of controversy about whether or how a rule applies. You can use phrases-that-pay as an effective organizing principle: By focusing on one "phrase-that-pays" within each subsection of the argument, you ensure that you are focusing on one issue or sub-issue at a time, and you make it easier for the court to understand your argument. Thus, if one or more of your legal issues is governed by well-established rules, you can begin to structure your argument by reviewing those rules and identifying the phrases-that-pay that are in controversy in your case.

③ You can often identify phrases-that-pay by turning your rule into an if-then statement. An "if-then" rule says, in essence, "if a certain condition exists, then a certain legal status results." The phrase-that-pays is almost always the "condition" that you are trying to prove the existence or nonexistence of. Thus, look for the phrases-that-pay in the "if" clause; that clause usually contains the narrow point that the writer is trying to explain or prove. For example, 18 U.S.C. § 2113(e), part of a federal bank robbery statute, was drafted to enhance punishment for bank robbers who took hostages as they fled, and it provided in pertinent part as follows:

> Whoever, in committing any offense defined in this section, or in . . . attempting to avoid apprehension for the commission of such offense . . . forces any person to accompany him without the consent of such person, shall be imprisoned not

② Sidebar: Sometimes rules exist, but no one has yet articulated them. Legal writers use "inductive reasoning" to find these rules. See Section 5.2.2.c below for advice on how to use inductive reasoning to find rules.

③ Sidebar: Note that you should not necessarily articulate your rule as an if-then statement in the argument itself; this technique is merely a method for identifying the phrases-that-pay.

KONRAD TISCIONE, LEGAL REASONING AND LEGAL WRITING, CH. 2 (7th ed., Aspen 2013).

2. *See, e.g.*, LAUREL CURRIE OATES & ANNE M. ENQUIST, THE LEGAL WRITING HANDBOOK §§ 22.3.2 (5th ed., Aspen 2010).

less than ten years, or if death results shall be punished by
death or life imprisonment.

In *Whitfield v. United States*, the petitioner was charged under that
statute. He was a failed bank robber who had sought refuge in a
nearby home and asked the homeowner to show him a windowless
room where he could hide. Shortly after they walked together to
that room, the homeowner had a heart attack and died. Stating the
relevant parts of the statute as an if-then statement would read as
follows:

IF death results after a person forces someone to accompany
him or her while attempting to avoid apprehension for
committing attempted bank robbery, THEN that person shall
be punished with death or life imprisonment.

A good way to identify phrases-that-pay is to ask what either side
would be arguing about. In *Whitfield*, the two sides were arguing
about whether walking together to the computer room meant that
Whitfield had "forced" the homeowner to "accompany" him. Thus,
"forced accompaniment" (and any alternate form of those two
words) is the phrase-that-pays.

Sometimes, one rule will have more than one phrase-that-pays in
controversy. To determine if this is true for a particular rule, consider
both how courts have interpreted the rule and how the rule relates
to a particular set of facts. For instance, in the previous example,
the petitioner might argue that he did not force the homeowner to
do anything "without her consent," since she responded immediately when he asked her where they could hide. Some courts might
conduct a separate analysis of "force" or forcing "without consent"
in those circumstances. If the courts have conducted these separate
analyses, it would be easy to divide the argument on this rule into
two parts: (1) whether the defendant "forced" the homeowner to do
something "without consent," and (2) whether walking eight feet
down the hallway constituted "accompaniment" for purposes of the
statute. On the other hand, if the courts have not addressed these
issues separately, it might not be worthwhile for you to do so.[3] The
court's analysis is usually a good starting point.

Whether your rule comes from a statute or the common law,
you may find that you can discover the true phrases-that-pay only
after further research. Sometimes a term in controversy has one
or more layers of judicial gloss, so that the actual focus of the

---

3. Of course, you may decide that courts should be analyzing issues that
they have not analyzed in the past.

controversy—and therefore the phrase-that-pays—is one or two layers away from the phrase-that-pays in the rule itself.

The Fourth Amendment, for example, provides that "[t]he right of the people to be secure in their persons, houses, papers, and effects, against unreasonable searches and seizures, shall not be violated, and no Warrants shall issue, but upon probable cause." Courts have long held, however, that "consent" is an exception to the warrant requirement. In some of those Fourth Amendment cases, the courts have explored whether certain behavior does or does not constitute consent; in others, the issue is not what consent *means*, but about whether the person who did the consenting was the appropriate person; if not, the consent may not have been *reasonable*.

In *Fernandez v. California*, for example, the issue was whether a domestic partner could consent to a search. When the police had come to the door, the defendant had objected to police entering, saying "I know my rights." The police suspected that the defendant had hurt his domestic partner (they had heard screaming coming from the home), and they arrested him and removed him from the scene. The police then asked the domestic partner for consent to search the apartment. Thus, the phrase-that-pays in that Fourth Amendment case was whether the *consent was reasonable*, even though the word *consent* doesn't appear in the Fourth Amendment itself.

As another example, 28 U.S.C. § 1332 gives federal district courts "diversity jurisdiction" over certain state-law lawsuits between "citizens of different states," if the amount in controversy is higher than a particular minimum. If you turn that standard into an if-then statement, you could get a rule that says something like this:

> IF the litigants on opposite sides of a state law case are citizens of different states, and the case meets a certain financial threshold [certain condition], THEN a federal court has diversity jurisdiction over the cause of action [legal status].

If you did not conduct further research, you might presume that you had to focus your analysis on the meaning of the term *citizen* as it applies to your client and his or her opponent. If you did conduct further research, however, you would discover that the courts define *citizenship*—for purposes of § 1332—as "domicile." You might then fashion an if-then rule that says something like this:

> IF a person is domiciled in a state [certain condition], THEN that person is a citizen of that state for purposes of § 1332 [legal status].

This rule makes it seem like your phrase-that-pays is *domicile*. You continue your research, and find that the courts explain that establishing a domicile under § 1332 requires that "a person must be physically present in the state and must have either the intention to make his home there indefinitely or the absence of an intention to make his home elsewhere."[4] So now your if-then rule looks like this:

> **IF a person is physically present in a state and either (a) has the intent to make a home there or (b) lacks intent to make a home elsewhere [certain condition], THEN that person is domiciled in that state [legal status].**

Upon looking at the cases addressing this rule, you see that courts analyze case facts to determine a person's "physical presence," "intent" to make a home in a state, or both, when determining whether the standard is met. An often-reliable test for the true phrase-that-pays is to identify the term that courts connect—or "apply"—to the facts of the case. In a diversity case, for example, courts typically move from the concept of "citizenship" to "domicile," and from "domicile" to "intent." If the court connects case facts to the terms "physical presence" and "intent" ("Mr. Kish was physically present in Illinois through much of the relevant time period, and stated at a press conference his intent to remain"), you can be pretty confident that for the rule determining diversity of citizenship, it would be appropriate to focus analysis on the phrases-that-pay "physical presence" and "intent to make a home there indefinitely or the absence of an intent to make a home elsewhere."

When deciding what points to argue in your brief, however, you must do more than identify the phrases-that-pay that exist within a rule; you must decide which phrases-that-pay are at issue. For example, you may have a diversity situation where a party to a case is obviously "physically present," but where there is some controversy as to whether he or she has the requisite "intent" to make a home in the state. In that situation, you would acknowledge that there is no controversy as to physical presence and focus your argument on establishing intent. We will discuss below how best to include uncontroversial issues within the argument.

Thus, to use rules to structure your argument, you must understand how the rules work *and* understand what controversies the rules present in your client's case. In the example above, we worked forward, starting with the statute and moving through common law rules until we found the language that the court applied to case facts. You could also work backward, however; in the example above, note

---

4. *See, e.g., Deasy v. Louisville & Jefferson Cty. Metro. Sewer Dist.*, 47 Fed. App'x 726, 728 (6th Cir. 2002) (court-designated unpublished decision).

that the court connected physical presence and intent, then note that these two factors constituted domicile, and then note that domicile constituted citizenship. This three-step process might help:

(1) See how courts apply the rule, moving forward or backward through as many layers as needed to determine what words or phrases the courts focus on when they connect legal concepts to the facts of the case.

(2) Determine how those words or phrases connected to the facts of the case relate to the rule or statute at issue (are the words part of the rule, part of the courts' definition of terms in the rule, or part of the courts' explanation of how the rule applies?).

(3) Determine which phrases-that-pay are at issue in your client's case.

When writing, you must be sure to clarify how the phrases-that-pay relate to each other and to the relevant statutes or common law rules. Once you have analyzed all of the applicable rules, identified their phrases-that-pay, and determined which phrases-that-pay are in controversy in your case, you can begin to draft a working outline of your argument.

5.1.2. Using Your Research to Help You Structure Your Argument

A second method of identifying argument structure is to use your research. Look at that stack of authorities (whether it is a stack of paper on the floor, or a list of authorities in a file in your computer). Each one of those authorities made it into the stack because it appeared to support some aspect of your argument. Some authorities may support more than one, or even several, aspects of your argument. Ideally, you will have used an organized note-taking system as you reviewed each authority. For cases, for example, you may have recorded procedural information such as court and date, and substantive information such as issue(s), facts, holding, and reasoning. Now you can review those notes, and the authorities themselves, and look for organizing principles for your argument.

One way to identify organizing principles is to identify argument points you can get from each authority. To do this, look at each authority and write out the ways in which the authority relates to or supports your argument. These points may be rules or policies that the court would need to consider in order to decide the case, or assertions that the court would have to agree with to decide the case in your favor.

This is a brainstorming technique, so don't worry about making the statements in perfect rule format, or even in formal language. Just use some method to list the holding(s) or other information from the authority that made you think the authority would be helpful to your argument, recording the source for each item. As you proceed through your authorities, you may discover that you have already written down the same assertion or a similar one from a different source. If that's the case, simply add the new source to that item, perhaps noting the difference in a parenthetical. You may also have some assertions in mind that you can't tie to a particular source at the moment; be sure to write those down as well.

Although many good writers compose at the computer keyboard, the computer may not be the best place to use this method. You may want to write the assertions on index cards so that you can shuffle them around later. You may want to write them on a big piece of paper or a whiteboard so you can think about how the statements from one authority connect to the statements from another authority, perhaps drawing arrows to make the connections more obvious to yourself. You may have a decision tree app that will let you simulate this kind of physical activity on the screen. Use whatever method works best for you.

For example, imagine you were trying to brainstorm your arguments for petitioner in the case of *Fernandez v. California*. In that case, as noted above, the issue was whether a domestic partner could consent to a search after an objecting resident had been removed. The facts indicated that after the objecting resident had been removed, the police put pressure on his domestic partner, implying that her children might be removed from the home if she did not consent to the search. In a previous case, *Georgia v. Randolph*, the United States Supreme Court had held that police cannot obtain valid permission from a co-occupant of a house to enter without a warrant when another co-occupant is physically present at the scene and expressly refuses to consent. The question in *Fernandez* was whether the co-occupant can give consent after the objecting occupant has been involuntarily removed from the residence. After doing your research, you might come up with the following list of points that the court would have to agree with for you to succeed:

Sample list of points my side needs the court to agree with (plus supporting authorities):

1. **The co-tenant's consent was invalid.**

   Georgia v. Randolph
   Ohio v. Smith

Kentucky v. Silver
California v. Enns
Virginia v. Ralph
Louisiana v. Hébert
New York v. Merritt

2. Once a co-tenant objects to a search of the home, that objection overrules the later consent of another co-tenant.

Georgia v. Randolph
Nevada v. Pollman
Illinois v. Brill
Ohio v. Mika
California v. Moylan

3. Removing the objecting co-tenant does not negate the objecting co-tenant's consent.

Hawaii v. Barnett
Pennsylvania v. Stanchi
Florida v. McGinley

4. The most sacred space protected by the Fourth Amendment is the private residence.

Indiana v. Contreras
Utah v. Chavez
Hawaii v. Silva
Vermont v. Bernstein
Ohio v. Zahm
Utah v. Puccinelli

5. A later-consenting co-tenant cannot overrule the earlier non-consenting co-tenant.

Georgia v. Randolph
Illinois v. Brill
Ohio v. Zahm
Utah v. Chavez
Texas v. Amari

6. Pressure to consent makes consent invalid.

California v. Thai
Hawaii v. Silva
Ohio v. Zahm

Michigan v. Dunn
Illinois v. Perek

7. The court should reverse the decision of the California Court of Appeals.

   Georgia v. Randolph
   California v. Thai
   Michigan v. Dunn
   Ohio v. Zahm

8. Allowing the objecting tenant to control the consent decision does not thwart effective law enforcement.

   Utah v. Chavez
   Hawaii v. Silva
   Vermont v. Bernstein
   Ohio v. Zahm
   Utah v. Puccinelli

9. The officers had time to get a warrant without risking destruction of evidence.

   California v. Thai
   Michigan v. Dunn
   Ohio v. Zahm

10. Affirming this decision will encourage officers to arrest parties who object to a search as a means of obtaining consent from others.

    Hawaii v. Silva
    California v. Thai
    Utah v. Puccinelli

After making the list, try to identify relationships between and among the points. For example, points 1 and 7 are really two sides of the same coin: if the co-tenant's consent was invalid, the decision below must be reversed. Some of the points may be repetitive of other points, and so they can be eliminated, or the two repetitive points can be synthesized into one point, for example, points 2 and 3. If you are in doubt, write up both points; doing so should teach you enough about their substance to reveal any overlap. Some points may be parts or subparts of other points, and so they should be grouped accordingly; for example, points 2, 3, and 5, or points 8, 9, and 10. Some points may be threshold issues, so you may decide that they should be addressed first. Other points may be policy arguments, like point 4, and you can place them wherever you think they will do the most good.

If you have listed these points on index cards, you might try moving the cards around to identify the relationships between and among the points. You might stack the cards that seem to make the same point. If you have listed these points on a piece of paper, whiteboard, or app, you might try drawing lines or circles to connect related points, or to identify a hierarchy among the assertions.[5] Once you have figured out, even tentatively, how the points relate to each other, you are ready to draft an outline.

5.1.3. Using Policy-Based Rules in Your Argument

Another method of creating an outline of your argument—or of identifying points to be included in your outline—is to identify relevant policy arguments. Legal writing is based on rules, and usually rules provide the best structure for legal analysis. Some writers, however, focus so much on the structure that the rules provide that they miss important policy arguments.

Policy arguments are based on a special kind of rule called a *public policy*. In law, *public policy* is defined roughly as a societal rule about how people should behave or how institutions should function in our society.[6] Even when policies remain the same, laws may change as human attitudes change or as scientific knowledge changes. For example, over the past 30 years, laws about smoking in public places have changed based on (1) the public policy or societal belief that one person should not cause harm to another and (2) the scientific knowledge about the harms of secondhand smoke. In many legal arguments, the policy arguments are implicit in the more formal legal rules that apply to the issues in the case, and they need not be addressed separately. Sometimes, however, the court will be more likely to agree with your ultimate conclusion if it can also be convinced—or reminded—of the importance of a policy that underlies your argument.

If you were arguing on behalf of Fernandez, for example, you might include a separate point addressing the historic "sanctity of the home" under the Fourth Amendment. If you were arguing on behalf of the state, in contrast, you might include a point about the

---

5. *See, e.g.*, Elizabeth Fajans & Mary R. Falk, *Comments Worth Making: Supervising Scholarly Writing in Law School*, 46 J. Legal Educ. 342 (1996).

6. *See generally* Ellie Margolis, *Closing the Floodgates: Making Persuasive Policy Arguments in Appellate Briefs*, 62 Mont. L. Rev. 59, 70 (2001).

importance of police discretion in deciding when it is appropriate to arrest a suspect and take him into custody. In the "sanctity of the home" argument, you might cite many different types of authorities, including historical analyses of the Fourth Amendment. You would also, however, want to find cases in which courts suppressed evidence because police had entered a home without a warrant or appropriate consent. If you were arguing about police discretion, however, you would highlight cases in which courts upheld challenged police actions based on the importance of deferring to on-the-job decisionmaking by police officers in dangerous situations.

Even if you make a policy argument separately from more traditional legal arguments, remember that policy arguments are not drastically different from traditional legal arguments. You may, but you are not required to, label them as "public policy" or "policy" arguments (e.g., you need not say, "For reasons of public policy, this court should . . ."). Further, policy arguments can and should be supported by references to outside authorities.[7] Although policy arguments might be more likely to include citations to extra-legal sources,[8] whenever possible, you should include citations to and analysis of cases in which courts referenced certain policies when deciding similar legal issues.

You may have started thinking about policy arguments as you tried to identify a theme for your argument. At this stage, you should make sure that the outline of your argument reflects your theme. As part of that step, note whether policy arguments that support your theme are worth addressing as separate points in your argument and whether there are authorities that would be useful support for these arguments. Not every brief needs a separate policy argument; as noted previously, policy arguments are often implicit in legal arguments. But when drafting a working outline, you may wish to tentatively identify policy arguments that could be incorporated into your argument.

5.1.4. Using a Reverse Roadmap to Structure Your Argument

Another method of identifying structure is to create an outline in paragraph form. Start with the ultimate point that you want the

---

7. *Id.* at 66.

8. For example, if you are arguing that traffic stops are dangerous for police officers, you might cite to statistical information about how frequently police officers are injured in the course of conducting traffic stops.

court to agree with, and then ask yourself what point or points the court must agree with to agree with *that* point, moving in reverse until you are at the smallest part of any test you might ask a court to apply. This method is more complicated because as you write the reverse roadmap paragraph, you must already have in mind some relationships between and among your points. The method might result in several branching paragraphs rather than just one. For example, if you were working on *Fernandez v. California*, part of your reverse roadmap outline might look like this:

> **This court should reverse the decision below. In order to decide to reverse, it has to agree that the consent was invalid.**
>
> **In order to agree that the consent was invalid, the court either has to agree that Fernandez's objection survived his removal from the home OR that pressure made his co-tenant's consent invalid.**
>
> **It might help the court to agree that Fernandez's objection survived his removal from the home if the court agreed that it's bad public policy for police to arrest and remove people who refuse to consent to a search.**
>
> **It might help the court to agree that Fernandez's objection survived his removal from the home if the court agreed that the sanctity of the home is the most important location to be protected in Fourth Amendment jurisprudence.**

As with the "list of assertions" method, this method might be more effective with pen and paper than with a computer. If you want to pick up a paragraph and move it around or draw lines connecting two or more paragraphs with each other, you may be better off with hard copy than digital copy. A reverse roadmap outline might be complete enough to let you start writing, or it may be a method you can combine with other methods to help you draft a working outline.

5.1.5. The Working Outline

After you have used some method or methods to identify the major rules, policies, and assertions that control your argument, you should analyze how they relate to each other and draft a working outline that shows those relationships as you currently understand them. If you were researching *Fernandez v. California*, you might come up with a working outline like the one below. (Note that these headings are not in perfect "point heading" form.)

Possible Working Outline for *Fernandez v. California*

1. The most sacred space protected by the Fourth Amendment is the private residence.

2. *Georgia v. Randolph* controls this case.

    2.1 Once a co-tenant objects to a search of the home, that objection overrules the later consent of another co-tenant.

    2.2 Removing the objecting co-tenant does not negate the objecting co-tenant's consent.

    2.3 A later-consenting co-tenant cannot overrule the earlier non-consenting co-tenant.

3. Pressure to consent makes consent invalid.

4. Reversing the decision would promote public policy.

    4.1 Allowing the objection to control does not thwart effective law enforcement.

    4.2 The officers had time to get a warrant without risking destruction of evidence.

    4.3 Affirming this decision will encourage officers to arrest parties who object to a search as a means of obtaining consent from others.

Of course, this outline is not carved in stone. As you write, you may discover that some arguments are incomplete, while others are not worth making. You may discover that some sections of your outline need to be divided into two subsections, that others are not worthy of a full discussion, or that you need to add certain arguments. As with the research questions, your goal is not perfection; rather, it's to create an outline that is complete enough to get you started on your writing.

If *any* type of prewriting outline is too difficult for you, you may want to try writing *before* you outline. Use written or unwritten prompts to keep going, like "What I want to say is…." or "My side should win because…." Keep your paragraphs to a reasonable length, and then, after you have written your argument, use the advice in Chapter Nine to write an effective topic sentence for each paragraph. Those topic sentences will reveal the main points you have made and the order in which you have made them. You can then use the topic sentences to evaluate the relationships among your points and to re-map your large-scale organization, perhaps using some of the techniques noted in this chapter.

5.2.   USING AN ANALYTICAL FORMULA

Once you have created a working outline, you can begin to draft your argument. Two kinds of formulas can help you draft your argument. The first formula is the formula of assertions and arguments that you create to answer the questions that your case presents. The working outline you created is your initial attempt to craft that formula, to decide how to structure your analysis of the issues and assertions relevant to your argument. That formula is unique to this set of facts and issues in this jurisdiction at this time; you might be able to reuse certain elements in the formula, but it is doubtful you would ever write another brief with that identical set of assertions and arguments. It is for one-time-use only.

The second kind of formula that can help you draft your argument is far from unique: it can be recycled forever, for as many times as you need it. As we discussed in Chapter Two, we call this formula CREXAC, which stands for Conclusion, Rule, EXplanation, Application, and Connection-conclusion. While various legal writers use various labels for these elements (you may be familiar with CRuPAC, or TREAT), the structure they recommend is similar for a very good reason: For every legal issue, legal readers want to know what the governing legal principle is (the Rule), how that rule operates or what it means (the EXplanation), how the rule does or does not apply to the relevant facts (the Application), and how that rule application connects to the case as a whole (the Connection-conclusion). Throughout your legal career, you will often use CREXAC units of discourse, at varying levels of depth, to explain how rules govern a set of facts.

Some writers have a hard time understanding the CREXAC formula. They may try to make the whole argument section one long CREXAC, or they can't decide which elements are worthy of a CREXAC analysis and which elements are not. At this stage of the writing process, let your working outline dictate the first phase of your writing process. Presume that you need to write a CREXAC unit of discourse for each point in your outline. Writing up the analysis will teach you about the point, and you may discover that some points are not controversial (and so do not need a CREXAC analysis), while other points are more complex than you realized (and thus may need to be divided into two or more CREXACs). *See* Illustration 5.1 for a guideline you can use to identify where you need to supply a CREXAC analysis within your argument. Each element of the CREXAC formula is explained more fully below.

ILLUSTRATION 5.1

Sample Argument Structure

1. This court should reverse because first major assertion
[introductory material and roadmap to Sections 1.1 & 1.2].
   1.1. First major assertion is true because first reason is true
[CREXAC analysis of 1.1].
   1.2. First major assertion is true because second reason is true
[introductory material & roadmap to sections 1.2.1 & 1.2.2].
      1.2.1. Second reason is true because first subreason is true
[CREXAC analysis of 1.2.1].
      1.2.2. Second reason is true because second subreason is true
[CREXAC analysis of 1.2.2].

2. Even if first assertion is not true, backup assertion is true
[CREXAC analysis of 2].

3. Policy reason is true
[CREXAC analysis of 3].

5.2.1. State Your Issue as a Conclusion (the First "C" of CREXAC)

In the first "conclusion" element of the formula, the writer articulates the specific issue that is being addressed, or articulates the problem (or part or subpart of the problem) that is being "solved" in this section of the document. The writer could articulate an issue from *Fernandez v. California,* for example, by stating affirmatively what the issue is:

> This Court must decide whether the consent exception to the Fourth Amendment's warrant requirement allows a co-tenant to overrule the express objection of a fellow tenant who has been removed from the home after his objection.

Although this method effectively tells the court the issue (and is preferable to neglecting to articulate the issue at all), it is not the best choice in a brief to a court because it is not argumentative.

Generally, in persuasive writing, you should make your arguments as if they are the only reasonable resolution to the issues before the court. Therefore, it is often best to state your issues as conclusions:

> Once the resident of a home has refused to consent to a search, the Fourth Amendment does not allow police officers to remove that tenant from the home and seek the consent of a co-tenant.

If your issue is more complicated, the conclusion may be longer than just a simple sentence. You may need to provide legal or factual context to help the reader to understand how the conclusion fits into your argument. In *Whitfield v. United States*, for example, the Court was asked to determine whether a failed bank robber "forced" a homeowner to "accompany" him in violation of an anti-kidnapping provision of a federal bank robbery statute. The statute imposes a harsh sentence—death or life in prison—if a person dies after or during forced accompaniment. A writer might therefore provide legal, historical, and factual context before using a conclusory statement to articulate the issue:

> When Congress federalized the crime of bank robbery in response to gangland activities that crossed state lines, it imposed mandatory harsh penalties on those who kidnapped innocent bystanders as part of their crimes. The petitioner here asked a homeowner to show him a place to hide, and then he walked down a hallway with her. This de minimis movement does not constitute "forced accompaniment" under the anti-kidnapping provision of the federal Bank Robbery Act.

By stating your issue as a conclusion, you begin to focus your reader not only on the issue that you will be addressing in that section of the argument, but also on the result that your analysis of the issue will reveal.

5.2.2. Provide the Rule (the "R" of CREXAC)

After you have focused the reader's attention on the issue being addressed, you should articulate the rule that governs the issue. As we noted in Chapter Two, a rule essentially says that "if a certain condition exists, then a certain legal status results." In legal writing, many sentences in your writing could be characterized as rules. When we talk about The Rule in a CREXAC unit of discourse, however, we are talking about the *governing* legal principle, i.e., the principle that articulates the condition that results in the legal status at issue in this CREXAC unit of discourse.

IF you are a human being [certain condition], THEN you are mortal [legal status].

The rule about not driving while intoxicated could be stated like this, for example:

IF you operate a vehicle while under the influence of a regulated intoxicant [certain condition], THEN you are guilty of violating State Code § 123.13 [legal status].

Most rules need not be stated in the argument using "if-then" terminology. However, articulating the if-then structure can help you to test the rules that you include in your brief.

If your rule comes from a statute or a well-established common law test, stating the rule may be simple. Stating the rule can be more complicated, however, if there is controversy about which rule applies, or if you must use inductive reasoning to "find" your rule. In those situations, as we explain below, your method of articulating your rule may lead you to change the structure of your argument.

a. Stating Established Rules

If the rule is derived from a statute or other enacted law, you may simply quote the pertinent language, as in this example from the anti-kidnapping provision noted above. If your rule comes from a statute, you may paraphrase the language of the statute that is not at issue in that section of the document. For example, in the *Whitfield* case, the brief writers had to address whether the defendant was attempting to avoid apprehension and whether he forced someone to accompany him. In the section on forced accompaniment, the only language in quotation marks is the language at issue in that section:

18 U.S.C. § 2113(e) imposes harsh penalties on any person who is attempting to avoid apprehension for the commission of an offense under the § 2113(a), and who "forces any person to accompany him without the consent of such person."

Similarly, if the rule is a well-accepted common law rule derived from a well-known authority, you may simply articulate the rule in its familiar language:

This court has already decided that a resident's objection to a search cannot be overridden, holding that "a physically present inhabitant's express refusal of consent to a police search is dispositive as to him, regardless of the consent of a fellow occupant." *Georgia v. Randolph*, 547 U.S. 103, 122-23 (2006).

④ If your case is more complex, stating one rule may not give the reader enough context. Some writers articulate The Rule for the CREXAC unit of discourse only after they provide a "rule cluster" that starts with a well-accepted general rule and moves to the more narrow rule that is the focus of that section of the argument. The following example is one way to open an argument section that argues that the petitioner's domestic partner had the authority to consent to the search after he had objected to the search and then been removed from the scene. Notice how the writer moves the reader from the general rule—the Fourth Amendment—to the narrow rule at issue, which will be The Rule for this section of the argument:

> **The Fourth Amendment to the United States Constitution guarantees "[t]he right of the people to be secure in their persons, houses, papers, and effects, against unreasonable searches and seizures." U.S. Const. amend. IV. The Fourth Amendment forbids the search of a home unless the government first obtains a warrant, based upon probable cause. *Id.* If a criminal suspect shares his home and is absent from the home when police arrive, a co-tenant may consent to the search. *Illinois v. McGuffin*, 222 U.S. 222, 230 (1999). However, if a criminal suspect is present in the home, and informs police of his objection to the search, that "express refusal of consent" to a search is dispositive as to him, "regardless of the consent of a fellow occupant." *Georgia v. Randolph*, 547 U.S. 103, 122-23 (2006). That authority to refuse consent must override any later consent that police seek from a co-tenant, regardless of whether the suspect is removed from or remains in the home. *See id.***

Thus, although the paragraph lists several rules, the writer is focusing the reader's attention only on the last rule in the list, which she gleaned from *Georgia v. Randolph*. She didn't start with that rule, because the reader would not have understood why it was relevant. Thus, she moved quickly from the Fourth Amendment, through other relevant rules, to the rule at issue in this case. This paragraph illustrates the difference between statements that are *"a rule"* and those that are The Rule. Many sentences in an argument could be characterized as rules and could be turned into if-then statements. Some of those "rules" may be parts of case descriptions, may be topic sentences, or may be part of your umbrella paragraph. Don't worry about the fact that they might also be thought of as rules. Just make sure to keep your focus on The Rule: the legal principle that is the main governing rule for the issue you are currently writing about.

④ The discussion below of "Tell" issues is relevant here because you are telling the reader what the rule is and that it is relevant in the given case. A rule cluster may also function as part of an argument's "backstory," as discussed in Chapter Nine. A rule cluster is one way to move the reader from what is known (established rules about the Fourth Amendment) to what is not known (the issue in this case).

b. Using a "Rule-Choice-Rule" When the Court Must Choose Among Two or More Rules

Some issues are governed by well-established rules, and the court needs to decide only how the rule applies to the facts of the case. Sometimes, however, a major debate between you and your opponent is a debate as to which of two or more rules the court should apply to the situation. If you have to convince the court to choose the rule that you want, as opposed to the rule that your opponent wants, you must include a section in your argument devoted to proving that "your" rule is the best rule to apply. Of course, that "rule-choice" argument must be based on a rule, as well.

If a court has chosen a particular rule to apply to a situation, it has done so because it has decided that the case has certain factors or raises certain issues that the chosen rule best addresses. You might think of the basic format for a rule-choice rule as follows:

> **IF factors or issues exist [certain condition], THEN a decision to apply the designated rule in this case results [legal status].**

Sometimes, courts state the "rule-choice rule" explicitly. For example, everyone who has taken a constitutional law course knows that when courts must decide whether a certain governmental action is constitutional, they have at least three choices. They can apply the "strict scrutiny test" (which they apply when certain fundamental rights are implicated or the rights of a suspect class are affected); they can apply the "intermediate or heightened scrutiny test" (which they apply in a variety of situations, including situations in which laws make gender-based distinctions); or they can apply the "rational basis test" (which they apply when a law does not affect fundamental rights or make questionable distinctions). Thus, if your case is about the constitutionality of a governmental action, you and your opponent might disagree as to whether the court should apply the rational basis test or the strict scrutiny test. In that situation, your first order of business is to argue about which rule applies, using the rule-choice rule that governs strict scrutiny and rational basis. For example, if you believed that strict scrutiny was appropriate, that section of your argument could be based on the following rule-choice rule:

> **IF a statute makes distinctions based on suspect classifications or infringes on fundamental rights [certain condition], THEN courts apply the strict scrutiny test [legal status].**

Of course, even if a rule-choice rule exists, you should use a CREXAC unit of discourse to prove how it applies *only* if the choice of rule is in controversy. If both sides agree that the strict scrutiny test applies, for example, then the brief need not establish this fact through a CREXAC analysis. The writer can simply introduce the strict scrutiny section by telling the reader the rule-choice rule and stating that it results in the use of strict scrutiny before moving on to a CREXAC analysis of the strict scrutiny test itself.

5 Thus, if the choice of rule is not controversial, a typical argument would have at least one CREXAC devoted to the rule, focusing on how it should apply in the current case. If the choice of rule *is* controversial, however, that controversy may affect the structure of the argument. The writer may need to include as many as three sections of the argument that address the rule-choice issue in some way. For example, the writer might first argue that the rule-choice rule requires that the preferred rule be applied. In the second section, the writer could argue that the client wins when the preferred rule is applied. In the third section, the writer could argue that the client wins even if the nonpreferred rule is applied. The following working outline shows the structure of an argument in which the parties disagreed as to the appropriate test in a case about the validity of a ballot design statute:

5 As noted above, you should devote one CREXAC unit of discourse to each phrase-that-pays in controversy. Section 5.3 below addresses how to handle elements that are required for your argument but that are not controversial.

1. Because this ballot design statute infringes on the fundamental right to vote, this court must apply strict scrutiny.

2. Under the strict scrutiny test, this court should find that the statute is unconstitutional.

    2.1. There is no compelling governmental interest in burdening some voters more than others in the voting booth.
    2.2. The ballot design statute is not narrowly tailored to meet the supposed goal of fair voting procedures.

3. Even if this court applies the rational basis test, the statute is still unconstitutional.

    3.1. The option of rotation shows that the voting burdens complained of are needless.
    3.2. Drawing names out of a hat is not a rational basis for imposing voting burdens.

If there are two or more competing rules and the courts have not yet labeled the "rule-choice rule," your job is to find and articulate that rule. You can "find" the rule by reasoning inductively from one or more cases in which a court has made the rule-choice decision.

The next section explains how to use inductive reasoning to find and articulate legal rules.

c. Using Inductive Reasoning to Find and Articulate Legal Rules

As many a frustrated first-year law student can attest, courts sometimes decide cases without explicitly articulating the rule that they are applying. Further, sometimes the rule that they are applying can be accurately stated more narrowly or more broadly. If the cases that are analogous to your case do not contain a clear rule, or if the applicable rule as it is currently envisioned would dictate a bad result for your client, you may have to "induce" a rule. Using inductive reasoning is appropriate for finding rules of all types, not just rule-choice rules.

If you don't know what inductive reasoning is, we'll take a moment to explain it. The etymology of the word "induce" includes the concept of "leading," and we induce rules when the law and the facts lead us to see that courts or legal systems are operating in a certain way. If we think of the Socratic syllogism about whether Socrates is mortal, imagine if we didn't know that all human beings were mortal. The facts in the world might "lead" us to induce that rule if we noticed that our grandparents were dead, and we thought about the fact that no human being lives much past 100 years old. From that data about the natural world, we might induce the rule that "all human beings are mortal."

It is not accurate to say that we are labeling a "new" rule when we use inductive reasoning. The rule was there all along; inductive reasoning simply lets us recognize it, label it, and present it more effectively to the court.

When you use inductive reasoning to find a rule, you are trying to read between the lines of court opinions, to notice patterns or factors that always or never predict certain results, or results that occur *only* when certain patterns or factors are present. Authors of law review articles might observe these patterns or factors in a vacuum, but you have a head start because you know what you are looking for. In an advocacy document, inductive reasoning frequently begins when you distinguish your case from the cases that apparently apply.

For example, in the statute at issue in *Whitfield*, the term "forced accompaniment" is not defined. Counsel for Whitfield might consult other cases in which courts interpret undefined terms and try to articulate a rule that would lead the court to interpret the term favorably. If multiple cases relied heavily on legislative history to interpret undefined terms, counsel might be able to articulate a rule like the following:

When a statutory term is both undefined and ambiguous, and the statute's legislative history expresses a single rationale for using that term, this Court will interpret that term in accordance with that unified congressional intent. *McGuffin v. McGriffin*, 132 U.S. 1702, 1709-10 (2012).

To explain that newly-induced rule, the writer would find examples of times when the Supreme Court—and perhaps other courts—interpreted a statute consistently with unified legislative history. Ideally, the writer might shore up the rule further by finding at least one case in which a court refused to follow legislative history because that history offered multiple rationales for use of a term.

However you find your rule, be sure to state it explicitly early within the appropriate section of the argument. In this way, you satisfy readers' expectations and allow them to understand your analysis more easily.

5.2.3. Explain the Rule (the "EX" of CREXAC)

After you have articulated the rule, you must provide your reader with any needed explanation of the rule. As we noted above, one way to structure your argument is to identify the controversial phrases-that-pay in the relevant rule(s) and to give each controversial phrase-that-pays its own CREXAC unit of discourse. Once you have identified the relevant phrase-that-pays for each CREXAC unit of discourse, you can test the analysis in each section of the CREXAC formula to make sure that each paragraph in that analysis relates somehow to that phrase-that-pays. In the explanation section, for example, you should define the phrase-that-pays, explain its meaning, show how it has been interpreted in earlier cases, or all of the above.

Explaining the phrase-that-pays in appropriate detail helps the reader to understand how the rule works. In persuasive documents like briefs, it is often useful to end the rule explanation by providing a "rule summary." The rule summary nails down exactly what you want the reader to take from the rule explanation, and it prepares the reader for the rule application. In this section, we will explain how to decide what "appropriate detail" means, and how to use a rule summary effectively.

a. Deciding How Much Rule Explanation Is Needed

When deciding how much explanation to provide for the phrase-that-pays in any particular section of your argument, consider two questions: (1) How ambiguous is the language of the phrase-that-pays? (2) How controversial is the application of the phrase-that-pays to the facts of this case? The more ambiguous and controversial the phrase-that-pays is, the more detailed your explanation should be.

Presumably, all of the issues analyzed in a brief will be controversial; if they were not controversial, they would not need to be analyzed.[9] When a phrase-that-pays is ambiguous, controversial, or both, you should "explain" its meaning, usually by illustrating how it has been applied in one or more authority cases.

The length of your explanation will vary depending on how abstract and/or controversial the rule is. Probably the best way to fully illustrate the meaning of a rule is to use at least one authority that illustrates what the rule does mean in the context of facts that are similar (or nearly similar) to the facts at bar, and at least one authority that illustrates what the rule does *not* mean in the context of facts that are similar to the facts at bar.[10]

The following example sets forth the rule, rule explanation, and rule summary of a CREXAC unit of discourse on behalf of the government as it might appear in *Fernandez v. California*. The writer is arguing that the search of the defendant's apartment was reasonable. The phrase-that-pays, which is "reasonable," is underlined throughout.

Good Example

A warrantless search is <u>reasonable</u> if police obtain valid consent. *Illinois v. Rodriguez*, 497 U.S. 177, 181, 183-84 (1990). Co-tenants "assume the risk" that other co-tenants might let police search common areas in their absence. *United States v. Matlock*, 415 U.S. 164, 171 n.7 (1974). Warrantless searches to which a co-tenant consents are <u>unreasonable</u> only if the other co-tenant (1) is physically present and (2) objects to the search. **6** *Georgia v. Randolph*, 547 U.S. 103, 120 (2006). **7** Here, the warrantless search of Petitioner's apartment was <u>reasonable</u> because Rojas consented, and Petitioner was not physically present and objecting at the time of her consent.

6 This sentence sets out *the* rule that the writer is focusing on.

7 Here is the initial Conclusion (or "thesis conclusion"). It need not be the first sentence of the first paragraph (although it's fine if it is), but it should usually appear within the first paragraph.

---

9. See discussion below and in Chapter Nine for examples of how to deal with issues that are not controversial, but that must be included in the analysis in some way because they are necessary elements of a statute, test, or other legal rule.

10. *See also, e.g.,* Laurel Currie Oates & Anne M. Enquist, The Legal Writing Handbook § 12.8.4 (5th ed., Aspen 2010).

⑧ A search is <u>reasonable</u> if consent is offered by anyone who jointly possesses premises or effects; the consent of absent possessors is not required. *E.g., Frazier v. Cupp*, 394 U.S. 731, 749 (1969). In *Frazier*, the Court found <u>reasonable</u> a search of the defendant's duffel bag based on the consent of defendant's cousin, noting the cousin "was a joint user of the bag" and thus "clearly had authority to consent to its search." *Id.* at 740. The court rejected defendant's argument that the cousin "only had actual permission to use one compartment of the bag and that he had no authority to consent to a search of the other compartments." *Id.* The Court declined to "engage in . . . metaphysical subtleties" and found that, "in allowing [his cousin] to use the bag and leaving it in [the cousin's] house," the defendant "must be taken to have assumed the risk that [his cousin] would allow someone else to look inside." *Id.*

⑨ When two persons possess joint authority over the premises, either may give effective consent for a <u>reasonable</u> search, even if police neglect an opportunity to seek consent directly from the tenant who is the suspect. *E.g., Matlock*, 415 U.S. at 169-72. The co-tenant's consent in *Matlock* was grounds for a <u>reasonable</u> search, even though the suspect was nearby; he had recently been arrested and was in a police car near the residence. *Id.* at 179 (Douglas, J., dissenting). Similarly, in *Rodriguez*, the consent of an apparent co-tenant resulted in a <u>reasonable</u> search even though the suspect was asleep in the residence at the time. 497 U.S. at 180. The Court found it sufficient that the officers <u>reasonably</u> believed that defendant's girlfriend was a tenant with apparent authority to consent, and the Court refused to require that officers should have roused defendant to seek his consent. *Id.* at 179, 173-80.

⑩ A search based on a co-tenant's consent is <u>unreasonable</u> only if the objecting co-tenant is both physically present and objecting at the time of the consent. *Randolph*, 547 U.S. at 170. The search at issue in *Randolph* was found to be <u>unreasonable</u> because police used the consent of a suspect's estranged wife to justify their entrance to the home even though the suspect was then present and objecting. *Id.* This Court emphasized the particular importance of "physical presence" to nullify another co-tenant's consent. *Id.*

⑪ The exception carved out in *Randolph* is a narrow one. The *Randolph* Court held that "a warrantless search of a shared dwelling for evidence over the express refusal of consent by a *physically*

⑧ This paragraph begins the rule explanation; it addresses a case in which the court found that the search was reasonable.

⑨ The rule explanation continues in this paragraph; note that the writer addresses two authorities in this one paragraph.

⑩ This paragraph continues rule explanation, focusing on a case in which the court found that a co-tenant's consent did NOT result in a reasonable search.

⑪ Here, the writer anticipates that the opponent will use *Randolph* in its argument, and lays a foundation to attack that reasoning in the rule application. When making counterarguments, consider what you and your opponent disagree about; here, one area of disagreement is the meaning and applicability of *Randolph*.

present resident cannot be justified as <u>reasonable</u> as to him on the basis of consent given to the police by another resident." *Id.* at 120 (emphasis added). In dicta, the Court indicated that a search might not be <u>reasonable</u> if police had removed a "potentially objecting tenant from the entrance for the sake of avoiding a possible objection." *Id.* at 121-22. The Court's **12** holding, however, rested on the Court's perception of "widely shared social expectations" and its observation that "a solitary co-inhabitant" typically has an absolute entitlement to "admit visitors, with the consequence that a guest obnoxious to one may nevertheless be admitted in his absence by another." *Id.*

12 Because the dicta seemingly favors the petitioner, the writer buries it in the middle of this paragraph and contrasts it with the court's holding.

13 This Court has long recognized the importance of consent as a basis for <u>reasonable</u> searches, noting that consent-based searches are part of "the standard investigatory techniques of law enforcement agencies" and are "a constitutionally permissible and wholly legitimate aspect of effective police activity." *Schneckloth v. Bustamonte*, 412 U.S. 218, 228, 231-32 (1973) (consent of suspect not in custody can be valid without showing that suspect knew of right to refuse consent). The *Schneckloth* Court emphasized that "the community has a real interest in encouraging consent, for the resulting search may yield necessary evidence for the solution and prosecution of crime, evidence that may insure that a wholly innocent person is not wrongly charged with a criminal offense." *Id.* at 243. The Court has thus sought to avoid "artificial restrictions" on consent searches that "would jeopardize their basic validity." *Id.* at 229.

13 This paragraph builds some policy argument into the rule explanation section. If the writer had sufficient ammunition on this point, it might be appropriate to pull this paragraph and create a whole section addressing the thesis that the ability to seek consent is a vital part of effective law enforcement.

14 Accordingly, the physical presence of an objecting co-tenant is the crucial factor here. The only way that Petitioner's objection could override Rojas's consent and make the resulting search <u>unreasonable</u> would be if Petitioner had been present in the apartment at the time of Rojas's consent. Because Petitioner was absent, his argument must fail.

14 This paragraph is the rule summary.

Illustrating what the phrase-that-pays means and does not mean sets the boundaries of the phrase-that-pays and gives the application of law to facts more validity. Chapter Six includes a discussion of how to use authority cases effectively in your explanation section.

b. Writing the Rule Summary

After you have shown the reader how courts have applied the phrase-that-pays in the past (or explained the rule in some other way), your reader should have a good idea about how the rule operates. Because a brief is a persuasive document, however, you may want to be sure that the reader understands the rule the same way you do. Thus, it is almost always effective to end your rule explanation with a brief rule summary that drives home what you were trying to teach the reader with the rule explanation. In the rule summary, you should *not* merely restate the rule as you articulated it in the beginning of the argument. The following, for instance, would be an ineffective rule summary for the example above:

> *Bad Example of a Rule Summary*
> Thus, warrantless searches to which a co-tenant consents are unreasonable only if the other co-tenant (1) is physically present and (2) objects to the search.

This rule summary merely restates the original rule. Instead, you should consider the facet of the rule that you were trying to expose or to emphasize and make that aspect of the rule the focus of the rule summary. In the example above, for instance, the writer was trying to emphasize the significance of simultaneous physical presence at the time of the co-tenant's consent to search. To emphasize that facet of the rule, she might write a rule summary that makes that point explicit:

> *Better Example of a Rule Summary*
> Accordingly, the physical presence of an objecting co-tenant is the crucial factor here. The only way that Petitioner's objection could override Rojas's consent and make the resulting search unreasonable would be if Petitioner had been present in the apartment at the time of Rojas's consent. Because Petitioner was absent, his argument must fail.

Note how the writer shifts from rule explanation to argument, first stating the rule and then indicating that the petitioner will fail. The rule summary thus helps the writer to lay a strong foundation for the rule application. The writer can use the phrase-that-pays, and perhaps significant facts, to create an expectation in the reader that the writer has an easy task, or that the writer's opponent has a difficult task. The writer can then fulfill that expectation in the rule application.

A rule summary may not be needed if your rule explanation is relatively short and straightforward. We advise, however, that you routinely draft a rule summary. If you decide that it appears overly repetitive, you can delete it. If, however, your rule explanation has advanced a more nuanced understanding of the rule, a rule summary can help the rule explanation have a greater impact.

5.2.4. Apply the Rule to the Facts (the "A" of CREXAC)

After you have articulated the rule and explained it as needed, it's time to apply the rule to the facts. In this step of your analysis, you are trying to show the reader how the phrase-that-pays intersects with the facts. How do the required elements or factors exist (or not exist) in your case? You should never substitute synonyms for the phrase-that-pays in any section, but particularly not in the application section.

15 You might think of the "A" in CREXAC as standing for "Argument," because it's true that rule application often provides the best opportunity for effective argument.

15 Brief writers face a few challenges when applying law to facts. First, some brief writers mistakenly substitute analogies for application of law to facts. Second, some do not exploit the foundation that they laid in the rule summary. Third, for issues that are "pure" questions of law—and courts of last resort often analyze questions of law—the facts may seem to be irrelevant. Finally, when analyzing statutory interpretation issues, the writers may believe that they don't have any real "facts." This section will address each of these challenges in turn.

a. Apply Rules, Not Cases

Begin the application section of your analysis by stating affirmatively how the rule does or does not apply to the facts. Essentially, you begin your application by saying "Phrase-that-pays equals (or does not equal) our case facts." If your case is not controversial, a short passage might be enough, as in this example, which is focused on the voluntariness of Rojas's consent:

> **Here, Rojas's consent was voluntary. Police did not seek her consent until almost an hour after Petitioner's arrest. She gave both oral and written consent to the request to search.**

Do *not* begin the application by drawing analogies; analogies may support the application of law to facts, but they do not substitute for it. Thus, this sentence would usually not be an effective way to begin rule application:

> *Ineffective Beginning to Rule Application Section*
> Like the co-tenant in *Matlock*, Rojas had joint authority over the apartment and thus her consent would make the search reasonable.

Instead, begin with a direct statement that connects the phrase-that-pays to the client's case. If the issue is at all controversial, you should be sure to provide details about the record facts[11] that support your assertion about how the law applies to the facts, as in this example (the phrase-that-pays, "reasonable" is underlined for emphasis, not as an example to follow):

More Effective Beginning to Rule Application Section
Here, the search of Petitioner's apartment was <u>reasonable</u> because Rojas had apparent and actual authority to admit visitors, and she consented to a search.

There are at least three different ways—alone or in combination—that you may expand your application section, if needed. First, you may expand it by providing more details about the facts:

Effective Continuation of Rule Application
Rojas gave Officer Cirrito her name and "stated that she lived there with her boyfriend, [Petitioner,] and her children." J.A. 66. Because Petitioner and Rojas were co-tenants of the premises, Petitioner would understand that he had assumed the risk that Rojas might admit guests "obnoxious" to him.

Second, you may expand the rule application—only if needed—by drawing analogies or making distinctions between your client's case and your authority cases:

Effective Continuation of Rule Application
Like the suspect in *Matlock*, who had been legitimately removed from the premises before police sought consent from the co-tenant, Petitioner had been legitimately arrested and removed from the premises before officers began seeking consent from Rojas.

We want to emphasize this point: you do not always have to draw *any* analogies or disanalogies between your case and authority cases. You almost never have to analogize or disanalogize *every* case cited in your rule explanation section. In general, avoid boring your reader by restating the obvious; save your analogies and

---

11. Be sure to cite to the record so that the court can verify each referenced fact.

dis-analogies for the times the connections and disconnections are more sophisticated. In this way, you can help to cement the reader's understanding of how a rule operates and of how it does or does not apply to your client's case.

The third way that you might extend your rule application is by directly attacking an opponent's argument. Do not attack the argument by restating the opponent's point:

> *Ineffective Attack on Opponent's Argument*
> The Petitioner has argued that this Court should extend *Randolph* to allow Petitioner's objection to continue even after he had been legally removed from the dwelling. Petitioner's argument is not valid because that argument fails to consider Rojas's interests and would read the Fourth Amendment to impose a prospective veto on a co-tenant's freedom to consent to entry, or indeed, to refuse to consent to it. Nothing in this Court's extensive consent jurisprudence would justify allowing an absent co-tenant to exercise such a veto.

Do not highlight your opponents' arguments by labeling them as your opponent's. Instead, directly refute the point they have made (or, if you are Petitioner, the point you expect them to make):

> *More Effective Attack on Opponent's Argument*
> Extending *Randolph* to allow Petitioner's objection to continue even after he had been legally removed from the dwelling would ignore Rojas's interests. The Fourth Amendment does not allow a tenant to impose a prospective veto on a co-tenant's freedom to consent to entry, or indeed, to refuse to consent to it. Nothing in this Court's extensive consent jurisprudence would justify allowing an absent co-tenant to exercise such a veto.

Notice that the substance of these two attacks is largely the same. The only difference is that the weaker example is framed as the opponent's argument, while the better example is just one more part of the writer's argument. Chapter Nine will give more guidance on how to frame your arguments effectively.

b. Application When the Issue Is a Question of Law

A legal question, or question of law, is a question about what the law should mean or how it should be interpreted. Should the law regulate all dog owners or only owners of dangerous dogs? Should the law governing "employers" include supervisors within the meaning of "employer"? Questions of fact, in contrast, ask whether the law should apply to a particular situation. Is a dog "dangerous" if it bites any person who tries to pet it? Is a person a "supervisor" if she is in charge of drawing up work schedules for all of the people in her section, but does not have the authority to hire and fire?

Even legal questions, however, are decided in a factual context. There is the hypothetical factual context of noting what will happen to certain categories of people and things if the case is decided one way or another, and there is the concrete factual context of noting what will happen to the parties in this particular case. Your application may focus on the broader legal question, but you may also want to include references to your case facts as a concrete example that shows a real-life impact.

In *Whitfield,* for example, the Court was interpreting the meaning of statutory language that imposes life in prison on attempted bank robbers who "forced" a person to "accompany" them. Although the question before the Court was whether *de minimis* movement could satisfy the rule, that legal question was decided in the context of a particular set of facts. Note how this writer talks in general about the merits of applying the rule in a certain way even as he brings in the specifics of his client's case:

Good Example of Rule Application of Question of Law
As a matter of law, Petitioner's de minimis movement of Mrs. Parnell does not satisfy the forced accompaniment requirements of § 2113.

16 The statute's movement requirement is clear: to meet the sentencing standard, a defendant must move another person a substantial distance or move the person into or out of some building. In the context of § 2113's overall structure and its sentencing scheme, moving a person a substantial distance or over a significant threshold would necessarily increase the risk of harm to that person. A defendant who causes this substantial movement is sufficiently culpable to warrant the imposition of the most severe sentence under § 2113, which imposes a mandatory minimum sentence of ten years and a maximum sentence of life in prison.

16 This paragraph and the one following justify the writer's legal conclusions about the meaning of the language in the statute.

Allowing de minimis movement to meet the standard would undermine § 2113(e)'s purpose of imposing the greatest penalties for the most egregious conduct because it would cause minor actions to result in major penalties. Further, a de minimis movement standard would convert § 2113(e)'s sentencing structure from a deliberate congressional choice to punish the worst offenders most severely and turn it into a blanket sentencing enhancement that applies to virtually all bank robbers irrespective of their level of culpability.

The circumstances here provide a vivid illustration. No **17** reasonable jury could have found that the "forced movement" at issue here was substantial. Even viewed in the light most favorable to the government, the evidence showed that Mrs. Parnell was **18** "forced" to move only a few feet, from one room to another inside of her own home, at the hands of an unarmed and frightened suspect. JA 65a (Court of Appeals acknowledgment that "Whitfield required Mrs. Parnell to accompany him for only a short distance within her own home, and for a brief period"). That forced movement was a far cry from the cases that led to the enactment of § 2113, where armed robbers abducted bank customers and pushed them into their getaway cars before driving them across state lines.

The movement here was instead equivalent to the *de minimis* forced movement that routinely occurs when a robber temporarily confines bank employees and customers during a robbery. That type of insubstantial movement over a few feet—movement that is essentially unavoidable whenever a victim is confined during a robbery—is not forced accompaniment.

Accordingly, a defendant must have forced substantial movement to satisfy the elements of forced accompaniment. Petitioner in this case did not satisfy the elements of § 2113(e) as a matter of law. Thus, his conviction must be reversed and his case remanded to the district court for resentencing.

Note how the writer refers to the client in the first paragraph, and how a later paragraph uses concrete details from the case to show the court the impact its decision will have in a specific case. Not every legal issue will need such a lengthy application section or such a detailed description of the client's facts. A good writer, however, will look for opportunities to use client facts to make abstract legal principles vivid.

c. When Statutory Language Is the "Fact" to Which the Law Applies

Another challenge that many student writers face when writing the application section is the problem of "no facts." If you are ana-

---

17 This paragraph highlights the sympathetic facts from the client's case and compares them to the facts that spurred the enactment of the statute in the 1930s.

18 The writer places "forced" in quotation marks to imply that she disagrees that any forcing was involved.

lyzing a statutory interpretation issue, it may seem to you that there are no facts—there is only the statute itself. Many students think of the term *facts* as referring only to tangible events, like a car accident, or a murder, or even an interrogation. For a statutory interpretation issue, however, the word *facts* refers less often to events and more often to realities like the statutory language at issue, other relevant statutory language, or the statute's legislative history. One guideline: if a rule speaks in terms of human or corporate behavior, it is likely that it applies to human or corporate events, and that's where you should look for the relevant facts. In contrast, if a rule speaks in terms of legislative behavior, it is likely that it applies to legislative events—such as the language of a statute, or the decisions a legislature made when enacting it—and that is where you should look for the relevant facts.

For example, a student writer who is arguing that Title VII's use of the word "employer" does not allow individual liability for supervisors could have several CREXAC units of discourse focused on rules of statutory interpretation. One section might be focused on the rule that words in a statute should be read consistently throughout the whole statute. She would explain that rule by showing how other relevant courts had read terms consistently in statutes. In the application section, it would be meaningless to talk about the events of alleged sexual harassment at the center of the lawsuit. Rather, the focus should be on how the term at issue, "employer," was used in the statute as a whole, and how that use demands a particular interpretation in this case:

Good Example of Rule Application in Statutory Construction Analysis

The use of the word "employer" in other sections of Title VII demonstrates that Congress did not intend that individual supervisors like Wendl could be held liable. In § 2000e-8(c), the act provides that *"every employer* is responsible for the execution, retention and preservation of certain employment records" (emphasis added). Likewise, § 2000e-10 states that *"every employer* shall post and keep posted in conspicuous places pertinent provisions of the subchapter" (emphasis added). Interpreting the word "employer" the same way throughout § 2000e(b) demonstrates that Congress did not intend the term to include individuals. It is extremely unlikely that Congress intended to impose such administrative duties on individuals in supervisory positions. It is far more reasonable to conclude that the word "employer" as used in §§ 2000e(b), 2000e-8(c), and 2000e-10, was intended to apply to employer-entities only.

This guideline does not mean that event-based facts are always irrelevant to statutory interpretation questions. As they can with other legal questions, event-based facts may provide helpful illustrations of how the legal policies at issue play out in concrete situations. Writers should be aware, however, that with statutory interpretation questions, they must think about the concept of "facts" more broadly: they are applying the rule of a canon of interpretation to the fact of the existing statutory language.

5.2.5. Make the Connection (the Second "C" of CREXAC)

After you have applied the rule to the facts, you should connect the application to your argument by articulating a connection-conclusion. As noted in Chapter Two, you may not need to begin a new paragraph if the application has been brief and the connection-conclusion is straightforward. For example, a good connection-conclusion may look something like this:

> **Therefore, because Mr. Lamb was abusing the dog when he was bitten, Ms. Zahm cannot be held liable for Mr. Lamb's injuries under Code § 111.1111.**

Stating a connection-conclusion explicitly at the end of your CREXAC analysis is an important part of the formula. Even though you stated a conclusion at the beginning of your CREXAC unit of discourse, and you said how the law applies to the facts at the beginning of the application section, the connection-conclusion serves a different purpose. It makes the reader aware of your conclusion, yes, but it also tells the reader that your analysis of this part of the discussion is finished and that you will soon be moving on to another point.

Further, as its name implies, the connection-conclusion shows the reader how this part of the analysis fits into, or connects with, the argument as a whole. If a section of your argument is about a dispositive point, the connection-conclusion should make the connection between that point and the ultimate result you seek. At the very least, you should connect your analysis of the phrase-that-pays (underlined in the following example) to the point that was at issue in that section of the argument:

> **Because Petitioner was not physically present when Rojas consented to the search of their shared apartment, the consent was valid and the search was therefore <u>reasonable</u>. Accordingly, this Court should affirm the decision below.**

This connection-conclusion connects the writer's point about the phrase-that-pays—that the search was "reasonable"—to the point of the section, which is that the petitioner's co-tenant validly consented to the search. Further, because that point is dispositive, the writer ends the connection-conclusion by asking the court to affirm the decision below.

5.3. WHEN *NOT* TO PROVIDE A CREXAC ANALYSIS

Above, we described how to complete a relatively thorough analysis of a legal issue. But not every issue needs a CREXAC unit of discourse. If an issue does not need the full treatment of a CREXAC, you must decide how much real estate, if any, to devote to the issue. As with most legal questions, an appropriate answer is "it depends." Some issues that would be controversial in one case will be obvious in another, and the depth of your analysis must change accordingly. Illustration 5.2 shows four labels you can use to describe how much discussion to include for each issue or sub-issue: Ignore, Tell, Clarify (CRAC), or Prove (CREXAC):

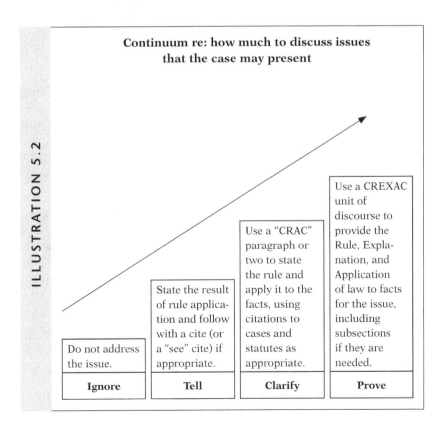

ILLUSTRATION 5.2

Continuum re: how much to discuss issues that the case may present

Ignore	Tell	Clarify	Prove
Do not address the issue.	State the result of rule application and follow with a cite (or a "see" cite) if appropriate.	Use a "CRAC" paragraph or two to state the rule and apply it to the facts, using citations to cases and statutes as appropriate.	Use a CREXAC unit of discourse to provide the Rule, Explanation, and Application of law to facts for the issue, including subsections if they are needed.

5.3.1. Ignore Issues

Some issues are obviously *not* relevant to the analysis. Others are relevant to the analysis, but they are so obviously not controversial that the reader does not need you to spend even one sentence discussing the issue. These are *Ignore issues;* that is, they are issues that you can *Ignore* in your written legal analysis.

For example, suppose that the statute forbidding drunk driving in your state contains this language:

> **Any person who operates any vehicle, streetcar, or trackless trolley within this state, may not, while operating the vehicle, streetcar, or trackless trolley, be under the influence of alcohol, a drug of abuse, or a combination of them, as specified in section B of this statute.**

Let us presume that you work for the state prosecutor, and you have brought charges against a defendant who was arrested while sitting in the driver's seat of her car, a Chevy Impala, parked on the side of a highway. She admitted that she drank four beers earlier that evening, and sobriety tests showed an illegal level of alcohol in her blood. In order to establish that she violated the statute, you would have to prove the following elements (words signaling elements are underlined):

> **Defendant is a <u>person</u> who was <u>operating</u> a <u>vehicle</u> while <u>under the influence of alcohol</u>.**

In your written analysis, you would not spend any time explaining that the defendant, as a human being, is a "person" under the statute. You could ignore this issue. Likewise, in this case, you would not expend even a sentence to say that "a Chevy Impala, an automobile, is a 'vehicle' under the statute." In another case, however, whether the person was operating a "vehicle" might well be at issue. In 2009, a man was arrested for operating a motorized barstool while intoxicated. In that situation, the state should not treat the "vehicle" element as an Ignore issue.

Thus, if an element is so obviously met that there could be no doubt in your reader's mind that it is satisfied in this case, you should ignore it. Do not, however, let yourself be lulled into a false belief that an issue is not controversial. For example, you might believe that "operating" a vehicle is the same as driving, and presume that someone sitting in a parked car is not legally operating the car. Research, however, might well reveal that "operation" includes sitting behind the steering wheel in a car whose gearshift is in park.[12]

---

12. *See, e.g., State v. Cyr*, 967 A.2d 32, 40 (Conn. 2009).

Be sure that you are confident about how the law works before deciding to ignore an issue.

5.3.2. Tell Issues

As its name implies, a writer includes a *Tell issue* in legal analysis by *telling* the outcome of application of law to facts and then citing to authority. There are two kinds of Tell issues. The first kind is an issue that is relevant but is not controversial. The second kind of Tell issue is an issue that could have been controversial, but that has been removed from controversy by some outside means, such as a party's concession.

For example, suppose that your client, Sam Bell, is a young man who was injured while intoxicated after "hell night" activities at his fraternity. A hometown friend, Marvin Kobacker, had taken him from a supervised "drunk room" at the fraternity and later left him alone in an off-campus apartment, where he fell and injured himself. You are wondering whether Mr. Kobacker is liable to Mr. Bell.

A common law rule in your jurisdiction provides that "a person assumes a duty of care if he or she takes charge of a person who is helpless." You look at the rule and realize that two phrases-that-pay are "take charge" and "helpless." Upon doing the research, you discover that there are several factors to analyze when determining whether someone "took charge" of another person. Likewise, there are several ways to prove that a person is "helpless." At first blush, it might seem that you need to complete two separate CREXAC units of discourse. One case from the highest court in your jurisdiction, however, states unequivocally that a person who is intoxicated is "helpless" under this standard. In this situation, Mr. Bell was unequivocally intoxicated. Thus, this required element is without controversy in your case, and you can treat it as a Tell issue:

> In Vanita, a person assumes a duty of care by "taking charge" of a person who is "helpless." *Jenkins v. Diamond*, 101 N.E.2d 104, 109 (Van. 2007). An intoxicated person is considered helpless. *Id.* at 111.

The second kind of Tell issue is one that has been removed from the controversy in some way. In a First Amendment challenge to a statute, for example, a court will use strict scrutiny to analyze a content-based restriction, while it will use a lower level of scrutiny to analyze a content-neutral restriction. If you and your opponent disagree as to whether the restriction at issue is a content-based restriction, you would probably need to use a CREXAC unit of discourse to argue that the statute does or does not impose a content-based restriction. However, if your opponent has conceded the issue—perhaps in a brief or in an oral argument to a lower court—you may treat the issue as a Tell issue, citing authority if possible:

> **As the petitioner concedes, the statute at issue criminalizes speech based on its content. Pet'r Br. at 16. Accordingly, this court should apply the strict scrutiny test when analyzing its validity.** *See Cornelius v. NAACP Legal Defense & Ed. Fund, Inc.*

19 You might keep Tell issues in mind when you answer exam questions. Even diligent students sometimes omit an issue for the mistaken reason that they think it is too obvious. When in doubt, treat it like a Tell issue and spend a sentence on it. If the professor wasn't looking for that issue, one sentence won't cost you too much time, but if the professor *was* looking for it, you have at least mentioned it. Further, sometimes in writing up the one-sentence Tell analysis, you may realize it needs a little more explanation.

Tell issues can be dealt with in different contexts, but they can usually best be placed in one of two places in the brief. First, as is discussed in Chapter Nine, the writer can deal with Tell issues in introductory material: when providing context for the argument as a whole, you may need to address one or more Tell issues to provide context and clear away the uncontroversial points. Second, Tell issues can arise when you are articulating the rule, either as part of a rule cluster or as an uncontroversial but significant facet of a governing rule. **19**

5.3.3. Clarify or CRAC Issues

A *Clarify issue* is similar to a Tell issue, but it is an issue that is a shade more complex. The term *Clarify* signals that the issue needs a bit more detail—about the law, the facts, or both—for the reader to understand either why the issue is not controversial or why the issue is not relevant.

For example, presume that your client, Old Testament Publishers, is an employer with eight full-time employees. A plaintiff has filed a suit under both state and federal age discrimination statutes. The federal statute applies only to employers with "20 or more employees for each working day in each of 20 or more calendar weeks in the current or preceding calendar year." In a memorandum in support of a motion to dismiss, you could conceivably treat the applicability of the federal statute as a Tell issue:

> **Because Old Testament Publishers has only eight employees, the federal Age Discrimination in Employment Act does not apply. 29 U.S.C. § 630(b) (defining "employer" as a person having "twenty or more" employees).**

On the other hand, if your client were an ice cream parlor in a tourist town, its employee count might take a little more time to make clear, because the employee count is not stable throughout the year. In that situation, the applicability of the statute would be a little more complicated, and you should treat the issue as a Clarify issue:

> Mr. Zawierucha cannot bring a cause of action under the federal Age Discrimination in Employment Act. The Act applies only to employers with "twenty or more employees for each working day in each of twenty or more calendar weeks in the current or preceding calendar year." 29 U.S.C. § 630(b). Admittedly, Ice Cream Dreams sometimes employs more than twenty people. During this calendar year, it has employed twenty or more people during ten calendar weeks. For the preceding year, it employed twenty or more people during twelve calendar weeks. Because it has never employed more than twenty employees for "twenty or more calendar weeks" in a calendar year, however, Mr. Zawierucha will be unable to bring a cause of action using this statute, and this court should accordingly dismiss Count IV of his complaint.

You might think of a Clarify issue as a CRAC issue, since it requires you to state a Conclusion, state the Rule, Apply the rule, and provide a Connection-conclusion.

It is difficult to give an exact formula for distinguishing between Tell issues and Clarify issues. You may presume that more is always better, but that is not always true. You will needlessly annoy some readers by giving a paragraph of analysis where a sentence plus citation will suffice. As you gain more experience in written legal analysis (and experience with various readers), you will develop your own sense of judgment as to the appropriate depth for your analysis.

In the meantime, there are a few factors you can consider. For example, is the language in the uncontroversial rule abstract or highly technical? The harder the rule is to understand on its own, the more likely it is that your reader will benefit from a Clarify analysis. Is the connection between the law and the facts complex enough that you want to take the reader by the hand to make sure that the connection is evident? Are you writing about an area of law with which the court may be unfamiliar? If so, it may be worth the extra sentence or two to clarify the outcome of the issue.

5.3.4. Prove or CREXAC Issues

Now we have come full circle. We use the word *prove* to describe the kind of analysis provided in a CREXAC unity of discourse—the most in-depth type of legal analysis.[13] An issue is a *Prove* or *CREXAC*

---

13. In their text, Professors Neumann and Tiscione use the term *rule proof* in much the same way that this text uses the term *rule explanation*. Richard

issue if (1) the issue concerns a required element of the analysis, and (2) the issue is controversial.

After you have analyzed the kinds of issues that your case presents, you should take another look at your working outline. Decide whether each issue listed is an Ignore, Tell, Clarify, or Prove issue, and mark each as appropriate. Consider whether you have omitted any issues that should be in your outline. You can leave an Ignore issue out of your outline, but you should list Tell issues, perhaps parenthetically, to make sure that you include them in your analysis, if needed.

5.4. DEALING WITH YOUR OPPONENT'S ARGUMENTS

A common dilemma for brief writers is whether and how to address their opponent's arguments. Some advocates believe that acknowledging the existence of an opponent's argument in any way is a sign of weakness that should be avoided. These writers may hope that their opponents will present only a weak case or that the court will not notice the gap. Judge Hamilton of the Fourth Circuit notes, however, that the best briefs "[address] head-on the opponent's best responsive argument, best supporting case law or statutory authority, and, if at issue, the opponent's listing of contrary evidence."[14] If these authorities are missing, the judge may draw negative conclusions, as Judge Parker of the Second Circuit observes:

> I would also like to recommend that all advocates distinguish contrary authority, even in their opening brief. If there is bad precedent out there for your case, you can assume your adversary will cite it to us, or we will independently find it. If the first time I see an adverse case is in the answering brief, then my initial reaction is that the appellant does not have a good explanation as to why that case is inapposite. While a response in the reply brief may dispel this initial impression, it may not. Therefore, by failing to mention contrary precedent in the opening brief, the advocate makes that precedent more weighty than it perhaps should be.[15]

K. Neumann, Jr. & Kristen Konrad Tiscione, Legal Reasoning and Legal Writing ch. 12 (7th ed., Aspen 2013).

14. Clyde H. Hamilton, *Effective Appellate Brief Writing*, 50 S.C. L. Rev. 581, 582 (1999).

15. Fred I. Parker, *Foreword: Appellate Advocacy and Practice in the Second Circuit*, 64 Brook. L. Rev. 457, 463-64 (1998).

Professor Kathryn Stanchi has analyzed the growing body of social science research that has investigated the impact of including negative information in various rhetorical situations.[16] Professor Stanchi concludes that, beyond following the ethical requirement to address directly contradictory authority,[17] attorneys must be very careful when deciding whether and how to bring up negative arguments.

Addressing negative authorities is a part of addressing your opponent's arguments, but it is not the only part. After you have crafted your working outline, make a list of what you consider to be your opponent's most likely arguments.[18] For each argument, you may need to make three determinations. First, you should identify the precise area of disagreement. Second, determine whether your argument as currently constructed contains any material that contradicts the particular argument. If it does not, your third step is to determine whether and how to introduce contradictory material.

First, determine the exact locus of the disagreement. The heart of the familiar CREXAC formula—Rule, EXplanation, and Application—can help you to do so. Perhaps you and your opponent disagree as to the particular rule that must be applied. In that circumstance, you may have to add one or more sections to your argument, using a rule-choice rule to argue that the court should apply your preferred rule.

---

16. Kathryn M. Stanchi, *Playing with Fire: The Science of Confronting Adverse Material in Legal Advocacy*, 60 RUTGERS L. REV. 381 (2008). The article, which is well worth reading, notes that "the decision to volunteer negative information depends on a complicated algorithm" that measures several overlapping factors. *Id*. at 433.

17. Rule 3.3(a)(2) of the ABA Model Rules of Professional Conduct provides that an advocate may not "fail to disclose" legal authority in the "controlling jurisdiction" that the lawyer knows is "directly adverse" to the client's position, unless opposing counsel has disclosed it. http://www.americanbar.org/groups/professional_responsibility/publications/model_rules_of_professional_conduct/rule_3_3_candor_toward_the_tribunal.html (last accessed Sept. 19, 2020). The American Bar Association notes that these rules "serve as models for the ethics rules of most jurisdictions." http://www.americanbar.org/groups/professional_responsibility/publications/model_rules_of_professional_conduct.html (last accessed Sept. 19, 2020).

18. Professor Stanchi warns against bringing up negative arguments pre-emptively unless you are fairly certain that your opponent will actually bring them up. Stanchi, *supra* note 16, at 427, 428. Of course, if you are a respondent, an appellee, or a party opposing the motion, you may be able to consult an actual brief to determine what those arguments are. Admittedly, this option is not always available in a law school setting.

For another issue, you may agree as to which rule should be applied but disagree as to what that rule means, perhaps because you disagree about which authorities best illustrate how that rule should operate. In that circumstance, the explanation section of a particular unit of discourse argument may be longer because you may need to address not only the significance of cases that you believe best illustrate how the rule operates but also the *in*significance of the cases that your opponent might proffer. You should take care to address what the authorities do *not* mean or do *not* say, and to justify your decisions. You should not make your opponent's arguments, as in this example:

Bad Example
The Respondent may argue that the *McGuffin* case applies here. Respondent may argue that *McGuffin* stands for proposition that . . .

Instead of spending valuable pixels on the opponent's actual argument, make your position as to that argument evident from the beginning. If you are writing a responsive brief or are otherwise certain that your opponent will be making a certain point or bringing up a certain authority, you may wish to tie the authority to your opponent, as in this example:

Better Example
Any argument that *McGuffin* applies here is invalid. The *McGuffin* court never addressed . . .

This type of argument has risks, particularly if you are writing the opening brief.[19] In the alternative, you can simply attack the negative authority. This type of argument is a method of portraying yourself as an educator.[20] For the court's benefit, you are describing the cases that are relevant and those that are not relevant:

Good Example
McGuffin does not apply here for two reasons. First . . .

---

19. *See generally* Stanchi, *supra* note 16, at 424-27 (discussing when and how to volunteer negative information).

20. Commentators have referred to this educational style as the "scholarly" style. Stanchi, *supra* note 16, at 391 (citing James F. Stratman, *Investigating Persuasive Processes in Legal Discourse in Real Time: Cognitive Biases and Rhetorical Strategy in Appeal Court Briefs*, 17 Discourse Processes 1, 8-10 (1994)).

Depending on the amount of detail needed, you may want to devote a paragraph or even a point-heading section[21] to the principle that a case or a series of cases is inapposite.

Finally, as to some issues, you and your opponent may agree as to what the rule is and to what it means but disagree as to how it applies. In that situation, your rule application section would need to be longer because you would need to provide more detail as to the significance of certain facts that promote your point of view and the insignificance of facts that your opponent might use to promote his or her argument. The rule application example from *Fernandez*, excerpted above, shows one way to attack an opponent's arguments as part of the rule application.

Your second step is to determine if your opponent is making or may make an argument that you cannot address within the confines of your argument as it is currently structured. Look at each of the opponent arguments on your list and determine whether your argument contains contradictory analysis. Sometimes the analysis may be indirectly contradictory: two rules are mutually exclusive, and your argument does the best possible job of explaining why and how a particular rule applies in your case. At other times, your argument may directly contradict your opponent; instead of just saying that rule A applies, you will argue that rule B does not apply, or argue that even if it does apply, it does not result in a finding for your opponent.

You may, however, identify opponent arguments that you have not addressed directly or indirectly, and you must decide whether to do so. If you have no effective response to an issue, it may be better to leave it out of your argument[22] and focus on making your strong arguments as effectively as possible. For other issues, you may decide to make a direct attack on your opponent's point of view.

20 This kind of argument may be less likely to be rule-based. Instead, you may be making a direct assertion that your opponent's argument misinterprets the law or the facts. Instead of *explaining* the meaning of a rule by illustrating how it has been applied in the past, you will, in a way, be providing *evidence* for the truth of your assertion about your opponent's argument. For example, you may

20 Note that we are using "evidence" in its colloquial sense. We are not suggesting that these arguments will necessarily include citation of testimony, exhibits, or the like (although in certain circumstances, they might).

---

21. In this situation, you may want to mentally substitute the word "Evidence" for the "Explanation" part of CREXAC. Your assertion that a certain line of cases is inapposite would be your "rule," and in the place of the explanation, you would provide evidence for the truth of that assertion by discussing the cases and describing how they do not provide the support that your opponent might suggest.

22. Stanchi, *supra* note 16, at 383.

be arguing that a particular interpretation of a statute is wrong. The evidence to support that assertion could be legislative (e.g., discussing legislative history or statutory language), judicial (describing on-point cases from appropriate jurisdictions), or empirical (citing studies that support the thesis behind the assertion).

Thus, depending on your assertion, your evidence may come from the record, from extra-legal sources, or, as in most CREXAC arguments, from relevant authorities that have applied a particular rule. For example, if you are arguing that a court misinterpreted a rule or a line of cases, your evidence for that assertion would likely consist of a correct analysis of those cases, perhaps showing how other courts had applied that rule. When making arguments of this type, choose your words carefully. If you are petitioner, it may be tempting to attack the lower court for its holding. It might be more tactful and more fruitful, however, to characterize your attack as an attack on the assertion behind the holding rather than on the court that made the holding. Thus, instead of saying, e.g., "The Eighteenth Circuit erred when it found that the Mousse Statute applied here," it might be better to say, e.g., "The Mousse Statute regulates desserts; it cannot be applied to snacks."

We close this section with two warnings about dealing with your opponent's arguments. First, addressing negative authorities almost never means that you should begin your argument by addressing negative authorities. Professor Stanchi's research shows that "it is clear that beginning with refutation decreases persuasive value."[23] Second, addressing negative arguments or authorities does not require you to attack opposing counsel or the courts below.[24] Instead of questioning the integrity or intelligence of opposing counsel, note a possibly tenuous connection and then refute it—e.g., "Although this statute, admittedly, governs some types of employment relationships, it is inapposite here. The statute's language. . . ." You increase your credibility when you accord appropriate respect to your opponents and the judiciary.

---

23. Stanchi, *supra* note 16, at 397.

24. *Id.* at 410 (citing Stratman, *Investigating Persuasive Processes in Legal Discourse in Real Time: Cognitive Biases and Rhetorical Strategy in Appeal Court Briefs*, 17 DISCOURSE PROCESSES at 44).

5.5. CONCLUSION

By creating a working outline and using the CREXAC formula to analyze every controversial element in your argument, you give the court the information it needs to understand the validity of each element of your argument. An important part of your job as an advocate is to identify which issues need a full CREXAC analysis and which issues should be addressed more succinctly or summarily. Further, you must be sure that, whenever possible, your argument addresses your opponent's best points. Your goal is to write a brief that addresses—in appropriate depth—both the strengths of your arguments and the weaknesses of your opponent's arguments. The more effectively you do so, the more you increase the chances that the court will understand why the law demands the result that you seek.

Using Cases Effectively

Did you take torts in your first year of law school? (We're betting that you did.) Do you know the legal standard for civil assault? (We're betting that you have a general answer for that question.) Do you know the legal standard for civil assault in your state? (We're betting you're not 100% sure that it's the same.) If you fell asleep in class, would it constitute civil assault in your state if your teacher woke you by slamming a heavy con law textbook down two inches from your dozing head? (We're betting that your answer is no more specific than "maybe.")

Your increasingly less-specific answers are why you need to include rule explanation sections in motion memos and appellate briefs, and to include case descriptions for the cases cited within those rule explanations. Even when judges know the law generally, they need you to specify the precise standards at issue; when the issues are controversial, they need you to include enough specifics in case descriptions to help the judges understand how those standards work in specific fact situations.

1 As every law student (and former law student) knows, case law is one of the pillars of the American legal system. Cases are the basis for common law, and they provide judicial gloss on statutory and constitutional law. Good legal writers must learn how to read cases effectively; just as importantly, they must learn to describe cases to others. We use the term "case description" to refer to the information about an authority case that you include in a legal document.

The way you write a case description will depend on the document you are including the case description in, how you are using the case, and the audience for the case description. If you are writing to a non-lawyer, you might use very general language, because giving some specifics without others might confuse someone not familiar with court procedure. If you are writing to a judge, it may be tempting to leave things out, with the idea that the "judge knows everything." You should resist that temptation, however. This chapter provides a formula to help you decide which details are and are not necessary and appropriate.

2 Since some courts now require that attorneys include hyperlinks to cited authorities, you may think that even if a judge doesn't know everything, the judge or the judge's clerk can just click through to the authorities you cite, and thus you don't need to provide any relevant information in court documents. While it may be true that your reader *can* click through to the cited authority, your reader should not *need* to click through. We imagine that the hyperlink requirements are there to allow courts to verify the information in your document; do not treat them as a substitute for the necessary work of providing a good case description.

Because cases and case descriptions are such an important part of legal writing, this chapter covers a lot of ground. The chapter will address: (1) the case description formula; (2) how to make case descriptions as succinct as possible; (3) how to write and use parenthetical case descriptions; (4) how to make sure your case descriptions are accurate; (5) how to use quotations in case descriptions; and (6) how to use language precisely when analogizing and distinguishing cases.

1 As you know, lawyers refer to the written record of a court's decision using a variety of labels, including *case, decision,* and *opinion.*

2 We do not recommend including hyperlinks in the body of a document unless a court rule specifically requires them. In a way, hyperlinks serve as an invitation to leave the document; and as you know from your own experience with hyperlinks, readers may not always come back once they click on that first link. If you are uncertain, include hyperlinks in the table of authorities. This placement will allow the judge or law clerk to access your authorities easily without interfering directly with their reading process.

6.1. FORMULA FOR EFFECTIVE CASE DESCRIPTIONS

When you cite a case in a persuasive document, it will most likely be for one of two reasons. You may be using the case to provide "rule authority"; that is, you are citing the case to provide authority for the existence of a rule. More often, however, you are citing the case as "illustrative authority"; that is, you believe that the case effectively illustrates how the rule has been applied in a meaningfully similar case. While the depth of your case description may vary depending on whether it is being used as a rule authority or an illustrative authority, you should almost always provide some description for each case you cite. As the Chief Justice of the Colorado Supreme Court has noted, "[i]f [a] case is important enough to cite, it should be analyzed within the brief or, at least, within a parenthetical."[1]

Case descriptions are about providing context. As one judge has noted, "[c]iting to sentences out of context and, thus, misrepresenting the holding of the court . . . will not be good for your legal career."[2] Articulating a court's statement about the meaning of the word "resident," for example, isn't helpful unless the reader knows what that court was looking at when it made that statement: was the term "resident" from a statute regulating school districts, from a regulation about public benefits, or from an insurance contract?

To write effective case descriptions, you need to learn how to focus your descriptions appropriately, providing the relevant details and omitting the rest. In most situations, if you are citing a case, the reader should be able to understand or infer at least three or four elements from your case description. This does not mean that you must devote a sentence to each of these elements or even that you must state each one directly. Whether you state elements directly or leave readers to infer them will depend, as do most decisions, on the context in which the case descriptions appear.

With that warning, here are the elements:

(1) **The relevant issue.** Be sure that the reader can identify which of the case's many issues and sub-issues you are using the case to illustrate. You should also provide the legal context in which the court analyzed that issue, *if it is different from the context of the case at bar or the cases under discussion in that section of your argument.* Likewise, if you will be analogizing or distinguishing the case based on some particular facet of the legal issue, be sure to provide sufficient detail so that the reader can understand that facet of the issue.

(2) **The disposition of that issue.** Make clear how the court disposed of that narrow issue and, if relevant, how it disposed of

---

1. Nancy E. Rice, *Tips on Legal Writing*, Colo. Law., May 2015, at 61.
2. Judge James R. Wolf, *Taking a Swing at Appellate Brief Writing*, Fla. B.J., September/October 2011, at 39.

the entire case. Thus, if you are discussing the issue of breach, don't just tell the reader what the court considered or analyzed. Be explicit: "The court found that defendant had breached his duty of care when he failed to. . . ."

(3) **The facts relevant to that issue.** Include enough of the legally significant facts for the reader to understand how the court applied the law to reach its holding on the issue and how the case is analogous to the case at bar. If you wish to draw an analogy to these facts or to distinguish your case based on its facts, provide more detail. Try to describe the facts in a way that highlights similarities or dissimilarities by writing at the appropriate level of abstraction or concreteness; remember that your rule explanation is laying the foundation for the rule application. For example, if the statute at issue in your case regulated drinking, it might be appropriate to analogize it to a statute that regulated gambling. In describing that statute and the cases analyzing it, you might refer to the gambling statute as a statute that governs "highly-regulated addictive **3** behavior." If you wanted to distinguish the gambling statute, you might talk about it as regulating gambling *behavior*, so that you can later contrast it with a statute regulating alcohol *consumption*.

3 Including this description does not mean that you won't explain any specifics about the statute; rather, you would provide the specifics as needed but be sure to highlight (e.g., in a topic sentence and elsewhere) the fact that the statute governs highly-regulated addictive behavior.

(4) **The reasoning relevant to that issue.** Include enough information to give the reader a basic understanding of why the court decided the issue before it in the way that it did. If either the case or the reasoning behind the court's decision is significant, provide more detail. Again, you are laying a foundation for the rule application. If the court's reasoning highlighted a detail that is distinct from the details in your case, you should highlight that reasoning in your case description. For example, suppose you were one of the lawyers in the *Fernandez* case, in which police went to the door of a battery suspect and then arrested him for domestic violence after he said that the police could not enter. After the suspect was gone, the police asked his domestic partner for consent to enter. Each side might cite the *Randolph* case, which said police could not seek consent from one tenant if another was present and objecting to police entry. Counsel for the government would highlight the reasoning of the *Randolph* court about the significance of the objecting tenant's presence at the scene. Counsel for Fernandez would highlight the part of the reasoning where the court noted that the presence rule was appropriate "[s]o long as there is no evidence that the police have removed the potentially objecting tenant from the entrance for the sake of avoiding a possible objection."

When writing a case description, your default mode should be to include all four of these elements. Admittedly, on some occasions, it may be appropriate to include only three; at times, the facts may be omitted in a section devoted to an issue of law, particularly in a situation in which the writer cites two or more cases with similar fact situations. Likewise, when an argument turns on a question of fact, it may be permissible to omit a court's reasoning. When in doubt, however, include all four elements. Note that including these four elements in a case description is not all that the effective brief writer must do. To ensure that the brief is effective, you must be sure that your case description is as succinct as possible; you must use verb tenses accurately; you must choose when to use parenthetical case descriptions instead of textual ones (and do so effectively and appropriately); and you must be certain that the case description is accurate.

6.2. MAKING CASE DESCRIPTIONS AS SUCCINCT AS POSSIBLE

Including the issue, the disposition, the facts, and the reasoning in a case description may seem to require a long description. Actually, all four of these elements can often be conveyed in a parenthetical description, and they can certainly be conveyed in a textual description of two sentences. Of course, if a relevant aspect of the case is complex or particularly significant, or if you need to highlight certain details from the case to lay a foundation for your rule application, you may need to provide more detail.

There are two keys to succinct case descriptions. The first key is focus. You must understand the focus of the argument you are currently making and make sure that the case description has that same focus. The second key is efficient use of language. You must work to convey the most information in the fewest words.

6.2.1. Focus

The case description below is from a brief about whether a search was valid under the state's Fourth Amendment jurisprudence. In the fictional state of Vanita, those in police custody are entitled to a type of warning called a *Conner* warning before being asked to consent to a search. If a person is in police custody and is asked to consent to a search without being given a *Conner* warning, the search is invalid. The issue being addressed in the relevant section of the document is whether the defendant had been in custody at the time of the search for purposes of a *Conner* warning.

Good Example

4 This phrase signals the issue.

A defendant is in custody for purposes of a *Conner* warning **4** if police imply that the defendant is obligated to submit to a search in order to be free to leave. *Helmond v. State*, 101 R.E.2d 358, 365 (Van. 2006). In *Helmond*, the police never answered defendant's questions about her right to refuse consent, told defendant that it was in her "best interest to cooperate" with them, and that they would "allow" her to go on her way if they did not find anything. **5** *Id*. at 364-65. The court found the consent invalid, holding that defendant was in custody because a person in her position would not believe that she was free to disregard the police request. **6** *Id*.

5 This sentence describes the legally significant facts.

6 Here the writer provides the disposition of the custody issue, followed by the court's reasoning.

One method you can use to test the focus of your case descriptions is to look for the phrase-that-pays for that section of the document. If your case description includes the phrase-that-pays, chances are good that you have at least focused the description on the right legal issue. In the previous example, the phrase-that-pays "in custody" appears twice in the case description. The following case descriptions are from an argument that an employer took an "adverse action" against an employee in retaliation for her exercise of protected conduct under Title VII. Note how the writer takes care to connect the phrase-that-pays, "materially adverse," to each of the case descriptions (the phrase-that-pays is in small capital letters):

Good Example

7 Issue.

Reassignment of duties within the same job description can qualify as a MATERIALLY ADVERSE **7** action when the employee is moved from one position into another which is objectively worse. *Burlington Northern & Santa Fe Railway Co. v. White*, 548 U.S. 53, 70 (2006). In *Burlington Northern*, the plaintiff, who was the only woman in her department, had been moved from her forklift operator position to standard track laborer tasks after she complained of sexual harassment. **8** *Id*. at 53. The court found that the transfer was a MATERIALLY ADVERSE action **9** that would deter a reasonable employee from making complaints to supervisors, noting that the duties of a track laborer were more grueling and dirtier than the duties of a forklift operator. **10** *Id*. at 54.

8 Facts.
9 Disposition.

10 Reasoning.

11 Issue.

Examples of MATERIALLY ADVERSE actions **11** also include heightened supervisory scrutiny, selective enforcement of policies, and being disciplined more harshly than similarly situated coworkers. *Ford v. Gen. Motors Corp.*, 305 F.3d 545, 553 (6th Cir. 2002).

In *Ford*, the Sixth Circuit found that a plaintiff who had filed an EEOC complaint had faced MATERIALLY ADVERSE actions **12** when he showed that he had subsequently faced an increased workload and increased scrutiny from his manager. **13** *Id*. Likewise, a Black employee who had filed race discrimination complaints **14** established MATERIALLY ADVERSE actions **15** when he showed that he was later denied the opportunity to attend a training program which his white coworkers attended on the company's dime. *Laster v. City of Kalamazoo*, 746 F.3d 714, 719-20 (6th Cir. 2014). The *Laster* court reached this conclusion even though the plaintiff was later allowed to attend the training, noting that the employee was required to pay for half of the costs, while his coworkers were not required to pay for any of their expenses. **16** *Id*. The court found that this disparate application of policies regarding training opportunities **17** constituted a MATERIALLY ADVERSE action. *Id* at 732.

12 Disposition of issue.

13 Facts.

14 Facts.

15 Disposition of issue.

16 Facts.

17 Reasoning.

If the court has not been thoughtful enough to use the phrase-that-pays that you have identified for that section of the argument, you can make the connection yourself, as long as you do it honestly. If you do make the connection yourself, be sure to justify the connection by quoting language that makes the connection obvious. The word *apparently* is often helpful when describing a connection that is implicit rather than explicit, as in this description of a court's reasoning in a fictional case:

> *Good Example*
> The Court apparently believed that the company's behavior constituted a materially adverse action, because it noted that "any employee would think twice about complaining if they knew that the result would be assignment to the worst job in the building." *McGuffin v. Vineyard Electric*, 101 U.S. 101, 103 (2013).

When trying to decide how much detail to give the reader within the case description, first assess how you are using the case. If you are using the case as rule authority and plan to discuss it in depth in your explanation section, you may give only a "naked cite." On the other hand, you may be using a case as rule authority only because it is from a court of mandatory jurisdiction or it is well known as the source of a particular rule, rather than because of its relevance to your client's case. (Presumably, you plan to use other cases to illustrate the rule.) If that is the situation, you should provide a parenthetical description:

18 Facts.

19 Issue and disposition of issue.

20 Facts.

For an employer's behavior to be found to be an "adverse action," a plaintiff must show that a "reasonable employee would have found the challenged action materially adverse, which in this context means it well might have dissuaded a reasonable worker from making or supporting a charge of discrimination." *Burlington Northern & Santa Fe Railway Co. v. White*, 548 U.S. 53, 70 (2006) (finding reassignment to "dirtier" and "worse" job duties **18** was materially adverse **19** even though pay rate was the same **20**).

A last reminder about focus: As noted above, your casebook courses may have taught you to search for the main point of the case, or the point that the case "stands for" in the development of a legal rule. In advocacy, in contrast, your case descriptions must focus on the *relevant* issue, facts, disposition, etc., even if that issue is not the main point that the court addressed. In your research (and thus in your case descriptions), you may need to go beyond—or even ignore—the case's main point.

For example, suppose you are researching the issue of breach in a negligence case based on a defendant's duty to another after the defendant has "taken charge" of that person. You find a court opinion that reviewed a finding on the merits in another take-charge negligence case in which the trial court found for the plaintiff and awarded punitive damages. The court mentioned the facts and the finding of negligence, but focused its opinion on the legal standard for punitive damages and whether those damages were appropriate in that case. It might be tempting to skip over that opinion, because the main point of the case was the rule about punitive damages.

Of course, if there was a decision for the plaintiff on the merits, the trial court had, by definition, found duty, breach, causation, and harm. Accordingly, you should review the opinion to see if the facts of the case are relevant to yours in a way that would allow you to argue that your case should or should not be decided in the same way. Admittedly, the opinion might be more helpful if the court laid out some reasoning that you could use, but the mere description of the relevant facts with the holding can give you room for argument. For example, suppose the appellate court noted that the trial court had held that defendants breached their duty of care, that they knew plaintiff's decedent was heavily intoxicated and unconscious, and that they refused to seek medical help or call her parents. Just knowing these facts would allow you to infer that knowledge of the victim's dangerous condition was significant, and you might be able to use that case to support your argument about whether breach had occurred in your client's case.

6.2.2. Using Language Effectively

Even when using a textual case description or when you must give the reader more detail, do not make your case description needlessly long. Provide only the information that the reader needs about each of the four elements. In many case descriptions, writers run into trouble in the first sentence. One way to avoid this trouble is to concentrate on the subject-verb combination. The first sentence you write about a case should tell the reader something that the court did or something about why the court did what it did. It should *not* tell the reader what the case *involved*, *regarded*, or *concerned*, or what the court *addressed, considered, examined*, or *dealt with*. Notice how the first sentence in the following case description wastes the reader's (scarce) time and energy:

Bad Example
In *Burlington Northern & Santa Fe Railway Co. v. White*, 548 U.S. 53, 70 (2006), this Court examined whether certain employer behaviors were "materially adverse."

This description tells the reader that the court examined an issue, but it leaves the reader in suspense as to what happened as a result of the examination. Suspense is the enemy of good legal writing. Instead of saying only that the court "examined" the issue, the writer should say something about a court's ultimate ruling or, if relevant, a particular finding in the case. Verbs such as *held* and *found* are more likely to get your reader to the point of the case:

Good Example
This Court has held that reassigning an employee to the worst duties in her job description **21** was a "materially adverse" action **22** **23** for purposes of a Title VII retaliation claim. *Burlington Northern & Santa Fe Railway Co. v. White*, 548 U.S. 53, 70 (2006).

21 Facts.

22 Disposition.

23 Issue.

If you do not need to emphasize which court made the decision, a sentence like this can be even more effective:

Good Example
Reassigning an employee to the worst duties in her job description **24** is a "materially adverse" action **25** **26** for purposes of a Title VII retaliation claim. *Burlington Northern & Santa Fe Railway Co. v. White*, 548 U.S. 53, 70 (2006).

24 Facts.

25 Disposition.

26 Issue.

The bad example told the reader only the issue that the court addressed in *Burlington Northern*. The good examples, on the other hand, tell the reader the issue, the legally significant facts, and the disposition of the issue. The writer can add any needed reasoning in a second sentence.

6.2.3. Verb Tense in Case Descriptions

Many writers get confused as to the appropriate verb tense when describing cases. This confusion results when courts mix legal rules that are currently in force—properly stated in the present tense—with case facts, findings, and holdings—properly stated in some form of the past tense.[3]

Within a case description, use an appropriate form of past tense to describe events that happened before the case began as well as events that happened in the case. The court's holdings as to specific parties should also be described using the past tense:

Good Examples
The plaintiff had filed a sex discrimination claim against two of her supervisors.

The officer testified that he had provided the defendant with *Miranda* warnings.

When the ship captain saw the Coast Guard approaching, he threw the crate of undersized fish overboard.

The plaintiff alleged . . .

The defendant argued . . .

The court found . . .

The court reasoned . . .

When you are stating a general rule that the court articulated, however, use the past tense only to describe the court's action, and use the present tense for the rule itself:

Good Examples
Applying that standard, the court held **27** that "[s]ervice of process upon a defendant's adult child who is an overnight resident in the house of defendant's usual abode, and then the sole occupant

27 Past tense: statement of what the court did in the past.

---

3. A detailed discussion of the sequence of tenses is beyond the scope of this book; for an excellent explanation of how verb tenses are used in legal writing, see ANNE ENQUIST, LAUREL OATES & JEREMY FRANCIS, JUST WRITING: GRAMMAR, PUNCTUATION, AND STYLE FOR THE LEGAL WRITER (5th ed. 2017), at §§ 8.3, 10.1.2.

of it, is **28** reasonably calculated to accomplish notice to the defendant." *McGuffin v. Zahm*, 101 R.E.2d 222, 228 (Van. 2020).

The court held **29** that the service of process on the defendant's adult child in the defendant's home provided **30** valid notice to the defendant. *McGuffin v. Zahm*, 101 R.E.2d 222, 228 (Van. 2020).

The correct verb tense may not make or break your argument, but using the wrong verb tense distracts the reader at best. At worst, it confuses the reader and slows comprehension.

28 Present tense: general rule about when service of process is valid.

29 Past tense: statement of what the court did in the past.

30 Past tense: statement of how the rule applied to specific facts in a specific case.

6.3. WRITING AND USING EFFECTIVE PARENTHETICAL DESCRIPTIONS

Parenthetical case descriptions are a useful alternative to in-text, or textual, case descriptions. "Parentheticals" can save both space and the reader's time, but the writer must be careful to remember the principles of focus and completeness. Incomplete parentheticals tend to be ineffective because they give the reader only a snippet of information. Often, unfortunately, the snippet does not contain enough information to make the case useful to the reader, who must decide whether the cited case provides authority for a ruling in the case at bar. The following parentheticals, for example, would not be helpful in an explanation section discussing what plaintiff behavior constitutes "protected activity" under Title VII:

Bad Example
See generally EEOC v. New Breed Logistics, 783 F.3d 1057, 1066 (6th Cir. 2015) (plaintiff made oral complaints to supervisors); *McGuffin v. Ostrander Services, Inc.* 894 F.3d 1111, 1199 (6th Cir. 2020) (plaintiff sent email to supervisor's administrative assistant).

These parentheticals merely hint at the issue (something about the significance of reports to a supervisor) and the facts (who made the reports, how they were made, and who they were made to), but they do not tell the reader how the court resolved the issue or why the court resolved it the way it did. This type of snippet parenthetical may be effective, but *only* if the surrounding text—usually the text before the citation—supplies sufficient context. For a parenthetical to be effective, either the parenthetical alone *or* the parenthetical and the surrounding text will give the reader information about at least three, and preferably four, of the required elements: the relevant issue, its disposition, the relevant facts, and the relevant reasoning. In the first example below, the text before the citations provides the disposition, the issue, and the reasoning; the parentheticals, therefore, need include only the legally significant facts. In the second example, in contrast, which has no introductory text, the parenthetical includes all four elements:

Good Examples

As long as the evidence indicates that managerial employees knew or should have known about a plaintiff's complaint, **31** courts have found various manners of and audiences for reporting to be valid "protected activities" **32** under Title VII. *See, e.g., EEOC v. New Breed Logistics*, 783 F.3d 1057, 1066 (6th Cir. 2015) (oral complaints to supervisors **33**); *McGuffin v. Ostrander Services, Inc*. 894 F.3d 1111, 1199 (6th Cir. 2020) (email to supervisor's administrative assistant with request to forward to supervisor **34**).

31 Reasoning.

32 Issue and disposition of issue.

33 Facts.

34 Facts.

McGuffin v. Ostrander Services, Inc. 894 F.3d 1111, 1199 (6th Cir. 2020) (finding protected activity **35** when plaintiff sent email to supervisor's administrative assistant with request to forward to supervisor, **36** because supervisor "knew or should have known" about the complaint **37**).

35 Issue and disposition of the issue.

36 Facts.

37 Reasoning.

As with textual descriptions, parenthetical descriptions are more helpful when they use language effectively and focus on the phrase-that-pays.

Knowing how to write effective parenthetical case descriptions is important, but the writer must also know *when* to use a parenthetical description. Deciding when to use a textual or a parenthetical description for a cited case is really a question about how much detail to provide. If little detail is needed, as when you are citing to a case only for rule authority, you can easily use a parenthetical description. Ultimately, your decision will be based on the answers to two questions: (1) How is the case significant to your argument? (2) What information does the reader need to have to understand the case's significance?

The more significant an authority case is, and the more important it is for the reader to understand its facts and reasoning, the more detail you need to provide *in your argument*. If the issue or the authority case is more straightforward, on the other hand, you can provide a shorter textual description *or* a parenthetical description. Note that you should generally *not* provide both a parenthetical and a textual description for the same case. You may appropriately have a sentence with introductory text that precedes a citation with a parenthetical description. Generally, however, if you need more than a sentence of introductory text, you should use a textual description rather than a parenthetical one. Likewise, it is usually not appropriate to follow a parenthetical case description with further textual description of a case.

As noted in Chapter Five, the ideal explanation section within each unit of discourse in your argument includes at least one case in which a court found that the rule applied to a certain set of facts, and at least one case in which a court found that the rule did *not* apply to a certain different set of facts. In most situations, you will want to provide a textual description of both of those cases. A sensible compromise is to provide one or two more detailed case descriptions, followed up—when appropriate—by citation to one or more illustrative cases with parenthetical descriptions.

38 Of course, you should not use this method as an excuse to bombard the reader with 10 authorities when one would suffice. Cite an additional authority only when it illustrates some relevant facet of the rule that your previous authorities did not illustrate, or when it proves that the interpretation you are illustrating is well established.

The following example shows a case description to be used in an "adverse action" discussion. Unlike the case descriptions above, which describe cases in which the court found that an adverse action existed, this case description illustrates when a court is *not* likely to find the existence of an adverse action. Some writers seem to think it is dangerous to let the court see any case in which a court ruled "against" their client's interest. Effective writers, however, realize that if a so-called negative case is distinguishable, it can be used very effectively to argue against a particular result.

Because the writer of this case description plans to argue that the defendants did take an adverse action, he lays the foundation for that argument by using the rule explanation to highlight the negligible impact of the alleged adverse action in the authority case:

Good Example
De minimis employment actions and those not supported by evidence do not usually constitute adverse employment actions. *McGuffin v. Summerlin Indus.*, 700 F.3d 701, 711 (6th Cir. 2003). The court in *McGuffin* held that the plaintiff failed to provide sufficient evidence to show that his employer took adverse employment actions against him in retaliation for filing complaints of racial discrimination. *Id.* at 723. The plaintiff claimed that the

38 For example, if knowledge were at issue, and a party had demonstrated knowledge by words and actions, you might include a case description of one case in which words demonstrated knowledge, and another in which actions demonstrated knowledge.

employer had failed to immediately remove a performance letter from his file, failed to give him a cash advance, singled him out for supervision, and denied him overtime. *Id.* at 267. While acknowledging that the denied overtime could constitute an adverse action, the lack of evidence for that fact (beyond a bald statement by the plaintiff) was not sufficient for his claim to survive summary judgment. *Id.* at 267.

Because the writer will be arguing that his client has sufficient evidence for her claim, he highlights the court's concerns about lack of evidence in the authority case. Although any needed analogy and distinction will occur in the rule application, remember that you are laying the foundation for the rule application in the rule explanation.

6.4. ACCURACY IN CASE DESCRIPTIONS

As noted above, an effective case description includes the relevant issue, disposition, facts, and reasoning. It should go without saying that legal writers should not misrepresent any of these elements. Say it we must, however. When we chat with judges and law clerks and quiz them about their legal writing pet peeves, many mention wordiness and poor organization. Almost all of them, however, complain about attorneys who misrepresent the facts or the law. Law clerks describe the many times that they have read in a brief that a case stands for one proposition, only to consult the case and find that it stands for some wholly unrelated point, or worse, that it contradicts the very point the attorney was using the case to make.

39 Admittedly, some lawyers do not take this seemingly obvious step. Take note and be sure to do so with your own opponents. It is both satisfying and effective to be able to say to a court—in an oral argument, a responding brief, or a reply brief—that the very case that your opponent cites actually hurts rather than helps their argument.

39 So the first thing you need to remember about accuracy is that someone will be checking your work. And don't count on escaping scrutiny if you are submitting a brief to an overworked and understaffed trial court; at the very least, your opponent should be checking the validity of your cited cases. Don't be tempted to misrepresent case law, either through negligence or willfulness. The momentary satisfaction of presenting an argument with a veneer of validity is not worth the cost in reputation and future credibility. Further, you may face sanctions; ABA Model Rule 3.3(a) provides that a lawyer shall not "knowingly make a false statement of fact or law to a tribunal."

Accordingly, let us presume that you are not going to knowingly misrepresent cases; how can you avoid doing so negligently? First, avoid two common shortcuts that often lead to mistakes; second, be careful to avoid characterizing dicta as holdings, particularly when describing certain categories of cases. Finally, write with an awareness of common inferences, and prevent wrong inferences as appropriate.

40 First, beware the shortcut. One shortcut to avoid is relying on how others have characterized cases. If you read a memo, brief, or court opinion that characterizes a case in a certain way, it is tempting to repeat that characterization yourself. Certainly, you may reason, that attorney or that judge would not have misrepresented the law. Resist the shortcut. Take the time to click through to the cited case and to read it for yourself to verify that it says what you think it says. Further, be sure to use Shepard's, Keycite, and the like, and to conduct further research to verify that the case is still valid law. Even if the judge or attorney did not misrepresent the law, more recent authorities may have changed the validity of that case. Thus, read it and update it yourself; don't rely on the work of others.

Another shortcut to avoid is using a case as authority when you have read only an isolated paragraph or two. Modern computer research can often send legal researchers on a cavalcade of clicking, jumping from one source to another to another, and from one use of a search term to the next. Thankfully, both Lexis and Westlaw now send graphic signals to alert you when you are reading material in a dissent, and Lexis signals other non-majority opinions. And of course, whether you are citing to material from the majority or the dissent, be sure to take the time to discern the relevant issue, disposition, facts, and reasoning.

The second way that writers may negligently misrepresent the law is by failing to distinguish dicta from holdings, especially in what we have referred to as *kickback cases*. As we have noted, we use the label *kickback case* for a case that comes to a court of appeals after the trial court has granted a motion to dismiss or a motion for summary judgment. If the court of appeals reverses and remands the decision, it in essence "kicks it back" to the court below. But a decision to reverse and remand does not necessarily mean that the court made any *findings on the merits* as to how the law applies to the facts. In reversing a grant of a motion for summary judgment, the court may be doing no more than finding that a dispute exists as to the material facts. When reversing a grant of a motion to dismiss, the court is merely finding that the pleadings were sufficient to state a claim, not that the pleadings were true or that the plaintiff will necessarily succeed in his or her cause of action. It is particularly important to remember that the motion standard when a court decides on a motion to dismiss requires a court to presume that a complaint's factual allegations are true. This presumption does *not*

40 Of course, in law school, an academic honor code may forbid you to consult attorney briefs, or to use them without citing them as the source of your analysis. Even if it were permissible to use them without citation, however, you should not rely on their validity.

mean, however, that the allegations are in fact true or that the plaintiff will be able to establish at trial that they are true.

A careless writer, trying to explain the rules about what constitutes willful and wanton misconduct in allegations about injuries that occur during team sports (in this case hockey), might misrepresent the court's holding by quoting a partial sentence with a misleading introduction:

Bad Example

The court held that the defendant players' actions, when they "checked" plaintiff from behind while he was bent over with his head facing the boards, were "not only violations of the rules, but, given [plaintiff's] vulnerable position and the 'STOP' warnings on players' jerseys, that they went beyond conduct ordinarily accepted during the course of competition and into willful and wanton conduct." *Karas v. Strevell*, 860 N.E.2d 1163, 1173 (Ill. App. 2d Dist. 2006), *aff'd in part, rev'd in part*, 884 N.E.2d 122 (Ill. 2008).

The *language* is quoted accurately; the context, however, is not accurate. A law clerk who went to read the full sentence surrounding the quotation would find that three words missing from the sentence create a vastly different impression of the case (the emphasis is added):

Instead, *plaintiff alleges that* Strevell's and Zimmerman's actions were not only violations of the rules, but, given Benjamin's vulnerable position and the "STOP" warnings on players' jerseys, that they went beyond conduct ordinarily accepted during the course of competition and into willful and wanton conduct.

The state appellate court did not find that the defendants' conduct had been willful or wanton or that the facts were accurate as pleaded. It merely restated the plaintiff's argument and found that the complaint was adequate to state a cause of action. In contrast, notice how the writer in this example accurately portrays the disposition of the issue and uses the word "may" to indicate the lack of a legal holding:

Good Example

41 Issue.

Violations of rules may constitute willful and wanton misconduct **41** of either players or coaches in a league if the players have not been appropriately taught the rules of the game. *Karas v. Strevell*, 860 N.E.2d 1163, 1173 (Ill. App. 2d Dist. 2006), *aff'd in part, rev'd* *in part*, 884 N.E.2d 122 (Ill. 2008). In *Karas*, the court found a complaint sufficient to state a cause of action **42** when the plaintiff alleged that a hockey league had not taught or enforced new rules against checking from behind and that two players checked a vulnerable player from behind despite the player's "vulnerable position" and the existence of warnings on the back of players' jerseys that said "STOP" in large letters. **43** *Id*. at 1174.

42 Disposition of issue.

43 Facts.

Thus, you can still cite to a kickback case; you must, however, accurately portray the issue and its disposition in any case description.

Finally, because readers will make inferences, writing accurate case descriptions sometimes means preventing or correcting those wrong inferences. Apply a two-part standard: if it is foreseeable that typical readers would make a mistaken inference, and if they would be angered or confused upon finding out that they were wrong, use a few words to launch a preemptive strike against that inference.

For example, if you are analyzing the meaning of "resident" in a statute governing school districts and cite cases about the meaning of the term "resident," the reader will infer that the cases are about school district residents. Accordingly, if you cite a case analyzing the term in another context, you must be explicit, e.g., "Analyzing the use of *resident* in a regulation governing medical benefits, this court concluded. . . ."

44 Likewise, if you make a legal assertion and follow it with a citation, your readers instinctively conclude that the citation is to a mandatory authority, merely glancing at the citation information to verify that conclusion. Here are some bad examples from a brief written to a federal district court within the First Circuit:

44 Because readers need to take that brief but important verification step, we disagree with those who recommend putting citations in footnotes in court documents. Cites in footnotes are fine in some contexts, but not when part of the job of the citation is verifying the validity of the cited material by noting the date of the decision and the jurisdictional authority of the court.

Bad Examples

Refusing to allow individual liability for supervisors under Title VII is "manifestly inconsistent" with Title VII's "underlying rationale and primary goals." Tracy L. Gonos, *A Policy Analysis of Individual Liability—The Case for Amending Title VII to Hold Individuals Personally Liable for Their Illegal Discriminatory Actions*, 2 N.Y.U. J. Legis. & Pub. Poly. 265, 270 (1998-1999).

With Title VII, Congress intended not only to make discriminatory acts by both employers and their agents actionable, but also to make "those who discriminate"—both employers and their agents—jointly and severally liable for their discriminatory acts. *Wyss v. General Dynamics Corp.*, 24 F. Supp. 2d 202, 206 (D.R.I. 1998) (citation omitted).

With both of these examples, the statements are relevant legal assertions that are followed by a citation and are not preceded by a qualifier. In both situations, readers would instinctively presume that the citation provides authority for the validity of the statement, and they would be frustrated or angered to see the nonauthoritative citation following the statement. To avoid this problem, simply use qualifying language that reveals that the source is not authoritative. Generally, it is *not* appropriate to announce to the court that a particular source is not authoritative:

> *Bad Examples*
> Although not authoritative, a commentator has noted that refusing to allow individual liability for supervisors under Title VII is "manifestly inconsistent" with Title VII's "underlying rationale and primary goals." Tracy L. Gonos, *A Policy Analysis of Individual Liability—The Case for Amending Title VII to Hold Individuals Personally Liable for Their Illegal Discriminatory Actions*, 2 N.Y.U. J. Legis. & Pub. Pol'y 265, 270 (1998-1999).

> A persuasive court has found that Congress intended for Title VII not only to make discriminatory acts by both employers and their agents actionable, but also to make "those who discriminate"—both employers and their agents—jointly and severally liable for their discriminatory acts. *Wyss v. General Dynamics Corp.*, 24 F. Supp. 2d 202, 206 (D.R.I. 1998) (citation omitted).

Judges and their clerks know that commentators and nonauthoritative courts are only persuasive authority. A better and more elegant way to make them aware of the nonauthoritative nature of the statement is to succinctly reveal the source in text. If possible, you should also give the court a reason to find value in the statement:

> *Good Examples*
> One commentator has argued that refusing to allow individual liability for supervisors under Title VII is "manifestly inconsistent" with Title VII's "underlying rationale and primary goals." Tracy L. Gonos, *A Policy Analysis of Individual Liability—The Case for Amending Title VII to Hold Individuals Personally Liable for Their Illegal Discriminatory Actions*, 2 N.Y.U. J. Legis. & Pub. Pol'y. 265, 270 (1998-1999). Title VII's underlying rationale is revealed in Section . . .

> Another district court in the First Circuit has faced this same issue and agreed that Congress intended to make discriminatory

acts by both employers and their agents actionable under Title VII. *Wyss v. General Dynamics Corp.*, 24 F. Supp. 2d 202, 206 (D.R.I. 1998) (citation omitted). That court further noted that Congress also intended to make "those who discriminate"—both employers and their agents—jointly and severally liable for their discriminatory acts. *Id.*

In the first example, the writer tries to increase the value of the source by tying its assertion to specific statutory language. In the second example, the writer tells the court why it should care about this nonauthoritative source by stating that the court was addressing the same issue that the court is currently addressing.

Accurately describing authority cases is one of the best ways to give a court confidence that your legal arguments are valid. You promote accuracy when you make sure to (1) provide sufficient information about the issue, disposition, facts, and reasoning; (2) focus the information on the issue currently under discussion; (3) use language efficiently to avoid unnecessary wordiness; (4) use parenthetical rather than textual descriptions as appropriate for rule authorities or less significant cases; and (5) take care to avoid misrepresenting the cases you cite.

6.5. USING QUOTATIONS EFFECTIVELY IN CASE DESCRIPTIONS

Quotations can be used very effectively to provide proof and support for the brief writer's assertions. When using quotations from cases, however, it's good to keep a couple of points in mind. First, don't use too many quotations; you should generally prefer paraphrases to quotes. Of course, whether you are quoting or paraphrasing, be sure to provide appropriate citations. Providing sufficient context, as described below, can help readers to understand why the language is included.

Writers' problems with quotations from cases tend to fall into three categories. The first category is "needless quoting," i.e., providing a quotation when a paraphrase would be more appropriate. The second two categories are "not enough" and "too much." Some writers drop quotations into their arguments without giving the reader enough information about the case. Without sufficient context, the quotation is meaningless. Other writers give the reader too much quoted language, leaving the reader to complete the writer's job of sifting through the language and sorting out its meaning. Police your writing to avoid these problems.

6.5.1. Avoid Needless Quoting

As indicated above, you should generally prefer paraphrasing to quoting. Quotation marks draw the reader's attention, and you want to save that special attention for important statements. Generally, use direct quotations only (1) when you are stating rules or other language at issue, or (2) when you are justifying a conclusion you have drawn about the meaning of an authority. Even when quoting a rule, you can and should focus the reader's attention as appropriate. Further, remember that using quotations may demand energy of the reader. Beginning or ending a paragraph or section with quoted material, for example, may require the reader to work to figure out the writer's purpose for the quoted language. In the following example, the writer is addressing duties that landowners owe to people on their land. The plaintiff in this case was a trespasser, so the analysis was focused on duties that landowners do and don't owe to trespassers. The bad example leads the reader to believe that the plaintiff might have been an invitee, a licensee, or a trespasser.

Bad Example

"Entrants upon land are divided into three classifications: invitees, licensees, and trespassers." *Rhodes v. Illinois Cent. Gulf R.R.*, 665 N.E.2d 1260, 1268 (Ill. 1996). This court has defined a "trespasser" as "one who enters upon the premises of another with neither permission nor invitation and intrudes for some purpose of his own, or at his convenience, or merely as an idler." *Id.*

The example above does not focus the reader's attention. The following example, in contrast, paraphrases the uncontroversial language and focuses the reader on the term at issue and its definition:

Better Example

This court has used three classifications for an entrant upon land: invitee, licensee, and "trespasser," which is defined as a person who enters onto the premises of another "with neither permission nor invitation and intrudes for some purpose of his own, or at his convenience, or merely as an idler." *Rhodes v. Illinois Cent. Gulf R.R.*, 665 N.E.2d 1260, 1268 (Ill. 1996).

This example paraphrases the non-controversial language and focuses the reader's attention on the words that are crucial to the controversy. You may be confused by our use of the word "paraphrase," since some of the unquoted language in the second example is identical to the quoted language in the first example. As a general rule in legal writing, you are allowed to use identical language without quoting it as long as the language meets two requirements: (1) it is cited appropriately, and (2) it is not a unique turn of phrase or remarkable for some other reason.

6.5.2. Provide Sufficient Context for Quotes

If, like us, you were an English major as an undergraduate, you may have become enamored with the power of a pithy quotation. Remember that in law, a quotation is only as meaningful as its source and its relevance. If the source of the quote is not meaningful to the reader (e.g., if the source is from secondary or optional authorities) or the writer hasn't given enough context to demonstrate the relevance of the quote (e.g., for a case, the issue, the rule, and the facts), the reader can't begin to understand the significance of the quote without consulting the source. And since most readers don't have time to read the cases cited in the briefs, the quote may have a negative impact: the reader will be annoyed at being given insufficient or misleading information.

Thus, when using a quotation from a case, be sure the reader can glean the relevant issue, the disposition of that issue, and the facts and/or reasoning of the opinion. Do not drop a quotation into your argument like a chocolate chip into batter. Note the following example, which discusses an exception to the rule about a landowner's duty of care to a trespasser:

> *Bad Example*
> The *Rhodes* court refused to accept the "place of danger" exception argument because the "safe location was [not] transformed into a place of danger by the mere fortuity that an injured trespasser came to rest there." *Id*. at 1269.

The reader does not have enough context to understand what the exception is and why the plaintiff's argument would make all premises a "place of danger." Further, although this writer's alteration of the quotation was honest, adding a "not" to a quotation does not fill the reader with confidence. Presumably, the writer included the quoted language because she wants to attack her opponent's argument using similar reasoning. That method can be effective, but make sure the case description includes the details that give context for the quotation:

Better Example

45 Issue and
disposition of the
issue.

46 Facts.

The "place of danger" exception imposes a higher duty on a
landowner only if the landowner's property has certain dangers
that would exist for all trespassers. *E.g., Rhodes*, 665 N.E.2d at
1268. The *Rhodes* court refused to apply that exception **45** when
the landowners found the plaintiff's decedent—who was intoxicated, injured, and unconscious—in a warming shelter on the
defendant's property. **46** *Id.* Noting that the shelter promoted
safety for those on the property, the court rejected the plaintiff's
argument, observing that a safe place does not become a place
of danger due to the "mere fortuity" that "an injured trespasser
came to rest there." *Id.* at 1269.

Quotations can also be used effectively in parentheticals:

Good Example

The Illinois Supreme Court has refused to apply the "place of
danger" exception broadly, rejecting its use when the location
was otherwise safe and the trespasser's injury occurred before
he arrived on the premises. *Rhodes v. Illinois Cent. Gulf R.R.,*
665 N.E.2d 1260, 1269 (Ill. 1996) ("We do not agree that this safe
location was transformed into a place of danger by the mere fortuity that an injured trespasser came to rest there.").

By making a quotation part of a coherent case description, you
make it more likely that the quotation will do the job of convincing
the court that the case stands for the proposition you say it does.

6.5.3. Avoid Overlong Quotes

Some writers are so enamored with the court's language or so
fearful of paraphrase that they are loathe to break the shackles
of the quotation marks. Instead, they simply provide page after
page of excerpted quotes and let the reader determine the significance of the quoted language. "Overquoting" creates two problems. First, the writer is not doing his or her job. The writer is not
supposed to provide the raw material to the readers and let them
sort out what it all means. The writer's job is to research the law,
synthesize the available information, and write up the analysis in
a way that allows the reader to understand the situation with a
minimum of effort.

The second problem is related to the first. A reader who is constantly asked to consume and digest lengthy quotations may lose
the thread of the argument. As a practical matter, many readers

(including some of the people reading this book) skip long quotations. Judges who are reading briefs may do so because they know that the quotation says nothing about the case currently before the court; instead, it talks about another case, which must somehow be connected to the current case. Writers who overuse long quotes frequently do so because they have not figured out that connection and thus cannot make the connection within the argument. They compensate by giving the reader background reading that may, with luck and some work, allow the reader to reach the conclusion that the writer espouses. Since the writer, rather than the reader, is supposed to do the work, it is usually ineffective to use lengthy quotations.

The following example is adapted from a brief that references the *Rhodes* case cited above. The writer is trying to argue that the defendants, who had merely contacted the authorities about an injured person, had not voluntarily assumed a duty of care to render services to another. The writer wants to use language from *Rhodes* to argue that public policy supports a "no duty" finding.

Bad Example

In a factually similar case, *Rhodes v. Illinois Central Gulf Railroad*, 665 N.E.2d 1260 (Ill. 1996), a passenger boarding a train informed the conductor that someone was lying in the unmanned waiting room station. *Id*. at 1263. The conductor called his supervisor on his radio and reported that a man lying in the waiting room needed assistance. *Id*. The supervisor in turn relayed the information to the police dispatcher, who contacted the patrolman on duty and the Chicago police department. *Id*. at 1264. Six hours after the initial call was made by the conductor, the plaintiff's decedent was taken to the hospital, where he died the next day from a brain injury. *Id*. at 1266.

In *Rhodes*, the plaintiff alleged that the defendant Railroad voluntarily undertook a duty to aid plaintiff's decedent and did so negligently by failing to follow up on the Chicago police department's response to its call. *Id*. at 1273. However, the Illinois Supreme Court found no voluntary undertaking on the part of ICG which gave rise to a duty. *Id*. The court held that, at most, the defendant Railroad undertook to report plaintiff's decedent's presence to the Chicago police department and performed that undertaking by placing several calls to that department. *Id*. The Illinois Supreme Court found "nothing to indicate that ICG, by that action, voluntarily undertook to do anything more, such as ensuring that aid would be provided." *Id*.

Furthermore, the court in the *Rhodes* case noted as follows:

> As a matter of public policy, we do not think it appropriate to hold that a party voluntarily undertakes a legal duty to rescue an injured stranger by simply calling the police. Such a holding would discourage citizens from taking even this most basic action to obtain assistance for an injured stranger. We therefore reject the appellate court's voluntary undertaking theory as a basis for ICG liability in this case.

Id.

> Accordingly, plaintiff's argument goes against public policy because it would discourage people from helping those in need by making them fearful of legal liability.

Readers who skipped the quote (and many would) would have no way of knowing where the writer's "accordingly" came from. Even readers who read the quote would have to figure out for themselves the significance of the quoted language, not to mention who "ICG" was. If you are tempted to use a lengthy quotation, try one of two tactics to help ensure that your readers will understand your message.

The first and perhaps most obvious solution is to try to shorten the quote. Start by underlining the language that is most significant to your argument:

> As a matter of <u>public policy</u>, we do not think it appropriate to hold that a party voluntarily undertakes a legal duty to rescue an <u>injured stranger by simply calling the police</u>. Such a holding would <u>discourage citizens from taking even this most basic action to obtain assistance for an injured stranger</u>. We therefore reject the appellate court's voluntary undertaking theory as a basis for ICG's liability in this case.

Then, quote only the underlined material (after removing the underlining), and incorporate a paraphrase of the rest of the quotation into your argument. The revised example below also shortens the case description by using words economically and incorporating multiple concepts into each sentence as appropriate.

Better Example
Calling the police to report an injured person, without more, does not constitute voluntarily assuming a duty. *See Rhodes v.*

Illinois Central Gulf Railroad, 665 N.E.2d 1260, 1273 (Ill. 1996). The defendant in *Rhodes* was a railroad whose employees had informed the police, via several phone calls, of passenger reports that a person was lying in the train company's unattended waiting room station. *Id.* at 1263. Six hours after the initial call was made by a conductor, the plaintiff's decedent was taken to the hospital, where he died the next day from a brain injury. *Id.* at 1266. The Illinois Supreme Court found defendant had not participated in any voluntary undertaking that gave rise to a duty to follow-up with the police. *Id.*

In rejecting the plaintiff's argument, the court observed that public policy favors a rule that encourages people to report injured persons to the police, noting that, "[a]s a matter of public policy . . . simply calling the police" should not create a legal duty to rescue. *Id.* The court believed that imposing liability in those circumstances would "discourage citizens from taking even this most basic action to obtain assistance for an injured stranger." *Id.*

Accordingly, plaintiff's argument goes against public policy because imposing liability on defendants in this case would discourage people from helping those in need by making them fearful of legal liability.

In the alternative, you may determine that the lengthy quote is absolutely necessary for your argument. If this is the case, promote the effectiveness of the quotation by articulating the conclusions you want the reader to draw from it and putting those conclusions into the body of your argument. We recommend using what we refer to as an *NPR Introduction* before the quotation.

An NPR Introduction is an introduction that focuses the reader's attention on the point the writer is using the quotation to prove or establish. We call it that because of the way in which reporters on NPR and other broadcast outlets constantly introduce little snippets of interviews or public events. In much the same way, a long quote is a little snippet of an opinion or other legal document. Legal writers, unfortunately, often give readers unfocused introductions like, "The Court noted," or, as in the previous illustration, "the court in the *Rhodes* case noted as follows." In contrast, newscasters almost never give introductions like, "The President said," or "The Senator noted." Instead, they give the audience some context and essentially tell them what to listen for when they hear the quoted language.

The illustration below is from a broadcast in which a reporter on *Morning Edition* on NPR excerpted pieces of interviews with people who had knowledge of changes in climate in Mongolia. One particular change in the climate, referred to as a *dzud*, refers to five types of extreme winter weather that made it much more difficult for Mongolian herders to maintain their livelihoods; the *dzuds* led many to move to the city from the country. The excerpt below focuses on discord at a UN Programme as to the impact of the *dzuds*. Notice how the (italicized) language leading up to the final quotation paraphrases the message of the quote to prepare the audience for what is to come:

Good Example

"There is a tragedy of the commons happening in Mongolia," says Tungalag Ulambayar, a dzud researcher and Mongolia country director for the Zoological Society of London. "The primary role of institutions is to restrict people's actions. You can't do whatever you want. You have to obey traffic laws. The same issue applies to rangeland management."

During the 2009-2010 dzud, Tungalag oversaw a disaster response team for the United Nations Development Programme. *At first, she says, her colleagues in Geneva were wary of characterizing dzuds as natural disasters.*

"'Shelters weren't destroyed. No one died. So it's not a disaster,' they said. And we said, 'No, it is a disaster. Someone is losing total livelihood, and that causes huge psychological trauma to human well-being.'"

In the same way, you should prepare your audience for a long quotation by stating the conclusion you want the reader to draw from it:

Better Example

The Illinois Supreme Court has refused to find that persons assume a duty to protect an injured stranger when they inform the police about the injured stranger. *Rhodes v. Illinois Cent. Gulf R.R.*, 665 N.E.2d 1260, 1273 (Ill. 1996). The court based this opinion on the public policy that it is good for bystanders to seek assistance for people who are injured:

> As a matter of public policy, we do not think it appropriate to hold that a party voluntarily undertakes a legal duty to rescue an injured stranger by simply calling the police. Such a holding would discourage citizens from taking even this

most basic action to obtain assistance for an injured stranger. We therefore reject the appellate court's voluntary undertaking theory as a basis for [defendant]'s liability in this case.

Id. Accordingly, plaintiff's argument goes against public policy because imposing liability on defendants in this case would discourage people from helping those in need by making them fearful of legal liability.

Use an NPR Introduction to help the reader to get the most out of lengthy quotations. The focused introduction will encourage the reader to read the quote by directing the reader's attention and making it easier to understand the point of the quotation. Even if the reader does skip the quote, the writer has still articulated the point of the quotation in a place that increases the likelihood that the reader will see it and in a way that the reader can understand.

6.6. USING LANGUAGE PRECISELY WHEN ANALOGIZING AND DISTINGUISHING CASES

As we noted in an earlier chapter, writing a good rule application section does not require you to analogize or disanalogize each case you cited in the rule explanation section. When used appropriately, however, analogies and dis-analogies can be an effective part of rule application. By showing the reader how a case is like or unlike a relevant case, a writer can convince the reader to apply the rule in a way that will achieve the desired result. Note that your application section *should not begin* with the analogy or distinction. Instead, begin with an explicit assertion about how the law applies to the facts (generally, "phrase-that-pays equals or does not equal case facts"). Use the relevant cases as needed to support that assertion. Do not begin your application this way:

Bad Example of Beginning of Rule Application
This case is like *McGuffin*.

Instead, begin by telling the reader how the law applies to the facts:

Better Example of Beginning of Rule Application
Mr. Pillion had not voluntarily assumed a duty to protect the Plaintiff. He had merely come upon an injured person while out jogging, and he called the police so that the person could be helped. Like the defendant in *McGuffin*, Pillion . . .

Your case analogies and distinctions will be most effective if they are *precise*. Do not analogize a specific fact to a whole case:

Bad Examples
Like *Rhodes*, the Defendant here had merely contacted the police.

Like the situation in *Rhodes*, the Defendant here had merely contacted the police.

Like in *Rhodes*, the Defendant here had merely contacted the police.

These comparisons are inapt because one defendant, by definition, cannot be "like" a whole case, or a whole situation. Focus your analogy or distinction on the narrow category that you are comparing or contrasting. Compare defendants to defendants, and other actors and things to their specific counterparts in the authority case. These illustrations make the comparisons explicit:

Better Examples
In the present case, Defendant, like the defendant employees in *Rhodes*, had merely contacted the police after he became aware of an injured stranger.

Like the warming shed in *Rhodes*, the defendant's bus shelter was not an inherently dangerous location.

Unlike the train tracks at issue in *Rosmarin*, a bus shelter is not an inherently dangerous location.

These examples also provide details from the client's case that make the analogies and disanalogies vivid. The writer must do more than make the bare statement that "this case is like (or unlike) *McGuffin*" if the reader is to see the connection or the disconnection between the two cases. In the next example, the writer takes care to provide the details that will clarify the distinctions between the two cases:

Good Example
In this case, the Village Clerk did nothing more than alert police to the possibility of an injury. Like the passengers who alerted defendant employees in *Rhodes*, in this case, an anonymous person called the Sirius Village Clerk to report that a truck had driven off a roadway and into a ditch. (See Plaintiff's Amended Complaint, C57.) The Village Clerk then relayed that information

to the Morgan County Sheriff's Department, (C48) which eventually notified the Block Island County Sheriff's Department. (C45). The only voluntary action undertaken by Sirius Village and its Village Clerk was to pass along to the Sheriff's Department the accident report regarding plaintiff's decedent. Like the record regarding the defendant employees in *Rhodes*, the record here contains no facts that indicate that either the Village Clerk or Sirius Village voluntarily undertook to do anything more.

Therefore, neither the Village nor the Village Clerk can be liable to Plaintiff for any failure to provide aid to the Plaintiff's decedent.

This application provides the details necessary for the reader to understand how the law applies to the facts, and it uses analogy to highlight the client's important facts.

Analogies and distinctions are not always needed. Some legal writers believe that if you have cited a case in the rule explanation, you must analogize or distinguish it in the rule application. We disagree with that philosophy. If the connection between the authority case and your client's case is obvious, you may waste the reader's time by presenting a belabored analogy or distinction.

Bad Example
Like the defendant in *McGuffin*, who met the relevant standard due to his three previous convictions, the defendant here has also met the relevant standard due to his four previous convictions.

Better Example
The enhanced sentencing rule applies to the defendant. It provides that "any prior conviction that has not been invalidated" will result in an enhanced sentence. Because all four of the defendant's previous convictions are currently valid, this court should impose an enhanced sentence on the defendant.

Save analogies and distinctions for situations in which there is some nuance to the rule, its application, or the connection (or lack of connection) between your client's case and the relevant authority case:

Better Example
Vanita's enhanced sentencing standard requires the state to establish that the defendant has a "significant criminal record" to even be eligible for enhanced sentencing. Unlike the defendant in *McGuffin*, who had three felony convictions—two of them for

violent felonies—the defendant's four convictions are all for misdemeanors, and three of these are traffic-related misdemeanors. Accordingly, there is no reason to conclude that defendant has a "significant criminal record," and this court should find that he is not eligible for enhanced sentencing.

Thus, before providing analogies or distinctions, make sure that they are worth the reader's time. When you do include them, focus them on the specific people or things that you want to compare. Second, make sure that you provide the details that allow the reader to understand both the comparison and the application of law to facts.

6.7. CONCLUSION

If you do litigation writing, you will spend a lot of your time citing to case authority. Use this chapter to learn the most effective ways to give your readers the right amount of information about those cases, and to provide it in the most efficient and effective way possible.

Persuasion with Statutes as Authority

When most legal writers think about authority for arguments, they think first about cases. This is especially true in the civil context because we think of most civil claims as being based in common law. While it is true that contracts and torts claims rely mostly on case law, many civil law claims find their origins in statutes. And virtually all arguments in criminal law cases are based on statutes or constitutional provisions. So, in either the civil or the criminal context, a writer will often engage with statutory law as well as case law.

Let's say that you have identified a statute that impacts a claim you are making or opposing on behalf of a client. Let's also say that you know that statutory interpretation begins with the plain meaning of the statute's language. You might erroneously assume that you must head off on a completely different path than the one you would take were no statute involved. In the case-law-only scenario, you would look for cases, preferably from courts whose decisions are mandatory authority for you, that establish or clarify rules governing the relevant claim. We are here to tell you that the research path you will follow when a statute applies is the same for the most part, although the existence of the statute adds a preliminary step and some possible additional avenues for argument that don't exist in the case-law-only scenario. We'll get to those differences soon.

For now, remember that the search through cases for guidance in interpreting statute-based rules is still the biggest part of your task.

You already know that statutes are *primary* authorities and that they are *mandatory* authorities within the jurisdictions in which they are enacted. If a statute governs the legal question you are analyzing, you will not have to look far to find the starting point for your research: the statutory language. The language of the statute is rarely the ending point, however.

In this chapter, we will identify some of the methods you will pursue to enlighten yourself and your reader when you are working with the mandatory authority of a statute. You may already have encountered a hierarchy of approaches to statutory interpretation, beginning with the plain meaning of the statute's language and continuing through judicial interpretations, legislative history, policy implications, canons of construction, and occasionally other considerations. Lawyers use these tools to interpret statutes because courts have told us that these are the appropriate ways to learn what statutory language means. In fact, when courts interpret statutes, they begin with plain meaning and progress, as appropriate and necessary, through the other tools they have identified.

So, before we begin to consider how you might construct an argument when a statute governs or impacts the claim, let's look at how a court applies the statutory interpretation tools. A useful example is the United States Supreme Court case *Marx v. General Revenue Corp.* 568 U.S. 371 (2013), a student loan case in which the Court explicitly worked through several of the means of statutory construction. The Court analyzed certain language in the Fair Debt Collection Practices Act.

We will reproduce parts of that opinion here to illustrate our discussion of persuasive writing when statutes are the authority or an authority. Perusing this excerpt and our annotations should give you a good introduction to methods courts use when they analyze statutes:

> **1** As in all statutory construction cases, we "'assum[e] that the ordinary meaning of [the statutory] language accurately expresses the legislative purpose.'" *Hardt v. Reliance Standard Life Ins. Co.*, 560 U.S. 242, 251 (quoting *Gross v. FBL Financial Services, Inc.*, 557 U.S. 167, 175 (2009)) (alteration in original).
>
> * * *
>
> **2** As the Tenth Circuit correctly recognized, Rule 54(d)(1) codifies a venerable presumption that prevailing parties are entitled to costs. Notwithstanding this presumption, the word "should" makes

1 The Court begins with *plain meaning*, which it calls "ordinary meaning." Because plain meaning is the Court's starting point, you will often begin arguments based on statutes with the plain meaning of the statutory language in question.

2 If the plain meaning of a statutory phrase has often been the subject of earlier litigation, courts may have already settled on the plain meaning of the words that concern you. In other instances, you may find that courts have not agreed on whether the meaning is plain or that they have agreed that the meaning is plain but not on what that "plain" meaning is.

clear that the decision whether to award costs ultimately lies within the sound discretion of the district court. *See Taniguchi v. Kan Pacific Saipan, Ltd.*, 566 U.S. 560, 565 (2012).

* * *

3 Prior to the adoption of the Federal Rules, prevailing parties were entitled to costs as of right in actions at law while courts had discretion to award costs in equity proceedings. *See Ex parte Peterson*, 253 U. S. 300, 317-318 (1920).

* * *

4 Marx and the United States as *amicus curiae* suggest that any statute that specifically provides for costs displaces Rule 54(d)(1), regardless of whether it is contrary to the Rule. Brief for Petitioner 17; Brief for United States as *Amicus Curiae* 11-12 (hereinafter Brief for United States). The United States relies on the original 1937 version of Rule 54(d)(1), which provided, "Except when express provision therefor is made either in a statute of the United States or in these rules, costs shall be allowed as of course to the prevailing party unless the court otherwise directs.'" *Id.*, at 12 (quoting Rule). Though the Rules Committee updated the language of Rule 54(d)(1) in 2007, the change was "stylistic only." Advisory Committee's Notes, 28 U.S.C. App., p. 734 (2006 ed., Supp. V). Accordingly, the United States asserts that any "express provision" for costs should displace Rule 54(d)(1).

We are not persuaded, however, that the original version of Rule 54(d) should be interpreted as Marx and the United States suggest. The original language was meant to ensure that Rule 54(d) did not displace existing costs provisions that were contrary to the Rule. Under the prior language, statutes that simply permitted a court to award costs did not displace the Rule.

* * *

5 General Revenue contends that the statute does not address whether costs may be awarded in this case—where the plaintiff brought the case in good faith—and thus it does not set forth a standard for awarding costs that is contrary to Rule 54(d)(1). In its view, Congress intended § 1692k(a)(3) to deter plaintiffs from bringing nuisance lawsuits. It, therefore, expressly provided that when plaintiffs bring an action in bad faith and for the purpose of harassment, the court may award attorney's fees and costs to the defendant. The statute does address this type of case—i.e., cases in which the plaintiff brings the action in bad faith and for the purpose of harassment. But it is silent where bad faith and purpose of harassment

3 Here, the Court addresses legislative history, focusing on the status of the law prior to the enactment of the statute (a federal rule). Legislative history often includes information about what a legislature or its members said, did, or considered when they proposed or debated legislation. It may also include a common law rule that the statute was meant to codify or to amend.

4 Statutory amendments are a form of legislative history that can show legislative intent. Note both (1) how the language has been amended and (2) pre- and post-amendment court decisions about the statute's meaning.

5 As indicated here, legislative silence is often at the root of statutory ambiguity. Likewise, if a court amends a statute after it has been interpreted many times, but does NOT amend language that has been interpreted, that silence — i.e., that refusal to amend — can also be significant.

are absent, and silence does not displace the background rule that a court has discretion to award costs.

6 Canons of statutory construction are generally accepted principles, but not laws. Like any other legal principle, if a court applies it, it becomes law in that context. Courts may turn to canons of construction after analyzing plain meaning and legislative history. There are too many canons to list here, but commonly-applied canons are *expressio unius* (seen here), *in pari materia*, and *ejusdem generis*. The names of canons can be good search terms, but courts seesaw between English and Latin phrasing and may use their own phrasing. You will encounter many other canons as you read cases; in fact, we began this chapter with one: the plain meaning canon.

6 Marx and the United States take the contrary view. They concede that the language does not expressly limit a court's discretion to award costs under Rule 54(d)(1), Brief for Petitioner 10; Brief for United States 19, but argue that it does so by negative implication. Invoking the *expressio unius* canon of statutory construction, they contend that by specifying that a court may award attorney's fees and costs when an action is brought in bad faith and for the purpose of harassment, Congress intended to preclude a court from awarding fees and costs when bad faith and purpose of harassment are absent. They further argue that unless § 1692k(a)(3) sets forth the exclusive basis on which a court may award costs, the phrase "and costs" would be superfluous. According to this argument, Congress would have had no reason to specify that a court may award costs when a plaintiff brings an action in bad faith if it could have nevertheless awarded costs under Rule 54(d)(1). Finally, the United States argues that § 1692k(a)(3) is a more specific cost statute that displaces Rule 54(d)(1)'s more general rule.

The context surrounding § 1692k(a)(3) persuades us that General Revenue's interpretation is correct.

* * *

7 Courts commonly analyze similar language in other statutes, if they find a legally significant similarity in either the statutes themselves or in the language at issue. Thus, when doing statutory research, search for the language at issue in other statutes that may have a meaningful connection.

7 Finally, the language in § 1692k(a)(3) sharply contrasts with other statutes in which Congress has placed conditions on awarding costs to prevailing defendants. *See, e.g.,* 28 U.S.C § 1928 ("[N]o costs shall be included in such judgment, *unless* the proper disclaimer has been filed in the United States Patent and Trademark Office prior to the commencement of the action" (emphasis added)); 42 U.S.C § 1988(b) ("[I]n any action brought against a judicial officer . . . such officer shall not be held liable for any costs . . . *unless* such action was clearly in excess of such officer's jurisdiction" (emphasis added)).

* * *

As the above discussion suggests, we also are not persuaded by Marx's objection that our interpretation renders the phrase "and costs" superfluous. As noted, *supra*, at 383, the phrase "and costs" would not be superfluous if Congress included it to remove doubt that defendants may recover costs when plaintiffs bring suits in bad faith. But even assuming that our interpretation renders the phrase "and costs" superfluous, that would not alter our conclusion.

The canon against surplusage ⑧ is not an absolute rule, *see Arlington Central School Dist. Bd. of Ed. v. Murphy*, 548 U.S. 291, 299, n. 1 (2006) ("While it is generally presumed that statutes do not contain surplusage, instances of surplusage are not unknown"); *Connecticut Nat. Bank v. Germain*, 503 U.S. 249, 253 (1992) ("Redundancies across statutes are not unusual events in drafting . . . "), and it has considerably less force in this case.

First, the canon against surplusage "assists only where a competing interpretation gives effect to every clause and word of a statute." *Microsoft Corp. v. i4i Ltd. P'ship*, 564 U.S. 91, 106 (2011) (internal quotation marks omitted). But, in this case, no interpretation of § 1692k(a)(3) gives effect to every word. Both Marx and the United States admit that a court has inherent power to award attorney's fees to a defendant when the plaintiff brings an action in bad faith. Because there was, consequently, no need for Congress to specify that courts have this power, § 1692k(a)(3) is superfluous insofar as it addresses attorney's fees. In light of this redundancy, we are not overly concerned that the reference to costs may be redundant as well.

Second, redundancy is "hardly unusual" in statutes addressing costs.

* * *

Finally, the canon against surplusage is strongest when an interpretation would render superfluous another part of the same statutory scheme.

* * *

⑨ Lastly, the United States contends that § 1692k(a)(3) "establishes explicit cost-shifting standards that displace Rule 54(d)(1)'s more general default standard." Brief for United States 17; see also *EC Term of Years Trust v. United States*, 550 U.S. 429, 433 (2007) ("'[A] precisely drawn, detailed statute pre-empts more general remedies'" (quoting *Brown v. GSA*, 425 U.S. 820, 834 (1976))). Were we to accept the argument that § 1692k(a)(3) has a negative implication, this argument might be persuasive. But the context of §1692k(a)(3) indicates that Congress was simply confirming the background rule that courts may award to defendants attorney's fees and costs when the plaintiff brings an action in bad faith. The statute speaks to one type of case—the case of the bad-faith and harassing plaintiff. Because Marx did not bring this suit in bad faith, this case does not "fal[l] within the ambit of the more specific provision." Brief for United States 13; *see also RadLAX Gateway Hotel, LLC v. Amalgamated Bank*, 566 U.S. 639,648 (2012) ("When the conduct at issue falls

---

⑧ The canon against surplusage prefers an interpretation that gives meaning to all words in a statute over one that would make some of the words meaningless (or "surplus"). Courts must often reconcile so-called *dueling canons*, i.e., canons that would lead to opposite results.

⑨ In so-called "policy analysis," courts interpret statutory language by identifying a statute's purpose or underlying policy, choosing the meaning that best serves that purpose or policy. When a legislature has not explicitly identified a statute's purpose, opinions can become a free-for-all of competing policies. When courts must choose between dueling canons, a policy analysis may be the tie-breaker.

within the scope of *both* provisions, the specific presumptively governs . . ." (emphasis in original)). Accordingly, this canon is inapplicable.

Marx, the United States, and General Revenue also spar over the purpose of § 1692k(a)(3). Brief for Petitioner 14-16; Brief for United States 21-28; Reply Brief 11-14; Brief for Respondent 30-43. Marx and the United States contend that Congress intended to limit a court's discretion to award costs to prevailing defendants because Debt Practices Act plaintiffs are often poor and may be deterred from challenging unlawful debt collection practices by the possibility of being held liable for the defendant's costs. This purposive argument cannot overcome the language and context of § 1692k(a)(3), but even if it could, we find it unpersuasive. Rule 54(d)(1) does not *require* courts to award costs to prevailing defendants. District courts may appropriately consider a Debt Practices Act plaintiff's indigency in deciding whether to award costs. *See Badillo v. Central Steel & Wire Co.*, 717 F.2d 1160, 1165 (7th Cir. 1983) ("[I]t is within the discretion of the district court to consider a plaintiff's indigency in denying costs under Rule 54(d).").

7.1. THE "HIERARCHY" OF STATUTORY INTERPRETATION

As you have seen, when courts write about statutory interpretation, they often set out a list of means or methods of interpretation. These methods include the following:

(a) conducting *exegesis*, or analysis, of the *plain meaning* of the language;
(b) interpreting the words and phrases used in the statute by reference to definitions in statutory and common law;
(c) clarifying the meaning of the statute by observing how it has been applied by courts;
(d) examining legislative history to ascertain the intent of the legislature that enacted it;
(e) considering canons of construction and the policy underlying the statute; and
(f) looking for analogous statutes and interpretations.

You might think of all of these methods as tools in a toolbox. You will use some of these tools every time you work with a statute: plain meaning and case-law or statutory definitions, for example. You will pull out others, including, for example, canons of construction, legislative history, and policy, only when the main tools do not resolve your questions definitively *and* favorably. You will use these tools in the rule explanation portion of your analysis. Sometimes you will merely be explaining how courts have applied that statute. At other times, you will be showing how courts have used the tools in the toolbox to interpret statutes that are similar or statutes that have similar features. Sometimes, your goal will be to identify a rule you want the court to use to interpret the statute (as with the rule-choice rule we discussed earlier, in Chapter Five). At other times, you will use the rule explanation to support a thesis about how the statute should be interpreted. Your overall goal is always to show that the method of interpretation, or the interpretation itself, will lead to an interpretation of the statutory language that is consistent with public policy, legislative purpose, or both.

7.2. STATUTORY AND CASE-LAW DEFINITIONS

The first stage of your search for the meaning of a word or phrase in a statute is research for authority defining the word or phrase. That search begins in the statute containing the word or phrase, but it will often also lead you to case law and general statutory provisions. Below, we will illustrate each possible aspect of that search.

7.2.1. Plain Meaning and Definitions in the Statute Itself

The starting point for the interpretation of any statute is its *plain meaning*. Courts routinely say that they give effect to the plain meaning of the statute when that meaning is evident from an ordinary understanding of the words and phrases chosen by the legislative body that enacted it. When you interpret any statute, you should begin by thinking about the ordinary understanding of the words and phrases and whether they are open to various interpretations. Often, you will have a clear, general understanding of what each word and phrase means as a layperson would interpret it. You may also recognize that a word or phrase in a statute may have a very different impact depending upon how it is interpreted.

A common-sense interpretation of the text rarely ends the inquiry for a court, and it should never end your inquiry as you conduct research into the proper interpretation and application of the statute. In other words, your argument about the meaning of words, without support, will not convince the court. So, while you must address plain meaning at the beginning of any argument about the language of a statute, you will be on the safest footing after you have located authority for the interpretation that best serves your argument.

If you are like most educated people, your first thought about the best authority for the meaning of words is "dictionary." We're sorry. While courts sometimes cite dictionaries when they assign meanings to words, they are courts, and you are a non-court. As a non-court, you should stick to legal authority whenever it exists. The first legal authority you should consult is *the statute itself*.

Here is an example: suppose that you represent a client who has been sued for violating provisions of the Fair Debt Collections Practices Act, the federal statute that was the subject of *Marx v. General Revenue Corp.* Your client has attempted to collect a debt that is owed to it by making frequent telephone calls to the debtor's place of employment. The debtor claims that your client has violated the Act by engaging in abusive telephone harassment.

Once you have located the statute, your first thought is likely to discover whether repeated telephone calls to an employer may violate the Act. Searching the statute, you find this provision: "a debt collector may not communicate with a consumer in connection with the collection of any debt . . . at the consumer's place of employment if the debt collector knows or has reason to know that the consumer's employer prohibits the consumer from receiving such communication."[1] You recognize that, depending upon the debtor's employer's policies, telephone calls at work may violate the Act.

The next question you may have is whether your client is a *debt collector*. If you were to apply a common-sense understanding of the two words that make up the phrase, you would likely conclude that your client is covered by the Act because it acted to collect a debt. A quick flip through a dictionary would back you up. Because you know something about statutory interpretation, however, you are pretty sure that you can't stop there.

This is where a very important part of your due diligence comes in. When legislatures enact new laws, they often also enact definitions for important terms in the laws. Obviously, these statutory definitions are very helpful to you as a lawyer attempting to interpret the law. When you are working with a claim based on a statute, you always hope that the legislature has defined the words or phrases that will determine whether, and how, the statute affects your client.

---

1. 15 U.S.C. § 1692a(6).

So, instead of thinking about the search for statutory definitions as a time-consuming nuisance, you will think of it as a treasure hunt.

Statutory definitions sometimes appear in the same section of the law as the substantive provisions, but, more commonly, they appear in a separate section at the beginning or the end of a group of sections covering related topics. In the Fair Debt Collection Practices Act, the definitions appear in a separate section near the beginning of the group of sections that make up the entire Act. Having found the definitions section, our hypothetical selves are thrilled to discover that Congress has enacted a definition of "debt collector": "any person who uses any instrumentality of interstate commerce or the mails in any business the principal purpose of which is the collection of any debts, or who regularly collects or attempts to collect, directly or indirectly, debts owed or due or asserted to be owed or due another." This definition gives us a ray of hope that our client may not be a debt collector because it was collecting its own debts; it did not attempt to collect debts *owed or due to another*.

Our search is not finished. As you remember, we said that the research path you will follow when you work with a statute is much the same as the path you would follow when a statute does not govern or affect your claim. Do you also remember that we said that the path in the statutory law scenario includes a preliminary step? We have now completed the preliminary step: we have identified at least some of the key words or phrases that the statute includes, and we learned that the statute defines the phrase that we found. We are not ready to construct an argument, but we know what at least part of the argument will be about: the words "owed or due to another." We are now ready to step onto the familiar case law research path.

7.2.2. Judicial Interpretations of Statutory Definitions

Whether you have found a definition in the statute itself or not, your efforts at interpreting a word or phrase in a statute are not complete before you have looked for judicial authority interpreting those words. You are looking for cases in which courts have interpreted the same words in the same statute or, failing that, the same words in similar statutes. So, for example, if your position in a case requires you to argue that the word "knowledge" in a statute means "active or real awareness," your research goal is to find cases in which courts have interpreted the word "knowledge" in the same statute to have that meaning. If you are successful, you will be able to argue effectively that the plain meaning of "knowledge" in the statute is "active and real awareness." Your authority is the plain meaning of the word *as interpreted by a court or courts*. You would look for this judicial authority even if the statute includes a definition in order to discover whether courts have applied the definition from the statute as you believe it will be applied.

10 Statute numbers can be great search terms. Because *1692a(6)* will rarely occur other than within a discussion of that statute, it can be a main feature of a strong Boolean search. Note that if a statute is referred to by a common name in addition to a number, you should add *or [common name]* to your search.

10 Even definitions enacted by a legislature are open to interpretation, and a careful lawyer will always conduct research to learn how courts have treated the legislature's definition. Because we are working with statutory law, we know one useful search term: the statute number. Our search for judicial interpretations of "debt collector" on behalf of the client attempting to collect its own debt would begin with a search for cases using the statute number 15 U.S.C. § 1692a(6).

The other useful search term would be one that limits search results to cases in which the party attempting to collect the debt also owns the debt. Although lay people seldom talk about "owning" debt, that term is the one that is used by debt collectors, and therefore courts. Accordingly, "own!" within three words of "debt" (own! /3 debt) is a good starting point because it will capture cases using the noun *owner*, the verb *to own*, and the modifier *owned* or *own*. Conducting this search in the United States Supreme Court and United States Court of Appeals databases yields a number of helpful cases, including the recent Supreme Court case *Henson v. Santander Consumer USA Inc.*, 137 S. Ct. 1718 (2017), in which the Court engaged in a lengthy plain-meaning analysis and concluded that Congress intended to exclude the owners of debts from the definition of "debt collector." The Court's interpretation of the statute means that our client is not subject to the prohibitions of § 1692a(6) of the Fair Debt Collection Practices Act, and we can cite the mandatory authority of that statute and *Henson* in support of a motion to dismiss the claim.

Wonderful, isn't it? Statutes are so easy. Well, wait a second. The meaning of this statute was pretty easy to nail down, but legislatures and courts are not always so helpful.

First, legislatures do not always include definition sections in the laws they pass. Even when they do include a definition section, they do not always define every term that may be the subject of litigation. And, if you are lucky enough to find a statutory definition for the word or phrase in question, that definition may not be as clear as it could be.

Second, it is not always easy to find cases that analyze the words and phrases we want them to. We were lucky with this search; in the *Henson* debt collection case, the Supreme Court engaged in a multi-page analysis of the meaning of the *definition* of "debt collector." Even though the statute defined "debt collector," the plaintiff argued that the definition does not mean what it appears to mean by the words "debts owed or due or asserted to be owed or due another" but instead means any debt owed to any other person, including the person collecting the debt.[2] The Court rejected that argument.

If you were researching this issue in real life, you could end your research now. If *Henson* is still good law, you will argue that the plain meaning of the statute excludes your client from the definition of "debt collector." You will cite the definition from the statute and *Henson* as mandatory authority for that definition. Your CRAC or CREXAC argument will begin with the conclusion that the section of the Fair Debt Collection Practices Act on which the plaintiff relies does not apply to your client because your client is not a debt collector. The rule will be that an entity attempting to collect its own debt is not a debt collector for purposes of the statute. The application will follow from there. You have been lucky.

What if you are not so lucky, and no mandatory authority has defined the relevant terms from your statute? You may still find guidance from statutes and case law. Your search will require more creativity, however.

7.2.3. Definitions from General Provisions

Suppose that the statute that governs or affects your claim does not include a definition for a critical word or phrase. You may be thinking that your search for a definition now turns to cases, but you would be wrong. In fact, your search for mandatory statutory authority is not complete and may yet yield fruit. An example from a Nevada statute will help to illustrate the next step of your search.

Assume that you represent a young client who opposes the division of her high school into two separate schools in response to overcrowding. The student posted a vague warning about an "explosion" at the school on social media. She included words suggesting that the school board was going to cause the explosion and urged readers to attend the upcoming school board meeting where the board would hear opposition to the plan. The student is now charged with making a threat of terrorism under Nevada Revised Statutes § 202.448, which prohibits a person from "knowingly" using a means of written communication to make a threat of an act of terrorism.

Once again, your efforts would begin with the plain meaning of the relevant language from the statute. You recognize that the definition of "knowingly" is likely to be critical to the outcome of the charge against your client because she did not intend to make a threat of an act of terrorism but only to galvanize opposition to the

---

2. 15 U.S.C. § 1692a(6).

impending division of the high school. In essence, she would argue that she may have accidentally implied a threat of terrorism but that she did not do so intentionally. So, you hope that the statute has defined "knowingly" to require a form of intent or at least active awareness. Alas, § 202.448 does not define "knowingly." So, your efforts have not panned out as they did in the search for a definition of "debt collector." Still, you should not abandon the search for statutory definitions.

You went to law school and studied criminal law, so you know that criminal statutes are full of variations of the word "knowingly." You may wonder whether "knowingly" has the same meaning whenever it is used in Nevada criminal law. The answer is "maybe," and the place to look is the general statutory provisions.

11 Regulations are another potential source of mandatory authority defining statutory language. State and federal departments, commissions, and agencies are executive branch bodies that may "promulgate" regulations to give effect to statutes; legislatures often delegate definitional tasks to these bodies. Definitions in regulations are mandatory authority to the extent that they do not conflict with the language of the statute. Cite them as you would cite a statute, and look for cases in which courts have applied the regulatory definition. Chapter Two offers guidance on finding relevant regulations.

11 A *general provision* is a statute that applies broadly to a set of more specific provisions. A classic example is a set of definitions that apply throughout the criminal law of a state (to the extent that they do not contradict the language of a specific provision). In your case involving the terrorism charge, you would be looking for a Nevada statute that provides definitions to be applied throughout Nevada criminal law. And, you are in luck. Nevada Revised Statutes § 193.017 provides a definition that applies to all Nevada criminal statutes that include "knowledge" as an element and do not define "knowledge" internally: knowledge is defined as "knowledge that the facts exist which constitute the act or omission of a crime, and does not require knowledge of its unlawfulness." The definitional statute further provides that knowledge of a fact may be inferred from the knowledge of such other facts as should put an ordinarily prudent person upon inquiry. So, as we did in the "debt collector" scenario, we have a statutory definition, although its source is a general provision and not the specific statute defining the crime. The general provision is still mandatory authority, however. Your research now moves onto the familiar path of case law research—or in this situation, two paths: you need to learn how the Nevada courts have interpreted "knowingly" in Nevada Revised Statutes § 202.448 and how they have applied the definition of "knowledge" from Nevada Revised Statutes § 193.017.

7.2.4. Definitions from Case Law

So far, our search for mandatory authority defining important words or phrases in statutes has taken us to the statutes themselves and to general statutory provisions, and we have been lucky enough to find answers there. Sometimes, however, we will not be so lucky. Even when legislative bodies do not help us by defining the critical terms, however, our search for definitions in mandatory authority is not complete. Sometimes courts enter the vacuum created by legislative inaction by providing their own definitions for statutory language. When the decisions of those courts are mandatory authority, we may rely on their definitions in constructing our arguments based on the meaning of the words or phrases.

Once again, allow us to illustrate. Suppose that your young client who opposes the division of her high school faces the same charge under Nevada law. Let's assume that Nevada statutes do not include the general provision defining "knowledge." In the absence of any statutory definition, our search for a definition in mandatory authority turns to judicial interpretations of the statute. We are not just looking for cases in which courts have applied the statute; instead, we are looking for a case in which a court whose decisions are mandatory authority has told us what "knowingly" means as it is used in Nevada Revised Statutes § 202.448. Our search includes the statute number and "knowingly" as terms.

If we are lucky, our search will identify a case in which the court has defined "knowingly." Let's say that we have found a case from the Nevada Supreme Court called *State v. Celeste* in which the court held that the word "knowingly" in § 202.448 means "intentionally." Assuming that the court has applied that definition to resolve the case before it, we can rely on the court's definition, as well as the language of the statute itself, as mandatory authority for an argument that our client did not violate the statute because she did not intend to make a threat of terrorism. The rule portion of our argument might look something like this: "The statute requires that the state prove that the defendant acted 'knowingly,' and knowledge requires intent to make a threat of terrorism." We would cite the statute and *State v. Celeste*.

If we are less lucky and do not find a case from a court whose decisions are mandatory authority, we may still find support for our argument from a judicial definition. Suppose that our search for mandatory case-law authority has been fruitless. We should not abandon the search until we have also looked at persuasive case-law authority interpreting "knowingly" in § 202.448. If we were to find, for example, a decision from a Nevada trial court defining the term as requiring intent, we would be able to cite the language of the statute as mandatory authority and the trial court decision as persuasive authority for an interpretation of "knowingly" that requires intent. The rule portion of our argument might look something like this: "The statute requires that the state prove that the defendant acted 'knowingly,' and, while the Nevada Supreme Court has not considered the question, at least one lower Nevada court has defined 'knowingly' to require intent." We would cite the statute and the trial court decision.

In summary, words and phrases do not always mean what they appear to mean. Thus, even if you believe that you understand exactly what a statute means upon carefully considering its language, your inquiry cannot stop there. The interpretation of the statute will often lead to an understanding of the words and phrases that is very different from the plain meaning. Accordingly, your task is to determine what those words and phrases mean as they are used in the statute. You will look to various sources in order to identify those as-used definitions. The first two are (1) definitions within the statute or general provisions and (2) definitions from judicial applications of the statute. You will hope to find cases from courts whose decisions are mandatory authority. When mandatory authority is elusive, your search will move to persuasive authority interpreting the language. You will treat that authority as you would any other persuasive authority: it may be helpful, in varying degrees, but a court may choose to ignore it. Remember, however, that your argument will begin with the mandatory authority of the statute. Whether or not you find persuasive authority that provides definitions, you will also look at the ways in which courts have applied the language in order to clarify its meaning.

7.3. WHEN AUTHORITY DEFINING THE WORD OR PHRASE IS NOT AVAILABLE

We have talked about two possible scenarios: (1) the statutory law of the relevant jurisdiction provides a definition of the word or phrase that you must interpret in your argument and (2) the statute does not define the word or phrase in question, but the courts have defined it. A third scenario is possible: neither the statute nor the courts has defined the crucial word or phrase. Now is the time to pull out one or more of the secondary statutory interpretation tools we identified at the beginning of this discussion. We describe them below in roughly the order of the frequency with which you are likely to use them. The question of which of these tools is the right one in a situation depends on two factors: (1) which tools are available and (2) which tool is most favorable and persuasive for your side. Often, one or more of these tools is not available because, for example, no court has applied the language in question in a published decision, or the legislative history is silent about the meaning of the term you want to define. Once you have identified tools that *are* available in a given situation, you will rely on those that support the definition that best supports your argument and are most likely to persuade the court.

7.3.1. Help from Judicial Applications of the Statute

Even when a court has not defined the words and phrases in a statute, you can gain a clearer understanding of their meaning by observing how the court has applied the statute. As always, the most helpful common law authorities will be those that are mandatory. Your target cases will be mandatory cases in which the courts have applied the word or phrase you are examining in a manner that is consistent with a particular meaning and inconsistent with any other.

Consider for example, a civil trespass statute that requires "knowledge" but does not define it. Your client did enter onto private property while hiking in a state park, but he did not know that he had left the park. Suppose you find a decision from a court whose decisions are mandatory authority in your jurisdiction in which the court has held that a defendant was not liable for civil trespass damages and has given as its reason the fact that the defendant was not aware that he was on private property and did not intentionally enter onto private property. If the decision is good law, you may rely upon that decision as authority for the proposition that liability under the statute requires *intent*. The mandatory authority is the language of the statute *as applied by the court*. The rule and rule explanation portions of your argument might look something like this:

> A person is not liable for civil trespass damages under Vanita law unless the person *intentionally* entered onto the privately-owned land of another. *Mephisto v. Sepulveda*, 224 R.E.2d 337, 342 (Van. 2012). The Vanita civil trespass statute provides that a person is liable for damage caused after "knowingly entering upon the private property of another." Van. Rev. Stat. § 2218.62(b). The statute does not define "knowingly," but the Vanita Supreme Court has clarified that the knowledge requirement is not satisfied unless a person intentionally enters onto private property. *Mephisto*, 224 R.E.2d. at 342. The defendant in *Mephisto* had crossed the unmarked boundary between a highway berm and private property and trampled some soybean plants. *Id.* at 340. The court held that the defendant could not be liable for civil trespass damages because he did not intend to enter onto private property and did not know that he was on private property. *Id.* at 342. By suggesting that intent is a predicate to liability, the court

clarified that "knowingly" in the Vanita civil trespass statute means "intentionally." *See id*.

As you gain more experience, you will gain more confidence in your ability to ascertain the meanings of words and phrases from court actions. At first, you may feel comfortable only when the court has been explicit about its reasoning by saying something like this: "The statute requires knowledge, and the defendant cannot be held liable because he did not have actual knowledge." In time, you will learn how to take a court's application to its logical conclusion. When you find an application that would not be consistent with one possible interpretation of a word or phrase in the statute, you will reason by negative implication that the other interpretation must therefore be correct. As you may know, this process is called "drawing an inference." When a court says something directly, you can cite its opinion directly. When you draw an inference from the court's language, or the combination of the ruling, the law, and the facts, you use a *see* signal before the citation, to signal that you drew an inference.

For example, suppose that a defendant had received a notice in the mail but had not opened it. Further, suppose that the court finds no liability because the knowledge element is not satisfied. You will become comfortable with the interpretation of "knowledge" in that case as meaning actual knowledge because the court's decision would be inconsistent with an interpretation requiring only a negligent failure to know.

When judicial applications clarify the meaning of a statute to a degree that allows you to be confident in your understanding, your inquiry may be finished. If you have found several consistent applications that are favorable to your position, and none that are inconsistent, you will likely stop looking for guidance about how to interpret the statute. If the common law does not give you the favorable answers you seek, however, you may turn to other sources for help.

7.3.2. Help from Legislative History

The analysis of a statute always begins with the plain meaning of the words and phrases used by the legislature. As we have established, however, the inquiry rarely stops there, either for the court or for you. When statutory and common law definitions are unavailable and the courts have not interpreted the language clearly, consistently, or favorably, the next tool you may use to define an important statutory term is the legislative history of the statute. Your goal is to gain an understanding of the legislature's intent in enacting ⑫ the statute with the hope that the legislature's intent supports your desired interpretation of the language.

One major category of "legislative history" consists of documents and records generated or gathered by the legislature and its staff in the course of considering proposed legislation. It may take the form of reports by committees or staff, testimony of witnesses who testified before the committee or the full legislature, and statements of legislators. Legislative history also includes the changes in a statute as it is amended over the years. Those amendments are often persuasive evidence of how the legislature intends the statute to be interpreted or applied. Legislative history is most reliable when it is included in the official legislative record.

Let's look at two examples of rule/rule explanations incorporating legislative history as persuasive secondary authority for a particular interpretation of statutory language. To keep it simple, we'll use the same fictitious statute for both examples. The first example illustrates the use of legislative history in the form of the legislative record. The second illustrates the use of legislative history in the form of changes to the statute over time.

Assume that our client's employer demoted her to a position in which she has no contact with the public after she returned from a religious retreat with a new tattoo of a diamond on her forehead. The employee sued under the Religion Discrimination Act provision that prohibits discrimination based on an employee's expression of religious belief. The statute in question contains a nonexclusive list of expressions of religious belief, and that list includes "tattoos." Our client claims that her religion encourages small forehead tattoos of any kind as expressions of devotion and that her employer's action violated the Religion Discrimination Act.

The employer has moved for dismissal of our client's claim, and the arguments center around the meaning of the word "tattoo." The Religion Discrimination Act does not define "tattoo." While the plain meaning of "tattoo" may be obvious, the employer has moved to dismiss our client's claim because the symbol depicted in her tattoo is not inherently religious. The employer argues that a non-religious tattoo cannot be an expression of religious belief for purposes of the Religion Discrimination Act.

Our research does not uncover a single case in which a court has considered the meaning of the word "tattoo" as used in the Religion Discrimination Act, so we turn to legislative history for guidance on the meaning of "tattoo." In the legislative record, we find only one item related to the word "tattoo": a report by legislative staff showing that a few religions encourage followers to display geometric or other decorative tattoos in visible places and that a growing number

⑫ Legislative history is secondary authority: courts are never required to follow it. Interestingly, when courts use legislative history, they often note that it is "consistent" with other interpretive tools. Thus, if you find some juicy legislative history that supports your theory, find some backup, and cite the backup first. Then begin your discussion of legislative history by saying something like "The legislative history is consistent with this interpretation. . . ."

of constituents had complained to their congressional representatives about adverse employment actions based on such tattoos. Our research also reveals that the statute originally listed "religious tattoos" but was recently amended to just "tattoos." Here are the two rule/rule explanation examples (the citations are fictional):

First Example

The Religion Discrimination Act prohibits discrimination against an employee for displaying any tattoo as an expression of religious belief. The word "tattoo" in the Religion Discrimination Act is not limited to religious-themed tattoos. Congress included tattoos as a form of religious expression because employers had begun to treat employees adversely when they exercised their religion, in part, by displaying non-religious tattoos. *See* H.R. Rep No. 105-452, at 7 (1998). Therefore, Congress did not limit the types of tattoos that could be considered forms of religious expression to only religious-themed tattoos.

Second Example

The Religion Discrimination Act prohibits discrimination against an employee for displaying any tattoo as an expression of religious belief. The word "tattoo" in the Religion Discrimination Act is not limited to religious-themed tattoos. Indeed, when Congress first enacted the Religion Discrimination Act it included "religious tattoos" in a list of forms of religious expression. Religion Discrimination Act, Pub. Act 99-795, 1999 Laws 2408. In 2016, Congress amended the statute, eliminating the word "religious." The amendment clarifies that any tattoo may be a form of religious expression.

The mandatory authority in both of these examples is limited to the statute itself. The references to legislative history are merely efforts to persuade the court about the meaning of the mandatory authority.

13 You are probably most familiar with legislative history as it relates to federal statutes. Some states provide similarly complete legislative history, but not every state does.

13 Legislative history rarely provides the clarity that courts and lawyers desire when they are attempting to define words and phrases within statutes. In many of your searches, you will find no legislative record. On the other hand, you may find the legislative record but find nothing that relates to the part of the statute you need to interpret, or you may find that the record contains contradictory statements or testimony. It may contain documents or statements that are directly on point but show no indication of agreement by the legislators. In short, while you may find some guidance as to what the legislature intended when it enacted the statute, the legislative history will rarely be definitive. In many instances, you will find yourself on safer footing when you rely on the policy underlying the statute, even when that policy is not explicit in the statute or the legislative history.

7.3.3. Help from Policy and Canons of Construction

Policies come in many forms. Some relate to specific statutes and include the purposes for the statute or the underlying societal reasons for the passage of the statute. Others relate more generally to the ways in which we interpret or apply statutes. We refer to the first category as public policy and the second as canons of construction. Neither category constitutes mandatory authority for one interpretation of a particular statute over another, but both are tools you may use to support an argument for a favorable interpretation of statutory language.

a. Public Policy

When a legislator introduces a bill, the legislator may be motivated by one or more policy objectives. Other members of the legislature may support the same bill for their own policy reasons. These reasons may be explicit in the language of the eventual statute or in the legislative history, but more often they will not be. Whether explicit or implicit, these policy foundations may be useful tools in the interpretation of the statute.

In the absence of mandatory authority that specifies a particular interpretation, a court will generally try to interpret a statute in a way that serves the policy that motivated its enactment. When a court perceives that the policy underlying the statute was the broadening of a right, the court is likely to interpret the statute in such a way that the right is broadened. When the policy is the protection of innocent civilians, the court will likely interpret the statute in a way that advances the protection of civilians.

You may already be thinking that the policy underlying a statute will often appear to be different to different observers. You are right, of course. Statutes that criminalize behavior almost always serve a public protection policy. That policy may suggest a broad application. When the same statute provides minimal penalties, however, a second possible policy may be narrow application. A prosecutor may rely on the broad public protection policy to argue that the court should apply the statute to behavior that does not quite fit within the statute's plain meaning, while a defense attorney may argue that the narrow application policy would not support any application other than those spelled out explicitly in the language. The good news for you as a lawyer is that you will almost always be able to conceive of a policy that supports your position. The bad news is that your opponent is likely in the same position. So, plain meaning, statutory and common law definitions, and common law applications, all of which are less susceptible to competing interpretations, are far more reliable guides to statutory meaning.

Like many research trails in the context of statutory interpretation, this trail leads us first to a search in surrounding statutes for an explicit statement of the purposes underlying the provisions in question. As we have already mentioned, legislative bodies will often make the purposes or policies underlying a statute a part of the statute itself. We are certainly on safer footing in identifying public policy when the legislature has been transparent about its motivations. Let's consider an example of an explicit statutory purpose provision and how a lawyer might use it to support a favorable interpretation of statutory language.

Let's suppose that we represent a client who is visually impaired and whose employer has assigned her to a team comprising only visually impaired employees. The employer pays those employees at the same rate as employees who are not visually impaired and affords them the same benefits. Our client, nevertheless, wants to challenge the segregation under the Americans with Disabilities Act. The governing provision of the Act is 42 U.S.C. § 12112(a), which provides that an employer may not discriminate against a qualified employee on the basis of disability "in regard to job application procedures, . . . hiring, advancement, . . . or other terms, conditions, and privileges of employment." Let's further suppose that our search for helpful statutory or case-law definitions has been fruitless and that we have not found a single case in which a plaintiff has advanced the theory that segregation of employees with disabilities, without any other detriment, violates § 12112(a). So, the only available mandatory authority is the statute.

Our client acknowledges that her employer routinely hires and promotes visually impaired people, so we believe that our best hope is to focus on the "other terms, conditions, and privileges" language. We want to argue that segregating employees with disabilities is discrimination in other terms, conditions, and privileges; so, our search for support now takes us to public policy.

As we did when we looked for statutory definitions, we must often look beyond the substantive provisions of the statute to find any legislative purpose statement. Often, but not always, purpose provisions appear at the beginning of the group of statutes comprising the act of which they are a part, and this is true of the Americans with Disabilities Act. Congress included an explicit statement of the purposes underlying the Act in 42 U.S.C. § 12101, which is entitled "Findings and purpose." There, we discover this language among the "findings": "historically, society has tended to isolate and segregate individuals with disabilities, and . . . such forms of discrimination . . . continue to be a serious and pervasive social problem."

If we find no other support for our argument, our rule and rule explanation might look something like this:

> The Americans with Disabilities Act prohibits discrimination against qualified employees with disabilities in the terms, conditions, and privileges of employment. 42 U.S.C. § 12112(a). The Act does not identify every prohibited form of discrimination; however, Congress made clear that one of the principle problems to be solved by the Act was that "society has tended to isolate and segregate individuals with disabilities," and that this isolation and segregation were "forms of discrimination." 42 U.S.C. § 12101(2). Accordingly, employer actions that segregate employees with disabilities because of their disabilities are incompatible with the Act and must constitute impermissible discrimination.

You have probably noticed that we have not attempted to claim that the "findings and purpose" provision is mandatory authority for our interpretation of "other terms, conditions, and privileges of employment." Rather, we have identified the congressional finding as persuasive authority for our interpretation.

As we have told you, we are always on safer footing when the legislative body has identified the public policy underlying a statute, but we can incorporate public policy in an argument for a favorable interpretation of statutory language even when the legislature has not been so helpful. The following example illustrates the use of public policy that is not explicit in the statute.

Let's change the previous example by pretending that the "finding and purpose" section of the Americans with Disabilities Act does not exist. Once again, we have decided that the "other terms, conditions, and privileges of employment" language is the best part of the statute for our client. Our task is now to identify a favorable public policy that would be served by that language. One possibility is the public policy against stigma associated with disabilities. We are, of course, safest when we identify a policy about which near-universal agreement is assured. Our rule and rule explanation might look like this:

> The Americans with Disabilities Act prohibits discrimination against qualified employees with disabilities in the terms, conditions, and privileges of employment. 42 U.S.C. § 12112(a). The Act does not identify every prohibited form of discrimination; however, the Act reflects that Congress recognized the stigma associated with disabilities and the unjustified perception that individuals with disabilities are not capable of enjoying the same employment terms, conditions, and privileges as their peers who are not disabled. One of the chief benefits of the Act is the elimination of separate classifications for disabled and non-disabled individuals. Any employment action that serves to re-segregate employees with disabilities runs afoul of that purpose and must constitute discrimination in violation of § 12112(a).

You may find this version of the rule to be less compelling than the previous one, and you would not be alone. The first version is more compelling because it finds support in a policy identified by Congress. The second feels somewhat less reliable because it is obviously nothing more than the writer's preferred interpretation of the policy underlying the statute. So, when you identify a policy that your interpretation of a statute would advance, you should not just present your bald assertion of that policy without first looking for cases in which courts have mentioned that policy as being significant. The ideal case would be a decision by a mandatory court in which that court has identified the policy as a reason for interpreting the relevant statute in the way that you want it to be interpreted. Of course, as we have observed, courts do not always cooperate by writing opinions that are tailored to your precise future research needs.

You now understand that public policy is a tool that you will use with caution. Public policy may be the basis for a persuasive argument about how a court should interpret a statute, but it is not mandatory authority. You should always prefer mandatory authority when it is available. The same caveat applies to the other form of policy: canons of construction.

b. Canons of Construction

Canons of construction represent another form of policy. You may think of them as judicial policy to distinguish them from public policy, which we have just discussed. As a form of policy, canons of construction are not mandatory authority. As with any form of persuasive authority, their persuasive force may be substantial or negligible. Proceed with caution.

Earlier in this chapter, we identified a few of the most commonly cited canons of construction, but we barely scratched the surface. You may wonder why we did not include an exhaustive list and place the various canons into helpful categories. Trust us when we say that you don't really want that. Scholars of the canons have created lists that go on for pages and include such arcana as the *desuetude canon*.

The most important thing for you to remember about canons of construction is that they are policies of interpretation that may guide courts in the absence of better authority for the interpretation of statutory language. Because they are policies and not rules, a court is not required to apply any particular canon to the interpretation of any particular statute. Often, several canons arguably apply. Most legal writers seem to believe that the most appropriate canon in any case is the one that supports the writer's preferred interpretation.

You are probably getting the idea that canons of construction are weak authority in an argument about the meaning of statutory language. We will not belabor the point beyond providing a couple of guidelines and an example:

First, you should always prefer mandatory authority. Canons are not mandatory authority. Unless a court whose decisions are mandatory authority in your case has identified a particular canon as a basis for interpreting the language in question, your argument based on a canon is nothing more than a suggestion.

Second, before identifying a canon as support for your argument about statutory language, you must do sufficient research to ensure yourself that no other canon is more obviously applicable. If you identify a canon, you invite your opponent or the court to do the same. If theirs is more obviously applicable, you may have lost an argument that you could have won on the basis of legislative history or public policy.

Naming a canon of construction may be fun, especially if it is in Latin, but the uninitiated may find that they are playing a new and very complex form of poker without knowing all of the rules.

Now that we have frightened you, allow us to provide a modest example of a rule and rule explanation incorporating a canon of construction as support for a particular interpretation of a statute. Before we get there, glance back at the excerpt from *Marx v. General Revenue Corp.* that appears earlier in this chapter. That excerpt gives you an idea of how one type of canon, a *textual* canon, may inform a court when it interprets statutory language. Textual canons relate to the way that words are to be read in the context in which they appear. Our example below illustrates a different type of canon: the *substantive* canon. Substantive canons favor statutory interpretations that support certain identified values that may have nothing to do with the content of the statute itself. The example relies on the *Charming Betsy* canon, which favors a statutory interpretation that prevents a violation of international law. You will notice that the statute itself has nothing to do with international law.

Suppose your client is a Japanese company doing business in the United States. The company includes a division that performs work related to Japanese national security. In that division only, your client prefers to employ Japanese nationals for security reasons. After your client rejected a well-qualified American citizen for a high-level position in the division, the disappointed applicant sued for national origin discrimination. Your client wants to argue that its preference for Japanese nationals in certain positions does not violate Title VII. Your rule and rule explanation may look something like this:

> Title VII permits an employer to discriminate on the basis of national origin when national origin is a "bona fide occupational qualification reasonably necessary to" the operation of its business. 42 U.S.C. § 2000e-2(e). Article VIII(1) of the Japan Friendship Commerce and Navigation Treaty permits a Japanese company doing business in the United States to hire experts of its choice. April 1, 1953, 4 U.S.T. 2063. The *Charming Betsy* canon of statutory construction permits an interpretation of § 2000e-2(e) that recognizes Japanese national origin as a *bona fide* occupational qualification for employees in sensitive positions in Japanese companies doing business in the United States. *Smith v. McGuffin Indus.*, 101 U.S. 101, 109 (1964).

You have not suggested that the canon is mandatory authority, but you may have persuaded the court that applying the canon serves a worthy judicial policy.

7.4. CONCLUSION

This long discussion may have overwhelmed you on the first read, and, still, we could say so much more about persuasive writing when a statute is the subject. If you take away nothing else, remember that (1) the statute itself is mandatory authority, (2) you are always on the safest footing when you rely on mandatory authority to interpret a statute, and (3) you should use the non-mandatory tools cautiously, and never as substitutes for mandatory authority.

Evidence in Persuasive Writing

Take a moment to think about a trial. Conjure one up in your mind. What do you see? Okay, your first thought might have been a brilliant closing argument. Go back in time and think about everything that happens after the opening statements and before the closing arguments.

That is evidence, folks, and it is the basis for the outcome in nearly every trial. Now that you are focused on the right part of the trial, think about what it includes: for the most part, witness testimony and exhibits. *Evidence* can be anything that tends to prove a fact, and it takes many forms. You will learn about most of them in your evidence class, which you should take whether you currently intend to litigate or not. For our present purposes, we will discuss only two types of evidence: testimony and exhibits.

You know, and we know, that very few cases go to trial, yet evidence is central to the disposition of many cases. Let's think first about how and why this is so and then about how our use of evidence in persuasive writing is similar to and different from how we use evidence at trial.

8.1. THE POST-DISCOVERY PHASE: SUMMARY JUDGMENT, TRIAL, AND APPEAL

By now, you may be familiar with persuasive writing in the form of a motion to dismiss and the memoranda that follow. In the context of a motion under Rule 12(b)(6) or a parallel state procedural rule, the parties argue about whether the plaintiff's allegations state a claim upon which relief may be granted. The focus is on the complaint. In fact, Rule 12(d) of the Federal Rules of Civil Procedure prohibits a court from considering any matters outside the allegations in the complaint when ruling on a motion to dismiss for failure to state a claim. *Matters outside the allegations of the complaint* include evidence. So, in considering a motion to dismiss, a court may not consider evidence even if some evidence is already in the court record. Once a case proceeds beyond the motion to dismiss stage, however, the focus of the litigation shifts from *the allegations* to the *evidence*.

Rule 56 is the Federal Rule of Civil Procedure that governs a court's consideration of the evidence in support of a claim prior to trial. Any party in a case may assert a claim, and that party bears the burden of proving that claim. For the sake of simplicity, we will use the term "plaintiff" to refer to the party bearing the burden of proof. Rule 56 permits either party to ask for summary judgment, but, in practice, the defendant, or the party without the burden of proof, is almost always the movant (that is, the person *moving* or *filing a motion* for summary judgment), and the gist of the motion is that the plaintiff cannot prove the claim or claims.

Under Rule 56, a court may "grant summary judgment if the movant shows that there is no genuine dispute as to any material fact." Rule 56 explicitly instructs courts to consider only certain items when deciding a motion for summary judgment. Rule 56(c) (1)(A) specifies that those items may include "depositions, documents, electronically stored information, affidavits or declarations, stipulations (including those made for purposes of the motion only), admissions, [and] interrogatory answers." That list includes items obtained by the parties during discovery. Discovery does not begin in most cases until after the opportunity to move for dismissal under Rule 12(b)(6) has ended. So, for a court, a motion for summary judgment typically marks the shift from considering only the allegations of the complaint to considering evidence. This fact is the reason for Rule 56(b)'s instruction that "[u]nless a different time is set by local rule or the court orders otherwise, a party may file a motion for summary judgment at any time until 30 days after the close of all discovery." In practice, a court will not ordinarily consider a motion for judgment based on the evidence until the parties have had a full opportunity to obtain all relevant evidence through discovery.

Accordingly, the parties' motions and memoranda in connection with a motion for summary judgment under Rule 56 mark the court's first official view of the evidence in a case. Up to that point in the litigation, the court would have confined its consideration to the allegations of the complaint. If the court grants the motion for summary judgment (and if that decision is not reversed on appeal), the motion for summary judgment is also the final time that the trial court views the evidence in a case. Its decision to grant summary judgment ends the litigation. No trial follows. If the losing party appeals the trial court's decision, the court of appeals will consider the same evidence that the trial court considered and nothing more. If the appellate court affirms the decision to grant the motion for summary judgment, the picture of a trial that you conjured up at the beginning of this chapter never becomes a reality. Witnesses do not take the stand; the attorneys do not brandish exhibits before the jury. Nothing that you envisioned as evidence comes into the court's view. Still, the evidence, and only the evidence, has been the basis for the court's decision. Whatever was obtained in discovery was the only evidence that existed in the case.

Now, let's assume that the case takes a different course. Let's imagine that the court has denied the motion for summary judgment, or that an appellate court has reversed a grant of summary judgment, or that the parties have not filed motions for summary judgment, so the case proceeds to trial. Like a summary judgment motion, a trial takes place after discovery is complete. At trial, the basis for the outcome of the case is only the evidence presented at trial, however, and not everything obtained in discovery. Even if, on summary judgment, the court reviewed deposition testimony or affidavits, the trial court or the jury would not consider those documents unless the parties have made them part of the evidence at trial. Instead, the witnesses who gave the depositions or affidavits will testify at trial about the same matters. If, after the trial court issues its verdict, the losing party appeals the trial verdict, the court of appeals will also confine its review to the evidence that the parties presented at trial. So, in their briefs to the appellate court, the parties must confine their arguments to the evidence that was presented at trial and may not rely on other evidence obtained in discovery but not presented at trial.

With that background, we are ready to explain how and why lawyers use evidence in persuasive legal writing. We will address the two main contexts in which lawyers write about evidence: the summary judgment stage and the appellate stage.

8.2. EVIDENCE IN SUMMARY JUDGMENT MEMORANDA

As you now know, parties are generally discouraged, if not prohibited, from filing motions for summary judgment until after the end of the discovery period. The reasons for this delay are, perhaps, obvious to you. A court wants to give each party a full opportunity to use the discovery process to obtain evidence in support of a claim before it decides that a party cannot prove a claim. Once discovery has ended, however, a court will entertain motions for summary judgment, which are nothing more than an invitation by a party (usually the defendant) to the court to examine the evidence and determine whether the other party (usually the plaintiff) can possibly prove its claim. The motion for summary judgment stage is essentially a party's opportunity to ask the court to conduct a trial on paper rather than in a courtroom.

As you think about the court's consideration of a motion for summary judgment as a trial on paper, go back to your imagination as you did at the beginning of this chapter and envision a trial. This time, allow yourself to imagine both the attorneys' arguments and the presentation of evidence. In essence, a trial is the presentation of evidence and the attorneys' arguments about what that evidence proves. One side argues that the evidence supports the plaintiff's claims, while the other side offers conflicting evidence or attempts to identify holes in the evidence that prevent the plaintiff from proving those claims.

The attorneys in the trial are well aware of what the plaintiff must prove: they know the essential elements of the plaintiff's claim or claims. The plaintiff's lawyer attempts to present evidence that proves each of those elements, and, at the end of the trial, the attorneys argue about whether the plaintiff has succeeded. The court or the jury decides whether the evidence presented by the plaintiff proves, usually by a preponderance of the evidence, each element of each claim. With many variations, minor and major, that is the trial.

If the motion for summary judgment stage is a trial on paper, it must include the same basic elements as a trial: presentation of evidence in support of or opposition to the elements of the plaintiff's claim or claims, arguments of the attorneys about whether the plaintiff can prove each element, and a decision by the court. The court's decision is not part of the parties' persuasive writing, so we will focus our attention on the presentation of evidence and the parties' arguments.

① When you have read about, or thought about, or participated in motion practice, you have probably thought of the memoranda in support of and in opposition to a motion for summary judgment as arguments. They are. The attorneys craft arguments in an attempt to persuade the court that the evidence does or does not permit the plaintiff to prove a claim or multiple claims. You may not have thought about the role that evidence plays in the argument and instead have envisioned the arguments as being centered on what the law requires. What the law requires is the backdrop for, and a necessary part of, the written arguments, and sometimes a court will grant or deny a motion for summary judgment because a party has misperceived or misapplied the applicable law. More often, however, the controversy is about what the evidence will permit the plaintiff to show. So, once the applicable law is identified, the dispute will focus on the evidence.

No live testimony. No attorneys brandishing exhibits before a jury. So, what does the written presentation of evidence look like? Let's first identify what is the same about a live trial and a trial on paper. In both situations, the lawyer's first task is to identify a list of things that the plaintiff must prove. Those *things* are the elements of the plaintiff's claim or claims. The plaintiff's lawyer must then identify evidence that tends to prove each of those elements. The defendant's attorney will point out the gaps in that evidence or perhaps provide contrary evidence. At a live trial, that evidence will almost always take the form of either a witness's testimony or an exhibit, or both. In the trial on paper, the evidence will also generally take the form of a witness's testimony or an exhibit, or both. Below, we will examine the differences between live trials and paper trials for both kinds of evidence.

8.2.1. Testimonial Evidence

Having identified the similarities between the presentation of evidence at a live trial and the presentation of evidence in a trial on paper, we can now look at the differences. In a trial on paper, an attorney cannot call a live witness to offer testimony. The live witness's testimony is replaced by deposition testimony from that witness or the witness's affidavit. As we will explain below, both the deposition and the affidavit represent the witness's statements under oath. In that sense, they are the exact equivalents of the live testimony at trial. Of course, the court or jury cannot consider the demeanor of the witness while testifying when the testimony is

① In the summary judgment context, the party bearing the burden of proof argues that the evidence will permit it to prove a claim or that the evidence means the party will be able to prove its claim because it has presented evidence that tends to prove it. Contrast this focus with the trial, where the party must actually prove the claim. This distinction is why you must be very careful about the way you characterize holdings in trial court decisions granting or denying motions for summary judgment, and appellate decisions reversing or affirming those decisions.

written, but a court at the summary judgment stage is not deciding which evidence to *believe* but only whether some amount of evidence exists to support each element that the plaintiff must prove. So, if the witness's deposition testimony or affidavit tends to prove an element, the court may conclude that the plaintiff has shown that some evidence exists and that summary judgment is not appropriate, at least with respect to that element.

Rule 56 permits courts to consider depositions and affidavits equally. One of the main differences between the two is that the deposition includes the lawyers' questions as well as the witness's statements. A witness's statements in an affidavit are not tested through cross-examination and are not clarified through follow-up questioning. Still, if a witness's statement in an affidavit tends to prove an element of a claim, that statement will generally be sufficient proof to prevent summary judgment on the basis of that element.

Another difference between deposition testimony and an affidavit is the identity of the attorney guiding the subject matter and direction of the witness's statements. Some background information about how a person becomes a witness will help you to understand this distinction.

In almost every civil case, the court will require the parties to identify their witnesses in writing so that each party knows all of the potential witnesses of the other party. Once a party has identified witnesses, counsel for the opposing party will depose some or all of those people to learn and test what they know. So, in a deposition, counsel for the opposing party will generally control the direction of the questioning. The attorney who has identified the witness may also ask questions after opposing counsel has finished with the witness, but the opposing attorney will conduct the bulk of the questioning. So, you may think of a witness's deposition testimony as the statements made by that witness during cross-examination.

At a live trial, the attorney who calls a witness will almost always examine that witness first, however, and will elicit all the helpful information that the witness can offer on direct examination. So, the deposition testimony does not replace that live direct examination. That is the job of the affidavit.

An affidavit includes the favorable statements of a witness as prepared by the attorney who offers the witness. Those statements constitute some or all of the information that the attorney hopes to extract from the witness on direct examination at trial. They are a best-case scenario, of course, because the attorney will have drafted the affidavit and opposing counsel will not cross-examine the witness.

So, you may think of deposition testimony as the testimony of a witness on cross-examination and an affidavit as that same witness's testimony on direct examination. The dynamics of a deposition resemble those of a trial much more closely than do the dynamics of an affidavit. Deposition testimony is quite similar in format to trial testimony. The affidavit has no equivalent at trial. Witnesses are not permitted to take the stand at trial and make statements that have not been prompted by questions and that are not tested by cross-examination, as they may in an affidavit. Accordingly, attorneys generally use affidavits only to fill in gaps in deposition testimony with the expectation that the witness will fill those gaps at trial by testifying about all matters about which the witness has knowledge, including those that the witness covered in an affidavit and not in a deposition during the discovery phase. You may, in fact, accurately envision that some affidavits are the direct result of the writing process: while writing a memorandum in opposition to a motion for summary judgment, the lawyer realizes that none of the deposition testimony tends to prove one of the essential elements of the plaintiff's claim and crafts an affidavit to fill in the gap. Although affidavits are based on facts from witnesses, attorneys often write them with the goal of maximizing their persuasiveness. Thus, you should consider the lessons of the next chapter on framing your arguments, Chapter Nine, so that you can frame the facts in affidavits to your clients' best advantage.

The lawyer for a defendant who has drafted the motion *for* summary judgment will attempt to identify gaps in the evidence supporting the plaintiff's claim or claims. That lawyer may or may not cite any evidence in the memorandum in support. Obviously, the lawyer seeking summary judgment has no incentive to identify evidence that supports the other party's claims. Sometimes, however, a piece of evidence may undermine an element of a claim so completely that the moving lawyer will identify it and cite it in order to try to convince the court that the plaintiff cannot prove the undermined element and, therefore, that summary judgment is warranted. For example, consider a claim that requires a plaintiff to prove that the defendant breached a contract by failing to pay for services that the plaintiff provided. If the plaintiff testified at deposition that she had stopped providing services before the defendant was obligated to pay, the defendant's attorney will identify that testimony in its memorandum in support of its motion for summary judgment as evidence supporting its argument that the plaintiff cannot prove the breach element of her contract claim.

The party opposing the motion for summary judgment is much more likely to cite to witness testimony in the memorandum in opposition. That party bears the burden of proof and is required to identify evidence, almost always in the form of testimony, in order to show the court that it can support all essential elements of the contested claims. Remember that witness testimony may take the form of deposition excerpts or affidavits at the summary judgment stage.

The following sample is an excerpt from the rule application portion of a memorandum in opposition to a motion for summary judgment. In the excerpted portion of the argument, the plaintiff's lawyer relies on an affidavit and testimony from a deposition to show the court that a genuine issue of material fact prevents summary judgment for the defendant.

Example Relying on Affidavit and Deposition
Testimonial evidence from Plaintiff's affidavit and from her supervisor's deposition shows that a genuine issue of material fact exists as to the issue of pretext in the stated reason for Defendant's refusal to transfer Plaintiff to a position without a ten-pound lifting requirement; therefore, summary judgment in Defendant's favor is not appropriate. Plaintiff's supervisor has testified that no such position was available in December 2014. Shields depo., p. 22, lines 13-21. Ms. Tuey states, on the other hand, that she applied for an open position within her lifting restriction in December 2014, and Ms. Shields refused to consider her application. Tuey affidavit, ¶ 7. The evidence would, therefore, permit a jury to find that Defendant's stated reason for refusing to accommodate Ms. Tuey's disability by transferring her to a position she could perform is pretextual.

The rule explanation portion of a summary judgment argument might look much the same as the rule explanation in an appellate brief. In the application section, however, the plaintiff's attorney is likely to be citing evidence, as in the example above.

8.2.2. Exhibits

We have now thought about how depositions and affidavits serve the same function in a trial on paper that witness testimony serves in a live trial, and we are ready to think about the other main source of evidence: exhibits. Many live trials include only testimony, but in some cases exhibits form a part of the evidence upon which the parties rely in order to convince the court or the jury that the weight of the evidence favors their side. Exhibits take many forms, but, unlike witness testimony, they almost always exist before the dispute arises. In other words, they are not created for the purpose of proof. They exist independently and relate in some fashion to the parties' relationship before any lawsuit existed. Bills, photos of bruises, business records, damaged property, and many other items may serve as exhibits. They may serve as evidence at a live trial, and they may serve the same purpose in a trial on paper.

Often, attorneys can present exhibits in the trial on paper in the same form as they may present them at a live trial; in other situations, the attorney must provide the best possible paper version of the exhibit. In either instance, the attorney must actually include and identify the exhibit or the facsimile and may not rely on a mere assertion that the exhibit exists. In other words, the attorney must actually present the exhibit in the trial on paper. If the exhibit is a document or a photo, the attorney will refer to it in the argument about the evidence and attach it, or a copy of it, to the memorandum. If the exhibit does not exist on paper, the attorney may present it in the form of a photo or other reproduction of the exhibit, with the understanding that the actual item would be presented at a live trial.

8.2.3. Your Evidentiary Task at the Summary Judgment Stage

As we have already told you, the lawyer's goal in opposing a motion for summary judgment is to identify evidence in support of every essential element of the claims as to which the opposing party has moved for summary judgment. To achieve that goal, the lawyer must know what the essential elements are for each of these claims. A checklist is an effective way to keep track of those elements and the evidence that tends to prove them.

Well before a lawyer begins to draft the memorandum in opposition to summary judgment, the lawyer will have conducted the necessary research to identify the essential elements of the contested claims. The careful lawyer will create a checklist of elements to be proved and of the evidence that tends to prove each of those elements. These tasks will often take considerable time. The examination of the evidence, in particular, may take longer than the lawyer would like. In a case that includes multiple lengthy depositions, the lawyer will have to comb through the transcripts looking for every scrap of evidence that tends to prove an essential element of a claim. The lawyer may not have personally conducted or been present for all, or any, of the depositions and, therefore, may have no memory to draw upon in searching for the evidence. When you are in the position of that lawyer, you will allot plenty of time to the search for evidence.

Having completed these tasks, the lawyer will recognize any gaps in the existing evidence. Gaps will be elements for which the lawyer has not identified evidence. If the lawyer has completed the search for evidence with sufficient time remaining to secure affidavits to fill in those gaps, the fact that the existing evidence does not tend to prove every essential element may not be a problem. The lawyer may identify witnesses whose affidavits can stand in for other evidence in support of those elements. Of course, the gap will still be a problem if no identified witness can attest to a necessary fact. The lawyer cannot generate evidence, in the form of an affidavit or in any other form, that does not exist in the mind of any witness.

A checklist that identifies specific evidence for each essential element is an indication that the lawyer is ready to conduct the trial on paper by writing the argument and identifying the evidence in support of that argument. The *argument*, in this context, is an assertion that evidence supports each element that the plaintiff must prove and the identification of that evidence specifically. The lawyer will tell the court what the evidence tends to prove and then "show" the court the evidence by citing or quoting the specific testimony or exhibits.

How Do I Write About Facts?

When you write about how the law applies — or should apply — to facts, the *facts* you're talking about probably go by one of three labels: allegations, evidence, or findings of fact. There are slight differences in the way that you deal with each.

If you are writing a motion memo on either side of a *motion to dismiss*, your facts are the allegations that were made in the complaint. Allegations may or may not be true, but as we discussed in Chapter Three, they are taken to be true for the purposes of a motion. In writing about those "facts," your focus will not be on whether the plaintiff will or will not be able to succeed on the claims in the complaint. Instead, you must focus on whether the allegations state a plausible claim for relief, as required by the motion standard for a motion to dismiss. So, if the plaintiff must prove that the defendant was a *debt collector*, as that term is used in the Fair Debt Collection Practices Act, and you represent the defendant moving to dismiss under Rule 12(b)(6), the thesis-conclusion (first "C" of CREXAC) of your argument may look something like this:

Good Example
Plaintiff has failed to allege that Defendant was attempting to collect on a debt to another when its employees called Plaintiff

at her workplace and has not, therefore, stated a claim for relief under the Fair Debt Collection Practices Act. *See Henson v. Santander Consumer USA Inc.*, 137 S. Ct. 1718, 1721-22 (2017). Instead, Plaintiff has alleged facts that suggest that Defendant was attempting to collect on Plaintiff's debt to Defendant, in which case Defendant was not a *debt collector* for purposes of the Act. *See* Complaint, ¶ 10.

Notice that the focus of your argument is the allegations in the complaint and whether they state a claim upon which relief may be granted. The facts are the *allegations* in the complaint. From this opening, your argument would proceed through the rules pertaining to the term *debt collector* and an application of those rules to the facts as alleged in the complaint.

When writing a motion memo on either side of a motion for *summary judgment*, however, as you already know from this chapter, your facts are the evidence that each side has submitted in support of its motion memo. And once again, the truth of the *evidence* is not the focus. As noted in this chapter, the focus is whether the evidence is sufficient to permit the plaintiff to establish the claims articulated in the complaint. So, in the same Fair Debt Collection Practices Act scenario, the thesis-conclusion of your argument for the defendant will focus on the evidence and *not* on the allegations:

Bad Example
Plaintiff cannot identify a genuine issue of material fact because she has not alleged that Defendant was attempting to collect on the debt of another when its employees called Plaintiff at her workplace.

Good Example
Plaintiff cannot identify evidence showing that Defendant was attempting to collect on a debt owed to another when its employees called Plaintiff at her workplace and cannot, therefore, prove a claim against Defendant under the Fair Debt Collection Practices Act. On the contrary, the evidence shows that the Defendant's employees made the telephone calls in an effort to collect on a debt that Plaintiff owed to Defendant. *See* Erica Vance depo., p. 37, lines 18-33. Therefore, Defendant was not acting as a *debt collector* for purposes of the Fair Debt Collection Practices Act. *See Henson v. Santander Consumer USA*

Inc., 137 S. Ct. 1718, 1721-22 (2017). Even considering that evidence in the light most favorable to Plaintiff, the court will conclude that no genuine issue of material fact prevents the entry of judgment in Defendant's favor.

The focus of the argument in the summary judgment context is squarely on the evidence. Even if the plaintiff has alleged that the defendant was a debt collector, the court will ignore the allegation in deference to the evidence. In response to the defendant's summary judgment motion, the plaintiff must identify evidence in support of the contested aspect of the claim or lose the claim. From this opening, your argument would proceed through the rules pertaining to the term *debt collector* and an application of those rules to the evidence.

Finally, if you are appealing or countering an appeal of a decision on the merits (as opposed to a decision on a motion), you might be arguing that the court abused its discretion as to a procedural matter or made a clear error when it made its findings of fact. Unless that is the case, however, you are arguing about how the law should or should not apply to the findings of fact that the trial court made. In that situation, finally, you get to talk about what facts the plaintiff has established or failed to establish, instead of the qualified arguments that you need to make when arguing about whether allegations or evidence are sufficient.

Whatever kind of argument you are making, do your best to accurately characterize what the "facts" do and do not represent, and be precise in what you are asking the court to do.

8.3. "EVIDENCE" IN APPELLATE BRIEFS

Just as the summary judgment stage of the litigation is a trial on paper, the appellate briefs are an appeal on paper. Perhaps you have thought of appeals as arguments before a panel of judges. The oral argument is the showy part of the appeal, but it is rarely the whole deal. In fact, the oral argument is so limited in time and scope that it cannot provide the appellate court with all of the information that it needs to decide the matter. The appellate briefs are the appeal on paper that provides that information.

As you may know, an appeal often requires a court to decide whether a lower court or a jury correctly considered the evidence, even though no evidence is presented at the appellate stage of litigation. When you envision an oral appellate argument, you don't see parties, let alone witnesses or exhibits. So, you may wonder, when an appellate court reviews the evidence presented at trial or at the summary judgment stage, what does it look at?

2 Again, the task of identifying the "evidence" belongs to the lawyer who writes the appellate brief. Once again, the evidence generally takes two forms: testimony and exhibits. Exhibits that were presented at trial or at the summary judgment stage will be part of the record, as will the transcripts of witnesses' testimony at trial or depositions and affidavits that were identified as evidence at the summary judgment stage. On appeal, the lawyer's task in preparing the appellate brief in a case in which the trial court has considered evidence is to identify the evidence in the record that supports that lawyer's side.

An appellate court may consider only the evidence that the parties presented to the trial court, and, in preparing the appellate brief, the appellate lawyer must confine the arguments to the evidence that was presented below. Still, the appellate lawyer's task is not so different from the trial attorney's task in preparing the memorandum at the summary judgment stage: identify the evidence in the record or the gaps in the evidence that support the attorney's argument that the trial court or jury was correct in its view of the evidence or got it wrong. The pre-writing checklist of essential points and supporting evidence from the record makes the lawyer's task easier and prevents surprise gaps at the writing stage.

2 In many courts, it is customary on appeal for the parties to create a "joint appendix" in which they compile the aspects of the record that are relevant to their arguments on appeal. Having a joint appendix spares the court the burden of consulting the entire record, although it is typically still available if needed.

8.4. CONCLUSION

Once again, the chapter is finished, but your reading is not. A sample affidavit follows. It includes the statements of a woman who has complained about disability discrimination by her former employer. Her specific claim is that her employer failed to accommodate her back injury by granting her request to transfer her to an available position that would not have required her to lift heavy boxes. You will quickly notice that the facts as set out in the affidavit are one-sided. They represent the favorable testimony that the attorney representing her interests would like to elicit from her at trial. Read the affidavit and consider the ways in which it supports the client's cause of action and the ways in which you might try to counter that testimony if you were on the other side of the case.

SAMPLE AFFIDAVIT

IN THE UNITED STATES DISTRICT COURT
FOR THE SOUTHERN DISTRICT OF OHIO
EASTERN DIVISION

Equal Employment Opportunity Commission, :

      Plaintiff,   :

v.   :   Case No. 2:15-CV-773

                               :   Judge Lowe

Mt. Gilead Exempted Village Schools,   :

      Defendant.   :

Affidavit of Barbara Breshear Tuey

1.   I reside at 42 Hill Street, Mt. Gilead, OH 43338. I am over the age of 18 and am not under any disability. I have personal knowledge of the facts set forth below.

2.   From 1999 to 2014, I worked in the cafeterias of Mt. Gilead Exempted Village Schools. In 1999, I began working at the elementary school as a server and was later promoted to cook. In 2009, I became the cook at the new high school cafeteria kitchen.

3.   The work in the high school cafeteria required me to work alone for the first time and to lift boxes weighing in excess of twenty pounds several times per day.

4.   In November 2014, I injured my back while lifting a heavy box at work. I experienced a sharp pain and temporary paralysis but eventually regained my mobility and continued working for the duration of the day with the voluntary assistance of a janitor who lifted the remaining boxes. I reported the injury to my supervisor, Angela Shields, and requested to continue working. Ms. Shields insisted that I take medical leave and see a doctor before returning to work.

5.   Throughout the rest of November and all of December of 2014, my doctor refused to release me to work as long as my job required me to lift boxes weighing more than ten pounds.

6.   On or about December 1, 2014, while I was still on medical leave, I learned that one of the elementary school cooks planned to leave her job at the end of the year. I asked Ms. Shields whether I could return to the elementary school cook's position because that job required lifting of no more than five pounds. Ms. Shields informed me that she could not move me to the elementary school position while I was on medical leave.

7.   On December 8, 2014, I saw the posting for the elementary school cook position. On December 9, 2014, I formally applied for the position. On that same date, I asked Ms. Shields by telephone whether she would assign me to the elementary school cook position so that I could avoid the lifting that my doctor would not release me to do. Ms. Shields told me that school policy prohibited her from considering my application while I was on medical leave. I asked Ms. Shields to identify a school policy that prohibited her from considering my application for a position that was consistent with the medical restrictions imposed by my doctor. She refused to do so.

8.   On December 19, 2014, my doctor told me that he would release me to work on January 2, 2015, if I suffered no setbacks. On December 20, 2014, I told Ms. Shields that I could return to work on January 2, 2015, and again asked her to consider my application for the elementary school cook position. I told Ms. Shields during this conversation that the elementary school position would be better for my back because of the reduced lifting requirement.

9. On December 21, 2014, I presented a letter from my doctor to Ms. Shields informing her that I would be permitted to return to work on January 2, 2015, if I did not suffer a setback before that date.

10. On January 2, 2015, I returned to work at the high school. On that same date, I learned that Ms. Shields had filled the elementary school cook position by hiring the daughter of her best friend. I asked Ms. Shields why she had not allowed me to fill the elementary school position, but she did not offer any explanation.

11. On January 4, 2015, I presented a return to work authorization from my doctor to Ms. Shields.

12. On January 5, 2015, Ms. Shields terminated my employment for returning to work before my doctor had released me.

Further affiant sayeth naught.

——————————————   ——————————————————————

Date   Barbara Breshear Tuey

STATE OF OHIO
COUNTY OF MORROW

I, the undersigned Notary Public, do hereby affirm that Barbara Breshear Tuey personally appeared before me on the ___ day of October 2017, and signed the above Affidavit as her free and voluntary act and deed.

———————————————————

Notary Public

3 When Monte first started practicing law, he prepared a set of detailed affidavits without this language at the end. The attorney who had assigned the work was livid. "How could you graduate from law school without knowing that you must say 'Further, affiant sayeth naught' at the end of an affidavit?" Monte had barely enough courage to ask why the language needed to be there. The supervisor responded, "Everyone does it; just do it. Always."

From our perspective, the language adds nothing meaningful to the affidavit, is not legally required, and is obviously antiquated. It is often untrue, as well, because the witness may have a great deal more to say on the matter. We invite you to omit it. Monte still includes it because he's still scared of that law partner.

CHAPTER NINE

Framing Your Arguments for Navigation and Persuasion

9.1. Reader Signals: The Template

    9.1.1. Roadmap Paragraphs and Umbrellas

    9.1.2. Headings

    9.1.3. Thesis or Topic Sentences

    9.1.4. Internal Conclusions or Connection-Conclusions

9.2. Conclusion

You've no doubt heard the old adage "you can't judge a book by its cover." That rule may be great as a metaphor for human relationships, but as for books, we disagree. The reality is that you *should* be able to judge a book by its cover; the cover is part of what helps you decide to read the book, along with its title, and any description you may find (you can be sure our publisher thought long and hard about what we should put on the front and back covers of this book). Further, if you were debating whether to buy a book or check it out from the library, you'd be glad to be able to look at its table of contents, so you could continue to judge it.

Judges judge briefs by their covers, and by a lot more. As we've discussed, readers of fiction tend to be linear readers, progressing through documents from beginning to end. Readers of briefs and of other expository documents, in contrast, are active readers: they have an agenda, and they often move around within a document, and move from one document to another and back again, in their quest for understanding or for specific information.

Because your readers are likely to be active readers, you should make sure your documents include appropriate "reader signals": tables of contents, headings, enumeration, and other organizational cues that help guide active readers and provide context for all kinds of readers. When you are writing persuasively, you should make sure that those reader signals also help to advance your persuasive agenda: because your readers are making judgments as they read (even if they aren't judges), you want to make sure each reader signal is as persuasive as possible.

In Chapter Fourteen, we will talk about how to present navigational signals to your readers. In this chapter, we're going to talk about how to write them.

9.1. READER SIGNALS: THE TEMPLATE

When you open a new document on your computer, your software probably offers you the option of opening a "template" instead of a blank document. These templates can be used in many ways; in general, they are meant to guide you to provide the information that readers of the document will be expecting you to provide, in the places in which they will be expecting you to provide it. While many of the formulas in this book could be thought of as templates (e.g., CREXAC, the case description formula, etc.), the template described in this chapter is a template of reader signals. By writing these template

ILLUSTRATION 9.1

Argument
If you break a unit of discourse into smaller units of discourse, insert an umbrella with a **roadmap** that signals the next layer of organization. Here, signal the content of Sections 1 and 2. Do *not* signal the content of Sections 2.1 and 2.2 in this roadmap.

1. Heading One
This heading has no subparts: begin the CREXAC unit of discourse. Template items in CREXAC units of discourse include **topic or thesis sentences** for each paragraph, and a **connection-conclusion** at the end of the CREXAC.

2. Heading Two
Between heading 2 and heading 2.1, insert an umbrella that includes a **roadmap** signaling the content of sections 2.1 and 2.2.

   2.1. Heading Two Point One
No subparts here, so note Heading One's guidance re: template items within CREXAC: **topic sentences** for each paragraph and a **connection-conclusion** at the end.

   2.2. Heading Two Point Two
No subparts here, so note Heading One's guidance re: template items within CREXAC: **topic sentences** for each paragraph and a **connection-conclusion** at the end.

items strategically, you can both help your readers to navigate your document and be sure to exploit opportunities for persuasion.

The template has four items: roadmap paragraphs, headings, topic sentences, and connection-conclusions. Of course, each of those items will be repeated as needed; they are shown in Illustration 9.1 as they might appear in a portion of a motion memo or brief.

"Installing" a template of these reader signals in your document can provide several benefits. First, creating the template forces you to break your document into smaller parts, and documents broken into sections are easier on the reader. Further, active readers can use the template items to help them find the information they need and to skip over what they don't need. Linear readers and active readers can both get context from the four template items, context that can help them to understand the text that follows. Likewise, both kinds of readers will look for connections in the template items so that they can understand how each section of the document relates to the other sections or to your overall thesis, thus increasing their understanding of your writing. Finally, because template items are in natural *positions of emphasis* in the document, they are ideal locations for a type of persuasion called *framing*.

Scientists who study persuasion have learned a lot about the way our brains work when we read, and two things they've learned are important here: (1) all readers pay more attention to information in certain positions in a document; and (2) all human beings are more vulnerable to persuasion at particular moments in the reading process.

1 When readers look at a document, their eyes are drawn to white space, which means they are drawn to beginnings and endings: the beginning and ending of each document, document section, and even paragraph. Their attention peaks at these locations, and thus they often subconsciously assign more importance to information in these locations. We refer to these locations as positions of emphasis. Good writers make sure to make the most of positions of emphasis by filling them with relevant information; in persuasive documents, they make sure to use those positions of emphasis persuasively.

1 Beginnings and endings of sentences can be positions of emphasis as well. We will discuss how to exploit those positions of emphasis in Chapter Fourteen.

Because readers pay more attention to the information in those positions of emphasis, what they read in those positions of emphasis often has an impact on how they feel about what they read. Scientists describe this impact as *framing*, because the information in the positions of emphasis *frames* the other information. Scientists also use the word *priming* to describe writing that is meant to provoke a certain reaction. As one scientist has noted, priming usually refers to *what* is being said, e.g., we are priming the reader to think positively about our client by providing certain details about our client. *Framing*, in contrast, usually refers to *where* the information is being presented. And just as a picture frame is outside of the picture, writers usually frame their arguments on the edges. As one scientist has noted, "framing sets a context around communicative content."[1]

Framing can be an effective persuasive technique because, as human beings, we always make decisions within a particular context. If the context changes, that may change the way we think about our decisions and thus change the decisions that we make.

In a famous experiment, psychologists asked people how they would choose between options if their community were facing a dangerous epidemic that was expected to cost up to 600 lives. The researchers asked respondents to decide which program they would adopt to fight the disease. Respondents were asked to review descriptions of one of two sets of two alternative programs; one alternative in each set was described in terms of certainty, while the other was described in terms of probability. More significantly, despite differences in descriptions, all of the programs would achieve approximately the same result: preventing 200 of the expected 600 deaths.

One pair of programs was described in terms of how many "people would be saved," while the other described how many "people would die." When deciding on a program described in terms of how many people would be saved, respondents were more likely to opt for certainty, rather than taking a chance that fewer people would be saved. When deciding on a program described in terms of how many people would die, they were more likely to opt for probabilities, because they were more willing to take a chance that fewer people would die.[2]

As a persuasive legal writer, you are almost always asking readers to make a decision; you may be asking opposing counsel to decide to settle, asking one judge to grant or deny a motion, or asking a judicial panel to vote to affirm or reverse. How you frame the decision process can have a significant impact on the decision. When you characterize the facts, how do you want to frame the behavior of the various actors in the case? When you describe the relevant rule and the authority cases, how do you want to frame the law? Of course, framing techniques cannot turn a losing case into a guaranteed winner; they can, however, improve the chances that your reader will give your argument its best shot.

---

1. John Sonnett, *Priming and Framing: Dimensions of Communication and Cognition*, THE OXFORD HANDBOOK OF COGNITIVE SOCIOLOGY (Wayne H. Brekhus & Gabe Ignatow eds.) ch. 13, at 226; *see also* Amos Tversky & Daniel Kahneman, *The Framing of Decisions and the Psychology of Choice*, 211 SCIENCE, Jan. 30, 1981, at 453-571, *available at* http://www.stat.columbia.edu/~gelman/surveys. course/TverskyKahneman1981.pdf.

2. *Id.*

The sections below will talk about each of the reader signals in the template and discuss their persuasive opportunities.

9.1.1. Roadmap Paragraphs and Umbrellas

Professor Linda Edwards has used the term *umbrella paragraphs* to describe the combination of introductory material and roadmap paragraphs that appear—or should appear—at the beginning of most arguments.[3] We think that in almost every situation, the umbrellas should have two facets. First, the writer should include any information that is needed to provide context that is (a) relevant to the document as a whole, or (b) common to all of the subpoints, or (c) needed to connect the subpoints to the writer's thesis. We call this context the legal *backstory*. Second, any time you break a section into subsections, you should provide some sort of roadmap. Sometimes the backstory and roadmap can be combined in one paragraph, while at other times you may need two or three paragraphs. Note that it would be extremely unusual to need more than a page for your umbrella.

Many legal writers mistakenly believe—consciously or subconsciously—that they do not need to provide legal readers with introductory material. Legal readers are smart, these writers think (and judges must be especially smart!); legal readers must be able to read a document and figure out for themselves how the pieces fit together. And on one level they are right; readers can often figure things out, if they have enough time. But even good legal readers are usually short on time, and good legal writing doesn't make readers figure things out: it provides them with the information they need when they need it.

And whenever you are dividing a part of a document into subsections, legal readers need two kinds of context: they need to know how this piece of the document fits into your thesis, and they need to know what's coming. The backstory fits the content into the bigger picture, and the roadmap tells them what's coming.

a. Using Backstory to Provide Context and Persuade

One way to explain how the information in any section of a legal document fits into your thesis is by connecting it to the relevant legal issues. Move from what the readers know about the law—general context—to what's going on in this document or this part of

---

3. Linda Holdeman Edwards, Legal Writing: Process, Analysis, and Organization 69-74, 133-37, 160-61 (5th ed., Aspen 2010).

the document—specific context. For example, if you are writing a demand letter, the reader knows by the letterhead that you are a lawyer. You start by explaining who your client is and what legal claims your client is bringing against the reader or the reader's client. If you are writing a motion memo or a brief, you start with the foundational legal rule—e.g., the Fourth Amendment, or a statute—and then move to the specific language of the specific rule at issue—e.g., whether a yoga teacher can give permission to search a client's gym bag, or whether laws governing "milk distributors" can be applied to people who distribute soy milk.

By providing backstory (with appropriate citations) you give the reader vital context for what follows. If you are saying that a yoga instructor has authority to consent to the search of a gym bag, don't dive into consent analysis, presuming that the reader knows how it is relevant to the defendant's rights. Instead, start with general references to the Fourth Amendment and the laws governing consent to search. Likewise, if you are arguing that milk distribution laws don't apply to soy milk distributors, start with general reference to the regulation of milk products, and then move to the definition of milk and to milk distribution regulations and their limits.

Broadly stated, the reader should be able to glean four elements from the legal backstory:

1. **The question that this part of the document is answering.** If you are writing the backstory for the whole document, you should address the question that the whole document is answering. If you are providing backstory for just one part of the document, focus on that part alone. In almost every situation, you should state this question as a declaration. Don't say, "The issue is whether the defendant's yoga instructor had the authority to consent to the search of defendant's gym bag." Instead, assert your conclusion: "The Fourth Amendment does not give a part-time yoga instructor the authority to consent to a search of a client's personal possessions."

2. **The legal rule or standard that is at the root of the issue being addressed in that part of the document.** As you know, many legal arguments are about the meaning of a particular phrase-that-pays—a word or phrase within a constitutional provision, statute, or legal rule. Even when there is a thick layer of judicial gloss on the original rule—as there is, for example, on the First Amendment—you should still note (or quote) the pertinent part of the First Amendment before moving to the concept of, for example, the existence of a chilling effect in a particular case.

3. **How the legal issue in this case (or section of the document) relates to the rule, if needed.** If the rule at the root of the issue is the rule at issue, you can skip this step. If the rule at issue is a different rule, move from the rule at the root of the issue to the rule or sub-rule currently at issue. Again, here, you are moving the reader from what is known to what is unknown. You may accomplish this goal in any of a variety of ways, including moving through a series of interconnected rules, stating a general rule followed by subparts, or stating a general rule followed by one or more exceptions to that rule.

4. **The current status of that issue in the relevant jurisdiction, if needed.** Although this piece of the backstory is not always needed, for some cases its inclusion is crucial. Most umbrellas will make evident how the rule operates in general. Include more details about the rule's status only if there are any controversies about this rule that are relevant to your argument. For example, perhaps you are arguing that the court should allow an exception to a particular rule when circumstance C exists. To identify the current status of the rule, you might point out that the court has previously created exceptions for circumstance A and circumstance B. In addition or in the alternative, there might be a split in the circuits as to the issue. If you are writing to a court other than a court of last resort, it might be appropriate to point out that sister states or sister circuits have adopted a particular rule but that your jurisdiction has not yet done so. You may fear revealing a potential weakness in your case, but by framing that potential weakness from your perspective, you may be able to reduce any negative impact.

Be honest in the legal backstory. For example, if there is a split in the circuits, it might be tempting to point out only that certain other courts have decided the case the same way you want the court to decide this one. Your credibility would suffer, however, when the court reads your opponent's brief and discovers the truth. In contrast, if you begin by laying out the complete backstory, you will do much to help the court and to burnish your own image as an honest dealer.

In a recent decision, for example, the United States Supreme Court decided that certain types of cell phone data may be accessed only with a warrant supported by probable cause.[4] The Court was asked to determine the validity of a federal statute that allowed access to this data only if law enforcement made a request based on "reasonable grounds."

---

4. *Carpenter v. United States*, 138 S. Ct. 2206, 2221 (2018).

You may have heard something about the case, but we're guessing you don't know the details. The example below shows how counsel for the defendant might persuasively move a reader from a general knowledge that the case relates to the Fourth Amendment and cell phones to the specific knowledge that will provide context for the roadmap and the brief. Note that this example is on the long side; often, the discussion of the legal backstory can be accomplished in a couple of sentences.

Good Example of Framed Backstory Written by Defendant's Attorney

The Fourth Amendment has always forbidden unreasonable searches and seizures. **2** Over the centuries of its existence, it has evolved—and it must continue to evolve—to recognize_new inroads on personal privacy. **3**

In 1986 Congress passed the Stored Communication Act (18 U.S.C. § 2703) **4**, which allows the government to access data from third-party providers without a warrant or probable cause; the government can obtain a court order granting access to this personal data as long as the government can "offer" **5** the court "specific and articulable facts showing that there are reasonable grounds to believe that the contents of a wire or electronic communication, or the records or other information sought, are relevant and material to an ongoing criminal investigation." **6**

This court must recognize that a government is conducting an unreasonable search **7** when, without a warrant or probable cause, it accesses cell phone records that may reveal a person's every location over a period of months. The circuits are split as to **8** whether people have an expectation of privacy in this type of cell-phone location information. *McGuffin v. Gaffigan*, 999 U.S. 989, 1001 (2022) (citing cases **9**). If they do, the request for court orders allowed under § 2703 must be supported with probable cause.

10 This court must reverse the decision of the Sixth Circuit for three reasons. . . .

The following example of legal backstory comes from a brief in opposition to a motion for summary judgment in a stalking case. In

---

2 Fourth Amendment language at the root of the legal issue.

3 Foreshadowing that the current situation represents one of those "new inroads."

4 The other legal rule at the root of this issue.

5 Quotation marks emphasize how meager this requirement is.

6 What we know: the Fourth Amendment protects against unreasonable searches, it evolves, and a statute allows some data searches with an offer of "reasonable grounds."

7 The conclusion the writer wants the court to reach.

8 What we don't know: whether people have an expectation of privacy in this type of cell phone record. The next sentence notes the consequence of a finding that the expectation of privacy exists.

9 This citing technique provides access to a string cite without including one.

10 Here, the writer moves to the roadmap.

the main backstory, the writer had laid out the jurisdiction's three-part test for stalking (in essence, pattern of conduct, resulting fear or distress, and intent) and then noted that the plaintiff had submitted evidence as to all three elements.

The excerpt below provides the backstory for the second element: that the pattern of conduct resulted in the plaintiff's fear or distress. This section of the argument requires an umbrella—that is, backstory and roadmap—because it will be split into two sections to demonstrate that the plaintiff can succeed on either of two alternative means of proof. The plaintiff must prove that, as a result of the defendant's pattern of threatening conduct, the plaintiff either (A) "reasonably feared for either his or her safety or that of an immediate family member," or (B) "suffered substantial emotional distress caused by a pattern of conduct that would cause a reasonable person to suffer substantial emotional distress." Because the writer has stated earlier the stalking rule at the root of the case, the backstory here need only refer to it; accordingly, the backstory can be quite succinct.

1.2 Plaintiff has submitted evidence to establish that Defendant's pattern of conduct caused reasonable fear for Plaintiff's safety and substantial emotional distress.

Plaintiff's evidence also shows **11** that she can establish the second element of the anti-stalking statute **12**, which has two alternate methods of proof relevant here **13**: a plaintiff must establish that the defendant's pattern of conduct caused her to reasonably fear for her safety, or that it caused her to suffer emotional distress that a reasonable person would suffer in reaction to that conduct. Van. Rev. Code 2904.12(B) **14**. Here, Plaintiff's evidence shows (1) . . .**15**

11 Framing the argument positively by asserting that plaintiff has met this standard.

12 Explicit reference to "the second element of the anti-stalking statute" references the rule at the root of the case and provides context for active readers who may read non-sequentially.

13 The "relevant here" phrasing signals that the statute includes other, non-relevant details. Here, the plaintiff was put in fear, but immediate family was not, so she does not mention that aspect of the element.

14 This citation and the paraphrase clarify the specific controversy in this section of the document.

15 Here, with backstory complete, the writer shifts to the roadmap.

By referring specifically to the second element and citing authority for it, the writer has ensured that the reader will be able to understand what rule is at the root of the controversy for this part of the argument. The status of the rule is not controversial, and so the writer merely relates the two needed facets of the element.

Whether your legal backstory is complex or simple, providing it will go a long way toward helping the reader to understand the rest of the argument.

b. The Roadmap

Roadmap paragraphs follow the legal backstory. As the name indicates, roadmaps lay out where you are going in the relevant section of your document. For purposes of narrative reasoning, roadmaps are needed because the backstory has set up a problem: The roadmap literally shows the court how it can solve the problem.[5]

Roadmap paragraphs are important in the template because they help confirm, and sometimes establish, the reader's expectations for the document. A good roadmap will also reveal the writer's position on the points to be addressed in the relevant sections or subsections. By writing an effective roadmap, the writer tells the reader how far this part of the document extends—how many points does the writer talk about before stopping? In addition, an effective roadmap lays out the document's large-scale organization by telling the reader the order in which the writer will address the main points. Even a poorly organized document will be easier to understand if the writer has provided a good roadmap.

It is tempting to skip this step, but providing the roadmap makes your writing more effective by reducing the reader's suspense. If the reader sees a "3" heading, followed immediately by a "3.1" heading, for example, the reader does not know how many subheadings will follow or how the subheadings connect to the writer's main point. By writing a backstory and a roadmap, the writer can make the connections explicit.

Although many writers are familiar with the law review style of roadmap paragraphs (*e.g.*, "this article will address three issues"), roadmaps in court documents can and should be more sophisticated. A simple technique is to provide the legal backstory and then focus on how you want the court to apply the relevant rules to the relevant facts.[6] The following example shows an umbrella that might have been written by counsel for Captain Yates of the *Miss Katie*, who was charged with violating the Sarbanes-Oxley Act's anti-shredding provision. The anti-shredding provision forbids trying to avoid being charged with a crime by "destroying" or "concealing" any "tangible object"; Captain Yates was accused of throwing some undersized fish overboard to avoid civil charges of illegally harvesting small fish in the Gulf of Mexico. The focus of the argument was whether fish were a "tangible object" under the meaning of a statute that was enacted in the wake of the excesses and accounting failures

---

5. *See* Kenneth D. Chestek, *The Plot Thickens: Appellate Brief as Story*, 14 Legal Writ. 127, 155-56 (2008) ("The 'road map' paragraphs . . . describe where the legal issues will be encountered in the remainder of the brief. They serve both as 'foreshadowing' of the conflict to raise in the coming pages and as a neat transition to the 'rising action' portion of the plot.").

6. *See* Laurel Currie Oates & Anne M. Enquist, The Legal Writing Handbook § 21.2.1 (4th ed., Aspen 2006).

of the Enron and WorldCom business scandals. Note how the writer frames the argument by trying to highlight the differences between the corporate focus of the statute and the nautical realities of the charged offense:

Example of a Possible Umbrella for **Yates v. United States**[7]

In 2002, Congress enacted the Sarbanes-Oxley Act **16** to promote integrity in accounting practices after the Enron scandal. Section 1519 of the statute—known as the "anti-shredding" provision—makes it a crime punishable up to twenty years in prison to knowingly destroy, conceal, or cover up "any record, document, or tangible object" **17** with the intent to impede or obstruct an investigation.

In 2007 Petitioner, captain of the ship, the *Miss Katie*, was found to have caught some 72 undersized fish by an officer of the Fish and Wildlife Commission who had boarded the *Miss Katie* and measured her catch. Before he reached port, Yates apparently ordered some of those fish **18** thrown overboard to avoid charges, though to no avail: he received an administrative citation for harvesting undersized fish in the Gulf of Mexico.

19 Three years after this incident, in 2010, a U.S. Attorney in Florida charged Yates with violating Sarbanes-Oxley's "anti-shredding" provision by throwing undersized red grouper into the Gulf of Mexico in 2007. This Court should find that the anti-shredding provision applies to records and documents, not fish.

When this Court interprets statutes, it has an obligation to ignore plain language when that language contradicts congressional intent or leads to absurd results. *McGuffin v. Brewer*, 101 U.S. 104, 108 (1955). Further, a statute is void for vagueness **20** when it fails to "define the criminal offense with sufficient definiteness that ordinary people can understand what conduct is prohibited." *Kolender v. Lawson*, 461 U.S. 352, 357 (1983).

21 This Court should reverse the decision of the Eleventh Circuit for three reasons:

(1) Congress expressly enacted Section 1519 to close legal loopholes contributing to corporate financial scandals, not

16 The statute at the root of the controversy.

17 The language at issue in this case.

18 Frequent mentions of *fish* highlight a distinction between fish and accounting practices.

19 Because the brief makes a due process argument based on the statute's vagueness, this paragraph again highlights the apparent absurdity of an anti-shredding statute regulating someone throwing fish into the Gulf of Mexico.

20 What we know about statutory interpretation — courts usually follow plain language, but there are exceptions. We also know that some statutes are void for vagueness. We don't know whether fish are tangible objects under these rules and the Sarbanes-Oxley Act.

21 The roadmap is presented in list form to make it visible to active readers.

_____

7. Our source materials for this example were some of the real party briefs and amicus briefs in this case.

to regulate fishermen. Therefore, the Eleventh Circuit erroneously construed the statutory term "tangible objects" to include red grouper.

22 The writer doubles down on the argument's absurdity theme by talking about "Woodsy Owl."

22 (2) Imposing federal criminal liability on Captain Yates would permit prosecutors to use Section 1519 to turn minor civil or criminal infractions into serious felonies, leading to absurd results not only in this case, but in others. For example, individuals who destroy a misappropriated image of "Woodsy Owl," *see* 18 U.S.C. § 711a, or a videotape of a false weather report, *see* 18 U.S.C. § 2074, could face up to twenty years in prison.

(3) Captain Yates did not have fair notice that throwing red grouper overboard would violate an anti-shredding provision in a non-maritime federal statute enacted to promote integrity in business accounting practices. Thus, imposing criminal liability on Captain Yates under § 1519 would violate his due process rights.

This Court should limit the scope of § 1519 to avoid absurd results and promote due process. Captain Yates's conviction should be reversed.

Some writers provide a roadmap to the entire argument within the summary of the argument. They then provide mini-roadmaps to each complex section of the document (*i.e.*, each section of the document that has subparts). The structure of the headings will dictate the structure of the roadmap paragraphs. If there are two main headings, there should be two points in the overall roadmap. If a main heading section contains three subsections with subheadings, then the mini-roadmap that introduces that section should have three points. Our next example repeats the legal backstory in the stalking case excerpted above, and is followed by a mini-roadmap to the two points supporting the plaintiff's argument on the "reasonable fear" element:

1.2 Plaintiff has submitted evidence to establish that Defendant's pattern of conduct caused reasonable fear for Plaintiff's safety and substantial emotional distress.

Plaintiff's evidence also shows that she can establish the second element of the anti-stalking statute, which has two alternate methods of proof relevant here: a plaintiff must establish that the defendant's pattern of conduct caused her to reasonably fear for her safety, or that it caused her to suffer emotional distress that a reasonable person would suffer in reaction to that conduct. Van. Rev. Code 2904.12(B). Here, Plaintiff's evidence shows the following:

> (1) Defendant's repeated threatening phone calls, texts, and written notes personally delivered to her home and office were a pattern of conduct that caused her to reasonably fear for her safety, both at work and at home.

> (2) Defendant's threats of physical harm, along with his repeated statements that he would "get her in the end" and that she "couldn't avoid him forever" would cause a reasonable person to suffer emotional distress, and Plaintiff's deposition and those of her sister and boyfriend show that these threats and statements did cause Plaintiff to suffer emotional distress.

Accordingly, this court should find that Plaintiff has submitted sufficient evidence as to the second element of her stalking claim.

You should almost always use enumeration when you present roadmaps. Your context goal can be met without enumeration, but your navigation goal is always enhanced when readers—especially active readers who are skimming and scrolling—can easily see this list of your important points.

Whether you use enumeration or not, your roadmap should be argumentative. An ineffective roadmap will say, in essence, "this court must decide three issues: (1) whether to rule for or against my client as to issue one. . . ." Because you know how you want the court to decide the case, make that hoped-for result the premise of your roadmap, as in the previous examples, saying in essence: "This Court should rule in favor of my client for three reasons." You should also review your headings and roadmaps together, to make sure that the roadmaps predict exactly the points you will address and echo language that you will use when you address each point. You should not copy and paste your exact headings into the roadmap, but the roadmap should certainly include words and phrases—particularly phrases-that-pay—that appear in the headings. The roadmap will create expectations in the reader; by using similar language in the roadmap and the headings, you can reassure the reader that you are fulfilling those expectations, and make it easier for the user to find needed information.

9.1.2. Headings

By this stage of the writing process, most writers will have identified where their headings belong and will have begun to draft headings as well. On those unusual occasions when you must churn out a brief without time for significant revision, however, you might use the template method to help you to turn a stream-of-consciousness draft into a readable document.

Inserting headings is one of the simplest steps a writer can take to improve the brief's effectiveness because headings allow the user to find the most important parts of the document. In an objective document, a heading can be simply a word or phrase that accurately describes the subject of the section or subsection—for example, "Causation," "Due Process Violation," or the like; because the writer is usually not pushing one conclusion or another, the headings can be merely objective labels. When writing an argument, however, resist the temptation to take the easy way out: take the time to draft argumentative point headings.

In general, an argumentative heading should be a statement about what you want the reader (*e.g.*, a court) to *do*, or what you want the reader to *believe*. If possible, you can also include information about the reason for that action or conclusion, but you should do so only if the resulting heading will not be too long (three lines long is a good maximum). A good way to test the persuasive value of your headings is to ask yourself if the heading could be appropriate in your opponent's document. For example, the following headings might appear in a brief on the *Yates* case:

Bad Example
Statutes should be interpreted to avoid an absurd result.

This heading might be logical, but it would not be effective in either brief because both sides agree that this statement is true. They disagree on whether the interpretation here results in absurdity. Better headings would make the writer's position evident:

Better Examples
When the "anti-shredding provision" of an anti-corporate malfeasance statute forbids the destruction of any "document, record, or other tangible object," it would be absurd to interpret that language to include dead fish.

23 If you ever learned it is wrong to start a sentence with *because*, you may ignore that advice. Just make sure to follow a because clause (a dependent clause) with an independent clause, as the writer does here.

23 Because a fisherman's accounting practices include counting his fish, it is not absurd to interpret a financial integrity statute in a way that forbids illegal destruction of a fisherman's catch.

Argumentative point headings are an important part of your template because they are so highly visible. Further this advantage by choosing highly visible typefaces and styles for your point headings. Boldfaced type is usually an excellent choice, unless local rules forbid it.

You may be told that local rules "require" all capital letters, but be sure to check the rules yourself. Often, local practice has interpreted phrases such as "conspicuous type" to mean "all capital letters."[8] In the examples below, note how much less readable the all-caps heading is:

Bad Example
2.3. THE BROADER STATUTORY CONTEXT IN WHICH SARBANES-OXLEY INCLUDES "TANGIBLE OBJECT" CONFIRMS CONGRESS'S INTENT TO RESTRICT ITS MEANING TO PAPER, A COMPUTER, OR OTHER INFORMATION-PRESERVATION DEVICE.

Better Example
1.3 The broader statutory context in which Sarbanes-Oxley includes "tangible object" confirms Congress's intent to restrict its meaning to paper, a computer, or other information-preservation device.

Many legal typeface customs evolved during the age of the typewriter. Writers used all-caps typefaces and underlined text because boldfaced and italicized fonts did not exist. Readers welcome being able to find new point headings easily as they skim through a document, and boldfaced headings will help them do this. Headings made up of all capital letters are easy to find, but they are usually difficult to read.[9] Accordingly, you should never use all caps for point headings unless the court requires it.

In addition to typeface concerns, consider the placement of your headings as well. Headings should indicate a shift to a new issue or

---

8. *See generally* Mary Beth Beazley, *Hiding in Plain Sight: "Conspicuous Type" Standards in Mandated Communication Statutes*, 40 J. Legis. 1 (2014) (describing how various courts and legislatures have mandated all capital letters with the phrase "conspicuous type," even though all capital letters make writing less legible).

9. *See e.g.*, Ralf Herrmann, *How Do We Read Words and How Should We Set Them?*, Wayfinding & Typography (June 14, 2011), http://opentype.info/blog/2011/06/14/how-do-we-read-words-and-how-should-we-set-them. This essay explains that we can see clearly only a few letters at a time, and that we use our more blurry peripheral vision to pre-read and decipher upcoming letters. It also shows that all-caps letters are indistinguishable when blurry and that use of all-caps lettering therefore slows comprehension.

sub-issue, but be aware of reader needs for organizational signals. If you have gone more than three or four pages without a new heading, scrutinize your text. If possible, create subsections to provide readers with needed structure and organizational signals.

9.1.3. Thesis or Topic Sentences

24 Monte calls them thesis sentences; Mary Beth calls them topic sentences. We disagree on what to call these sentences, but we agree about what goes in them.

24 A *thesis sentence* or *topic* sentence is a sentence that expresses the main point of a paragraph. Although most of us learned in grade school that the topic sentence could be the first, second, or last sentence in the paragraph, in legal writing the topic sentence should always come first. Putting the topic sentence first is vital because most legal readers decide whether to read a paragraph based on its first sentence. If the first sentence shows the readers how the paragraph is relevant to the issue under discussion, they will continue. If not, they may skip down to the next paragraph, looking for more relevant information.[10] Further, readers in active-reader mode may scan the topic sentences, looking for paragraphs that address the points they're interested in.

Topic sentences can also help the legal writer: when well written, they signal the document's organization and can be used to check organizational effectiveness. After you have used the guidelines below to write an effective topic sentence for each paragraph (and verified that each sentence in the paragraph is connected to that topic), you can make a "topic sentence outline" by copying and pasting the first sentence of each paragraph into a new document.

When you review the topic sentence outline, you should see logical groupings: first, you should find several topic sentences relevant to your first point, then several topic sentences relevant to your second point, and so on. To the extent that you find topic sentences that are out of place, decide whether to fix the topic sentence, move the paragraph to a new location, or remove the paragraph from the brief.

Two reminders can help you to write effective topic sentences in a brief. First, whenever possible, use the phrase-that-pays within the topic sentence. Second, focus particular attention on topic sentences for rule explanation paragraphs. Those paragraphs lay the

---

10. *See, e.g.,* Geoffrey B. Duggan & Stephen J. Payne, *Skim Reading by Satisficing: Evidence from Eye Tracking,* Proceedings of the SIGCHI Conference on Human Factors in Computing Systems 1141-50, 1147 (2011) (agreeing with a conclusion about eye-tracking studies showing that "skimmers begin every paragraph and continue reading until the rate of information gain drops below a threshold whereupon they skip to the beginning of the next paragraph").

foundation for your argument, and the topic sentences provide an important substantive and persuasive opportunity.

a. Include the Phrase-That-Pays in Each Topic Sentence

One objective method you can use to check the effectiveness of your topic sentences is to look for the phrase-that-pays. Using the phrase-that-pays in each topic sentence tells the reader that the paragraph is worth reading and that it will provide more information about the word or phrase that is the focus of that section of the document.

The phrase-that-pays is almost always the best way to show the paragraph's focus on the key topic. In the examples below, from a section of a (fictional) brief supporting Captain Yates, the writer was arguing that interpreting "tangible objects" to include fish would go against Congress's purpose, so "Congress's purpose" was the phrase-that-pays for that section. Notice how, in the first list of topic sentences below, the writer does not always use the phrase-that-pays. The words "Congress's purpose" or possible substitutes (if any) are *italicized*:

Bad Example
Petitioner's reading of the statute would frustrate *Congress's purpose* by rendering it less likely that whistleblowers will report misconduct.

Petitioner's reading of Section 78u-6 is flatly at odds with *Congress's purpose* in enacting Dodd-Frank.

In addition, Petitioner's reading of the statute makes the confidentiality protections illusory for individuals seeking anti-retaliation remedies.

Moreover, Petitioner's reading would produce the very result that industry urged the Commission to avoid: undermining internal compliance regimes.

Finally, Petitioner's reading does not serve the *statute's policies:* incentivizing and protecting whistleblowers to better protect investors.

Whenever you omit the phrase-that-pays or substitute synonyms for it, you risk burdening and alienating the reader. In the third topic sentence above, for instance, the reader must do some mental work to recognize that a statute that makes a statute's protections illusory therefore thwarts its purpose. Although most people would be able to make this connection with a little extra effort, your argument should not require the reader to make any extra effort. *You* should make the extra effort and incorporate the phrase-that-pays into each topic sentence to signal that the paragraph says something meaningful about the phrase-that-pays. In the list that follows, notice how small revisions allow the writer to incorporate the phrase-that-pays:

> *Better Examples*
>
> Petitioner's reading of the statute would frustrate *Congress's purpose* by rendering it less likely that whistleblowers will report misconduct.
>
> Petitioner's reading of Section 78u-6 is flatly at odds with *Congress's purpose* in enacting Dodd-Frank.
>
> Petitioner's reading of the statute also thwarts *Congress's purpose* by making the confidentiality protections illusory for individuals seeking anti-retaliation remedies.
>
> Moreover, Petitioner's reading would interfere with *Congress's purpose* by producing the very result that industry urged the Commission to avoid: undermining internal compliance regimes.
>
> Finally, Petitioner's reading violates *Congress's purpose* because it does not serve the statute's policies: incentivizing and protecting whistleblowers to better protect investors.

The small amount of work it will take to incorporate the phrase-that-pays is worth the trouble. Using the phrase-that-pays in a topic sentence increases the likelihood that an active reader will find the paragraph, and that a linear reader will actually read it. If I am anxiously reading a brief, looking for information about how a particular interpretation does or does not support Congress's purpose, I may skip a paragraph that doesn't vividly signal its connection to that point. Accordingly, topic sentences that use the phrase-that-pays increase the value of your argument by making it easier to read and easier to use.

b. Use Legally Significant Categories in Topic Sentences

In a brief, topic sentences can be used effectively in the summary of the argument and the fact statement, but their effectiveness is crucial in the argument section. In particular, the topic sentences in the rule explanation section have a job to do. At a minimum, an effective topic sentence in the rule explanation should tell the reader something about what the phrase-that-pays means, usually by showing how it has been applied in the past. A formula for an effective topic sentence in the explanation might be expressed as follows:

> Phrase-that-pays is established [or cannot be established] when category of facts or reasoning that reveals a new facet of the phrase-that-pays exists. *McGuffin v. McGiffin*, 101 R.E.3d 104, 107 (Van. 2020).

Many writers waste the beginning of a rule explanation paragraph with a sentence about the facts of an authority case, as in these (fictional) examples from a brief in which an appellant is arguing that the client should be eligible for punitive damages in a Title VII case:

Bad Examples

In *Kolstad v. American Dental Assoc.*, 527 U.S. 526, 546 (1999), the Supreme Court examined the standards for awarding punitive damages in a Title VII claim.

In *Kolstad v. American Dental Assoc.*, 527 U.S. 526, 546 (1999), a plaintiff appealed after the trial court had denied her request for a jury instruction on punitive damages.

These examples tell the reader that the paragraph is about punitive damages, and about the *Kolstad* case. While this information may be accurate on some level, the reader hopes that the paragraph is really about how the holdings from *Kolstad* are relevant to the client's case; i.e., when a plaintiff should be eligible for punitive damages. The following example identifies the category of facts that will enable a plaintiff to argue eligibility for punitive damages:

Better Example

Egregious conduct is not required for punitive damages under Title VII; plaintiffs are eligible for a punitive damages instruction if the employer had knowledge that it may have been acting in violation of federal law. *Kolstad v. American Dental Assoc.*, 527 U.S. 526, 546 (1999).

By using legally significant categories in the topic sentence, the writer focuses the reader's attention on the true point of the paragraph: the irrelevance of egregious conduct and the relevance of knowledge. In the bad examples, in contrast, the reader knew only that the writer would be talking about *Kolstad* and about punitive damages.

Being able to identify legally significant categories is an important skill in legal analysis, and you can use it to your advantage in topic sentences. For example, if you are planning to argue that the rule in the case(s) discussed in a particular paragraph should apply in the same way to your client's case, you will want to look for categories—and use framing language—that make it easier for the reader to see that connection.

In the examples below, the writer is arguing about the permissibility of roadblocks during a police investigation. The writer found many authorities about roadblocks in immigration cases and wanted to analogize immigration roadblocks to the police investigation roadblock in the client's case. A topic sentence that focused on the facts would be less effective:

Bad Example
This Court has found constitutional an objective intrusion upon motorists during the course of a roadblock intended to detect the smuggling of illegal immigrants into the United States. *United States v. Martinez-Fuerte*, 428 U.S. 543, 557-58 (1976).

Rather than focus on the details of the immigration case, the writer of the better example focused on the legally significant categories that were relevant to the court's holding:

Better Example
The Constitution permits roadblocks that are placed at a designated location and that have a scope and duration that is not overly broad. *See United States v. Martinez-Fuerte*, 428 U.S. 543, 557-58 (1976).

Notice that the writer has framed the case in terms of what the constitution "permits," because the writer's goal is to get the court to allow the roadblock. Counsel for the other side of the case, on the other hand, might frame this same case differently:

Better Example
The Constitution forbids roadblocks unless they are situated at a fixed location and are limited in scope and duration. *See United States v. Martinez-Fuerte*, 428 U.S. 543, 557-58 (1976).

Whenever it is appropriate, try to use framing words—such as "only," "rarely," "generally," "broad," "limited" or the like—that lead your reader to think of the law from your point of view.

Thus, in the rule explanation section, you can use the topic sentence as a tool to characterize the law in a favorable way. Two caveats apply here: first, be sure that your characterization is fair as well as persuasive; second, be certain that the case descriptions that follow your topic sentences provide support for the characterizations that appear there.

Effective topic sentences make it easier for you to check your organization. More importantly, they make it more likely that readers will keep reading and that users will find the paragraphs that they are looking for. Finally, when you review authority cases for analogous or distinguishable categories to use in your topic sentences, you may generate substance for your arguments.

9.1.4 Internal Conclusions or Connection-Conclusions

Just as writers should check their headings against their roadmap paragraphs to look for foreshadowing and consistency, they should also check their headings against their internal conclusions to make sure their connection-conclusions are explicit. The last paragraph before a new heading is a strong position of emphasis, and stating an explicit connection-conclusion is a good way to exploit that position of emphasis. The writer can easily check for connection-conclusions by looking for each new heading or subheading and then checking the paragraph above that heading; unless it is a roadmap, the paragraph should end on the writer's explicit conclusion as to the point under discussion within that heading or subheading, and it should connect that point as needed to any other points in the argument.

Although some writers end a point heading section by foreshadowing the next issue, this technique is usually not necessary in a document with headings. If making the connection between the points in two sections or subsections is important, try beginning the next section with a reference to the section that you have just finished.

For example, in a subsection about part one of a two-part test, some writers will end the subsection by saying, in essence, "Petitioner meets part one of the test. Next, it will be shown that Petitioner meets part two of the test." To use positions of emphasis more effectively, the writer could end the first subsection by saying, "Petitioner meets part one of the test." After an appropriate, persuasive point heading, the next subsection's text can begin by saying, *e.g.*, "In addition to meeting part one of the test, Petitioner also meets part two. . . ." In this way, the writer shows a connection between the two parts of the test, but also exploits the position of emphasis at the end of the first subsection by focusing on the point made in that subsection. This technique can also be useful as a way to support digital readers, who may be jumping to part two of the document and would otherwise have no context for the information.

The guidelines are slightly different if the point is dispositive, that is, if that point alone can result in a victory for your client. In that situation, you may want to include terms in your connection-conclusion that connect the point to your overall thesis and tell the court what it must do. The sample below is adapted from a brief arguing that the trial court correctly granted a motion for summary judgment in a Title VII retaliation action. A retaliation claim requires plaintiffs to prove each element of a multi-part test, including the element that the employer took a materially adverse action against the employee. Because the employee must establish each element to succeed in the cause of action, the employer can succeed by winning on even one element, as this example illustrates:

Good Example

A transfer that results in no decrease in pay or significant change to job duties and that actually reduces one's roundtrip commute is not materially adverse. The trial court correctly held that the temporary transfer alleged by Durano as retaliatory did not constitute an adverse employment action. Accordingly, Durano cannot establish her claim of retaliation, and this Court should affirm the decision below.

If the point is not dispositive, exploit the position of emphasis that a section ending provides to articulate a connection-conclusion that hammers home the point you are trying to make in that section. Too often, a section of a brief does not conclude, it just stops. **25**

25 Like this paragraph did.

The sample below is from the last paragraph of a section of a brief arguing that a district court wrongly granted a motion for summary judgment for an employer in a Title VII retaliation claim. The section at issue argues that the plaintiff had submitted sufficient evidence to establish that the defendant-employer had committed an adverse action against an employee. The heading for the section states that "A jury could find that Lincoln's suspension, referral for a needless mental fitness exam, and subsequent transfer were materially adverse actions." But the end of the section does not highlight the thesis of the section:

Less Effective Example

In holding that the transfer was not an adverse action, the district court cited a single case, *McGuffin v. Vanita State University,*

221 F.3d 444 (25th Cir. 2009). The court's reliance on *McGuffin* was misplaced. Contrary to the district court's analysis, *McGuffin* is inapposite, as it is a discrimination case holding that the plaintiff's lateral transfer did not constitute a constructive discharge because a reasonable person would not have found it intolerable. *Id.* at 455.

By focusing the ending on specific criticism of the court below, the writer wastes an opportunity to exploit a position of emphasis. A better connection-conclusion would have echoed the point in the section heading:

More Effective Example
The plaintiff submitted expert evidence that the doctor who provided the mental fitness exam found it to be "needless" and that he "did not understand why she had been sent to him." (Burgin depo. p. 2, lines 32-33; p. 3, lines 35-37). Her suspension and transfer were each directly related to this needless exam. (Diaz depo, p. 33, line 44; Green depo, p. 23, lines 24-28). Accordingly, a jury could find that the employer had committed materially adverse actions against Lincoln.

Both linear readers and active readers look to the last paragraph of a section to get a quick take on the point the writer was trying to prove in that section. Make sure your last paragraph does the job.

9.2. CONCLUSION

To make your document reader-friendly and user-friendly, first be sure that you understand how the parts of your argument fit together. Then, make sure to show explicitly how the pieces fit together, and make it easy for all readers to find the various sections of your argument. Use roadmaps, headings, topic sentences, and connection-conclusions to show all of your readers both where each section of the argument is and how each section relates to the whole.

CHAPTER TEN

Formal Requirements in Appellate Briefs and Motion Memos

Although the argument section may be the largest piece of any brief, there's a lot more to a brief than the argument section. This chapter addresses the other sections that judges require or expect to see in briefs and motion memos. Rightly or wrongly, many readers form an impression of your credibility based on whether you conform to the minutiae of court rules. Your willingness to learn and follow rules about document format and filing guidelines tells the court that you are a professional, and that you take court requirements seriously. More significantly, you may suffer sanctions—from having to fix offending portions of the brief to having your case dismissed—for failure to follow certain rules.[1] In addition to following the rules, of course, you will want to take advantage of persuasive opportunities within each required section of the document.

Most state and federal courts in the United States are governed by at least two sets of rules. The more significant rules are the rules of procedure that govern all courts within a certain jurisdiction: the Federal Rules of Civil Procedure, the Federal Rules of Appellate Procedure, and the rules of civil and appellate procedure for a state system, for example.

In addition, most courts also have so-called local rules that may deal with requirements such as filing rules, page length, certificates of service, service on opposing parties, citations, and the like. Obeying these rules is crucial to the effective practice of law. Courts may dismiss cases if briefs are not filed on time,[2] or if counsel has failed to comply with court rules.[3]

In addition to following local rules, you will want to learn about local practices—the customs and behaviors that are unwritten but practiced by experienced local lawyers. Courts that allow or mandate electronic filing may prefer to have counsel file additional hard copies.[4] Trial judges may have "standing orders" that lay out rules for counsel to follow in all trials in front of particular judges. Taking the time to read a judge's standing order (typically posted on the court's website) may provide you with valuable information that will save you time and trouble and help you to make a good impression on the court. Whenever you have to file a brief, make sure that you have copies of all of the written rules that apply to documents submitted to that court, and try to find out the local practices and customs by consulting court websites, more experienced colleagues, or both.

This chapter explains the format requirements that are common to appellate briefs and motion memos. For appellate brief requirements, we will usually refer to Supreme Court rules, but most of

---

1. Judith D. Fischer, *Bareheaded and Barefaced Counsel: Courts React to Unprofessionalism in Lawyers' Papers*, 31 Suffolk U. L. Rev. 1, 31 et seq. (1997) (this article also contains several examples of courts' reactions to misstatements of law and facts and other failings). *See also* Judith D. Fischer, Pleasing the Court: Writing Ethical and Effective Briefs (Carolina Academic Press 2005).

2. *Booher v. Sheeram, LLC*, 937 N.E.2d 392, 394 (Ind. Ct. App. 2010), cited in *Always Follow the Rules, Above the Law* (Dec. 27, 2013), http://abovethelaw.com/tag/booher-v-sheeram-llc/ (last accessed October 15, 2020).

3. *In re O'Brien*, 312 F.3d 1135, 1136 (9th Cir. 2002).

4. *See, e.g.,* King County Local Rule 7(b)(4)(F) (discussing working copies, and requiring paper working copies for documents of 500 pages or more).

the requirements listed are common in other appellate courts. For motion memo requirements, we usually refer to federal court rules. Of course, you should follow the rules of the court to which you are writing, or the rules of your professor.

We will begin by addressing issues that are common to all briefs: length, typeface, and filing requirements. We will then address the rest of the requirements in two separate sections. Section 10.4 and its subsections address requirements relevant to appellate briefs, while Section 10.5 and its subsections address requirements relevant to motion memos.

10.1. LENGTH REQUIREMENTS

Most courts impose length limits on documents submitted to them. Take those limits seriously. Presume that the limit is meant to provide more than enough space for most arguments, and also enough space for arguments of common complexity. Don't presume that the length limit is a goal that you must strive to meet or to approach. Your goal as a writer should be to write enough about each issue to answer the question each issue presents and to give the reader confidence that your answer is correct. You do not win any points from judges for padding simple arguments, making the same point in two or three different point heading sections, or describing five cases where one would make the point. On the contrary, most judges are grateful to read a brief that makes its points effectively and then stops.

Of course, your argument must be complete. Presume that your readers are intelligent but ignorant of the particulars of the current case. Give enough details about your case, and about the authorities that you cite, for the members of the court to understand your analysis without having to resort to other documents. Your job is not to give them the same in-depth knowledge of the case that you have. Rather, perform a cost-benefit analysis; for example, a well-written three-sentence case description will give the court a reasonable understanding of that case, and may give just as much insight as a much longer one.

Courts may express a length limit as a page limit, a word limit, or both. The page limits on briefs may vary by category; briefs on dispositive motions generally have higher page limits (e.g., 20 pages) than non-dispositive motions (e.g., 15 pages). Appellate briefs may have even higher page limits. If you are a student, of course, your professor's local rules will dictate your limits.

10.2.　TYPEFACES AND MARGINS

Many courts have imposed font size and margin requirements to thwart lawyers who try to avoid length requirements by using smaller margins or smaller fonts. Local rules sometimes make recommendations as well.[5] If the court to which you are submitting your brief does not specify anything beyond page limits, presume standard margins (one inch all around) and a standard font size (12-point, nonproportional spacing).

10.3.　FILING REQUIREMENTS AND NUMBER OF COPIES

Courts impose very specific filing requirements on brief writers, listing specifics for everything from the method of service to the number of copies filed. Although some requirements may seem overly detailed, make sure you follow them. This section explains some categories of common requirements, but be sure to consult jurisdictional rules, local rules, and local practices before filing a brief in any court.

In the past, all documents were filed in hard copy at the courthouse, and counsel attached a paper certificate of service (discussed below) to certify that service had been made on opposing counsel. These days, most courts allow or even require electronic filing, known as e-filing, as a substitute for hard-copy delivery. If you are planning on e-filing, be sure to check with the court about pre-filing procedures. You may have to register with the court in advance to use its system. After you file, the court may provide an electronic receipt that allows you to open your document to check it. Do not rely on the receipt itself: open the document and make sure that the document transmission was successful. Further, so that you can seek any needed guidance, it makes sense to file your brief during business hours (even if the filing deadline is midnight), especially the first time you file with a particular court.

As for number of copies, United States Supreme Court Rule 33.1(f) requires that 40 bound copies of the brief should be filed

---

5. *Requirements and Suggestions for Typography in Briefs and Other Papers* 4, http://www.ca7.uscourts.gov/forms/type.pdf (last accessed September 23, 2020) (citing Ruth Anne Robbins, *Painting with Print: Incorporating Concepts of Typographic and Layout Design into the Text of Legal Writing Documents*, 2 J. Ass'n Legal Writing Dirs. 108 (2004)).

with the court in most circumstances. It is common for appellate courts to require a large number of copies (if it requires the filing of hard copies) because a panel of judges and their clerks will all need to review the brief. Rule 31.1 of the Third Circuit Local Appellate Rules requires that "each party must file ten (10) paper copies (i.e., an original and nine copies) of each brief with the clerk for the convenience of the court" and serve one paper copy on opposing counsel unless counsel has agreed to electronic filing. In some courts, local practice dictates that when attorneys file their briefs, they must file "courtesy copies," "working copies," or "judges' copies" with the court. If a document is filed in hard copy, the official version of the document cannot be marked up by a judge or the judge's clerk. Thus, counsel may provide one or more extra copies to speed the court's consideration of the brief. Even when briefs are filed electronically, some courts may require either electronic or hard-copy "working copies."

Court rules may also specify particular typefaces or font sizes (to ease reading), method of binding (to prevent staple injuries), color of the brief cover (to allow easy retrieval of a particular brief), and method of service on opposing counsel. Whenever you file a document with a court, make sure that you are following all needed filing requirements. Doing so will impress the court with your professionalism, will avoid sanctions, and may help speed a decision in your case.

10.4. DOCUMENT AND FORMATTING REQUIREMENTS FOR APPELLATE BRIEFS

As you will see, appellate courts impose many very specific formatting requirements on the briefs that they read. Many of the requirements are meant to ease their reading and comprehension, while others aim to ensure the validity of the law that you cite. This section discusses requirements that are common to many courts, but you should be sure to check the local rules to make sure you are meeting both their requirements and expectations.

10.4.1. Introductions in Appellate Briefs

Writers of appellate briefs typically provide context and crystallize the relevant issue(s) by writing a formal question presented (sometimes known as an *Issue Statement*). Recently, it has become common in some jurisdictions to provide context with an introduction as well.

An introduction presents the issue in its legal and factual context. In the introduction, you should inform the court about the issue or issues before it and about the precise procedural step you are asking it to take. The introduction should be specific, mentioning parties by name, not just by procedural status; it should also clarify the issue that is before the court in the appeal.

Bad Example

Appellant David Paul appeals the district court's denial of his motion to suppress all evidence and statements arising from two unlawful searches. The vehicle search was unlawful due to the recent passage of Proposition 64; the home search was tainted by the vehicle search and was independently unlawful due to problems with the supporting affidavit.

This introduction provides bare procedural information in that it tells the court that it is being asked to reverse a district court's decision that refused to suppress evidence resulting from vehicle and home searches. The introduction does not provide sufficient legal or factual context.

Better Example

Appellant David Paul appeals the district court's denial of his motion to suppress all evidence and statements arising from two unlawful searches. First, his vehicle was searched by a California officer without a warrant, based solely on the odor of marijuana. This search was unlawful because California has passed Proposition 64, which legalized the possession, transportation, and use of 28.5 grams or less of marijuana.

Second, based on the vehicle search, the officers obtained a warrant for the search of Appellant's home, a warrant which was tainted by the unlawful vehicle search. The warrant was also independently invalid because the affidavit in support of the warrant contained material false statements and omissions, did not provide probable cause to believe that evidence of any crime would be found in Mr. Paul's home, and cannot be justified under the "good faith" exception to the exclusionary rule.

This introduction gives the reader more factual context. It also provides more specifics about the challenges to the two warrants, telling the reader that this appeal will challenge the vehicle search because its only probable cause came from the odor of a legal substance, and will challenge the home search both for a "fruit of the poisonous tree" problem and for multiple problems with the supporting affidavit.

By writing a clear introduction, counsel provides needed context to the court that will enable it to better understand the rest of the brief. Although the introduction is not the place for strident argumentation, you can absolutely use it to highlight your theme.

10.4.2. Questions Presented

Almost all appellate briefs use questions presented to articulate the issues before the court. All questions presented should include certain useful elements and should be appropriately persuasive.

a. Elements to Include

Generally, writers should include three elements when writing a question presented: the core question, expressed as a yes-or-no question; the relevant law; and the legally significant facts. Writers commonly use one of three formats: the "under-does-when" format, the "whether" format, and the "deep issue"[6] or "multi-sentence" format. The "under-does-when" format essentially asks the following:

Under-Does-When Format

Under relevant law, are people within this legal status when these legally significant facts exist?

1 Under relevant law, does this legal status include these legally significant facts?

The "whether" format contains the same elements, but the information can be arranged in a different order:

Whether[7] Format

Whether a certain legal status exists when relevant law governs the situation and these legally significant facts exist?

1 As these examples show, the "under-does-when" format does not always include those exact words to introduce the law, the core question, and the facts. "Under-can-when" and "under-does-include" are common variations.

---

6. *See* Bryan A. Garner, *The Deep Issue: A New Approach to Framing Legal Questions*, 5 Scribes J. Legal Writing, 1, 4 (1994-1995).

7. People who are particular about grammar often cringe at the "whether" format because lawyers use it as if it is a complete sentence, even though it is technically a sentence fragment. (If you wanted to use the format correctly from a grammar viewpoint, you would write, "The issue is whether . . ." and end the sentence with a period.) Lawyers, however, have adopted the "whether" format as a valid sentence (using either a question mark or a period) and seem unlikely to change.

Whether a certain fact situation results in a certain legal status under this relevant legal standard?

Likewise, the multi-sentence format often contains the same elements, but in multi-sentence form:

Multi-Sentence Format
The law in this area provides X. The relevant facts are these. The question is as follows: Does this legal status result from these facts?

Here is an example of the same question written in all three formats:

Under the ministerial exception to Title VII, which precludes claims of employment discrimination against a religious institution brought by its ministers, are employment decisions about a teacher covered by that exception when she received religious training, held herself out as a minister of her church, taught religious doctrine as part of her duties, accepted a formal call to religious service, and claimed a ministerial housing allowance on her taxes?

Whether a church's employment decisions about a teacher are exempted from Title VII under the ministerial exception when the teacher received religious training, held herself out as a minister of her church, taught religious doctrine as part of her duties, accepted a formal call to religious service, and claimed a ministerial housing allowance on her taxes?

Title VII bans employment discrimination, but religious organizations are exempt from Title VII claims brought by their own ministers. Respondent taught in Petitioner's school as a "called teacher," installed as such in a formal ceremony after receiving religious training from a church-approved institution. As a teacher, she held herself out as a minister of her church, taught religious doctrine as part of her duties, and claimed a ministerial housing allowance on her taxes. The question presented is as follows:

Is a teacher's claim of employment discrimination precluded by Title VII's ministerial exception when the teacher has been installed as a called teacher, has held herself out as a church minister, and has claimed a ministerial housing allowance on her taxes?

Some writers use the question presented to ask a question about a substantive legal issue, essentially asking, "Under relevant law, does a certain legal status exist when these legally significant facts are present?" as in this example:

> Under Title VII's "ministerial exception," which precludes employment discrimination claims by ministers against their religious organization, is a teacher a "minister" when (1) she has been formally installed as a "called teacher" after receiving religious training from a church-approved institution, (2) she has held herself out as a minister of her church, (3) she has taught religious doctrine as part of her duties, and (4) she has claimed a ministerial housing allowance on her taxes?

Some appellate brief writers put the legal issue in the context of the decision that the court is being asked to reverse, essentially asking, "Whether the court below was correct when it held that under the relevant law, a certain legal status existed when these legally significant facts were present?" as in this example:

> Did the Seventh Circuit correctly hold that the ministerial exception to Title VII precludes a teacher from bringing a discrimination suit against her former employer when she had been installed as a "called" teacher after formal religious training, taught religious doctrine as part of her duties, and claimed a ministerial housing allowance on her taxes?

In addition to deciding how to focus your question, you must also decide how to structure the question. The "whether" structure often moves the core question to the beginning of the question:

> Whether the court below erred when it held that this law applied in this way to the legally significant facts?

or

> Whether legal status exists when these legally significant facts exist and when this law applies?

The "under-does-when" format, on the other hand, puts less emphasis on the core question, putting the law at the beginning. It also allows the writer to shift the legally significant facts to the end of the question, which may help to emphasize positive facts, as in this example:

> Under the Fourth Amendment's privacy guarantees, does an invitee into a residence have a legitimate expectation of

privacy when the invitee's sole purpose for being present is to assist the resident in an illegal activity?

The multi-sentence method, perhaps obviously, puts the core question at the end, which is also a position of emphasis. When deciding which format to use, consider what information you would like in the positions of emphasis within the question. Generally, the beginning and the end of the question are positions of emphasis, with the end of the question being the strongest position.

b. Persuasive Questions Presented

The way you frame your question, and the words you use to characterize the parties and the relevant facts, are effective ways to make your question presented persuasive. A common piece of advice is that you should write your question so that a "yes" answer would be good for your client:

Under relevant law, does my preferred legal status exist when this perfectly appropriate set of facts exists?

An alternate and equally effective method, however, is to use the question presented to highlight the wrongness of your opponent's request:

Under relevant law, is this outrageous result appropriate when these facts exist?

For example, you might write a question presented in the ministerial exception case in a way that highlights the potential ludicrousness of a person denying the application of a ministerial exception while claiming taxation benefits for being a minister:

Under Title VII's ministerial exception, which precludes ministers from bringing discrimination lawsuits against their churches, can a teacher at a religious school deny that she is covered by the ministerial exception when

(1) she holds herself out as a minister after having been installed as a "called" teacher following formal religious training;

(2) she teaches religious doctrine as part of her duties; and

(3) she has claimed a ministerial housing allowance on her taxes?

The writer's goal in this example is to provoke a visceral reaction in the reader: "Of course not! That would be ridiculous!"

Even the words you choose to describe the parties and events in the case can have a significant impact on a question's persuasive value. Judge Ruggero Aldisert describes this method as the persuasive use of *enthymemes*. An enthymeme is an unstated premise[8]; by using words with certain connotations, you may be able to lead your reader to subconsciously accept certain premises that will be good for your client, as illustrated by these questions from opposite sides of a Fourth Amendment case:

> **Whether a suspect's objection to police entry into his shared apartment barred the police from seeking his co-tenant's consent for a warrantless search of the apartment after Petitioner had been removed from the premises for a domestic violence investigation and then lawfully arrested for a prior robbery.**

> Under Fourth Amendment warrant requirements, was a consent to search valid when (1) the resident of a home expressly told police that they could not enter his home; (2) police removed that resident from the scene against his will; and (3) police subsequently turned to another resident to receive the consent that the first resident denied them?

Although the best enthymemes are based on legal premises that any court would agree with, some effective enthymemes can be based on policy premises or even common-sense premises. Some enthymemes are conveyed through the focus of a question on a particular angle of the case, while others may be conveyed merely by the choice of one word over another.

In the first example shown previously, the writer is basing his or her arguments on at least three unstated premises: (1) that "suspects" have fewer rights; (2) that people who live in apartments have fewer rights; and (3) that the objection of a person is less significant if they are then "lawfully arrested."

The second example, written from the defendant's point of view, is based on some opposite premises: (1) that "residents" have more rights than "suspects"; (2) that "homes" are more protected than "apartments"; and (3) that police should not remove people from the scene "against their will" as a means of getting permission to conduct a warrantless search.

---

8. *See* Ruggero J. Aldisert, Winning on Appeal 142-43 (rev. 1st ed., Nat'l Inst. Trial Advoc. 1996).

If you can base your question on a premise that is both valid and applicable, you can go a long way toward getting the court to agree with your argument before it has even read your first point heading. Often, both sides will have valid and applicable premises on which to base their questions, and so both sides can exploit this technique to emphasize their point of view.

One warning about a common problem with questions presented: take care in the way that you include the law, the facts, and the phrase-that-pays when you write the question presented so that you avoid assuming as true an element that is at issue in the case. A question that assumes an element at issue often asks, in essence:

Bad Example
Will this court find that condition X exists when Appellant has established all of the factors necessary for condition X?

Even though you may firmly believe that all of the factors are established, your question should not assume away elements that your opponent legitimately disputes. Instead, include the facts and the law that you can use to prove that the court should decide in your favor.

For example, in the following question, the writer has assumed that the prison mandated the employment relationship:

Bad Example
Under the FLSA definition of "employee," which does not include prison laborers on work-release programs mandated by the prison, does the FLSA regulate an employment relationship when the prisoner's involvement was mandated by the prison?

Because the other side argued that the prison did not mandate the employment relationship, the writer's question should not have assumed that a mandate existed. Instead, the writer should have included the facts and law that the writer planned to use to show that the prison did mandate the employment relationship:

Good Example
Under the FLSA definition of "employee," which does not include prison laborers on work-release programs mandated by the prison, does the FLSA regulate an employment relationship when the prison required prisoners to participate in a work-release program but instructed them to "choose" their employer from a restricted list of only three businesses?

In this question, the writer details the facts that will be used to argue that the work relationship was mandated. The use of quotes around the word *choose* is meant to signal that the limits on the prisoners' choices make the decision less like a choice and more like a mandate.

One tell-tale marker of a question presented that assumes an element at issue is that the writer has included the phrase-that-pays in the "when" clause—in other words, the writer has presumed that the phrase-that-pays exists. If you find yourself doing that, move the phrase-that-pays to the core question (the *does* clause), and ask yourself what facts you will use to prove that the phrase-that-pays does or does not exist. Those are the facts that should be in the *when* clause.

In addition to violating rules of logic, questions that assume elements at issue needlessly annoy the judge or justice reading the brief by failing to clarify the issue; these questions also hurt the credibility of the attorney who submitted them. By avoiding the trap of assuming elements at issue, you can both preserve your credibility with the court and incline the judge or justice to rely on your brief for a fair analysis of the case.

10.4.3. Fact Statements in Appellate Briefs

The fact statement, or statement of the case, provides the court with information about the procedural life of the case before it, as well as about the relevant facts that led the parties to court. For this reason, it is known familiarly as *the statement*, *the fact statement*, and *the statement of the case*. Some writers of appellate briefs use these last two categories as headings to divide their statement into factual and procedural categories.

An effective statement of the case will make it unnecessary for the court to resort to the record or the joint appendix, providing a universe of facts to which the court can refer. With rare exceptions, the statement should include in sufficient detail any fact even *referenced* in the argument.

2 The statement of the case should include necessary procedural facts and relevant background information in addition to the facts needed for the argument. The advocate should tell (in appropriate depth) the story of the events that gave rise to the litigation and how it progressed through the court system on up to the current hearing. The statement should also include citations that will allow the reader to verify easily the information cited. Most of the information will come from a joint appendix or a record, and that information should be cited according to Supreme Court Rule 24.1(a)

2 For many Supreme Court cases, the appendix to the petition for the writ of certiorari also contains important factual information.

or the appropriate rule from the relevant jurisdiction. Information that comes from the lower court opinions in the case (when these are not part of the record materials), as well as any statutes that may be included in the fact statement, should be cited according to appropriate citation rules.

Citations in the fact statement are vital because many judges will not trust facts without an appropriate citation. As a Fourth Circuit judge noted, "Little else makes my blood boil quicker than reading an appellate brief that lacks appropriate citations to the appendix in the statement of facts and the argument components."[9] Note that it would not be unusual to have a citation at the end of every sentence in a fact statement. Because the use of "*id.*" is as appropriate for record citations as for any other kind of citation, these multiple citations need not be intrusive.

If this is the first time you are working with a lengthy record, you may be tempted to "treasure hunt" for facts that help your client or hurt your opponent's case. Hunting for treasure is fine, but be sure you have not found fool's gold. In an appellate brief, for example, be sure not to confuse findings of fact with testimony that was not part of the court's factual findings.

A good fact statement begins by providing the reader with the necessary context. Too many writers begin the statement with the first happening in the case's chain of events, or an unfocused procedural statement about what has happened most recently. Note the following opening paragraphs (with minor adaptations) from the respective statements of the petitioner and the respondent in *Yates v. United States*. The parties in that case debated the meaning of the phase "tangible object" in a statute that was written in response to corporate destruction of paper documents. The narrow issue asked whether the phrase "tangible object" in that statute included fish. See which opening paragraph does a better job of providing context for the reader:

Opening Paragraph from Yates's Statement
Petitioner John Yates was convicted under 18 U.S.C. § 1519 for directing his crewmen to throw undersized fish back into the sea, after receiving a civil citation and being told to bring the fish to dock to be destroyed. Section 1519, commonly known as the anti-shredding provision of the Sarbanes-Oxley Act of 2002, criminalizes the destruction, alteration, or falsification of "any

---

9. Clyde H. Hamilton, *Effective Appellate Brief Writing*, 50 S.C. L. Rev. 581, 586 (1999).

record, document, or *tangible object*," with the intent to obstruct or influence the proper administration of any federal matter. 18 U.S.C. § 1519 (emphasis added). Concluding that a fish is a "tangible object," the court below affirmed Mr. Yates's conviction. Mr. Yates seeks reversal of that decision because it is contrary to this Court's precedents, which require that the phrase be interpreted in the context of its surrounding terms and the statutory scheme.

Opening Paragraph of the Statement of the United States

Following a jury trial in the United States District Court for the Middle District of Florida, Petitioner was convicted on two counts relating to his destruction of undersized fish for the purpose of interfering with a federal proceeding under the jurisdiction of the National Marine Fisheries Service. Count 1 charged him with preventing federal officials from exercising their lawful authority to seize the fish, in violation of 18 U.S.C. 2232(a). Count 2 charged him with destroying or concealing the fish in order to impede the Fisheries Service's investigation and administration of the federal fisheries laws, in violation of 18 U.S.C. 1519. Petitioner was sentenced to 30 days' imprisonment, to be followed by 36 months' supervised release. The court of appeals affirmed.

Each example has its strengths. The first example highlights the language at issue ("tangible object"), taking care to note its corporate context. The government's brief highlights the fact that the petitioner destroyed the fish as a means of avoiding prosecution.

After providing context, the writer must decide how to organize the rest of the fact statement. Although chronological organization is often favored, sometimes a topical organization is more effective. You may have strategic reasons for choosing or avoiding chronological organization. If causation is at issue, for example, presenting information chronologically may send the implicit message that events that occurred earlier caused the events that occurred later. If you do *not* want to send that message, present the later events first (using topical headings as needed) and then move back to the earlier events.

Even if you plan to use a chronological organization, try to identify a set of topics that you can use as an organizing principle. Identifying topics can allow you to create useful topical headings within the statement; headings are particularly helpful if the statement is long. Although the writer must provide procedural as well as factual information, there is no requirement as to where in the fact statement the procedural information must be included. Some writers provide the information about court proceedings immediately after giving context; others progress chronologically from the facts that happened "in the world" to the facts that happened in court. Finally, some writers include internal headings to separate their "statement of the case" (including procedural information) from their "statement of the facts" (for factual information).

a. Making the Fact Statement Persuasive

3 When you read real-world briefs, you will read many briefs that include the argument within the fact statement. Sometimes those briefs resulted in victory. Be aware that the argument in the fact statement was not necessarily useful to the victory.

3 Most courts frown on the inclusion of legal arguments in the fact statement. They frown even more on lying, even if by omission, or on stretching the truth in the way that you characterize the facts. You should include all legally significant facts, even those that may hurt your case. Including all relevant facts is important both for moral reasons—your oath as an attorney requires it—and for practical reasons—your opponent will point out that you lied, and you will lose your credibility with the court.[10] Supreme Court Justice Ruth Bader Ginsburg advised that "[a]bove all, a good brief is trustworthy. It states the facts honestly."[11] Judge Parker notes that severe distortions of the facts "will actually make me stop reading the brief and go to the district court's opinion, or even the opposing brief."[12]

Nevertheless, you can use persuasive writing techniques to tell the story from your point of view, to highlight the facts that are in your favor, and to lead the reader to draw honest and favorable conclusions about your client's case.[13]

When drafting the fact statement, remember that your reader will not be a passive recipient of information, dutifully taking in whatever you have put on the page and doing nothing more with it. Most readers—yourself included—are constantly assessing, using inductive and deductive reasoning, leaping to conclusions, and, at times, mentally leaving the text entirely. In the argument, you will be announcing your conclusions to the reader and then supporting

---

10. *See, e.g.,* Hon. Fred I. Parker, *Appellate Advocacy and Practice in the Second Circuit,* 64 Brook. L. Rev. 457, 462 (1998).

11. Ruth Bader Ginsburg, *Remarks on Appellate Advocacy,* 50 S.C. L. Rev. 567, 568 (1999). *See also* Joel F. Dubina, *How to Litigate Successfully in the United States Court of Appeals for the Eleventh Circuit,* 20 Cumb. L. Rev. 1, 5 (1998/1999); Sarah B. Duncan, *Pursuing Quality: Writing a Helpful Brief,* 30 St. Mary's L.J. 1093, 1101 (1999).

12. Parker, *supra* note 10, at 462.

13. For an excellent discussion of persuasive writing techniques in fact statements, *see* Laurel Currie Oates & Anne M. Enquist, The Legal Writing Handbook, at §§ 17.7, 18.12 (5th ed., Aspen 2010).

them with your analysis. In the fact statement, on the other hand, you can provide information that the reader can put together to reach a conclusion. If you do it skillfully enough, the reader will have drawn a conclusion in your favor even before reaching the first page of the argument section.

Scholars who study narrative theory note that readers who jump to conclusions probably do so due to their conscious or unconscious awareness of "stock stories," or "schemas" that they have been accumulating all of their lives.[14] Readers use the details you include to jump to conclusions about the details you did not include, based on their own experience with or knowledge of similar situations.

Narrative reasoning may rely on schemas about human communication ("If the writer is bothering to include this fact, that must mean. . . .") or about human or institutional behavior ("In my experience, people who do X are trustworthy"). When you are writing a statement of facts, you are trying to tell a story. Recognize that including certain details may lead your readers to jump to conclusions—or refer to schemas—that may help or hurt your case. Aim to tell the story in a way that is consistent with and promotes your legal argument.

Legal writers can also use storytelling method to help their readers understand why certain parties have behaved in particular ways. Professor Ruth Anne Robbins notes that "people respond—instinctively and intuitively" to certain schemas and "character archetypes," and that lawyers should "systematically and deliberately integrate into their storytelling the larger picture of their clients' goals by subtly portraying their individual clients as heroes on a particular life path."[15] Professor Robbins advises against casting the client's opponent (or other antagonist) as a Voldemort-style villain.[16] Instead, she recommends a more benign role: The antagonist is someone who is frustrating the hero, barring him or her from achieving a goal.[17]

---

14. Linda L. Berger, *How Embedded Knowledge Structures Affect Judicial Decision Making: A Rhetorical Analysis of Metaphor, Narrative, and Imagination in Child Custody Disputes*, 18 S. Cal. Interdisc. L.J. 259, 263 (2009) ("We make sense out of new experiences by placing them into categories and cognitive frames called schema or scripts that emerge from prior experience.") (citations omitted). For further discussion of narrative theory and other persuasive writing techniques, *see* Michael R. Smith, Advanced Legal Writing: Theories and Strategies in Persuasive Writing (3d ed., Aspen 2012); Ruth Anne Robbins, Steve Johansen & Ken Chestek, Your Client's Story: Persuasive Legal Writing (Aspen 2012).

15. Ruth Anne Robbins, *Harry Potter, Ruby Slippers and Merlin: Telling the Client's Story Using the Characters and Paradigm of the Archetypal Hero's Journey*, 29 Seattle U. L. Rev. 767, 768-69 (2006).

16. *Id.* at 788.

17. *See id.*

You may want to tell your story in terms of a quest.[18] What does your client seek? Rather than thinking in pure procedural terms—that your client wants the court to grant or deny a motion, or to affirm or reverse a decision—think in terms of your theme.

In the case about the ministerial exemption, for example, the plaintiff could present herself as a person who wanted to work, but was being thwarted by a discriminatory employer. Her employer, a church, could present itself as wanting to enforce the tenets of its religion without needless government interference.

When planning your fact statement, you should identify the hero or protagonist (perhaps your client, perhaps a legislature, perhaps the Constitution) and the antagonists (perhaps your opponent, or some agent of your opponent).[19] Your protagonist, though, is frustrated; its goal has been thwarted by some outside actor or problem.[20] Seen from this perspective, the antagonist can be a person, a governmental body, or an "absurd" interpretation of a statute. Your client's goal is not merely a particular court decision; rather, the goal is an experience or status *made possible* by the court's decision.

Accordingly, when you are writing your statement of the facts, review your theme and the legal conclusions you want the reader to draw, and consider how those legal conclusions relate to the facts. Recognize conclusions that you might want to lead your readers to, and conclusions you want the reader to avoid. Consider what presumptions, schemas, or default images could be relevant to the case generally, and to people like your client or your opponent in particular. For example, has your client had several drug arrests? Could your readers have certain presumptions about police officers or corporate executives that you want to reinforce or rebut? You might want to add certain details that will lead your readers' thoughts in a good direction.

For example, if you want the court to overturn your client's criminal conviction, it might help the court to decide in your favor if it believes both that your client was treated unfairly and that your client is essentially an innocent person who was in the wrong place at the wrong time (a familiar schema). Your fact statement can include the details that will help the reader reach these conclusions independently.

---

18. *See id.* at 781-82.

19. Kenneth D. Chestek, *The Plot Thickens: Appellate Brief as Story*, 14 LEGAL WRIT. 127, 152-53 (2008) (describing strategies for choosing protagonists and antagonists).

20. Robbins, *supra* note 15, at 778 (discussing different types of heroes, from the innocent to the warrior).

Particularly if your client is a criminal defendant, your reader—a judge or a law clerk—may have a hard time understanding his behavior. The reader may be thinking that *she* would never break the law in such a way, and so she may find it hard to comprehend the reasoning behind the decisions your client made that put him into the court's jurisdiction.

In *Whitfield v. United States,* for example, the Supreme Court was asked to interpret a statute that would determine the prison sentence of a man who had committed an attempted bank robbery. If the first thing you learn about Mr. Whitfield is that he tried to rob a bank, you would probably form a negative opinion about his character. Counsel for Mr. Whitfield opened the factual description portion of the fact statement by trying to put his client's behavior into a more positive context:

> In September 2008, Larry Whitfield was a 20-year-old with a high-school diploma and no criminal record. His mother was serving an extended tour of military duty overseas, leaving Whitfield alone to care for himself and his younger brother. Unable to carry this burden financially and overwhelmed by the recent loss of his job and car, Whitfield decided—together with Quanterrious McCoy—to rob a credit union in Gastonia, North Carolina.[21]

This description does not absolve Whitfield of responsibility; it specifically notes that he "decided" to rob the credit union. It attempts to evoke sympathy, however, by reminding the court that the defendant had no previous record and that he was shouldering extra responsibilities while his mother was serving her country overseas.

After you have considered your theme, the conclusions you want the reader to draw, and the schemas you might want to exploit, make a list of all of the facts that are relevant to your case. Consult the abstract of the record, the record itself, the lower court decisions, and even the argument to come up with all of the legally (and emotionally) significant facts. (Be certain, of course, not to mischaracterize facts that were offered into evidence and rejected.) Perhaps divide your list into three parts: neutral facts, positive facts, and negative facts. As you tell your story, you can use some or all of the following persuasive techniques to highlight the positive facts and "lowlight" the negative ones.

---

21. *Whitfield v. United States*, 2014 WL 4244264 (U.S.), 3-4 (U.S. 2014) (petitioner's brief) (citation omitted).

b. Exploiting Positions of Emphasis

An easy and effective way to highlight information is to put it into positions of emphasis within the document. Readers subconsciously pay more attention to information that appears before or after a mental or physical break within the document. Thus, both the beginning and the ending of the fact statement are positions of emphasis, as are the beginnings and endings of any heading sections within the facts, and even the first and last sentences of paragraphs.

When writing your fact statement, strive to put your positive facts into positions of emphasis. You may even create positions of emphasis by inserting topical headings, by creating paragraph breaks, or by using headings to separate the introduction from the fact statement or the fact statement from the statement of the case.

c. Juxtaposing Good and Bad Facts

One way to think about the power of narrative reasoning is to compare it to pointillism, a painting technique developed in the nineteenth century by Georges Seurat. Instead of mixing red and blue paint on his palette to make purple paint, Seurat painted red dots next to blue dots and allowed the viewer's eye to "mix" the color. Legal writers can apply this technique to writing to try to control the way the reader sees information in the fact statement. If you put certain facts next to certain other facts, the reader's brain may "mix" the information to draw the conclusion that you want. When making your list of facts, try to identify facts that can be paired, either to lead the reader to draw a good conclusion or to prevent the reader from drawing a bad one.

For bad facts, use the "buddy system": Make sure that every bad fact that is included in the statement is paired with a good fact that explains (or neutralizes) its presence. Certain negative facts will look better if they are juxtaposed with a good fact, or even a neutral fact that readers can use to explain to themselves why the negative fact occurred or why it is not significant.

For example, in *Yates v. United States*, the petitioner was arguing that his destruction of fish did not fit within the "destruction of tangible objects" clause of the Sarbanes-Oxley Act. The petitioner could help the argument along by juxtaposing the "tangible object" language with the commonly-used label for the clause it appears in: the "anti-shredding provision." Because "shredding" reminds people of how they destroy paper, this juxtaposition leads the reader to think of that provision as being limited to paper records rather than fish.

d. Details or Aerial View?

To make sure that your readers remember the positive facts in your case, make them spend more time and less energy on them. Use several sentences to make a point instead of crowding the information into one sentence.[22] Be as concrete as you can be when describing a positive fact so that the reader doesn't have to figure out what happened. Conversely, when you want to deemphasize a fact, don't spend much time on it, don't go into a lot of detail, and don't use concrete language.

For example, if you were representing the plaintiff in the Title VII ministerial exception case, you would want to describe some of the facts more succinctly:

> Most of the plaintiff's work time was spent on secular rather than religious activities. She typically taught seven different subjects per day, six of them non-religious subjects such as math and reading. Defendant encouraged Plaintiff to participate in religious training to be eligible for a promotion and a higher rate of pay, and she participated in a ceremony upon the completion of that training. Although Defendant gave Plaintiff tax information and had her sign some paperwork after the ceremony, it never informed Plaintiff that she was forfeiting any legal rights by her decision to seek a promotion.

The reader would have to expend energy to identify the details that this brief description implies, and more than likely would not do so. Counsel for the defendant-employer, on the other hand, might describe certain events in greater detail:

> Plaintiff taught religion courses for an hour every day. After her first year as a teacher, Plaintiff paid to take a four-credit course in ministerial education. She received a "Diploma of Vocation" upon her successful completion of that course, and she submitted that Diploma to Defendant and asked to be considered for a position as a "Called Teacher." After the congregation voted to approve Plaintiff as a Called Teacher, Plaintiff participated in a Ministerial Ordination ceremony in which she and two other Called Teachers took vows that they would "teach faithfully the Word of God, the Sacred Scriptures," and "exemplify the Christian faith and life and

---

22. *See also* OATES & ENQUIST, *supra* note 13, at § 17.7.6 (discussing "airtime" and detail).

> lead others toward Christian maturity." As did the other
> Called Teachers, Plaintiff signed a ministerial certificate after
> that ceremony and received information about tax benefits
> that are available to ministerial employees.

Notice how the writer has unpacked the details to state explicitly information that is implicit in the first example. The first example notes that six of the teacher's seven daily courses were non-religious. This language implies that the seventh was a daily religion course; the second example makes that point explicit. Likewise, the second example gives more details about the religious nature of the training and the ceremony, with the probable goal of leading the reader to doubt that the plaintiff was ignorant of her role as a minister.

Of course, as with any persuasive method, use good judgment. If you go overboard in either direction, you will hurt rather than help your argument.

10.4.4. Summary of the Argument in Appellate Briefs

The summary of the argument follows the statement of the facts, and it signals an abrupt change. Up until this point, the writer has been describing the case, including its issues, the opinions below, and the facts. Now the writer begins to argue.

A summary of the argument is required for almost all appellate briefs, and it can play two roles. First, the summary can serve as a roadmap to the argument as a whole. The writer should succinctly state the major arguments relied on in the brief, in the order in which they appear in the argument section. Second, the summary can be used to present a holistic picture of the case, focusing more on policy and equity than on black letter law.

A good summary should grab the reader's attention in its opening paragraph. While the statement of facts should open with a somewhat objective statement of what the case is about, the summary of the argument can be more dramatic, identifying the underlying issues that the case presents.

In a 2019 case, for example, the Supreme Court had to consider whether a state's park commission violated the First Amendment by maintaining a 32-foot cross that had been erected in 1918 as a memorial to local residents who had died in World War I. The case presented each side with an opportunity for a dramatic opening.[23]

---

23. These examples are taken from briefs submitted in the case of *American Legion v. American Humanist Ass'n*, 139 S. Ct. 207 (2019).

Excerpt from the Brief Arguing No Violation
The Fourth Circuit's decision would compel the removal or destruction of a 93-year-old war memorial that was erected to honor the men who died in World War I, and that for nine decades has been used exclusively for that purpose, solely because it bears the shape of a cross.

Excerpt from the Brief Arguing a Violation
The central principle of the establishment clause is that the government cannot align itself with a single religion. When the government prominently displays a large Latin cross as a war memorial, it does more than just align the state with Christianity; it also callously discriminates against patriotic soldiers who are not Christian.

Each of these openings grabs the reader's emotions. When reading the first example, we instinctively reject the idea of destroying a war memorial. Likewise, when reading the second example, we just as instinctively reject the idea of discriminating against soldiers. These writers do an excellent job of presenting their arguments in a frame that highlights their theme.

A dramatic opening to the summary of the argument can be thought of as a "boom" opening, because it is meant to make a noise in the reader's brain to attract attention. Not every summary needs to have a boom opening, however. Sometimes, it can be effective to slow things down and to make the reader think for a moment. In *Young v. United Parcel Service*,[24] for example, the issue was the validity (under the Pregnancy Discrimination Act) of UPS policies that did not award certain workplace accommodations to employees who were pregnant. In their argument summaries, each party took a little time to provide details that presented the case in a positive context. You should be able to guess which example is from the UPS brief and which example is from Ms. Young's brief:

Example One
Petitioner asks this court to declare that employers must provide accommodations to women with pregnancy-related lifting restrictions, even if similarly situated nonpregnant employees do not receive such accommodations. While this type of accommodation might make for good policy, it is not required by the Pregnancy Discrimination Act.

---

24. 575 U.S. 206 (2015).

Example Two

UPS provides temporary accommodated work to three sizeable classes of drivers with work restrictions: those with on-the-job injuries, those with ADA disabilities, and those with conditions that render them ineligible for Department of Transportation certification. But it does not provide accommodated work to drivers who experience similar work restrictions due to pregnancy. That disparity violates the requirement of the Pregnancy Discrimination Act that "women affected by pregnancy, childbirth, or related medical conditions shall be treated the same . . . as other persons not so affected but similar in their ability or inability to work." 42 U.S.C. § 2000e(k).

These openings are effective because they each broaden the focus from the narrow decision to provide or not provide accommodations. The first focuses the reader's attention on what the statute does and does not explicitly require. The second juxtaposes the company's refusal to accommodate pregnant workers with its willingness to accommodate numerous other kinds of workers.

Most openings for the summary of the argument focus the reader on what the case is about. It can sometimes be appropriate, however, to focus on what a case is *not* about. In *United States v. Stevens*,[25] for example, the issue was the constitutionality of a federal statute that restricted creation and distribution of certain videos that included depictions of violence between or against animals. The statute was drafted to stop the creation of a category of videos that depicted the murders of puppies and kittens. The statute was challenged as overbroad by Stevens, a filmmaker whose films about pit bulls included some footage of dogfighting, which he opposed. Stevens could, no doubt, have started his summary of the argument with a boom opening. Instead, he slowed the pace and isolated the disagreement between himself and the government:

> This case is not about dogfighting or animal cruelty. The government and Stevens stand together opposing that. The question here is more fundamental: whether the government can send an individual to jail for up to five years just for making films—films that are not obscene, pornographic, inflammatory, defamatory, or even untruthful. They are controversial. But that is supposed to invigorate, not contract, the First Amendment's protection.

---

25. 559 U.S. 460 (2010).

This opening for the summary is effective because it disarms the emotional arguments that focus on animal cruelty and puts the focus on the less emotional—but equally important—issue of First Amendment guarantees.

Once the writer has written an appropriate opening, it is time to concentrate on the rest of the summary. Many writers clog up the summary of the argument with too much detail. This part of the document is meant to provide a *summary*. It should focus more on rules and how they apply than on detailed explanations.

In most situations, the summary of the argument need not contain numerous citations to authority. Of course, if a case, statute, constitutional provision, or other authority is at issue, it will be mentioned; likewise, if a particular issue is largely controlled by a case or other authority, that authority may be mentioned as well. Usually, however, the focus is on legal principles rather than on the authorities that are the source of those principles. Writing a paragraph for each major section of your argument should provide plenty of information for the reader.

10.4.5. Document Format Requirements and Service Requirements for Appellate Briefs

The United States Supreme Court rules specify the elements to be included in every type of brief submitted to it, from a brief petitioning for a writ of certiorari to a petitioner's reply brief on the merits. The Federal Rules of Appellate Procedure and rules of state supreme courts lay out similar guidelines. This section will focus on the document requirements of a petitioner's brief on the merits, which are described in Supreme Court Rule 24.

In practice, the party filing the responsive brief—whether it is an appellee's brief or a respondent's brief—is allowed to omit certain segments of the brief (e.g., the jurisdictional statement, the fact statement, or the opinions below) if that party agrees with the other party as to that information. In most appellate advocacy courses, of course, students on each side of the case are required to complete all segments of the document for pedagogical reasons. Whether in practice or in class, you must learn and follow the local rules.

a. Cover Page in Appellate Briefs

Supreme Court Rule 34.1 lists the elements that must be included on the cover page of the brief, including the docket number of the case, the name of the court in which the case will be heard, the caption of the case, the court of origin of the case, the type of document, and the name of the counsel of record. Similarly, Rule 341(d) of the Illinois Civil Appeals Rules, for example, lists the elements that must appear on the cover page of a brief, including the case number, the name of the court that is being appealed to and of the tribunal whose decision is being reviewed, the name of the case as it appeared in the lower tribunal, with the parties' identities indicating their status in both courts (e.g., "plaintiff-appellant"), the name of the trial judge entering the judgment to be reviewed, and the individual names and addresses of the attorneys and their law firms.

b. Page Numbers in Appellate Briefs

4 Lowercase or "small" roman numerals – e.g., iii, iv, ix, xv – are also known as romanettes. Preliminary pages in briefs have been numbered with romanettes because they are typically written or finalized *after* the body of the brief is written. In typewriter days, it would not have been possible to know what page numbers to use. We anticipate that the United States Supreme Court, like many other courts, will soon allow or mandate Arabic numbers for all pages.

4 Typically, a formal cover page is not numbered. If the caption is followed by text on the first page, however, it is appropriate to number that page. In United States Supreme Court briefs, the cover page is not numbered, and all pages until the page after the table of authorities are numbered with lowercase Roman numerals (i.e., the question presented appears on page i). Arabic numbering of the pages begins with the opinions below (*see* Section 10.4.5(g), *infra.*). Consult local rules for pagination guidelines for other appellate briefs; if pagination is not mentioned, you may presume that Arabic-numeral pagination is acceptable throughout.

c. Issues in Appellate Briefs

Appellate briefs designate the issue or issues before the court with a formal question or questions presented, which we described above. In Supreme Court briefs, the question presented appears alone on the first page after the cover page. However, in most other briefs, the question presented may be the fifth or sixth element of the brief; Rule 28 of the Federal Rules of Appellate Procedure places the statement of the issues after the jurisdictional statement and before the statement of the case. This placement may be why some attorneys are beginning their briefs with an introduction that identifies the issue. As noted in Supreme Court Rule 24.1(a), the brief may not raise additional questions or change the substance of the questions raised in the petition for the writ of certiorari; however, "the phrasing of the questions presented need not be identical with that in the petition for a writ of certiorari." Note that if your case has multiple questions, you should number the questions.

d. Parties to the Proceeding in Appellate Briefs

Appellate briefs may require a separate listing of "parties to the proceeding." In many cases, all of the parties to the proceeding have been listed in the caption on the cover page of the brief. If the parties are too numerous to list on the cover page, or if any of the parties have changed since the decision of the case below, Supreme Court Rule 24.1(b) requires you to include a separate page labeled "Parties to the Proceeding," which lists all parties (other than those on the cover sheet) who were parties to the proceeding in the court whose judgment is under review. Likewise, if any of the parties is a company with parent companies or non-wholly owned subsidiaries, you may need to add corporate disclosure information about that company here. Supreme Court Rule 29.6 describes corporate disclosure requirements.

e. Table of Contents in Appellate Briefs

Supreme Court Rule 24.1(c) requires a table of contents for all briefs that exceed 1,500 words. Generally, the table of contents contains a list of every element of the brief that has a title, from the question(s) presented, the opinions below, the argument *and* its sections that are labeled with point headings, to the conclusion, the certificate of service, and the appendix (if any). The table of contents should list only the first page on which each element appears. Note that some courts allow electronically filed documents to include hyperlinks to other portions of the same document;[26] if your court does, you may wish to link the items in the table of contents to their appropriate counterparts.

f. Table of Authorities in Appellate Briefs

Supreme Court Rule 24.1(c) also requires a table of authorities for all briefs that exceed 1,500 words. Rule 34.2 requires that the table of authorities include "cases alphabetically arranged, constitutional provisions, statutes, treatises, and other materials." Most attorneys use the categories listed in the rule as headings within the table, and some may subdivide any longer categories further. For example, they may group cases by court—United States Supreme Court cases, United States Circuit Courts of Appeals cases, and so on. This grouping may help the court to assess the brief's authority, but the rules do not require it.

The most important requirement is that the table should note *each* page on which each authority is cited. If an authority is cited so frequently that listing the individual pages would not help the court to find particular discussions of the authority, the table of authori-

---

26. *See, e.g.,* Third Cir. LAR 113.13.

ties may note *passim* (Latin for "throughout") instead of listing individual pages. *Passim* is often necessary to refer to a statute that is at issue because the statute may well be referenced on every page of the argument. Take care to use *passim* only when absolutely necessary; it is not an excuse for being too lazy to search through the brief to find the particular pages on which the citations appear.

Word processing programs may have a "table" function, which will allow you to create a table of authorities more easily. If you use this function, review the table after you generate it to be sure that it includes each needed authority and each needed page reference. Note that within the text of the brief, every case citation should have a pinpoint cite (also known as a "pincite"), which means that the first citation of the case will include the first page of the case and a specific "pinpoint" page. Be sure to review your table of authorities to remove that pinpoint. The table of authorities is one time that a case citation does not need a pinpoint.

Some courts allow electronically-filed documents to include hyperlinks to documents available on the Internet.[27] If your court does, we recommend that you include those links in the table of authorities (rather than within the document itself). Take care to follow rules about citation and appropriate paper copies.[28]

g. Opinions Below in Appellate Briefs

Supreme Court Rule 24.1(d) requires that the brief writer cite the official and unofficial reports of "the opinions and orders entered in the case by courts and administrative agencies." This section is usually designated "Opinions Below." If official citations exist, the writer must provide them; if the opinions are also (or only) available in the joint appendix or some other document submitted to the Court, the writer should make that clear as well — e.g., "The decision of the Second Circuit Court of Appeals is found at 101 F.3d 101 and at page 73 in the Joint Appendix." With this section, the Supreme Court brief writer begins Arabic page numbering with page 1. Some attorneys (notably, the United States Solicitor General's Office) reprint the caption of the case before this element; although Rule 24.1 does not specify this requirement, reprinting the caption helps the reader to distinguish between front matter and the body of the brief.[29]

---

27. *See, e.g., id.*

28. *See, e.g., id.* at 113.13(b) (noting that links "may not replace standard citation format") and 113.13(c) ("Hyperlinks do not replace paper copies of the appendix").

29. *See, e.g., National Ass'n of Mfrs. v. Department of Defense*, 2017 WL 3412010 at *1 (2017) (appellate brief) (note that the internal caption is shown

h. Jurisdiction in Appellate Briefs

In Supreme Court briefs, the jurisdictional statement, required by Rule 24.1(e), is usually rather straightforward. The rule asks for the "time factors" on which jurisdiction rests, and the attorney should therefore include the date on which the judgment being reviewed was entered, the date on which the petition for certiorari was filed, and the date on which the petition was granted. These items are necessary because they show that a final decision has been entered and that the petitioner has followed the necessary procedural steps and met any deadlines. The brief should also include the statute or statutes that give the reviewing court the authority to hear this type of appeal.

In cases in other appellate courts, the jurisdictional statement may be more complex. For example, Rule 28(a)(4) of the Federal Rules of Appellate Procedure requires that an appellant's brief include the basis for the district court's jurisdiction, including a citation to the statute and a statement of relevant facts; the basis for the court of appeals' jurisdiction, with similar inclusion of law and facts; relevant filing dates; and an assertion that the appellant is appealing a final appealable order. Jurisdictional issues can be raised for the first time at any point in the proceedings; thus, in practice, be sure that you understand the court's jurisdiction in your client's case.

i. Relevant Enacted Law in Appellate Briefs

Rule 24.1(f) requires the attorney to set out—"verbatim with appropriate citation"—the constitutional provisions, treaties, statutes, regulations, and ordinances (in that order) at issue in the case. Thus, this section should include only those statutes or other enacted laws whose language or application is in controversy. This section should *not* be used to reprint any statute *cited* in the brief. Rather, you should include statutes or other enacted laws only if you are asking the court to interpret or apply them (or not to apply them) in this case. Label this element according to whatever it happens to contain, e.g., "Relevant Constitutional Provisions" or "Relevant Statutes" or "Relevant Constitutional and Regulatory Provisions."

If only one paragraph of a lengthy statute is in controversy, you can quote only the pertinent part, but be generous: do not quote merely the sentence at issue. In general, when excerpting enacted law in a section of this type, you should quote at least a paragraph,

---

only on the "original [.pdf] image," and not on the Westlaw version of the document).

and be sure to include introductory material that provides sufficient context (e.g., "Section 125 defines 'stevedore,' and provides in pertinent part: . . .").

If printing the entire text of the relevant provisions would take up too much space (more than a page), simply include the citations and explain that the full text is reprinted in an appendix.[30]

j. Standard of Review in Appellate Briefs

As you read in Chapters Three and Four, the standard of review is the framework within which a court makes its decision. You must tell the court what standard of review applies to any decision you are asking it to review. The United States Supreme Court does not require that the standard be laid out in a separate section, but some courts are allowing or requiring separate inclusion of the standard. For example, the United States Court of Appeals for the Third Circuit, in Rule 28.1(b), requires counsel to specifically identify the standard of review and the claimed failure of the trial court: "whether the trial court abused its discretion; whether its fact findings are clearly erroneous; whether it erred in formulating or applying a legal precept, in which case review is plenary; whether, on appeal or petition for review of an agency action, there is substantial evidence in the record as a whole to support the order or decision, or whether the agency's action, findings and conclusions should be held unlawful and set aside for the reasons set forth in 5 U.S.C. § 706(2)."

Even if the court does not request a formal statement of the standard, it may be appropriate to include it. A good location in which to place this item is before the statement of the case, on the theory that knowing the standard of review may give the reader needed context for reading the fact statement. In the alternative, you could include the standard in introductory material. If different issues are subject to different standards of review, the introductory material preceding each issue should include the standard for that issue. In contrast, if the same standard applies to all issues, you could include it early in the argument section in your overall introduction, unless court rules require otherwise.

k. Statement of the Case in Appellate Briefs

Supreme Court Rule 24.1(g) asks for a "concise statement of the case, setting out the facts material to the consideration of the ques-

---

30. *See* Section 10.4.3(r) for discussion of Supreme Court rule requirements for the appendix.

tions presented." Methods for writing an effective statement of the case were discussed above.

l. Summary of the Argument in Appellate Briefs

Writing the summary of the argument is addressed above. The formal requirements are few, but some are quite particular. Supreme Court Rule 24.1(h) specifically notes that "mere repetition of the headings under which the argument is arranged is not sufficient." If you are arguing in a different appellate court, be sure to consult the local rules, as not all courts have this requirement.

m. The Argument in Appellate Briefs

Much has already been written about the argument; we will simply note here that Rule 24.1(i) asks that the argument exhibit "clearly the points of fact and of law presented and [cite] the authorities and statutes relied on." Some appellate courts may ask counsel to list any relevant authority that goes against counsel's argument. Thus, even though the method of written argument may not vary from court to court, you must still consult local rules about the argument itself.

n. The Conclusion in Appellate Briefs

The only requirement that the Supreme Court imposes on the conclusion, in Rule 24.1(j), is that it "[specify] with particularity the relief the party seeks." At a minimum, your conclusion should tell the court what you want it to do: affirm, reverse, reverse and remand, or vacate the decision below. Be precise when requesting relief. Ask the court to "affirm" or "reverse," *not* to "uphold" or "overrule" the decision below. Many lawyers write only one sentence as a conclusion, as in this example:

Good Example
For the foregoing reasons, this Court should reverse the decision below.

You will sometimes see flowery language in the conclusion, such as "Counsel for the Petitioner respectfully requests that the Court affirm the decision below." Although this language probably does not hurt counsel, it probably does not help, either. Because the words "respectfully submitted" appear in the signature block, just below the conclusion, you need not use "respectfully" in the conclusion itself. Indeed, briefs filed by the Solicitor General of the United

States typically have extremely short conclusions, consisting most often of an extremely short request for relief.

Good Examples
The judgment of the Court of Appeals should be reversed.
The judgment of the Court of Appeals should be affirmed.

Some courts will have little patience for a conclusion that is much longer than a paragraph. Make sure that you are aware of both local rules and local customs in this regard.

o. Signature in Appellate Briefs

The rules of the United States Supreme Court do not specifically require that attorneys sign briefs (although certificates of service must be signed). Rule 34.3 requires that the body of every document (i.e., information before any certificate of service or appendix) "shall bear at its close the name of counsel of record."

Although other courts have traditionally required an ink signature, that practice is changing with the rise of electronic service. The Third Circuit's Local Appellate Rule 46.4 provides that "[a]ll documents, motions and briefs must be signed by an attorney or by a party appearing pro se. Electronically filed documents must be signed with either an electronic signature or 's/typed name.'" Likewise, Local Rule 28.4 specifies that "[e]lectronic briefs may be signed with either an electronically generated signature or 's/ typed name' in the signature location. Counsel's state bar number, if any, and address and phone number must be included with the signature."

Unless rules specify otherwise, you should presume that a handwritten signature is required with a document filed in hard copy. Note that many courts require some sort of registration for those who wish to use electronic filing systems and thus electronic signatures; be sure to check local rules on this matter well before the filing deadline. Whether your signature is manual or electronic, you should include the phrase "Respectfully submitted" before the signature line.

p. Certificate of Service in Appellate Briefs

Most courts require that litigants who serve papers on the court also certify that they have served copies of those documents on opposing counsel. In this way, the court ensures that all litigants have copies of all of the documents in the case. Supreme Court Rule 29.5 specifies that "proof of service . . . shall accompany the document when it is presented to the Clerk for filing and shall be separate from it." The rule specifies several methods of certifying service, including "a certificate of service, reciting the facts and circumstances of service . . . and signed by a member of the Bar of this Court representing the party on whose behalf service is made."

Federal Rule of Appellate Procedure 25(b) provides that "[u]nless a rule requires service by the clerk, a party must, at or before the time of filing a paper, serve a copy on the other parties to the appeal or review. Service on a party represented by counsel must be made on the party's counsel." Some courts may allow service of opposing counsel after the brief is filed with the court, while others require that counsel file a certificate indicating that such service has already been accomplished.

If you are filing electronically, you may be able to serve your opponent electronically as well. Once again, be sure to consult local rules; electronic filing has added some wrinkles to the filing process. In some courts, only those who have registered with the court may use electronic filing services. Federal Rule of Appellate Procedure 25(c)(1)(D) provides that service may be made "by electronic means, if the party being served consents in writing." Along those lines, the Third Circuit's Local Appellate Rule 31.1(d) provides that "[a] party who is a Filing User as provided in L.A.R. Misc. 113.4 consents to electronic service of the brief through the court's electronic docketing system (cm/ecf). Service by alternate means must be made on all parties who are not Filing Users. The certificate of service must note what method of service was used for each party served." If your opponent is not able to receive electronic service, in other words, you may need to provide service using more traditional means. Be sure to find out service requirements well in advance of your filing deadline.

In general, the certificate of service should describe how service was accomplished. If you hand-deliver the document to opposing counsel's office, the certificate should say so and list the address. If the brief is filed electronically, as will typically be the case, the certificate should indicate that fact, and that certificate may be filed electronically as well. As always, consult local rules to find out the particulars.

q. Certificate of Compliance in Appellate Briefs

The certificate of compliance is a fairly new requirement; it seems to serve as a supplement to page-length and word-limit requirements. Modern word processing systems could make it difficult for a court to tell if an attorney has cheated a page limit, by, for example, using 11.8-point font instead of 12-point font. A certificate of compliance typically requires the attorney to certify that he or she has complied with court rules as to document length. (In a law school setting, you may also be asked to certify that you have complied with the honor code.) Although the certificate of compliance is a recent phenomenon, it is being required more frequently.

Federal Rule of Appellate Procedure 32(a)(7) requires that a brief must either comply with a page limit or with a word limit that is verified in a certificate of compliance. Federal Rule of Appellate Procedure 32(a)(7)(B) requires that the certificate state either the number of words in the brief or the number of lines of monospaced type in the brief. Local rules may add more requirements. Rule 31.1(c) of the Local Appellate Rules of the Third Circuit requires that counsel certify consistency between hard copy and electronic documents and allows for sanctions if an electronic document is infected with a computer virus.

Likewise, the United States Supreme Court now requires a Certificate of Compliance for all briefs filed in booklet format (and booklet format has been the typical format). Rule 33.1(h) requires that the certificate state the number of words in the brief (according to the word processing program) and state that the brief complies with the required word limits.

r. Appendix in Appellate Briefs

Few courts have rules that require an appendix for every brief. As noted previously, however, Supreme Court Rule 24.1(f) suggests an appendix (sometimes known as an "addendum") when legislation is too lengthy to reprint in the "applicable statutes" section of the brief. If an appendix is necessary, do not simply attach copies or .pdfs of statutes downloaded from a legal database. Instead, download the text into a word processing system and reformat the text, using typefaces and margins that promote readability.

Local rules and local practice—as well as the specific needs of your brief—will dictate the items that you include in the appendix. In general, you should include any information to which the court may need to refer while it considers the case, and which is not contained in the Joint Appendix or the Appendix to the Petition for the Writ of Certiorari. For example, you may include unpublished decisions, copies of documents (or segments of documents) that are at issue, and the like.[31] Note that some court rules may require an appendix in certain circumstances.

---

31. *See, e.g.*, Ruggero J. Aldisert, Winning on Appeal 84-89 (rev. 1st ed., Nat'l Inst. Trial Advoc. 1996); Carole C. Berry, Effective Appellate Advocacy: Brief Writing and Oral Argument 107 (3d ed., Thomson/West 2003).

10.5. DOCUMENT AND FORMATTING REQUIREMENTS FOR MOTION MEMOS

Trial courts rules do not typically impose many specific requirements on motion memos. This section describes the few elements that most courts require, and elements that we believe would enhance the quality and readability of any motion memo. Of course, you should check local rules. You must be sure to include any elements that are required, but you may certainly add elements that are not required, so long as the rules do not specifically forbid them. As you will see, many of the requirements are similar to those for appellate briefs.

10.5.1. Introductions in Motion Memos

5 Writers of motion memos typically articulate the issue before the court in a short paragraph under the heading "Introduction" or "Preliminary Statement." An introduction presents the issue in its legal and factual context. In the introduction, you should inform the court about the issue or issues before it and about the precise procedural step you are asking it to take. The introduction should be specific, mentioning parties by name, not just by procedural status; it should also clarify the issue that is before the court on the motion or in the appeal.

> **5** In some jurisdictions, the custom is to include or substitute a question presented. If this is true for your jurisdiction, consult Section 10.4.1 above.

Bad Example
This motion arises out of a Title VII action. Defendant has filed a motion to dismiss because Plaintiff has failed to state a claim upon which relief can be granted under Fed. R. Civ. P. 12(b)(6). This memorandum is filed in support of Defendant's Motion.

This introduction provides bare procedural information in that it tells the court that it is being asked to grant a motion to dismiss a Title VII action. It does not, however, clarify the narrow issue that is before the court, identify facts needed for context, or name the specific grounds for the defendant's motion, as the following example does:

Better Example
This Motion arises out of an action alleging sexual discrimination in violation of Title VII, 42 U.S.C. § 2000e-2. Plaintiff Laura Steger alleges Title VII violations by Defendant Second Christian Church, her former employer. Defendant has filed this Motion to Dismiss under Fed. R. Civ. P. 12(b)(6). The Complaint fails to

state a claim upon which relief can be granted against Defendant because Plaintiff served as a "Called," or Ministerial, Employee of the Church, and the Ministerial Exception to Title VII prevents government interference in a church's decisions about ministerial employees. Thus, Defendant's decision to terminate Plaintiff is not subject to Title VII. This Memorandum is filed in support of Defendant's Motion.

This introduction tells the reader that this is a sexual discrimination case, not just a Title VII case. It reveals that the ground for the motion is the assertion that certain employment decisions of religious organizations are not covered by Title VII.

By writing a clear introduction, counsel provides needed context to the court that will enable it to better understand the rest of the brief. Although the introduction is not the place for strident argumentation, you can absolutely use it to highlight your theme and be persuasive in other ways.

6 Because fact statements for briefs and motion memos have many similarities in form and function, much of the guidance here repeats the fact statement guidance in Section 10.4.2. If you have already read that section, you should focus your attention on the examples, which may be different.

6 10.5.2. Fact Statements in Motion Memos

The fact statement, or statement of the case, provides the court with information about the procedural life of the case before it, as well as about the relevant facts that led the parties to court. For this reason, it is known familiarly as *the statement*, *the fact statement*, or *the statement of the case*.

Fact statements for motion memos present some unique difficulties. The author of an appellate brief often has a well-developed record, with findings of facts articulated by the court below. In contrast, the writer of a motion memo may be working from a complaint (in the case of a motion to dismiss) or from numerous discovery documents (for a motion for summary judgment).

An effective statement will make it unnecessary for the court to resort to the record, providing a universe of facts to which the court can refer. With rare exceptions, the statement should include in sufficient detail any fact even *referenced* in the argument. A motion memo is usually written at a very early stage in the litigation. The writer must provide procedural information as to how the lawsuit began and how it has progressed, but this information is usually not lengthy and is thus not a significant part of the statement.

The statement should also include citations that will allow the reader to verify easily the information cited. This means that you are likely to be citing to the complaint or to discovery documents. You should take care, however, to cite precisely to the documents on which you have relied for your information, and to be sure the court has access to those documents as well. We recommend that your citation be as precise as possible: if the lines are numbered, your citation should include the page and line numbers. If the paragraphs are numbered, cite to the paragraph. If neither of these items is numbered, cite to the page. Of course, for any of these items, you must cite to the document as well, whether it is a complaint, an affidavit, a deposition, or some other document.

Good Example

This lawsuit arose from a dispute over the management and direction of RoFlo, a closely-held corporation. In 1985, Robert Kress and his then-wife, Florence Kress, obtained title to approximately 1,200 acres in rural Shelby County. Aff. of Robert Kress at ¶ 4 (Mar. 3, 2016). Sometime shortly before or after they obtained title to the 1,200 acres, Robert and Florence also acquired UHO. Id. at ¶ 5.

Citations in the fact statement are vital because many judges will not trust facts without an appropriate citation. As a Fourth Circuit judge noted, "Little else makes my blood boil quicker than reading an appellate brief that lacks appropriate citations to the appendix in the statement of facts and the argument components."[32] Note that it would not be unusual to have a citation at the end of every sentence in a fact statement. Because the use of "*id.*" is as appropriate for record citations as for any other kind of citation, these multiple citations need not be intrusive.

The first time you are working with a lengthy record, you may be tempted to "treasure hunt" for facts that favor your client or hurt your opponent's case. Hunting for treasure is fine, but be sure you have not found fool's gold. You may not rely on depositions in a motion memo in the same way that you would rely on findings of fact.

A good fact statement begins by providing the reader with the necessary context. Too many writers begin the statement with the first happening in the case's chain of events, or an unfocused procedural statement about what has happened most recently.

Ineffective Opening Paragraph from Motion
for Summary Judgment

Plaintiff was employed by Defendant from September 13, 2020 until August 26, 2021. (Pl. depo. p. 5; *Exhibit 2*, Employee Termi-

---

32. Clyde H. Hamilton, *Effective Appellate Brief Writing*, 50 S.C. L. Rev. 581, 586 (1999).

nation Form.) During her entire tenure, Plaintiff was a salaried, exempt administrative assistant to Ken Crowe. (Pl. depo. pp. 6-7; Pl. Aff. ¶4.) Crowe was Defendant's controller and director of operations. (Crowe depo. p. 5.) He was the second-highest ranking employee behind Jason Taylor, who was Defendant's president. (Lively depo. pp. 7, 65.).

Reading this paragraph, the audience would be forced to try to figure out what legal issues this case is focused on. Noticing that the paragraph references an employee termination form, the reader might be able to figure out that this case is about some sort of employment law issue. The following opening does not make the reader work; it provides the legal context immediately.

Better Opening Paragraph from Motion for Summary Judgment

7 These acronyms refer to the Americans with Disabilities Act and its state counterpart, here, the Tennessee Disability Act. As a general rule, you should never use a new acronym. Here, *ADA* is an abbreviation familiar to all lawyers in the United States, and in this context, *TDA* is equally familiar.

7 Defendant's motion for summary judgment was filed in response to Plaintiff's employment discrimination complaint, which alleges disability discrimination under the ADA and TDA. At all times relevant to this action, Plaintiff had stage IV breast cancer. Defendant does not deny Plaintiff's allegation that at all times she had satisfactorily performed her job as the administrative assistant to Kenneth Crowe, Defendant's controller and director of operations.

The better opening begins with a specific reference to the legal context, that this is a claim about disability discrimination. It follows with a straightforward, but emotional, fact that describes the plaintiff's specific disability: she has stage IV breast cancer. The plaintiff ends the paragraph by noting a fact that the defendant has not denied: that she had performed her job satisfactorily. Thus, readers have both context and facts that may lead them to be sympathetic to the plaintiff.

After providing context, the writer must decide how to organize the rest of the fact statement. Although chronological organization is often favored, sometimes a topical organization is more effective. You may have strategic reasons for choosing or avoiding chronological organization. If causation is at issue, for example, presenting information chronologically may send the implicit message that the events that occurred earlier caused the events that occurred later. If you do *not* want to send that message, present the later events first (using topical headings as needed) and then move back to the earlier events.

Even if you plan to use a chronological organization, try to identify a set of topics that you can use as an organizing principle. Identifying topics can allow you to create useful topical headings within the statement; headings are particularly helpful if the statement is long. Although the writer must provide procedural as well as factual information, there is no requirement as to where in the fact statement the procedural information must be included. Some writers provide the information about court proceedings immediately after giving context; others progress chronologically from the facts that happened "in the world" to the facts that happened in court, i.e., the filing of the lawsuit.

a. Making the Fact Statement Persuasive in Motion Memos

8 Most courts frown on the inclusion of legal arguments in the fact statement. They frown even more on lying, even if by omission, or on stretching the truth in the way that you characterize the facts. You should include all legally significant facts, even those that may hurt your case. Including all relevant facts is important both for moral reasons—your oath as an attorney requires it—and for practical reasons—your opponent will point out that you lied, and you will lose your credibility with the court.[33] Supreme Court Justice Ruth Bader Ginsburg advised that "[a]bove all, a good brief is trustworthy. It states the facts honestly."[34] Judge Parker notes that severe distortions of the facts "will actually make me stop reading the brief and go to the district court's opinion, or even the opposing brief."[35]

8 When you read real-world briefs, you will read many briefs that include the argument within the fact statement. Sometimes those briefs resulted in victory. Be aware that the argument in the fact statement was not necessarily useful to the victory.

Nevertheless, you can use persuasive writing techniques to tell the story from your point of view, to highlight the facts that are in your favor, and to lead the reader to draw honest and favorable conclusions about your client's case.[36]

When drafting the fact statement, remember that your reader will not be a passive recipient of information, dutifully taking in whatever you have put on the page and doing nothing more with it. Most readers—yourself included—are constantly assessing, using inductive and deductive reasoning, leaping to conclusions, and, at

---

33. *See, e.g.,* Parker, *supra* note 10, at 462.

34. Ruth Bader Ginsburg, *Remarks on Appellate Advocacy*, 50 S.C. L. Rev. 567, 568 (1999). *See also* Joel F. Dubina, *How to Litigate Successfully in the United States Court of Appeals for the Eleventh Circuit*, 20 Cumb. L. Rev. 1, 5 (1998/1999); Sarah B. Duncan, *Pursuing Quality: Writing a Helpful Brief*, 30 St. Mary's L.J. 1093, 1101 (1999).

35. Parker, *supra* note 10, at 462.

36. For an excellent discussion of persuasive writing techniques in fact statements, *see* Oates & Enquist, *supra* note 13, at §§ 17.7, 18.12 (5th ed., Aspen 2010).

times, mentally leaving the text entirely. In the argument, you will be announcing your conclusions to the reader and then supporting them with your analysis. In the fact statement, on the other hand, you can provide information that the reader can put together to reach a conclusion. If you do it skillfully enough, the reader will have drawn a conclusion in your favor even before reaching the first page of the argument section.

Scholars who study narrative theory note that readers who jump to conclusions probably do so due to their conscious or unconscious awareness of "stock stories," or "schemas" that they have been accumulating all of their lives.[37] Readers use the details you include to jump to conclusions about the details you did not include, based on their own experience with or knowledge of similar situations.

Narrative reasoning may rely on schemas about human communication ("If the writer is bothering to include this fact, that must mean. . . .") or about human or institutional behavior ("In my experience, people who do X are trustworthy"). When you are writing a statement of facts, you are trying to tell a story. Recognize that including certain details may lead your readers to jump to conclusions—or refer to schemas—that may help or hurt your case. Aim to tell the story in a way that is consistent with and promotes your legal argument.

Legal writers can also use storytelling methods to help their readers understand why certain parties have behaved in particular ways. Professor Ruth Anne Robbins notes that "people respond—instinctively and intuitively" to certain schemas and "character archetypes," and that lawyers should "systematically and deliberately integrate into their storytelling the larger picture of their clients' goals by subtly portraying their individual clients as heroes on a particular life path."[38] Professor Robbins advises against casting the client's opponent (or other antagonist) as a Voldemort-style vil-

---

37. Linda L. Berger, *How Embedded Knowledge Structures Affect Judicial Decision Making: A Rhetorical Analysis of Metaphor, Narrative, and Imagination in Child Custody Disputes*, 18 S. Cal. Interdisc. L.J. 259, 263 (2009) ("We make sense out of new experiences by placing them into categories and cognitive frames called schema or scripts that emerge from prior experience.") (citations omitted). For further discussion of narrative theory and other persuasive writing techniques, *see* Michael R. Smith, Advanced Legal Writing: Theories and Strategies in Persuasive Writing (3d ed., Aspen 2012); Ruth Anne Robbins, Steve Johansen & Ken Chestek, Your Client's Story: Persuasive Legal Writing (Aspen 2012).

38. Ruth Anne Robbins, *Harry Potter, Ruby Slippers and Merlin: Telling the Client's Story Using the Characters and Paradigm of the Archetypal Hero's Journey*, 29 Seattle U. L. Rev. 767, 768-69 (2006).

lain.[39] Instead, she recommends a more benign role: the antagonist is someone who is frustrating the hero, barring him or her from achieving a goal.[40]

You may want to tell your story in terms of a quest.[41] What does your client seek? Rather than thinking in pure procedural terms—that your client wants the court to grant or deny a motion, or to affirm or reverse a decision—think in terms of your theme.

In the employment discrimination case excerpted above, for example, the plaintiff is presenting herself as a person who wants to continue to work, but who is being thwarted by a discriminatory employer. Her employer could present itself as wanting to make its own decisions about its workforce.

When planning your fact statement, you should identify the hero or protagonist (perhaps your client, perhaps a legislature, perhaps the Constitution) and the antagonists (perhaps your opponent, or some agent of your opponent).[42] Your protagonist, though, is frustrated; its goal has been thwarted by some outside actor or problem.[43] Seen from this perspective, the antagonist can be a person, a governmental body, or an "absurd" interpretation of a statute. Your client's goal is not merely a particular court decision; rather, the goal is an experience or status *made possible* by the court's decision.

Accordingly, when you are writing your statement of the facts, review your theme and the legal conclusions you want the reader to draw, and consider how those legal conclusions relate to the facts. Recognize conclusions that you might want to lead your readers to, and conclusions you want the reader to avoid. Consider what presumptions, schemas, or default images could be relevant to the case generally, and to people like your client or your opponent in particular. For example, has your client had several drug arrests? Could your readers have certain presumptions about police officers or corporate executives that you want to reinforce or rebut? You might want to add certain details that will lead your readers' thoughts in a good direction.

For example, if you want the court to grant your client's motion to dismiss in a criminal case, it might help the court to decide in

---

39. *Id.* at 788.

40. *See id.*

41. *See id.* at 781-82.

42. Kenneth D. Chestek, *The Plot Thickens: Appellate Brief as Story*, 14 Legal Writ. 127, 152-53 (2008) (describing strategies for choosing protagonists and antagonists).

43. Robbins, *supra* note 37, at 778 (discussing different types of heroes, from the innocent to the warrior).

your favor if it believes both that your client was treated unfairly and that your client is essentially an innocent person who was in the wrong place at the wrong time (a familiar schema). Your fact statement can include the details that will help the reader reach these conclusions independently.

Particularly if your client is a criminal defendant, your reader—a judge or a law clerk—may have a hard time understanding his behavior. The reader may be thinking that *she* would never break the law in such a way, and so she may find it hard to comprehend the reasoning behind the decisions your client made that put him into the court's jurisdiction.

In *Whitfield v. United States,* for example, the Supreme Court was asked to interpret a statute that would determine the prison sentence of a man who had committed an attempted bank robbery. If the first thing you learn about Mr. Whitfield is that he tried to rob a bank, you would probably form a negative opinion about his character. Counsel for Mr. Whitfield opened the factual description portion of the fact statement by trying to put his client's behavior into a more positive context:

> In September 2008, Larry Whitfield was a 20-year-old with a high-school diploma and no criminal record. His mother was serving an extended tour of military duty overseas, leaving Whitfield alone to care for himself and his younger brother. Unable to carry this burden financially and overwhelmed by the recent loss of his job and car, Whitfield decided—together with Quanterrious McCoy—to rob a credit union in Gastonia, North Carolina.[44]

This description does not absolve Whitfield of responsibility; it specifically notes that he "decided" to rob the credit union. It attempts to evoke sympathy, however, by reminding the court that the defendant had no previous record and that he was shouldering extra responsibilities while his mother was serving her country overseas.

After you have considered your theme, the conclusions you want the reader to draw, and the schemas you might want to exploit, make a list of all of the facts that are relevant to your case. Study the complaint and the appropriate discovery documents. Perhaps divide your list into three parts: neutral facts, positive facts, and

---

44. *Whitfield v. United States*, 2014 WL 4244264 (U.S.), 3-4 (2014) (petitioner's brief) (citation omitted).

negative facts. As you tell your story, you can use some or all of the following persuasive techniques to highlight the positive facts and "lowlight" the negative ones.

b. Exploiting Positions of Emphasis in Motion Memos

An easy and effective way to highlight information is to put it into positions of emphasis within the document. Readers subconsciously pay more attention to information that appears before or after a mental or physical break within the document. Thus, both the beginning and the ending of the fact statement are positions of emphasis, as are the beginnings and endings of any heading sections within the facts, and even the first and last sentences of paragraphs.

When writing your fact statement, strive to put your positive facts into positions of emphasis. You may even create positions of emphasis by inserting topical headings, by creating paragraph breaks, or by using headings to separate the introduction from the fact statement or the fact statement from the statement of the case.

c. Juxtaposing Good and Bad Facts in Motion Memos

One way to think about the power of narrative reasoning is to compare it to pointillism, a painting technique developed in the nineteenth century by Georges Seurat. Instead of mixing red and blue paint on his palette to make purple paint, Seurat painted red dots next to blue dots and allowed the viewer's eye to "mix" the color. Legal writers can use a similar technique to try to control the way the reader sees information in the fact statement. If you put certain facts next to certain other facts, the reader's brain may "mix" the information to draw the conclusion that you want. When making your list of facts, try to identify facts that can be paired, either to lead the reader to draw a good conclusion or to prevent the reader from drawing a bad one.

For bad facts, use the "buddy system": make sure that every bad fact that is included in the statement is paired with a good fact that explains (or neutralizes) its presence. Certain negative facts will look better if they are juxtaposed with a good fact, or even a neutral fact that readers can use to explain to themselves why the negative fact occurred or why it is not significant.

For example, in *Yates v. United States*, the petitioner was arguing that his destruction of fish did not fit within the "destruction of tangible objects" clause of the Sarbanes-Oxley Act. The petitioner could help the argument along by juxtaposing the "tangible object" language with the commonly-used label for the clause it appears in: the "anti-shredding provision." Because "shredding" reminds people of how they destroy paper, this juxtaposition leads the reader to think of that provision as being limited to paper records rather than fish.

d. Details or Aerial View?

To make sure that your readers remember the positive facts in your case, make them spend more time and less energy on them. Use several sentences to make a point instead of crowding the information into one sentence.[45] Be as concrete as you can be when describing a positive fact so that the reader doesn't have to figure out what happened. Conversely, when you want to deemphasize a fact, don't spend much time on it, don't go into a lot of detail, and don't use concrete language.

For example, a summary judgment case about the ministerial exception to employment discrimination reached the United States Supreme Court a few years ago. A main issue was whether a teacher in a religious K-8 school was or was not a minister under the law. If you were representing the plaintiff in that case, you would. want to describe some of the facts more succinctly:

> **Most of the plaintiff's work time was spent on secular rather than religious activities. She typically taught seven different subjects per day, six of them non-religious subjects such as math and reading. Defendant encouraged Plaintiff to participate in religious training to be eligible for a promotion and a higher rate of pay, and she participated in a ceremony upon the completion of that training. Although Defendant gave Plaintiff tax information and had her sign some paperwork after the ceremony, it never informed Plaintiff that she was forfeiting any legal rights by her decision to seek a promotion.**

The reader would have to expend energy to identify the details that this brief description implies, and more than likely would not do so. Counsel for the defendant-employer, on the other hand, might describe certain events in greater detail.

> **Plaintiff taught religion courses for an hour every day. After her first year as a teacher, Plaintiff paid to take a four-credit course in ministerial education. She received a "Diploma of Vocation" upon her successful completion of that course, and she submitted that Diploma to Defendant and asked to**

---

45. *See also* OATES & ENQUIST, *supra* note 13, at § 17.7.6 (discussing "airtime" and detail).

be considered for a position as a "Called Teacher." After the congregation voted to approve Plaintiff as a Called Teacher, Plaintiff participated in a Ministerial Ordination ceremony in which she and two other Called Teachers took vows that they would "teach faithfully the Word of God, the Sacred Scriptures," and "exemplify the Christian faith and life and lead others toward Christian maturity." As did the other called teachers, Plaintiff signed a ministerial certificate after that ceremony and received information about tax benefits that are available to ministerial employees.

Notice how the writer has unpacked the details to state explicitly information that is implicit in the first example. The first example notes that six of the teacher's seven daily courses were non-religious. This language implies that the seventh was a daily religion course; the second example makes that point explicit. Likewise, the second example gives more details about the religious nature of the training and the ceremony, with the probable goal of leading the reader to doubt that the plaintiff was ignorant of her role as a minister.

Of course, as with any persuasive method, use good judgment. If you go overboard in either direction, you will hurt rather than help your argument.

e. Special Considerations for Motion Memo Fact Statements

The writer of a motion memo faces some special challenges. If you are writing a brief in support of a motion to dismiss, you may be arguing about a question of law. Nevertheless, you cannot ignore the facts in the complaint, even though they may consist of negative characterizations of your client. The aforementioned techniques for deemphasizing negative facts may be helpful, but you must always balance the desire for persuasion with the need for credibility. If you are too abstract in your description of the underlying facts, the court may distrust you.

The following example comes from a defendant's brief in support of a motion to dismiss. The defendant has been accused of racial discrimination based on numerous instances of racial insults and harassment. The description here is technically correct, but it would be very ineffective in a motion memo.

Bad Example from Defendant's Brief
Plaintiff, Stevie Wendl, claims that he experienced racial discrimination during his employment. Compl. ¶ **7.**

The court gets only a vague idea of what happened in the case and would be surprised when it reads the plaintiff's version of events.

Good Example from Plaintiff's Brief
Mr. Wendl worked for Defendant Marvin-Kobacker for 18 months, during which time Defendant allowed a racially hostile work environment to exist. Compl. ¶ 7. Immediately after Plaintiff's division participated in racial sensitivity training, Plaintiff's supervisor stopped by Plaintiff's workspace, looked directly at him, and said, "I guess I see why we had to have that training today." Compl. ¶ 8. On another occasion, when Plaintiff entered a semi-darkened room where two employees were chatting, one of the employees said, "Smile, Stevie, I can't see you." Compl. ¶ 8. Plaintiff reported these incidents to HR, along with several incidents in which Defendant's employees told racially insensitive jokes in Plaintiff's presence. Compl. ¶ 9. During the last month of Plaintiff's employment, Plaintiff entered a conference room for a meeting. Plaintiff's supervisor looked at Plaintiff and then said, "Better be careful what you say, folks, or someone's going to run to HR!" Compl. ¶ 10.

On the other hand, the statements in the complaint are merely allegations, even though they must be taken as true for purposes of the motion. Thus, if you are counsel for the defendant, you should not write your fact statement as if you believe that the statements are true. Instead, put these allegations in the plaintiff's "mouth"; that is, make clear that these are allegations in the complaint:

Good Example from Defendant's Brief
Mr. Wendl worked for Defendant Marvin-Kobacker for 18 months, and he alleges the existence of a racially hostile work environment during that time period. Compl. ¶ 7. Plaintiff's allegations include allegations of two hostile statements from his supervisor Compl. ¶¶ 8, 10; an allegation of one hostile statement from a co-worker, Compl. ¶ 9; and allegations of "numerous" racially insensitive jokes. *Id*.

This paragraph does not hide the fact that the defendant is accused of tolerating numerous incidents showing the existence of a racially hostile work environment, but it characterizes the allegations as what they are: allegations.

In addition to the controversial facts, there will likely be facts in the complaint that will help the court to understand the arguments, but which both sides agree on. These facts can be stated without labeling them as the allegations of one party or another.

Good Example from Defendant's Brief
Both Wendl and Zahm were employed by Marvin-Kobacker during the time of the alleged racial harassment. Compl. ¶ 4. Marvin-Kobacker employs over 200 individuals in its Foster, Rhode Island, location. Compl. ¶ 2.

These facts are not in dispute and are not controversial, and it is not worth the writer's time or the reader's energy to try to shade them in any way.

f. Special Considerations for Fact Statements in Summary Judgment Motion Memos

In many summary judgment motion memos, the statement of facts is similar to those in any other motion memo or appellate brief: the writer seeks to tell the facts in a narrative style, emphasizing good facts and de-emphasizing bad ones, and cites to appropriate sources for those facts. In the case of a summary judgment motion, the sources will typically be discovery documents.

In some courts, however, those who write motions for summary judgment title the fact statement "Statement of Undisputed Facts," and the statement includes numbered paragraphs of facts, much as a complaint does. Unlike a complaint, however, the facts in a summary judgment motion will be based on discovery documents, and those documents should be cited. The party replying to the motion must then either admit each paragraph or explain the dispute, again with citations to the appropriate discovery documents. In a 2008 employment discrimination case, the plaintiff alleged both discrimination and retaliation. Part of her claim was that she had been wrongly denied a trainee position. Below, you will see the first five paragraphs from both the defendant's "Statement of Undisputed Facts" and the plaintiff's corresponding response (names have been changed):

9 *Excerpt from Defendant's "Statement of Undisputed Material Facts"*

1. Ms. McCoy began working for Union Pacific in Train Service in Abbeville, Louisiana in 2002. Stuart Affidavit, Exhibit A.
2. Frank Stuart, the Manager of Terminal Operations for Union Pacific in Abbeville, hired Ms. McCoy. Stuart Affidavit.

9 This writer will be arguing that all of the material facts are undisputed, and the writer highlights that argument with this title. Unless this label is commonly used in the court to which you are submitting your motion memo, take care with this technique; overusing it can hurt your credibility.

3. In late July 2004, Mr. Stuart requested that Union Pacific employees wanting to be considered for a Yardmaster Trainee Position located in Abbeville, Louisiana submit written bids for the position to him no later than 12 noon, Tuesday, August 3, 2004. Stuart Affidavit.

4. Ms. McCoy, who then was Ms. Hébert, and others submitted bids for the position. At that time, Ms. McCoy had been with Union Pacific for approximately 2 years. Stuart Affidavit.

5. Although Mr. Stuart considered Ms. McCoy, Mr. Stuart selected Owen Duhon for that job because he had approximately 14 years with Union Pacific and had worked for Mr. Stuart as a yardmaster in the past. Stuart Affidavit.

10 Note that the plaintiff has not acceded to the defendant's use of the label "undisputed facts." Indeed, the very purpose of this fact statement is to highlight those material facts that *are* in dispute and to convince the court that it should deny the motion for summary judgment.

10 *Excerpt from Plaintiff's "Response to Statement of Material Facts"*

1. Admitted
2. Admitted
3. Admitted
4. Admitted
5. Admitted in part, denied in part. Plaintiff admits that she was qualified for the position (Deposition of Plaintiff, Exhibit 4 at 40). Nevertheless, Owen Duhon was selected for the job, although he had been fired from his previous managerial position (Deposition of Plaintiff, Exhibit 4 at 122). Plaintiff denies that seniority and/or years working with Union Pacific are criteria for selection for the yardmaster position (Deposition of Stuart, Exhibit 2 at 28). In 2006, Stuart selected an individual for yardmaster who only had "a couple of years" with Union Pacific (Deposition of Stuart, at 132, 133). The yardmaster position was to go to the person most qualified (Deposition of Plaintiff, Exhibit 4 at 37, 38; Deposition of Stuart, Exhibit 2 at 28). Furthermore, as stated in the union guidelines, Duhon was ineligible to be hired as a yardmaster (Deposition of Plaintiff, Exhibit 4 at 122).

Throughout any motion memo supporting or opposing a motion for summary judgment, the writer will be citing to discovery documents. Note that you help your argument's credibility when you can cite to your opponent's statements to support your points, as plaintiff's counsel does here.

Accordingly, when writing your fact statement, you should (1) decide what conclusions you want the reader to draw after reading the facts and note which presumptions the reader might bring to the fact statement; (2) collect the facts, noting which facts are positive, negative, and neutral vis-à-vis the conclusions you want the reader to draw; (3) organize the facts; (4) make the facts persuasive by exploiting positions of emphasis, context, level of detail, and specificity; (5) take care not to violate ethical or logical rules; and (6) make sure that you cite to appropriate sources for your facts as needed.

10.5.3. Summary of the Argument in Motion Memos

The summary of the argument follows the statement of the facts, and it signals an abrupt change. Up until this point, the writer has been describing the case, including its issues, the opinions below, and the facts. Now the writer begins to argue.

A summary of the argument is required for motion memos of a certain length (see local rules); if your brief does not require a summary, you may still include one if you believe doing so would advance your argument. The summary of the argument can play two roles. First, the summary can serve as a roadmap to the argument as a whole. The writer should succinctly state the major arguments relied on in the brief, in the order in which they appear in the argument section. Second, the summary can be used to present a holistic picture of the case, focusing more on policy and equity than on black letter law.

A good summary should grab the reader's attention in its opening paragraph. While the statement of facts should open with a somewhat objective statement of what the case is about, the summary of the argument can be more dramatic, identifying the underlying issues that the case presents.

In a 2019 case, for example, the United States Supreme Court considered an appeal of a summary judgment ruling about whether a state's park commission violated the First Amendment by maintaining a 32-foot cross that had been erected in 1918 as a memorial to local residents who had died in World War I. The case presented each side[46] with an opportunity for a dramatic opening:

Example One
The Fourth Circuit's decision would compel the removal or destruction of a 93-year-old war memorial that was erected to honor the men who died in World War I, and that for nine

---

46. These examples are taken from briefs submitted in the case of *American Legion v. American Humanist Ass'n*, 139 S. Ct. 207 (2019).

decades has been used exclusively for that purpose, solely because it bears the shape of a cross.

Example Two
The central principle of the establishment clause is that the government cannot align itself with a single religion. When the government prominently displays a large Latin cross as a war memorial, it does more than just align the state with Christianity; it also callously discriminates against patriotic soldiers who are not Christian.

Each of these openings grabs the reader's emotions. When reading the first example, we instinctively reject the idea of destroying a war memorial. Likewise, when reading the second example, we just as instinctively reject the idea of discriminating against soldiers. These writers do an excellent job of presenting their arguments in a frame that highlights their theme.

A dramatic opening to the summary of the argument can be thought of as a "boom" opening, because it is meant to make a noise in the reader's brain to attract attention. Not every summary needs to have a boom opening, however. Sometimes, it can be effective to slow things down and to make the reader think for a moment. In *Young v. United Parcel Service*,[47] for example, the issue was the validity (under the Pregnancy Discrimination Act) of UPS policies that did not award certain workplace accommodations to employees who were pregnant. In their argument summaries, each party took a little time to provide details that presented the case in a positive context. You should be able to guess which example is from the UPS brief and which example is from Ms. Young's brief:

Example One
Petitioner asks this court to declare that employers must provide accommodations to women with pregnancy-related lifting restrictions, even if similarly situated nonpregnant employees do not receive such accommodations. While this type of accommodation might make for good policy, it is not required by the Pregnancy Discrimination Act.

Example Two
UPS provides temporary accommodated work to three sizeable classes of drivers with work restrictions: those with on-the-job

---

47. 575 U.S. 206 (2015).

injuries, those with ADA disabilities, and those with conditions that render them ineligible for Department of Transportation certification. But it does not provide accommodated work to drivers who experience similar work restrictions due to pregnancy. That disparity violates the requirement of the Pregnancy Discrimination Act that "women affected by pregnancy, childbirth, or related medical conditions shall be treated the same . . . as other persons not so affected but similar in their ability or inability to work." 42 U.S.C. § 2000e(k).

These openings are effective because they each broaden the focus from the narrow decision to provide or not provide accommodations. The first focuses the reader's attention on what the statute does and does not explicitly require. The second juxtaposes the company's refusal to accommodate pregnant workers with its willingness to accommodate numerous other kinds of workers.

Most openings for the summary of the argument focus the reader on what the case is about. It can sometimes be appropriate, however, to focus on what the case is not about. In *United States v. Stevens*,[48] for example, the issue was the constitutionality of a federal statute that restricted creation and distribution of certain videos that included depictions of violence between or against animals. The statute was drafted to stop the creation of a category of videos that depicted the murders of puppies and kittens. The statute was challenged as overbroad by Stevens, a filmmaker whose films about pit bulls included some footage of dogfighting, which he opposed. Stevens could, no doubt, have started his summary of the argument with a boom opening. Instead, he slowed the pace and isolated the disagreement between himself and the government:

> This case is not about dogfighting or animal cruelty. The government and Stevens stand together opposing that. The question here is more fundamental: whether the government can send an individual to jail for up to five years just for making films—films that are not obscene, pornographic, inflammatory, defamatory, or even untruthful. They are controversial. But that is supposed to invigorate, not contract, the First Amendment's protection.

This opening for the summary is effective because it disarms the emotional arguments that focus on animal cruelty and puts the

---

48. 559 U.S. 460 (2010).

focus on the less emotional—but equally important—issue of First Amendment guarantees.

Once the writer has written an appropriate opening, it is time to concentrate on the rest of the summary. Many writers clog up the summary of the argument with too much detail. This part of the document is meant to provide a *summary*. It should focus more on rules and how they apply than on detailed explanations.

In most situations, the summary of the argument need not contain numerous citations to authority. Of course, if a case, statute, constitutional provision, or other authority is at issue, it will be mentioned; likewise, if a particular issue is largely controlled by a case or other authority, that authority may be mentioned as well. Usually, however, the focus is on legal principles rather than on the authorities that are the source of those principles. Writing a paragraph for each major section of your argument should provide plenty of information for the reader.

10.5.4. Document Format Requirements and Service Requirements for Motion Memos

Typically, trial courts designate few requirements for motion memos, so the most important format advice we can give you is to check the local rules of the court to which you are submitting the motion memo. One federal court requires that "[a]ll motions and applications tendered for filing shall be accompanied by a memorandum in support thereof that shall be a brief statement of the grounds, with citation of authorities relied upon." A state court rule requires that "[a] party filing a motion must also serve and file with it a memorandum of points and authorities in support of each ground thereof. The absence of such memorandum may be construed as an admission that the motion is not meritorious, as cause for its denial or as a waiver of all grounds not so supported." These rules focus on the legal requirements because many motions focus on procedure rather than facts.

Despite the lack of formal rules, memos supporting dispositive motions and other significant motions (e.g., motions to suppress evidence) often look much like appellate briefs, containing formal introductions or issue statements, fact statements, and the like. The most important guideline is to check the local rules, and find out all that you can about local practices and customs. Review motion memos submitted to the court in the past to see what elements local lawyers typically include. Don't be afraid, however, to adapt your motion memo if doing so (a) will not violate any court rules and (b) will help your client. In the following sections, we will describe ways that you can meet the court's formal and informal expectations when you file a motion memo.

a. The Caption in Motion Memos

Take a look at the sample motion memo at the end of Chapter Three. The top half or so of the first page is what we call the "caption." It tells the reader the who, what, and where of the case: where the case is being heard (the formal name of the court typically appears at the top of the page), who is suing who (typically on the left-hand side of the page, under the name of the court), what document is being filed (typically on the right-hand side of the page), and who is filing the document (typically included in the name of the document, e.g., "Defendant Monte Smith's Motion to Dismiss as to Himself"). Because trial courts are so busy, and because they receive a wide variety of documents, they have very specific requirements for captions, even though instructions may be pretty loose for the rest of the document. Rule 5.2 of the local rules for the United States District Court for the Southern District of Ohio is typical in its specificity:

> Except for the original complaint, all pleadings, other papers, and exhibits shall be identified by a title that contains the name and party designation of the person filing it and the nature of the pleading or paper; for example: "Defendant John Smith's Answer to the Amended Complaint," "Plaintiff Richard Roe's Answer to Defendant Sam Brown's Motion to Dismiss," "Affidavit of Joan Doe in Support of Motion for Summary Judgment," or "Exhibits in Support of Plaintiff John Smith's Motion for Summary Judgment." The names of the District Judge and Magistrate Judge to whom the case has been assigned shall be placed below the case number in the caption.

Just as some trial courts require requests for jury trials to be included in the caption of a complaint, many require oral argument to be requested in the caption of a motion. A Florida federal district court, for example, notes that oral argument is the exception rather than the rule, and that it must be appropriately requested:

> (j) Motions and other applications will ordinarily be determined by the Court on the basis of the motion papers and briefs or legal memoranda; provided, however, the Court may allow oral argument upon the written request of any interested party or upon the Court's own motion. Requests for oral

argument shall accompany the motion, or the opposing brief or legal memorandum, and shall estimate the time required for argument.[49]

11 Any teacher knows this feeling; if you ask your students to put their names in the top right-hand corner of the front page, and you are flipping through dozens of papers checking off names, you are not pleased with the students who ignore the request and thus slow down your work.

Thus, when filing a motion, don't rely on past experience or even this text: check the local rules and make sure the caption includes all the right information, and that it is in the correct location. If you are a clerk or a judge reviewing dozens, or even hundreds, of documents during a typical workweek, you have trained yourself to look for certain information in a certain location on the page. When the information is not where it belongs, it's easy to get frustrated, and most writers don't want to frustrate their readers. Follow the rules. **11**

b. Page Numbers in Motion Memos

Unlike appellate briefs, motion memos are numbered with Arabic numerals from beginning to end. As noted in the previous section, check the rules: some courts want those page numbers in a specific location on the page (e.g., bottom center).

c. Table of Contents in Motion Memos

12 As of this writing, the best way to do this is to make your document a .pdf and to make every heading a "bookmark." File your document with the Navigation Window open to increase the chances that your reader will read it this way.

Court rules tend to require a table of contents only when a brief exceeds a set number of pages, such as 20 or 30. Once your document exceeds 10 pages (some would say five), your reader will benefit if you include a table of contents. A formal table of contents contains a list of every element of the brief that has a title, from the introduction and statement of facts to the argument *and* all of the sections within the argument that are labeled with point headings, to the appendix (if any). The table of contents should list only the first page on which each element appears. Note that some courts allow electronically filed documents to include hyperlinks to other portions of the same document; if your court does not explicitly forbid this linking, you may wish to link the items in the table of contents to their appropriate counterparts. Likewise, be sure to use your word processing software to set up the table of contents as a "guide on the side" that your reader can use to promote comprehension and navigation. **12**

---

49. R. 3.01(j), Rules of the District Court of the United States for the Middle District of Florida, https://www.flmd.uscourts.gov/sites/flmd/files/local_rules/flmd-united-states-district-court-middle-district-of-florida-local-rules.pdf.

d. Table of Authorities in Motion Memos

As with the table of contents, a table of authorities is usually required only when the motion memo exceeds a certain length. Again, we would recommend that you include one in any document in which the argument exceeds five pages. A table of authorities typically includes "cases alphabetically arranged, constitutional provisions, statutes, treatises, and other materials" (as described in the United States Supreme Court rules). The most important requirement is that the table should note *each* page on which each authority is cited. If an authority is cited so frequently that listing the individual pages would not help the court to find particular discussions of the authority, the table of authorities may note *passim* (Latin for "throughout") instead of listing individual pages. *Passim* is often necessary to refer to a statute that is at issue because the statute may well be referenced on every page of the argument. Take care to use *passim* only when absolutely necessary; it is not an excuse for being too lazy to search through the brief to find the particular pages on which the citations appear.

Word processing programs may have a "table" function, which will allow you to create a table of authorities more easily. If you use this function, review the table after you generate it to be sure that it includes each needed authority and each needed page reference. Note that within the text of the brief, every case citation should have a pinpoint cite, which means that the first citation of the case will include the first page of the case and a pinpoint. Be sure to review your table of authorities to remove that pinpoint. The table is one time that a case citation does not need a pinpoint.

Some courts allow electronically-filed documents to include hyperlinks to documents available on the internet. If your court does, we recommend that you include those links in the table of authorities (rather than within the document itself). Take care to follow rules about citation and appropriate paper copies.

e. Issue Statements or Introductions in Motion Memos

As noted above, writers of motion memos include the document's issue(s) in a few different ways, most typically in an "introduction" or "preliminary statement" that appears immediately after the table of authorities, if one is included, or after the caption, if one is not. Formal issue statements sometimes appear after the summary of the argument as a way to re-focus the reader's attention before moving to the argument. Note, of course, that this repeating of the issues is not required; it may be appropriate only if the case is complicated and the facts are lengthy.

f. Relevant Enacted Law in Motion Memos

Because the controversy in many cases is focused on the meaning of language in statutes or other enacted law, it can be appropriate to quote the relevant language in a separate section of the document. Particularly if you are using a digital document with a guide on the side, using this method allows the reader to click back to that language and see it in context without having to leave your document. If you do include such a section, plan to include any constitutional provisions, treaties, statutes, regulations, and ordinances (in that order) *that are at issue in the case*. That is, this section should include only those statutes or other enacted laws whose language or application is in controversy. This section should not be used to reprint any statute *cited* in the brief. Rather, you should include statutes or other enacted laws only if you are asking the court to interpret or apply them (or not to apply them) in this case. Label this element according to whatever it happens to contain, e.g., "Relevant Constitutional Provisions" or "Relevant Statutes" or "Relevant Constitutional and Regulatory Provisions."

If only one paragraph of a lengthy statute is in controversy, you can quote only the pertinent part, but be generous: do not quote merely the sentence at issue. In general, when excerpting enacted law in a section of this type, you should quote at least a paragraph, and be sure to include introductory material that provides sufficient context (e.g., "Section 125 defines 'stevedore,' and provides in pertinent part: . . .").

If printing the entire text of the relevant provisions would take up too much space (more than a page), simply include the citations and explain that the full text is reprinted in an appendix.

g. Motion Standard (Standard of Review) in Motion Memos

As you read in Chapters Three and Four, the standard of review is the framework within which the court makes its decision. You must tell the court what standard of review applies to any decision you are asking it to review. Again, as noted in those chapters, calling a motion standard a standard of *review* is a misnomer, for the court is not *re*-viewing anything. Thus, we recommend that you refer to these standards as *motion standards*.

Most trial courts do not ask for a formal statement of the motion standard, but we believe it is wise to include one, with two caveats: first, put the standard in a separate section, visibly labeled. Second, be sure to craft your articulation of the standard to highlight the aspect(s) of the standard significant to your argument. For example, the motion standard for a motion to dismiss allows a court to grant a motion to dismiss if the plaintiff has not plead a set of facts that would plausibly allow it to obtain relief. Courts have held that plaintiffs must provide sufficient factual detail, and that a complaint that offers merely "labels and conclusions" or "a formulaic recitation of the elements of a cause of action" will not survive. If you are arguing that the statute does not apply to people like your client, your argument is about plausibility, and your motion standard should focus on the plausibility language. If, however, you are arguing that the plaintiff has not pleaded sufficient facts, you should focus on the formulaic recitation language.

We make these recommendations because most courts will not bother to read those paragraphs unless the application of the standard is particularly controversial. If it is, they will be grateful that you have labeled the section with the motion standard, making it easy for the court to consult its guide on the side and click back to that section (or flip back to the beginning of a paper document). If you provide the court with mere boilerplate that is irrelevant to your argument, you will have wasted your time and the court's time. If, however, you have highlighted language that is particularly useful to your document, you will make it easier for the court to decide in your favor.

h. Statement of the Case in Motion Memos

Although many courts do not specifically require a fact statement, you should include one in any motion memo for a dispositive motion, or any motion memo that is more than five pages long. Methods for writing an effective statement of the case were discussed above, in Section 10.5.2.

i. Summary of the Argument in Motion Memos

Writing the summary of the argument is addressed above, in Section 10.5.3. In general, courts require a summary of the argument for a motion memo only if the document exceeds a certain number of pages; we would recommend one if the argument is longer than 10 pages. The formal requirements are few, and they vary from court to court. While many experts advise writers to cite authorities only sparingly in a summary of the argument, at least one court requires citation, noting that briefs of a certain length may include a "succinct, clear, and accurate summary, not to exceed five pages, indicating the main sections of the memorandum and the principal arguments and citations to primary authority made in each section, as well as the pages on which each section and any subsections may be found."[50] Be sure to consult the local rules.

j. The Argument in Motion Memos

Much has already been written about the argument; we will simply note here that you should once again consult local rules. Although some courts refer to motion memos as "Memoranda of Points and Authorities," it is obvious that they have more than just bare "points" in mind. One trial court notes in its rules that "[e]very motion, opposition, countermotion, and reply shall include points and authorities supporting each position asserted. Points and authorities lacking citation to relevant authority, or consisting of bare citations to statutes, rules, or case authority, do not comply with this rule."[51] You should make your points and explain them by citing to authorities, and then apply the law to the facts (yes, we just slipped in a plug for CREXAC).

k. The Conclusion in Motion Memos

While conclusions are almost never required in motion memos, you would be wise to include one to highlight the specific relief that you seek. At a minimum, your conclusion should tell the court what you want it to do: grant or deny the relevant motion. Be precise when requesting relief. Ask the court to "grant" or "deny," *not* to "uphold" or "overrule" the motion. Many lawyers write only one sentence as a conclusion, as in this example:

Good Example
For the foregoing reasons, this Court should grant Defendant's motion to dismiss.

You will sometimes see flowery language in the conclusion, such as "Counsel for the Defendant respectfully requests that the Court grant the motion to dismiss." Although this language probably does not hurt counsel, it probably does not help, either. Because the words "respectfully submitted" appear in the signature block, just below the conclusion, you need not use "respectfully" in the conclusion itself. Don't *say* you are respectful; *be* respectful.

It can occasionally be appropriate to highlight a specific argument in the conclusion, as in these examples:

---

50. S.D. Ohio Civ. R. 7.2.
51. Nev. R. Prac. 8th Jud. Dist. Ct. 5.503.

Good Examples
Because Section 123.123 does not apply to part-time employees, this Court should grant the motion to dismiss.

Admittedly, Section 123.123 does not apply to part-time employees; however, Plaintiff should be considered a full-time employee according to the language in Section 123.124(b). Accordingly, this Court should deny the motion to dismiss.

Some courts will have little patience for a conclusion that is much longer than a paragraph. Make sure that you are aware of both local rules and local customs in this regard.

l. Signature in Motion Memos

You are probably tired of our recommendation that you consult local rules, but here, we will give it a twist: consult the local rules *as soon as possible* if this is the first time you are submitting a brief to this court. Current court rules typically require electronic submission of documents, and those submissions include an "electronic signature," which may mean a signature on the document, or a method of electronic submission and verification. Electronic submission usually requires registration, and you may not be able to register at 11:00 p.m. before you must submit a motion memo that is due at midnight.

Even if your "signature" is merely electronic verification, you should include a formal signature after the conclusion, with the phrase "Respectfully submitted" before a signature line, which may consist of a typed or electronically signed version of your name.

m. Certificate of Service in Motion Memos

Most courts require that litigants who serve papers on the court also certify that they have served copies of those documents on opposing counsel. In this way, the court ensures that all litigants have copies of all of the documents in the case. Typically, you must submit to the court a document verifying that you have served the motion memo on your opponent; this document is called a *certificate of service*. Consult the Electronic Case Filing, or "ECF" rules of the relevant jurisdiction to learn the requirements of service, and of the certificate of service.

If you are filing electronically, you may be able to serve your opponent electronically as well. Once again, be sure to consult local rules; electronic filing has added some wrinkles to the filing process. In some courts, only those who have registered with the court may use electronic filing services to file documents with the court or with other counsel. Note that if your opponent is not able to receive electronic service, you may need to provide service using more traditional means. Be sure to find out service requirements well in advance of your filing deadline.

n. Certificate of Compliance in Motion Memos

The certificate of compliance is a fairly new requirement; it seems to serve as a supplement to page-length and word-limit requirements. Modern word processing systems could make it difficult for a court to tell if an attorney cheated a page limit, by, for example, using 11.8-point font instead of 12-point font. A certificate of compliance typically requires the attorney to certify that he or she has complied with particular court rules as to length. (In a law school setting, you may also be asked to certify that you have complied with the honor code.)

Virginia court rules, for example, require that any document that has a word count limit "must include a certificate by the attorney, or unrepresented party, that the document complies with the applicable word count limitation."[52] This rule, like most similar rules, allows the attorney to rely on the word processing system's word count.

o. Appendix in Motion Memos

Few courts have rules that require an appendix for every motion memo. If an appendix is necessary, download the text into a word processing system and reformat the text, using typefaces and margins that promote readability.

Local rules and local practice—as well as the particular needs of your brief—will dictate the items that you include in the appendix. In general, you should include any information to which the court may need to refer while it considers the case, and which is not easily available to the court. Note that some court rules may require an appendix in certain circumstances; some trial courts require that counsel attach copies of unpublished decisions or of decisions from courts of another jurisdiction.

---

52. Va. Sup. Ct. R. 5A:4.

10.6. CONCLUSION

We know that this chapter includes some fussy requirements. Try to imagine how many documents courts and their support staff receive every day. The more uniformly documents are formatted, the easier it is for courts to spend time focusing on substance, rather than on figuring out whether the documents have been filed in the correct court and meet the significant procedural requirements. In other words, these seemingly fussy requirements allow the courts to spend more time focusing on the law. Your client is worth the fuss.

Oral Argument

When most people hear the words "motion" and "appeal," they conjure up lawyers and judges in a courtroom. Even lawyers sometimes respond this way. We have come to imagine a lawyer's efforts at persuasion as an oral exercise. In part, we can blame television and movies for this perception. All of the great scenes involving lawyers in persuasion mode include oral argument. The best written argument does not make for high drama. We can also blame history. In earlier times, oral argument occupied a much larger role in the legal persuasion process than it does today.

In the modern American system, motions and appeals are nearly always written. Oral argument occupies a very minor role in the adjudication process. In fact, most motions are decided without oral argument, and oral argument is increasingly rare in appeals. Still, litigators and appellate lawyers must understand the role of oral argument in various contexts and how to prepare for each. In this chapter, we will begin with oral argument in the appellate context, where it is more common and follows a more standardized format. We will then discuss the various forms of oral argument in the trial courts.

11.1. ORAL PERSUASION IN APPELLATE COURTS

Oral argument is increasingly the exception in appellate courts. Many courts in which oral argument once occurred in every case now limit oral argument to a small percentage of their cases. In 1999, Justice Ginsburg observed that the Fourth, Tenth, and Eleventh Circuits had then dispensed with oral argument in about 70 percent of cases.[1] As of 1995, almost two-thirds of the appeals filed in the Fifth Circuit were decided without oral argument.[2]

But oral argument still plays an important role in many appeals. Judges use oral argument to clear up lingering questions in their own minds and to attempt to convince judicial colleagues of their positions. Even a judge who is somewhat firm in her convictions about a case after reading the parties' briefs will listen for any reason to change those convictions. Oral argument rarely decides the outcome of an appeal, but it often helps the court to focus and shape the opinion that will result.

A thoughtful appellate lawyer will approach oral argument with two goals. The primary goal will be to persuade any undecided or open-minded judge to the lawyer's point of view. The equally important secondary goal will be to assist the court in framing a decision that favors the lawyer's position without overreaching or doing violence to precedent. The guidance that follows is our long-winded way of helping you to think about how to achieve those two goals.

11.1.1. Purpose of Oral Argument

Oral argument is not just motivational speaking. The lawyer's goal is to motivate, but the focus is *not* whatever inspirational theme is most likely to generate sympathy or passion. Instead, the appellate advocate's goal is to motivate by bringing attention to the

---

1. *See* Ruth Bader Ginsburg, *Remarks on Appellate Advocacy*, 50 S.C. L. Rev. 567, 568 (1999).

2. *See* Jacques L. Wiener, Jr., *Ruminations from the Bench: Brief Writing and Oral Argument in the Fifth Circuit*, 70 Tul. L. Rev. 187, 189 (1995).

most legally compelling aspects of the case. The legally compelling aspects of a case are likely to include facts and legal principles and may also include policy.

The lawyer's goal is also to eliminate anything that stands between the client and a favorable outcome. So, the well-prepared appellate advocate has identified the most likely roadblocks to that outcome in the minds of the judges and aims to help the judges to clear those roadblocks by identifying a path through the facts and the law. The court may identify its concerns through questioning during oral argument, but the well-prepared lawyer will have thought about these concerns well before the argument and will address them, whether or not the court identifies them.

The goal of most of the judges hearing an appeal is to test their own points of view about the case. Most judges will have read the briefs before the argument and will often have reached a tentative decision about the case. Judges will ask questions to verify their understanding of the facts and the ways in which existing authority applies to those facts. Their questions may appear to be designed to trip lawyers up or paint them into corners, but their goal is almost always to identify the limits of an argument or of a rule the lawyer wants the court to adopt, expand, or contract.

11.1.2. Format

In appellate arguments, the petitioner (or appellant) argues first, standing at a podium or lectern, and facing a panel of judges. The petitioner may reserve some of the allotted time for rebuttal. Counsel for the respondent (or appellee) follows, after which counsel for petitioner may present a rebuttal. Time allotted to each side for argument varies from 10 to 30 minutes; in many courts, each side is allotted 15 minutes, and counsel for the petitioner may reserve one, two, or three of those 15 minutes for rebuttal. Counsel for the respondent does not have the opportunity for rebuttal.

The typical method for oral argument is for the lawyers to deliver prepared remarks from a podium while addressing any questions the judges ask during the remarks. In other words, the judges will interrupt the lawyer to ask the questions. The court typically uses strict timekeeping methods and will not allow the lawyers to go beyond their allotted time. The court will allow only the first speaker to present a rebuttal.

11.1.3. Preparation for Appellate Argument

Appellate lawyers who both write the briefs and argue the appeals are at an enormous advantage in preparing for oral argument. They have completed the most important preparation for the oral argument by writing the brief. Brief writing requires careful exploration of the facts in the record, the legal issues, the authorities that control or impact the case, and the lower court's (or courts') actions in the case. All of that work provides the basis of knowledge from which the oral advocate works.

An appellate lawyer who has not written the brief must duplicate that preparation by learning the facts in the record, identifying the legal issues, studying the governing authority, and understanding the lower court's (or courts') actions. That preparation will require significant time and mental focus.

Some additional preparation is unique to the oral argument. The oral advocate must decide which points of fact or law to highlight during the very limited time allotted for the argument. He must also gather the information that he may need to respond to the court's questions and his opponent's arguments from the podium.

a. Deciding What Points to Argue

We have already told you that writing the appellate brief is the best possible preparation for gaining the necessary knowledge to present the argument. One small drawback in that preparation is that by the time a lawyer has finished writing the brief, everything in it feels critically important. But the limitations of oral argument do not allow the advocate to stand at the podium and summarize every point from the brief. So, the oral advocate must identify the points of fact and law that are most critical to the result she seeks.

The most critical points are those on which the court's decision is likely to turn; that is, the points that the court could resolve in either party's favor. These are the most controversial or unsettled points. So, the advocate's first task is to identify the most controversial and decisive points and to put other points aside for the time being. For example, if a claim requires that the plaintiff prove four elements, but the defendant has not seriously contested two of the elements, the plaintiff's appellate lawyer may have included arguments about all four in her brief in the interest of completeness. At oral argument, she will focus on those contested points and not spend much (if any) time on the points that are not seriously contested. By the same token, if the parties agree about the law that controls the outcome of one of those elements but disagree about what the evidence showed at trial, the careful oral advocate will not spend time arguing about the law. She will state the governing legal principles and then argue about how those principles apply to the facts.

Experienced appellate advocates often prefer to reduce their oral arguments to no more than three or four points. A way to identify those points after careful review of the facts and the law is to finish this sentence: "I will win if I can convince the court of these three things. . . ." The rest of the sentence provides the basic outline for the oral argument.

b. Adjusting the Analytical Formula for Oral Argument

In the appellate brief, the advocate may have followed a CREXAC (Conclusion, Rule, Explanation, Application, Connection-Conclusion) model of analysis. When planning the oral argument, she should think in terms of a pared-down version of that model: "CRAC," if you will. That is, first, she should state the point, or the conclusion, that she wants the court to agree with. Then, she should support that conclusion by stating the rule or rules that govern the issue. If a case or statute is significant to her argument, she may mention it, but in oral argument, the rule is more important than the citation to authority for that rule. On the other hand, the advocate must be thoroughly familiar with all of the relevant authorities so that she is able to answer any questions the court may have about them. In addition, in some cases, the relevant authorities become an important part of the argument.

Generally, the explanation part of the formula (the EX of CREXAC) that was so important in the brief may be all but eliminated in the oral argument. The judges' eyes may glaze over during any lengthy recitation of authority case facts and holdings unless it is given in response to a specific question. How much support the advocate should give for the rule varies from issue to issue. If the meaning of a rule, or which rule to apply, is at issue, the advocate may need to spend more time talking about relevant authorities and explaining why one authority or set of authorities is more relevant (or correct) than the other. In contrast, if the argument centers on how an established rule applies to the facts in a case, the advocate should plan to go into more detail about her client's facts. Again, she must still be prepared to discuss the relevant authorities if the court asks her questions about those authorities or about how they might apply to hypothetical situations.

After the advocate has stated the rule and supported it (if needed), she must apply the rule to the facts by naming the particular facts that mandate the result that she seeks. The advocate must remember that the meaning of the word *facts* in this context may vary from issue to issue. If the meaning of statutory language is at issue, for example, the facts may consist of the words from the statute. While the explanation section of the CREXAC formula may be all but non-existent in an oral argument, the advocate should not skimp on the application of law to facts. The judges will be particularly interested in why the facts of the case mandate the application of the rule in the manner that the advocate suggests. Similarly, they will benefit from a detailed discussion of the result that occurs when the rule is applied to those facts.

Although planning the argument is useful, every experienced oral advocate realizes that the judges will often control the topics to be covered in the argument. Nonetheless, a careful oral advocate should outline a full discussion of each of the points he plans to make during the argument. Doing so teaches him more about his case as he prepares to face the panel. The outline is the default argument, and the advocate will make that argument if the court permits him to do so, although he will rarely be permitted to proceed through the argument of an entire point without interruption.

c. Gathering Information

1 When we refer to a question of law in this context, we mean a question about which law applies or what the law means. When a case presents a pure question of law, answering that legal question decides the case. A pure question of law is one in which the facts are not controversial. As soon as the court decides what the law is, the outcome will be clear without any argument about the facts.

1 Once the appellate lawyer has identified the points she must make and win, her next task is to gather all the information necessary to make those points. *Information* is a very broad concept, and we use the word intentionally. *Necessary information* will include legal authority, of course. If the lawyer has identified three must-win points that are questions of law, gathering authority may be the entire task, because the entire argument will be about the law. More often, however, the must-win points include legal and factual controversies. So, in most cases, the necessary information includes legal authorities and facts. Before planning the content of the oral argument, the lawyer will study the relevant authorities, making sure that she knows the issues her case presents and all mandatory authorities that say anything about that issue. She will also be familiar with important non-mandatory authorities that were cited by the parties in their briefs or the lower courts in their opinions.

The *necessary information* also includes the facts and procedure of the case. The oral advocate must know which facts support her arguments on the must-win issues. She will use some of these facts to support her argument, but she will know the entire factual and procedural history of the case in preparation for responding to the court's questions. A well-prepared oral advocate is able to answer the court's questions about the details of any relevant facts or procedure and to tell the court where in the complaint, the record, the decisions below, or the joint appendix certain facts have been recorded. Another part of the oral advocate's preparation is to identify any problematic facts and prepare to explain why those facts do not undermine the advocate's position. Problematic facts are often those on which the opponent relies in making the contrary argument.

Finally, and perhaps most importantly, the careful oral advocate must figure out what he is asking for. What rule is the advocate asking the court to create or apply? What are the boundaries of that rule? That is, what kinds of situations does the rule apply or not apply to? What will be the impact of that rule on future cases? Knowing the impact of a favorable decision, or an unfavorable one, will enable the advocate to respond effectively to hypotheticals posed by the court.

To sum up, at the end of her intellectual preparation for an oral argument, the well-prepared advocate should have a command of the issues she plans to discuss, the boundaries of the rule she is advocating, the facts of her case, and knowledge of the cases and other authorities relevant to her argument and that of her opponent.

d. Written Preparation

At a minimum, the well-prepared appellate advocate should bring three things to the courtroom: the briefs that have been filed in the appeal, the joint appendix or other record materials that are before the court, and her argument notes. In the unusual (but not unheard of) event that the court should ask for information on a particular page in the record or a brief, the advocate will want to have the materials there with her. If there is not enough room at the podium, the advocate will leave those materials at counsel table and ask for permission to retrieve them if needed.

It is appropriate to bring an outline or some form of notes up to the podium, but these materials should be succinct. Notes, in whatever form, should be as close to invisible as possible. Any shuffling or turning of pages is likely to draw the judges' negative attention. If an outline is written or typed, it should occupy no more than two pages, which can be placed before the advocate on the podium and then left alone.

It is the tradition at many law schools for students to use a manila folder for their notes; the students either write their outline on the inside of the folder or prepare it on a word processor and tape or staple it in place. The advantage of a manila folder is that the pages make little noise when opened and stay in order even if dropped. Also, two pages is about the maximum amount of space that the advocate should try to fill with an outline or bullet points for the argument. The advocate may use the outside of the folder for information that she may need but that is not part of her prepared argument. That information may include names, citations, and facts of important cases about which the court may ask and citations to important parts of the record.

2 The oral argument emergency that students fear most is the completely blank mind. That understandable fear rarely materializes, and the fact that the written notes will include some opening sentences and bullet points for the argument should alleviate that fear. The most common emergency is that the court asks about the facts of a case that you cannot immediately recall. If the outside of the manila folder or a third page in a binder is devoted to short summaries of important cases with names and citations, you need not fear. You will calmly flip to that part of the prepared materials and answer the question.

2 An alternative to the manila folder is a *slim* three-ring binder. The binder looks more professional, but there are drawbacks. The pages in a binder are more difficult to turn and make more noise than the stiffer folder. Further, having a binder that allows multiple pages may tempt the advocate to write a more detailed outline, or even to write out the entire text of the planned argument. Even an advocate who uses a binder should plan to limit the notes for the prepared argument to just two pages; the binder will remain open throughout the argument and will not require any page-turning, except in an emergency.

Beginning oral advocates are often tempted to write out a script for an entire argument. No one should give in to that temptation for many reasons. We will identify the three most important reasons here.

First, and most importantly, reading from a prepared text is likely to antagonize the court. United States Supreme Court Rule 28.1 notes, delicately, that "[o]ral argument read from a prepared text is not favored." Judge Williams has made the point more directly, suggesting that reading the argument hurts both its style and its substance:

> The worst thing you can do is deliver a stiff presentation by attempting to read your argument verbatim. Such a presentation style is tedious and makes it difficult for you to answer questions from the bench. If you spend your time looking down at the podium reading your argument, you are likely to miss signals from the bench, and you cannot engage in a dialogue with the judges. Try to argue extemporaneously, or at least leave us with the impression that you are.[3]

Thus, when preparing materials to bring up to the podium, an advocate should think in terms of words, phrases, and lists, rather than sentences, paragraphs, or pages. A lawyer who writes in full sentences will be tempted to read them because she will presume that a prefabricated sentence will sound better than an extemporaneous remark. But judges expect oral arguments to be spontaneous dialogues. Most judges would rather hear an imperfect sentence from

---

3. Karen J. Williams, *Help Us Help You: A Fourth Circuit Primer on Effective Appellate Oral Arguments*, 50 S.C. L. Rev. 591, 598 (1999).

an advocate who is engaged in conversation with the court than perfect prose from a reader. An oral argument is a conversation, not a speech.

Second, when an advocate writes out a script word-for-word, the temptation to cut and paste from the appellate brief is too great. Reading an entire brief aloud would take much more time than the oral advocate is allotted. Further, the sentence structures we use when we write are often more complex than those we use when we speak. Any portion of an oral argument that is copied from a brief is likely to suffer both from long-windedness and unnecessary complexity. The best strategy to prepare for a concise, understandable argument is to write out an outline or a list of bullet points and to plan to speak in an educated but spontaneous manner about the topics included in the outline or list.

Third, an advocate who plans to write out a complete script is unlikely to prepare as carefully as effective oral argument requires. The act of reducing full text to a set of bullet points requires rumination about what must be said and in what order. Committing to an outline or list of phrases or words is committing to thoroughly understanding everything that falls in the gaps. Practicing to deliver a complete argument from that outline or list allows the advocate to test that understanding. The crutch of the complete script is no comfort when a judge's question reveals a lack of deeper understanding.

11.1.4. Presenting the Argument

The basic form of the oral argument is quite simple: an introduction, the argument itself (in three-ish points), and the conclusion. The argument is, obviously, the bulk of the presentation, but a well-planned introduction is critical to setting the context and the tone of the argument, and an effective conclusion ensures that an otherwise successful argument does not end with a thud or a whimper.

a. Introduction

The best introductions are concise but substantial. The goal is an introduction that takes up only one to two minutes of an advocate's time and goes beyond introducing the advocate and the topic of the argument. An effective introduction fulfills several important functions: it tells the court who the lawyer is, who his client is, and what his client wants; it outlines the argument and provides sufficient factual context to inform the court of the basis for the result the lawyer seeks; and it grabs the court's attention by focusing the court on a compelling theme.

Traditionally, advocates begin their arguments by saying, "May it please the court," although "Good afternoon, your honors" or any other respectful greeting will probably be acceptable to most judges. Of course, a careful advocate will review local rules to see if they require any particular opening, and, whenever possible, observe some arguments in that court to learn local customs. In the United States Supreme Court, for example, advocates never introduce themselves, and they traditionally begin their arguments by addressing the Chief Justice directly, saying, "Chief Justice, and may it please the Court."

However an advocate begins, she should never start without having the attention of the chief judge or justice. This requirement may mean that a lawyer waits while the judge finishes with notetaking from a previous advocate, but the benefit it provides in professionalism is well worth any cost in time. The advocate stands at the podium and waits in silence for the judge to nod or give some other signal telling her to begin. The advocate should stand still and look patient, watching for signals from the judge, and should not take notes or review notes while waiting.

The appellant or petitioner may need to reserve rebuttal time at this point. The manner for reserving rebuttal varies from court to court. In the United States Supreme Court, for example, the advocate does not formally request rebuttal time; instead, he must attempt to end his argument with time remaining. That remaining time may be used for rebuttal. In many other appellate courts, advocates may reserve rebuttal time before the argument begins. In some courts, the advocate may need to both request time from the bailiff or courtroom deputy *and* make the request orally from the podium. We will provide more detail below on preparing and making the rebuttal argument.

3 One of the first tasks of the appellate advocate is to introduce herself and her client. This introduction should be as short and simple as possible: the lawyer's name and the client's name and position in the case. This part of the introduction may be something like "May it please the court: I am Monte Smith, and I represent the appellee, Dynamic Industries, which was the defendant in this lawsuit." Many lawyers begin their appellate arguments with this sort of introduction. Others choose to begin with a one sentence thematic opening to grab the court's attention and then follow with their names and the identities of the clients. Whichever order an advocate chooses, she should aim to keep the introduction simple.

The thematic opening, when well-conceived, can set a favorable context for the entire argument. Some lawyers skip the thematic opening and move directly to a quick list of points they will make,

3 If you are worried about going blank at the beginning of an argument, write out the first sentence or two so that you have something to read in the unlikely event that you cannot remember how to start. No one really needs to be reminded of her name, but the knowledge that your opening sentences are in the notes verbatim may have a calming effect. This advice comes with a strong warning: Do not read the first sentences just because they are available. Beginning with strong eye contact is one of the favors the effective oral advocate does for herself.

but preparing a thematic opening can be a useful exercise even if the advocate decides to omit it from the beginning of the actual argument. Every appellate advocate should think carefully about the most favorable characterizations of his argument. This characterization will often lead to a compelling theme. As an obvious example, a lawyer who represents victims of child abuse would miss a great opportunity to provide context for his case were he not to inject a theme of "protecting innocents" or "deterring predators" at the outset. Lawyers who represent individuals against corporations or small companies against much larger ones rarely miss the opportunity to inject a level-the-playing-field theme. The possibilities are nearly limitless, and almost every case presents several possible themes. Whether or not an advocate intends to lead with a theme, he should think through the favorable categories and characterizations because doing so will likely affect how he couches the arguments he will make on behalf of his client.

The argumentative roadmap is an essential part of every introduction and is likely to consume the greatest amount of time within the introduction. An *argumentative roadmap* is a list of points the advocate intends to make, stated in an argumentative fashion. An effective advocate presents a roadmap of the points she plans to cover for two important reasons. First, the roadmap gives the advocate at least one opportunity to make those points. If the court becomes involved in the argument by asking questions early and often, that opportunity may be the only one. Second, a roadmap provides the obvious benefit of telling the court the points an advocate plans to address and the order in which she plans to address them. Some courts will let the advocate proceed with her argument if she has named the points that the court is interested in; if an advocate fails to present a roadmap, however, a judge may interrupt to ensure that the advocate intends to cover a point that is important to that judge.

4 The *argumentative* roadmap is not a list of major points stated neutrally. In other words, the advocate does not say, "First I will address the burden of proof; then, I will address the first element of the claim; finally, I will address causation." Rather, the advocate makes a mini-argument about each major point: "First, I will explain why Ms. Gimenez failed to satisfy her burden of proof on the breach element of her negligence claim because she did not even attempt to introduce evidence showing that my client's actions deviated from the standard of care in the industry; second, I will explain why Ms. Gimenez cannot satisfy the duty element of the claim because a manufacturer has no duty to protect consumers from injuries resulting from obvious misuse of a product; finally, I will explain why Ms. Gimenez suffered no injury apart from the

4 We purposely say "explain" rather than "argue." The court knows that you are making an argument; don't remind it that you are biased. Using the term "explain" also frames your presentation as an educational one: you are here to help explain these controversial concepts to the court.

injury to her head, which could not have been caused by my client's knee pad, which she wore around her neck." If the advocate is never able to return to one or more of those points, she has taken one shot at telling the court why it should rule in her favor.

An effective introduction will include facts only as they are necessary to a complete understanding of the mini-arguments in the roadmap. The advocate who presented the argumentative roadmap above would not have separately identified a list of facts. Still, the court would have learned the critical facts: Ms. Gimenez suffered an injury to her head while wearing a knee pad around her neck; the knee pad was manufactured by the advocate's client; and Ms. Gimenez did not offer evidence in an attempt to show that the advocate's client deviated from a standard of care in the relevant industry. Many advocates spend too much time providing factual context. An oral argument does not have a formal statement of the case the way a brief does. An advocate should presume that the court has read the briefs and is familiar with the record. The advocate should not use precious time reciting facts that are available to the court and are not critical to the court's understanding of the advocate's major points. The advocate should be prepared, of course, to answer questions about the facts and to back up general characterizations of the facts with details.

b. Argument

The bulk of the advocate's time during oral argument will be spent in two ways: delivering the prepared argument and answering questions. Once the advocate has finished the introduction, he simply moves to the first point of the argument, which the advocate presents in CRAC form. The briefest pause to signal a shift is appropriate, and the advocate will certainly want to reestablish eye contact if it has been lost during the introduction. The advocate should not wait for the court's permission to go on.

Some advocates provide a full sentence of transition between introductory material and the argument: "Your honors, I will now move to the first point of my argument." That formal shift is not necessary and consumes time. If an advocate has prepared effectively, she can proceed to her first point, the rule governing it, the support for that rule (if needed), and the discussion of how that rule applies to the facts. (Handling questions from the bench during that presentation is discussed in Section 11.1.5, below.)

c. Conclusion

Although the court will often control the amount of time an advocate spends talking about particular points, the good advocate is aware of the passage of time and tries to provide an effective conclusion. Some courts use a podium light to signal the passage of time: a green light is displayed throughout most of the argument; a yellow light signals that time is running short (how short varies from court to court); and a red light signals that time is up. An advocate should never stop the court from asking questions in order to conclude. However, if the court is quiet, and the yellow light is on, an advocate may decide to conclude rather than to launch into a new point for which insufficient time remains.

Like the conclusion to a brief, the conclusion to an oral argument should be short and sweet. At a minimum, it should tell the court what the advocate wants it to do. In an appellate argument, the advocates will typically be asking the court to affirm, reverse, or reverse and remand a decision. In many cases, the entire conclusion may be something like this: "Your honors, I ask you to affirm the trial court's decision." If more time is available, the advocate may want to recap the main reasons that support his conclusion, as in the following conclusion:

> In conclusion, Ms. Gimenez did not prove her case at trial. She failed to introduce evidence of a standard of care that would have required my client to warn her that wearing a knee pad around her neck would not protect her head in a motorcycle collision. If no such duty of care existed, then my client could not have deviated from that duty. Finally, Ms. Gimenez did not offer evidence to show that the knee pad itself caused her head injury. For all of these reasons, this court should affirm the jury's verdict in my client's favor.

If an advocate is still in conversation with the court when his time elapses, he must not deliver a conclusion without acknowledging that time has run out and asking for permission to conclude. If the court is asking a question when time elapses, the advocate must wait for the court to finish the question, inform the court that time is up, and then ask for permission to answer the question. Most courts will grant permission to conclude; nearly all courts will grant permission to answer their pending question.

If the court has granted permission to conclude, the advocate should deliver a simple one-sentence conclusion, even if he has a longer and more dramatic conclusion planned. The one-sentence conclusion will be along these lines: "Your honors, for these reasons we ask you to affirm the trial court's decision recognizing that my client is not liable for the injuries to Ms. Gimenez. Thank you." If the advocate feels that he has made all of his points clearly and no question is pending, he may even decide not to ask for time to conclude, and end by saying "I see that my time has expired. Thank you."

If the court has granted permission to answer a question after time has expired, the advocate should not extend that permission to add a conclusion. At most, he should answer the question and finish with "So, we ask you to affirm; thank you, your honors."

11.1.5. Responding to Questions from the Court

The best preparation for oral argument is preparation that allows the advocate to anticipate and prepare for the court's questions. The advocate who knows her case well will recognize the opponent's best arguments and the points of controversy on which the court's decision is likely to turn. She will forecast how the court will explore those points of controversy and be prepared to respond as persuasively as possible. She will even attempt to head off some of those likely questions by addressing them in her prepared argument. When a judge opens her mouth to ask a question, the prepared advocate will relish the opportunity to allay that judge's concerns and will not quake in the fear that the judge is about to expose the advocate's lack of knowledge or understanding.

The oral advocate's job is to address the court's concerns that may stand in the way of a favorable outcome, so she should hope to be interrupted and given the opportunity to hear what troubles one or more judges. An advocate who attempts to race past likely spots for questions in hopes that judges will not find room to insert themselves misses her one opportunity to talk to the court about the apprehensions that may stand in the way of a favorable outcome. An advocate's task at oral argument is not to get through her prepared points. Finishing a speech that is of no interest to the court is not a victory.

Experienced oral advocates say that they *prefer* answering questions to presenting arguments. Their experience has taught them that judges often give them important information about where they stand by the manner in which they ask their questions. On multi-judge panels, judges frequently use counsel to advance an argument that they already agree with, in hopes of gathering more votes. So, a judge who is hoping to convince a colleague may ask friendly questions that are designed to elicit the points that the judge believes to be most important. The alert advocate will bring greater focus to those points because she has recognized that the judge's question signals where the real controversy is.

The skillful oral advocate listens carefully to questions and thinks about the reason for the question and the most effective and complete way to answer before jumping into the response. Beginning advocates often fear the silence following a question and fill it with whatever comes to mind. Judges don't mind a pause if it is followed by an answer that fully addresses the concern underlying the question. The experienced advocate thinks about what the judge is asking for. Some questions ask for concessions, and the advocate will think through the implications of the concession before responding. At other times, as noted previously, a judge may try to advance a point of view by asking a question designed to reveal the best argument on that point or the strongest facts in support of an outcome. A careful lawyer will recognize what the judge is doing and will oblige by making the argument or identifying the facts. Some questions ask the advocate to identify or explain a policy supporting her position or seek information about a case or other authority. The effective advocate will listen carefully and pause to assess what the court is asking before answering.

As humans, judges sometimes ask very complex, convoluted, or poorly worded questions. Judges are rarely offended when an advocate asks for clarification. Ideally, the advocate will try to articulate what he believes the court has asked, e.g., "If I understand your question correctly, I believe that you are asking whether this court has ever required manufacturers to place warning labels on protective gear." This statement does not demand an answer from a court, but it allows the court to restate the question if the advocate has misunderstood. The advocate should make the statement in a respectful tone that does not give away any annoyance at the court's lack of clarity. If the court does not restate or clarify the question, the advocate should proceed to answer it.

Third, the effective advocate answers questions directly. Judge Williams has recommended that advocates "[r]espond immediately to a question with a 'yes,' 'no,' 'it depends,' or 'I don't know.'"[4] The court will almost always permit the advocate to elaborate on a direct answer once he has given it, but it may not tolerate the advocate's refusal to answer directly. If a "no" answer is harmful, an effective advocate will follow immediately with the "but" that softens the blow. The court will appreciate the advocate's candor and will be interested in the advocate's attempts to explain why the concession does not undermine his case.

The best answers connect the question to the advocate's prepared argument and provide support from the record or the authorities. So, if a response to a question touches on a point that the advocate

---

4. Williams, *supra* note 3, at 599.

intended to make in any event, the advocate should use the opportunity to advance that point to its end. If a fact in the record or a reference to an authority supports an answer, the well-prepared advocate will refer to it directly and provide a citation, if possible. For example, the advocate may respond as follows: "Yes, your honor, Ms. Gimenez testified at trial that she knew that the item was a knee pad but put it around her neck anyway, and that can be found at page 137 of the record." Or, when referring to authority, she may respond, "Yes, your honor, and other appellate courts, including the Fourth Circuit in *Swartz v. Jamison Co.*, have repeatedly held that the Act does not extend to debt holders collecting on their own behalf."

After answering the question and explaining the answer, the advocate should move back to her prepared argument without asking for, or waiting for, the court's permission. If the court is not asking a question, the advocate has the floor and sets the agenda. The advocate must decide whether to return to the point she was making or continue on to another point.

If the court has asked a question that moves an advocate to an issue other than the one he was addressing when interrupted, the advocate may be wise to complete the answer and continue with the second issue. The court may be signaling that it is not interested in the first issue, either because it already agrees with the advocate's position or because it will never agree with the advocate's position. In either circumstance, time is better spent on an issue in which the court has shown its interest.

If the court has asked about an issue that the advocate believes is irrelevant to the case, the advocate must still answer the question if he is able. He may let the court know that he thinks the question is irrelevant by respectfully pointing out the fact, legal rule, or other information that shows that the resolution of the case does not require resolution of the issue that it asked about, *e.g.*, "Yes, your honor, that is true, but, in this case, Ms. Gimenez testified that she *did know* that the product was intended for use on the knee and not the neck."

One warning: hypotheticals are not irrelevant questions. The wise advocate answers hypothetical questions thoughtfully and completely. Justice Ginsburg has expressed dismay over advocates' repeated dismissals of hypothetical questions with the pat answer, "That is not this case, your honor": "[The judge] knows, of course, that her hypothetical is not this case, but she also knows the opinion she writes generally will affect more than this case. The precedent set may reach her hypothetical."[5] When judges pose hypotheticals,

---

5. Ginsburg, *supra* note 1, at 569-70.

they are testing the boundaries of the rule you suggest. The good advocate knows the boundaries of the rule he or she recommends and is able to explain how the proposed rule would govern the hypotheticals posed by the court.

11.1.6. Safe Harbors

In nearly every case, each side has a few points sure to go in their favor. These points may not decide the outcome of the case, but they are relevant to that outcome and are safe topics for the advocate on that side. The advocate may think of these topics as *safe harbors*. As a safe harbor to a boater is a haven during a storm, a place where the raging waves and wind cannot reach her, a safe harbor in an oral argument is a statement about the law or the facts that is true even in the face of the opponent's best point or the court's toughest question. A well-prepared oral advocate will recognize her safe harbors and retreat to them to regain footing whenever she feels threatened during the argument.

The most likely safe harbors are the important and uncontroverted facts that support the advocate's position and the points of law that give the advocate the most comfort. In the product liability case involving the knee pad worn around the injured woman's neck, an obvious safe harbor for the manufacturer's attorney is that the plaintiff admitted at trial that she knew that the item was not designed to protect the head. A safe harbor based in the governing law may be that a manufacturer is not liable for failing to warn a consumer about the dangers of misusing a product when the warning would not have prevented the injury. Whenever the manufacturer's advocate feels the he is being backed into a corner, he may retreat to one of those harbors: "Yes, your honor, Ms. Gimenez did rely on my client's product to protect her head, *but she admitted at trial that she knew that the knee pad was not designed for the head.*" In the face of a hypothetical question suggesting liability for failing to warn about possible injury from misuse of a product, the manufacturer's counsel may retreat to the other safe harbor: "Yes, but here, your honor, Ms. Gimenez knew that she was misusing the product, so the warning would not have prevented her injury."

Advocates must choose safe harbors carefully. They must be points of fact or law that advance the advocate's position. In other words, they must be legitimate reasons for a decision in the advocate's favor. Because safe harbors are intended to stop a threatening line of questioning or to negate a strong argument from an opponent, they must also be *unassailable* points. An unassailable point is one for which no obvious comeback exists. So, if the safe harbor is based in the facts, it must be a clearly established fact. If the safe harbor is a legal principle, it must be one about which general agreement exists. The advocate does not help herself by retreating to a fact about which controversy exists because the court or the opponent will be quick to point out the contrary fact.

A well-prepared advocate will have identified one or two safe harbors for each point in her argument and be prepared to weave them into her argument in response to strong points from the opponent or into answers in response to challenging questions from the court. The best way to identify safe harbors may be to consider the case from the opponent's point of view and to ask which aspects of the facts or the law are likely to scare the opponent the most.

11.1.7. Rebuttal

5 Sometimes, of course, you might not reach an important point during your main argument and want to slip it into rebuttal. That's fine, but be elegant: tie the point in some way to a point brought up during your opponent's argument.

5 Rebuttal is the final chance that the petitioner or appellant has to address the court's concerns and questions. It should be the advocate's best shot at silencing any reservations that the court has expressed about the advocate's position or blunting any blows scored by the opponent. Counsel for the petitioner or appellant should, therefore, plan to spend most or all of the rebuttal time responding to what she has heard during the argument that has just taken place. She should not reserve important *arguments* for rebuttal. United States Supreme Court Rule 28.5 provides that "counsel making the opening argument shall present the case fairly and completely and not reserve points of substance for rebuttal." In any event, counsel should not simply repeat the same arguments that she has just made in her argument in chief.

Although final decisions about what to say in rebuttal must be made on the spot, some guidelines help advocates to present the most effective rebuttals. First, any point that an advocate makes on rebuttal should be a response to a point made during the opponent's argument. Some courts will interrupt counsel who try to use rebuttal to "finish up" the main argument, saying, "Counselor, do you have any rebuttal to offer?"

Second, even though an advocate must use rebuttal to respond to statements that opposing counsel has made during the argument, he should prepare for rebuttal while he prepares his argument. A well-prepared advocate will have anticipated most of the strong points that his opponent will make. In a moot court argument, a student might identify the points to which he has a powerful response. In real life, of course, the advocate should identify the points that are most crucial to his argument and address them as persuasively as possible, even if they are not his strongest points. Because the well-prepared advocate is aware of his opponent's strongest points, he can plan ahead by preparing short compelling rebuttals to several of those points and then make the final selections while listening to his opponent's argument. He may also tailor the selections to the specific wording of the opponent: "Your honors, counsel for Ms. Gimenez attempts to pin the blame for her head injury on my client by arguing that 'nothing came between her head and the pavement' except for our knee pad. That argument misses the point that Ms. Gimenez testified that the knee pad did not cause her head injury and that she knew it was not intended to be worn on the head or neck."

The most effective oral advocates plan to make only a few very concise points on rebuttal. They make those points and then sit down. The advocate begins the rebuttal with a very brief roadmap: "Your honors, I have two points on rebuttal." Then, she makes those two points and stops, even if time remains. Every successive thing that the advocate might say to fill up the remaining time will be weaker than the point made before.

11.1.8. The Right Words

Although the model for an oral argument is a conversation rather than a speech, in most cases it will be a more formal conversation than most people are accustomed to. Because most law students have never seen an oral argument before law school, some may imitate lawyers' oral presentations that they have seen on television. Unfortunately, these presentations are almost always opening and closing arguments during a trial, and the guidelines for an oral argument are different. For example, during an opening statement in a trial, counsel for each party may talk about what they will "show": "We will show you that the defendant was not anywhere near the scene of the crime. . . ." This statement refers to the testimony and exhibits that counsel plans to offer into evidence. It is inappropriate to imitate this language in an appellate argument because counsel will not be presenting evidence. Thus, he will not be "showing" the court anything.

Similarly, some students think they sound more lawyer-like if they speak in terms of "contentions," saying, *e.g.*, "Appellee contends that the law does not require it to warn about every possible misuse of its product." Although this phrasing may have a lawyerly ring to it, most experienced attorneys do not use phrases like this. Announcing what one contends only reminds the court that the statement is a mere contention, rather than the truth. The effective advocate will just make the assertion without preface: "The law does not require a manufacturer to warn about every possible misuse of its product."

Of course, no one expects a flawless presentation. Experienced oral advocates accept that they will use the wrong word from time to time. If they have actually misspoken, they take the time to correct themselves: "The Fourth Amendment, excuse me, I mean to say the First Amendment. . . ." They do not bother to correct errors that are not misstatements. A nervous student sometimes begins a sentence by saying something like "I contend that. . . ." The student immediately realizes that he should not have referred to himself, and his face shows his chagrin. Then, the student will attempt to correct himself: "I mean the Petitioner contends that. . . ." Suddenly, he remembers that he is not supposed to use labels of any kind, and he freezes in dismay. No court will rule against an advocate's side for a style error. The advocate should attempt to make the presentation as smooth as possible but not become hypersensitive to the imperfections in her phrasing. Unless she has said something offensive, she should just keep going. The court is interested in the content of your presentation and not the perfection of your delivery.

11.1.9. Summary

This detailed advice boils down to a few key points. (1) Know what you're asking the court to do and what the impact of its holding will be. (2) Know the facts and authorities behind your case so that you can answer questions about them. (3) Treat the oral argument like a conversation, let the court interrupt you, and be willing to answer all of the court's questions.

11.2. ORAL PERSUASION IN TRIAL COURTS

As we said earlier, an oral argument in a trial court is not standardized in the same way as an oral argument in an appellate court is. By that, we mean that an oral argument in a trial court can take one of many forms. Those forms can be nearly identical to the form of an appellate argument, somewhat similar, or so different that the two have next to nothing in common.

Before we get to some of the forms that a trial court oral argument may take, let's talk about the two main reasons for the differences between appellate oral argument and oral argument at the trial level.

The first difference relates to the different roles of the two types of courts. Appellate courts do one thing: they decide appeals of lower courts' judgments. Because the appellate oral argument has developed to accomplish one task, its form has become more or less standard in all appellate courts. The deviations from that standard are pretty minor; for example, some courts allot more argument time per side than others. But, in many respects, a lawyer who has participated in one appellate oral argument has already advanced significantly up the learning curve. In contrast to appellate courts, trial courts perform many functions. They resolve cases by ruling on dispositive motions, of course, and in that role, they resemble appellate courts somewhat. Trial courts also preside over discovery; preside over pretrial conferences; and preside over trials, including management of the jury selection process, the presentation of evidence, and the crafting of jury instructions. In all of those roles, and others, trial courts consider motions. Those motions may be in writing, but lawyers also make oral motions at various stages of litigation. Because trial courts consider so many different types of motions at so many different stages in a case, the forms that oral argument may take are almost limitless. We'll provide some examples after we have talked about the second reason for differences between appellate oral argument and oral argument at the trial court level.

6 Appellate judges have very little control over the form that any appellate argument takes because they do not schedule the arguments or dictate how they will proceed, but trial judges are not bound by those limitations. Appellate judges sit in panels. In many state and federal courts, the intermediate courts of appeals hear cases in panels of three judges. Like the United States Supreme Court, most state supreme courts sit in panels larger than three. No single judge on an appellate panel is responsible for scheduling an oral argument or describing the issues to be argued. The judges are given the schedule and the briefs for each set of arguments, or appellate docket, and prepare for an argument that will follow the standard format for that court. The issues for argument are dictated by the parties. In a trial court, on the other hand, oral argument occurs only because the trial judge has ordered it. When a trial court decides to hear oral argument on a motion, it may prescribe the form and the subjects of that argument in any way it chooses, either before or during the argument. Trial judges often exercise that authority by tailoring the form and subject matter of an argument to meet their own needs and to prevent the situation in which they must listen to 20 or 30 minutes of argument about issues they have already resolved in their minds.

With that explanation for the differences out of the way, let's talk about some of the forms that oral argument may take in a trial court. As you already know, dispositive motions (motions to dismiss

6 The United States Supreme Court and many state high courts may decide before oral argument that they will not hear all of the issues that the petitioner has raised in its notice of appeal. When courts limit the issues, they inform the parties of the specific issues as soon as possible, so that the attorneys know what issues to brief and present at oral argument.

and for summary judgment) are similar to appellate briefs in several important ways. Oral argument in support of a dispositive motion may also resemble oral argument in support of an appellate brief. So, we will begin our discussion of oral persuasion in trial courts with the dispositive motion argument, which is, at least sometimes, predictable in form, and then move to some guidance for trial court arguments in other contexts.

11.2.1. Oral Argument on Dispositive Motions

In its traditional form, an oral argument on a dispositive motion typically looks very much like an appellate argument. Each side is allotted a prescribed amount of time and uses that time as it chooses to highlight important facts, authorities, and policy considerations. Judges interrupt to clarify, explore, test, and challenge the lawyers' points. The movant begins and ends the argument. Most of the advice we have included on oral argument in the appellate setting applies equally to the traditional oral argument at the trial court level. The traditional oral argument in the trial court setting is exceedingly rare, however.

Most trial judges never ask for oral argument before deciding dispositive motions. Some judges see a request for oral argument as an indication of some sort of failure in the briefs: the only reason to ask for oral argument is that the motion memos did not address or clearly explain an aspect of the case that is necessary to the judge's decision. While some judges may use oral argument to provide a quick supplement to the briefs, a litigator should presume that he will rarely participate in an oral argument on a motion and write the motion memo accordingly.

7 If a court does hold an oral argument on a dispositive motion, the format may resemble or differ from the traditional format in several important ways. The argument may have all the formality of an appellate argument, with strict time limits, rebuttal for the moving party, and interruptions for questions by the judge. The argument may be as formal as a traditional argument, but the court may limit the topics to be covered. The court may decide not to impose time limits, allowing each side to argue for as long as it chooses to cover all of its points. The judge may interrupt frequently or may sit silently and listen to the entire argument without interjecting.

On the other hand, the argument may bear little resemblance to the formality or format of a traditional oral argument. The trial court may summon the lawyers to argue a motion and then lead an informal discussion of the issues, facts, and law. We could never prepare you for every permutation, but we do want you to be aware

7 Most good litigators would agree that oral argument sharpens their focus on the most critical aspects of their case. The time limits of an oral argument, along with the opportunity to hear a judge's concerns, force lawyers to recognize the most important facts and most contentious issues. Thus, if possible, hold a mock oral argument before you complete the final version of your memo or brief. Focusing on the most contentious aspects of your argument will help you to focus your written argument in a way that the normal editing process will not.

of the fact that trial court oral arguments may take many different forms. Some guidance about the fundamentals will help you to be prepared for any type of motion argument.

a. Presenting a Formal Motion Argument on a Dispositive Motion *without* Information that Indicates a Particular Focus

If you are asked to present a formal motion argument on a dispositive motion and you are not given information that indicates you should limit your focus, prepare for the oral argument as you would for an appellate argument. Start with an argumentative statement about what you want the court to do and a roadmap of two or three of the most significant reasons why:

> This court should grant defendant's motion to dismiss for two reasons: First, plaintiff's discharge does not jeopardize any recognized public policy of the state. Second, the plaintiff has failed to allege sufficient facts to support her allegation that the cause of her termination was her written complaint to the Occupational Safety and Health Administration.

It may be tempting to present uncontroversial points as a way of avoiding hostile questions. Recognize, however, that presenting an uncontroversial point may lead the court to spend time asking you about that point, time you could have spent on more significant issues. An oral argument presents the best opportunity to tip the court in your favor. Accordingly, you should focus your time on those points that are most controversial:

> In paragraph seventeen of Plaintiff's complaint, she alleges that her supervisor fired her on January 18, 2014. According to paragraph nineteen of the complaint, this termination occurred one day after she had filed a written complaint with OSHA, the Occupational Safety and Health Administration, of her concerns about toxins at the defendant's workplace. What Plaintiff does not allege, and cannot allege, is that the defendant had any knowledge of her complaint to OSHA. As this court knows, temporal proximity alone is not sufficient to establish causation: the plaintiff must allege and establish that Defendant had knowledge of the supposedly protected activity. It is not plausible to believe that OSHA representatives were yet aware of her written complaint on that date, let alone that they had contacted the defendant, or Plaintiff's

direct supervisor, to inform them of Plaintiff's concerns. Further, Plaintiff does not allege that she or any other employee had informed the defendant of her complaint, or of her plans to file a complaint.

This excerpt from the defendant's oral argument addresses head on the fact that is most obviously in the plaintiff's favor: the plaintiff was fired one day after filing a written complaint with a federal agency. Note how the defendant, in addressing that "bad fact," uses the phrases-that-pay from both the legal standard and the motion standard. First, "knowledge" is a facet of (and a phrase-that-pays of) the causation element in that particular claim. Second, the motion standard for a motion to dismiss provides that courts must dismiss claims that do not make allegations that "plausibly" state a cause of action. Counsel makes the connection between the legal standard and the motion standard, making it easier for the court to understand why it has the authority to dismiss the complaint.

b. Presenting a Formal Motion Argument on a Dispositive Motion *with* Particular Focus

If you are asked to present a formal motion argument on a dispositive motion and you are told how to limit your focus, prepare for an oral argument of this type in the way that you might prepare for a short, focused presentation. This type of argument occurs, most often, when the court schedules a motion hearing and identifies a specific issue or a list of specific issues to be covered. For each issue identified by the court, you will state the law and the facts that support the points you must address, and do so directly and succinctly, using legal authorities, as appropriate:

The court has asked us to address only the causation element. *Smith v. Beazley* specifies that establishing causation requires the plaintiff to allege more than temporal proximity; at a minimum, the plaintiff must also allege knowledge. Paragraph seventeen of Plaintiff's complaint alleges that her supervisor fired her on January 18, 2014, and paragraph nineteen alleges that on January 17, 2014, she had filed a written description of her concerns with OSHA, the Occupational Safety and Health Administration. Plaintiff has not alleged, however, that the defendant had any knowledge of her complaint to OSHA. The alleged temporal proximity alone is not sufficient to establish causation. As this Court knows, it must dismiss claims that are not plausible. Here, it is not plausible to believe that even the OSHA representatives were yet aware of her written complaint on the day after it was filed, let alone that they had contacted Defendant, or Plaintiff's supervisor, to inform them of Plaintiff's concerns. Further, Plaintiff does not allege that she, or any other employee, had informed Defendant of her complaint, or of her plans to file a complaint. Accordingly, Plaintiff has not sufficiently alleged facts in support of the causation element. Because she must establish causation to establish the claim as a whole, this failure alone warrants a dismissal of the case.

If the court has identified more than one issue, it may allow the moving party to make its arguments on all points before allowing the opposing party to respond, or it may hear argument on each issue separately, allowing both parties to argue about one issue at a time.

11.2.2. Participating in an Informal Motion Argument without the Court's Guidance on Particular Issues to Address

If you are asked to participate in an informal motion argument on a dispositive or a non-dispositive motion and the court does not provide guidance about the issues to be addressed, be ready for anything. Be able to cite the rule that governs the type of relief you are seeking and be ready with all relevant facts in support of your request. Try to anticipate both the court's and your opponent's objections to your request, and be ready with justifications to counter their concerns.

For non-dispositive motions, the judge may merely conduct a conversation, asking each party in turn to explain the basis behind the motion or to address particular areas of concern. Even in formal arguments, a judge deciding a motion may strictly limit the focus of the oral argument, asking each attorney to address a list of specific questions, rather than asking for a formal argument designed to highlight the case's strong points.

11.2.3. Making or Responding to an Oral Motion

If you find yourself making or responding to an oral motion, be prepared to identify the governing law and the facts or procedural events that support your argument. Attorneys make oral motions most often in the context of previously scheduled conferences, hearings, or trials. Examples are oral motions to exclude certain evidence during pretrial conferences, motions to strike testimony during trial, and motions relating to the content of jury instructions. Lawyers make these motions in the middle of ongoing events, and the court is unlikely to delay progress while the lawyers go back to their offices and draft written motions. So, the court will usually ask the lawyers to state the applicable legal principles and then make their arguments on the spot, using the facts and procedural history with which they are already very familiar.

11.2.4. The Special Situation of the Temporary Restraining Order or Preliminary Injunction Hearing

8 A temporary restraining order goes by the nickname "TRO" or "T.R.O."

9 In fact, a court may grant a TRO ex parte, i.e., without notice to the non-moving party, though it will usually do so only with assurances from the moving party that it has tried, and failed, to give notice to the non-moving party. So, a hearing on a TRO motion may be one-sided. A court will not grant a preliminary injunction without ensuring that the non-moving party has notice or that the moving party has exhausted all available means to provide notice.

8 **9** One special circumstance bears separate mention. The Federal Rules of Civil Procedure and parallel state rules allow a party to seek immediate relief upon filing a complaint. That relief takes the form of a temporary restraining order or, somewhat later but still very early in the litigation, a preliminary injunction. Either of those forms of relief is extraordinary, and the bar for showing that the relief is warranted is high. When a party asks for such relief, the court in which the case is pending may conduct a hearing on the motion almost immediately after it is filed.

A court will issue a temporary restraining order or a preliminary injunction only after finding that the moving party is likely to succeed on the merits of the case, the requested relief is necessary to prevent immediate or ongoing harm, the harm would become irreparable if the court were not to grant the requested relief, and the likely harm to the moving party outweighs the harm to be inflicted on the non-moving party if the court grants the request. A hearing on a motion for a temporary restraining order or a preliminary injunction may take many forms, depending upon the aspect or aspects of the moving party's burden on which the court requires more information before ruling.

Sometimes, when the parties agree about the facts but disagree about whether the law affords the moving party the relief it requests in its lawsuit, an oral argument on a motion for a temporary restraining order or preliminary injunction may resemble an appellate oral argument in which both sides present their positions *on the law*. Once the court has resolved the legal questions to its satisfaction, it will apply the law to the known facts and rule on the motion.

Often, however, a court cannot decide the motion without knowing more about the facts. In those situations, the court may conduct a hearing that resembles a trial more closely than an argument. The parties may present the evidence they have obtained to date, may characterize the evidence to the best of their ability at this early stage in the litigation, and may present opening and closing arguments. In very complex matters, these fact hearings may last for hours or days. **10** They may, of course, also include arguments about the law. Because the court must focus on the moving party's likelihood of success on the merits *and* the nature of the harm that would occur absent immediate relief *and* the potential harm to the nonmoving party if the court grants the relief, the variety of forms that the facts may take are almost limitless.

We cannot prepare you for every possible permutation of the temporary restraining order or preliminary injunction hearing. We do want you to be aware of a few guidelines, however. The party who seeks the relief must prepare its motion with the expectation that the court may conduct a hearing immediately upon receiving it. That means that a court may summon counsel to argue a motion for a temporary restraining order on the day of its filing. In preparing the motion, counsel should also be thinking about the arguments she will make and the evidence that is available to her in the event of an immediate hearing. A party seeking a preliminary injunction should gather evidence as she prepares the motion because the court may not afford time for evidence-gathering after the motion is filed. Careful motion preparation will reduce the inevitable stress associated with preparing for a hearing on a motion for a temporary restraining order or preliminary injunction a bit.

> **10** Note that this hearing takes place before discovery. The parties must do their best to present accurate information about the facts even though they have not had an extended opportunity to discover them.

11.3. PUBLIC SPEAKING

This point appears last because the most important public speaking tips have been made previously in this chapter: (1) don't read, and (2) maintain eye contact. The court is much more interested in the law and the facts of the case than it is in any particular style. That said, a few general pieces of advice will help any advocate to make the oral argument more effective.

First, speak loudly enough and slowly enough to be heard and understood. If possible, visit the court before the day of your argument to find out what kind of amplification system, if any, is in use, and how effective it is. If you are unable to visit the court, contact the court's bailiff or courtroom deputy clerk to ask whether the courtroom is large and whether amplification is provided. If you see several arguments in which the court is easily able to understand counsel who speak normally in front of a microphone that is six to eight inches from them, you can presume that you do not need to hold the microphone up to your lips in order to be understood.

Make sure, however, to adjust the microphone so that it is pointing at your face, rather than your shirt front or the air above your head. If you realize you are speaking too quickly, try to slow down. If this is not possible, try to pause briefly between sentences to give the judges a chance to catch up and to ask you questions.

Second, avoid distracting gestures, mannerisms, and dress. Most courts appreciate normal hand gestures. They are distracted, however, by both arms waving at once or by hands going beyond the boundaries of the podium (e.g., pointing at the judges). You should maintain a professional posture before, during, and after your time at the podium. While at the podium, stay *at the podium*. Most judges (and court recording systems) expect that the attorney will stand behind the podium for the entire argument. Generally, it is good advice not to touch your face or your clothes: don't adjust your collar or tie, run your fingers through your hair, scratch your ear, or jingle the coins in your pockets. If you are unsure whether you have any of these mannerisms, make a video of a practice argument, and then run through it at high speed. Any overused mannerisms will become obvious.

The standards for dress vary somewhat from court to court and are constantly evolving. When you are a student, choices like this affect only yourself and perhaps your grade; in practice, they may affect your client as well. Your goal should be to dress professionally, in a way that will not distract the court from your message. You must determine how to meet that standard in your particular courtroom. You might want to take a look at your outfit in the mirror to see how it looks not only when you are standing still, but also when you are sitting, bending, moving, and gesturing. Raising your arms above your head is a good test; so is squatting down to pick something up from the floor. Wear shoes that will not cause you discomfort as you stand still for the duration of your argument.

Third, just as you use sentence variety when writing, use vocal variety when speaking. Vary your speed and your tone of voice. Try not to speak in a monotone or to engage in uptalk. Pause occasionally to let an important point sink in. Likewise, if a point is important, speak slowly to draw the court's attention to it.

Finally, a word about your face. Realize that you are "on stage" from the moment you enter the courtroom until the moment you leave it. When you are at the podium, keep a poker face or smile. Don't reveal your feelings, even if you are upset or confused by a question. In law school settings, you probably did not choose which side to argue, but you must still act as if you are confident in your argument. Too often, students react to a probing question with a look that says, "You are right; I'm sorry that I'm on this side of the case." Practice controlling your reactions now; the skill will come in handy in a variety of situations in which you have to project more confidence than you feel.

Remember also that the court can see you even while you are at counsel's table, and you must act professionally there as well. Judge Wiener has aptly illustrated the unprofessionalism of an attorney who overreacts to his or her opponent's argument:

> Don't "act out" while seated at the counsel table during your opponent's turn at the lectern. Most judges resent being distracted by seated counsel's body language and nonverbal comment—shaking or nodding your head, rolling your eyes, grimacing, squirming in your chair, and the like—in response to your opponent's remarks from the lectern or our questions from the bench. Just sit still and pay attention to opposing counsel and the court. Likewise, don't make a big production out of taking notes while your opponent is arguing. When you must look at your papers or take notes, do so unobtrusively and discreetly.[6]

Because your goal on oral argument is to convince the court to adopt your point of view, you must take pains at every stage of the argument to impress the court with your credibility and your professionalism.

11.4. CONCLUSION

Although the oral argument causes many law students a lot of stress, most of them find it to be an enjoyable experience. The court is relying on your expertise, and it's satisfying to be able to explain why your clients deserve the result they seek. You'll be fine.

---

6. Wiener, *supra* note 2, at 205.

CHAPTER TWELVE

Complaints and Answers: An Introduction

12.1. The Complaint

    12.1.1. The Caption

    12.1.2. The Introduction or Preliminary Statement

    12.1.3. The Jurisdiction and Venue Section

    12.1.4. The Parties Section

    12.1.5. The Claims Section

    12.1.6. The Demand for Relief

    12.1.7. Local Rules and Special Situations

12.2. The Answer

    12.2.1. Admissions and Denials

    12.2.2. Defenses

12.3. A Word About Rule 11

12.4. Conclusion

1 The complaint is the first document filed in virtually every civil action. A complaint is the way a plaintiff initiates a lawsuit. You may also have heard of a "criminal complaint," but most criminal actions begin with a document called an *indictment*. Indictments are filed by government actors against people who may have violated criminal laws, while complaints are typically based on violations of civil law. The rules governing indictments are very different from those governing complaints in civil actions. Civil complaints are the focus in this chapter.

2 After a plaintiff files a civil complaint, the defendant has three response options: an answer, a motion to dismiss, and nothing. The third option, nothing, is a very bad idea. When a defendant fails to answer or move to dismiss within the time permitted, a plaintiff may ask the court to enter judgment for the plaintiff by default. In fact, default is required by court rules, including Rule 55 of the Federal Rules of Federal Procedure and parallel state rules of civil procedure. After a default ruling, the defendant has no right to present its side of the case, and the court will enter judgment against

1 In nearly every civil court, the plaintiff is required to pay a filing fee along with the complaint in order to initiate a case. The amount of the fee will be established by law or by court rule. Most courts require a civil cover sheet or similar document listing parties and counsel. Consult the court website and its local rules as needed to find the filing fee or the appropriate form for the civil cover sheet; in the alternative, call the office of the clerk of the relevant court to ask where to find the information.

2 In this sense, *default* means failure to answer. In sports, a player or team may lose by default for failing to show up. The application is the same in civil cases.

the defendant if the plaintiff is able to offer evidence to prove the essential elements of its claim.

So, when a complaint has been filed, the defendant named really has only two viable options: an answer and a motion to dismiss. The timing for either an answer or a motion to dismiss is governed by the applicable rules of civil procedure, and the deadline (the period within which a defendant must respond to the complaint in one of those two ways) is the same. In the federal system, the deadline is 21 days.[1] This chapter will address how to respond to a complaint by submitting an answer. (Motions to dismiss are addressed in Chapter Three.)

3 Although we focus on the federal rules, many state rules are modeled after the federal rules, and even those that aren't often have similar requirements. Of course, always consult the relevant rules before preparing a complaint for any court.

3 In both the federal court system and the individual state court systems, rules of civil procedure govern the basic contents of a complaint and an answer. In the federal court system, Rule 8(a) mandates that a complaint include (1) a short and plain statement of the grounds for the court's jurisdiction, (2) a short and plain statement of the claim showing that the pleader is entitled to relief, and (3) a demand for the relief sought. Rule 8(b) mandates that an answer include (1) any defenses to claims asserted and (2) an admission or denial of each allegation asserted against the party filing the answer.

12.1. THE COMPLAINT

Rule 8(a) never uses the word "complaint." Instead, it provides the standard for any "pleading that states a claim for relief." That language is broad enough to encompass complaints, which are the means by which most claims are asserted, but also includes counterclaims, cross-claims, and third-party claims, which are asserted after litigation has begun.

The kind of pleading required by Rule 8(a) is often called "notice" pleading because in the complaint, the plaintiff is required to give *notice* of the bases for jurisdiction and relief and of the facts giving rise to the plaintiff's claims. Notice pleading was a reaction to much more complex pleading requirements that predated the modern rules of procedure. Notice pleading, as prescribed by Rule 8(a) of the Federal Rules of Civil Procedure and most of the parallel state rules, has given rise to a more or less standard form of complaint. Not surprisingly, that form includes (1) a jurisdiction section (where the plaintiff asserts that the court has jurisdiction over the defendant and jurisdiction over, or authority to decide, the

---

1. *See* Fed. R. Civ. P. 12(a)(1)(A)(i).

issues in the complaint); (2) a claims section (where the plaintiff describes the facts giving rise to the asserted claim or claims); and (3) a demand for relief (where the plaintiff asks for money damages or other relief). All complaints also include a caption (which lists all plaintiff(s) and defendant(s)), and most include an introductory section and a section identifying the parties, although the rules do not require them.

The paragraphs of the complaint are numbered, beginning with the first paragraph in the preliminary statement and continuing through the claims section. The numbering of the paragraphs in the final section of the complaint, the demand for relief, begins again at 1. Although the rules do not require numbering, numbering the paragraphs makes it easier for the court and the attorneys in the case to reference particular allegations in the complaint. In practice, most attorneys keep the numbered paragraphs short, usually from one to three sentences about a single fact.

This chapter will explain the purpose of each section of the complaint and discuss complaint-writing strategies. Two sample complaints and a partial sample answer are included at the end of the chapter.

12.1.1. The Caption

The caption of the complaint includes the identity of the court in which the complaint will be filed and the names, and often the addresses, of all plaintiffs and defendants. While these components of the caption are all matters of fact, some thought may go into the order in which parties on each side are listed in a multi-party case. The first-listed plaintiff, and to a lesser extent the first-listed defendant, will be the parties whose names will be used most often to identify the case. Think of any famous case you have heard of: chances are good that you do not know whether the plaintiff by whose name the case is known was the only plaintiff in that case. The first-named plaintiff is known to history, while others are not. If a case is likely to generate publicity, a plaintiff's attorney may purposely choose, or purposely avoid choosing, a well-known person or corporation to be the first-named plaintiff. Other considerations may also affect attorneys' choices in the ordering of the parties in the caption.

12.1.2. The Introduction or Preliminary Statement

The introduction that begins most complaints is often called a "preliminary statement," and that is what we will call it here. As we have noted in Chapter One, legal readers always need context; in a complaint, the preliminary statement is where the writer provides that context. The preliminary statement is not required by the rules governing civil procedure, nor do the rules prescribe the form or content of a preliminary statement. In practice, preliminary statements do not follow a standard form. The most effective preliminary statements, however, tell a brief but compelling story about the events underlying the claims and provide a roadmap to the remainder of the complaint. Although a plaintiff may assert several claims, all of the claims are likely to center around a common theme. The preliminary statement is the spot in the complaint where the attorney introduces the theme that applies to the complaint as a whole.

When we talk about a "theme," we are talking about what a case is about. The theme is a big picture or summary way of describing the subject of a case. So, you might describe a case as a "civil rights action" or a "torts case." Those descriptions suggest themes, but they are very general. If you include or suggest a theme in the preliminary statement, you will want to think about a more compelling and case-specific theme than "a torts case."

In the first sample complaint at the end of this chapter, for example, the preliminary statement suggests two themes. The case is a lawsuit against a school district by a minor child and his family, claiming that the school district did not provide the child with an appropriate "free and fair public education" as required by the Individuals with Disabilities Education Act. You will notice that it first describes the subject matter of the case generally as "civil rights." The preliminary statement then suggests two more case-specific themes.

First, the preliminary statement suggests a little-guy-versus-the-uncaring-bureaucracy theme by repeatedly identifying the first-named plaintiff as a "minor child" and identifying the school district as the "institutional defendant." Using these labels allows the attorney to suggest a theme without coming right out and saying, "This is a case about a little guy who has been trampled by an uncaring bureaucracy." Using that kind of over-dramatic language would cause most readers to cringe, and your messaging would backfire. The more subtle suggestion of the same theme through careful labeling will not offend most readers, yet it still accomplishes the purpose of framing the complaint in a way that arouses favorable feelings from the reader at the outset.

The other theme suggested in the first sample complaint's preliminary statement is that the plaintiffs have consistently done all that the law requires while the defendant has refused to comply with the law. This theme is closer to the actual substance of the claims, and the attorney has suggested it more directly.

The preliminary statement is different from the claims section. In the claims section, the plaintiff must include all legally significant facts, *i.e.*, the facts necessary to demonstrate that the pleader is entitled to relief on each claim. In the preliminary statement, in contrast, the facts are presented more like a narrative designed to show that the complaining party has suffered a wrong and that the defending party is the source of that wrong. The "facts" included in the preliminary statement must be true to the drafter's best information, but they need not be limited only to those that are "necessary" in order to establish a claim. In the preliminary statement, therefore, the drafter of the complaint tells a compelling story about the events giving rise to the claims but need not include all legally significant facts and may include facts that are not legally significant.

A second important purpose that the drafter may accomplish in the preliminary statement is to set the stage for the claims in two ways: (1) by relaying background information about the context of the relationship or encounter that gave rise to those claims, and (2) by providing a roadmap to the complaint by signaling how the claims are organized and how they relate to one another. This purpose is particularly important when the complaint contains multiple claims, or when the law or the facts are complex for another reason.

For example, if the claims relate to an employment relationship, the preliminary statement is likely to identify one party as the employee or former employee and the other as the employer. The preliminary statement may also include the fact that the employment relationship has ended or has been altered in some fashion that will relate to all or many of the plaintiff's claims. Finally, the preliminary statement may indicate that one group of claims relates to events during the employment relationship while a second group of claims relates to the termination of the employment relationship.

In the preliminary statement, the drafter of the complaint is consciously attempting to present a story that compels a favorable or sympathetic response. At the same time, at this preliminary stage of the complaint, the drafter is establishing credibility and reliability as a source of information. In that spirit, the drafter avoids hyperbole and obvious plays for sympathy and adheres to a presentation style that is factual and calm.

12.1.3. The Jurisdiction and Venue Section

Rule 8(a) and its state parallels require a statement of the grounds for the court's jurisdiction. The jurisdiction statement is designed to establish that the federal or state court in which the complaint has been filed may properly exercise jurisdiction over the defendant and over the subject matter of the claims.

The allegations relating to personal jurisdiction will often include only a statement that the defendant or defendants are residents of the *forum*, which refers to the court's geographic jurisdiction (as opposed to its subject matter jurisdiction). Occasionally, a defendant's residence within the forum jurisdiction will not be obvious from its address alone. In such a case, the pleader will more carefully identify the bases in fact and law for the court's exercise of jurisdiction over that defendant. As the attorney for the pleader, you may have a visceral urge to gloss over controversial personal jurisdiction issues by baldly alleging that the court may exercise jurisdiction over the person of one or more of the defendants who are arguably not residents of the forum. In those closer cases, however, the burden placed upon you by Rule 8(a) is greater. The short and plain statement of the grounds for the court's jurisdiction must include sufficient factual detail to establish a legal basis for the court's exercise of jurisdiction over that defendant. Being accurate here is a wonderful opportunity to establish credibility; don't blow it.

Pleading subject matter jurisdiction in a federal court is almost always a matter of choosing one of two bases provided by the United States Code: federal question jurisdiction or diversity jurisdiction. If one or more of the claims arises under the "Constitution, laws or treaties of the United States," any U.S. district court may exercise jurisdiction over the subject matter of the claim, and any other claims relating to the same core set of facts, under 28 U.S.C. § 1331. If the requirements of federal question jurisdiction are not satisfied, a federal court may exercise subject matter jurisdiction over the claims only if the diversity requirements of 28 U.S.C. § 1332 are satisfied. As with personal jurisdiction, the pleader's obligation to provide a statement of the grounds for the court's jurisdiction is heightened when the basis for jurisdiction is not obvious from the facts alleged. In other words, if subject matter jurisdiction is likely to be a matter of controversy, the pleader is obligated by the rule and by careful practice to identify more completely the facts supporting the court's exercise of subject matter jurisdiction.

Attorneys often include a statement that the court in which the action has been filed is an appropriate venue, or location, for the litigation, even though Rule 8(a) does not require that the pleader address venue in a complaint. Venue is a narrower concept than jurisdiction in the sense that a court may have jurisdiction over the subject matter of the claims and yet not be an appropriate venue for those claims.

Venue in the U.S. district courts is governed by the federal venue statute, 28 U.S.C. § 1391. Section 1391(a) addresses venue for federal diversity actions; § 1391(b) addresses venue for federal actions based on federal question jurisdiction or a combination of diversity and federal question jurisdiction. Pleading venue involves little more than identifying which of the two subsections of § 1391 applies. As always, when venue may be controversial, the pleader's best defense against a motion to dismiss on the basis of improper venue is a complete recitation of the facts establishing that the chosen forum is a proper venue for the action.

12.1.4. The Parties Section

Rule 8(a) does not require that the complaint include a section devoted to the parties, but many attorneys routinely include one. You should not include a "parties" section unless you have thought about the best way to relay the information you would include in such a section and determined that a separate section is warranted. Your analysis may lead you to the conclusion that the caption includes all of the information about the parties that is necessary to establish the court's jurisdiction and provide a complete understanding of your client's allegations. In the alternative, you may decide that you can include any necessary information about the parties that is not part of the caption in the preliminary statement or in the jurisdiction and venue section. You may decide, however, that a separate section will allow you to include the information about the parties that you want to relay in the most coherent fashion while also allowing you to advance your chosen narrative about the parties and the claims.

Whatever other information you may choose to include in the parties section of the complaint, be certain to include the names of all parties and their relevant relationships to the other parties. For example, if a party is a defendant in the action and also the former employer of the plaintiff, include both of those facts in the parties section.

In the parties section of the first sample complaint at the end of this chapter, the attorney has included basic information about the identities and residences of the parties and their relationships to one another. That information could also have been included in the jurisdiction and venue section of the complaint. The attorney has added an allusion to the requirements of a federal statute and the defendant's alleged failure to comply with that statute. The attorney likely believed that those "facts" would be inappropriate in the jurisdiction and venue section and, therefore, added a parties section.

In the second sample complaint at the end of this chapter, the drafting attorney has used the "parties" section to identify each party's relationship to the subject matter of the claims. The attorney includes information about the parties' relationships to one another and the actions of each party that combined to give rise to the plaintiff's claim. Most of that information is also included in other sections of the complaint, but the attorney has chosen to highlight certain facts by including them in the parties section.

Because the governing rule does not prescribe a parties section, it also does not prohibit the inclusion of any particular kind of fact in that section. You may consider including any information related to the parties that you believe to be true and that also advances your theme.

12.1.5. The Claims Section

Most of the space in the complaint will be devoted to the "short and plain" statement of the claims. The facts that establish a plaintiff's right to relief on any particular claim are sometimes called the "cause of action," and some attorneys will use the term "cause of action," rather than "claim" in the claims section of the complaint. Although you may use either, we will use "claim" here.

The first step in determining what to plead or allege with respect to any claim is an understanding of the essential elements of that claim. If you are asserting a claim for discrimination under a federal anti-discrimination statute, for example, you must perform sufficient research to assure yourself that you know what your client will have to prove in order to establish the defendant's liability for that claim.

Most claims will have more than one essential element. Some claims will have elements that are all essential to the claim's success, while other claims will have some essential elements and some alternative elements. Only when you are certain that you have identified all of the elements of the claim should you turn your attention to determining which facts in your client's case will satisfy each element.

Until fairly recently, the pleading requirements of Rule 8(a) were generally satisfied by reciting each essential element of the claim and alleging that the element was satisfied in the facts of the plaintiff's case. A fact "conceivably" satisfied an element of a claim when an argument could be made that the fact, if established by evidence, would convince a trier of the facts that the element was satisfied. In 2009, however, the United States Supreme Court issued a decision, *Ashcroft v. Iqbal*, 556 U.S. 662 (2009), that heightened the pleading requirements without changing the language of Rule 8(a). Now, a plaintiff must plead facts in sufficient detail to convince a court that discovery is likely to uncover evidence in satisfaction of each essential element of the claim. The Court made clear that merely reciting the elements of the claim and alleging that the plaintiff's facts satisfy them will no longer meet the pleading requirements of Rule 8(a).

The two most important practical effects of the *Iqbal* decision are (1) an increased need for pre-litigation investigation to uncover as many supporting facts as possible and (2) an increased need for care in the drafting of the complaint to ensure that the allegations in support of each essential element of each claim plausibly satisfy that element. Of course, those practices have always been useful and advisable. An attorney who has thoroughly investigated facts before drafting a pleading and who has carefully drafted the allegations will be more aware of the strong and weak points in a claim, may identify additional potential claims, and will know at the outset where discovery must be focused. Because a defendant is required to respond to every allegation by admitting or denying it, a carefully drafted complaint will also yield a more informative answer.

If you are the plaintiff's attorney, the most obvious source of information about the events surrounding the claim is your client. Your client may also be able to identify other people who have knowledge about those events and who will be willing to talk to you about those events before you draft the complaint. Public records, including those found on the Internet, may also provide useful information. Before filing a complaint, an attorney has an obligation to exhaust those sources, and perhaps others. When you sign your name to a complaint, you are assuring the court that you have exercised due diligence in verifying the facts that your client presented to you. It is not appropriate for an attorney to base a complaint on the client's word alone.

Typical fact investigation techniques require finding documentary evidence that is consistent with the story the plaintiff has told the attorney. For example, the first sample complaint at the end of this chapter claims that the school district refused to provide a minor child with an appropriate education. A diligent attorney would ask to see letters or emails showing the district's refusal.

4 In the first sample complaint at the end of this chapter, the plaintiffs' claim is that the defendant has failed to comply with the terms of an offer of judgment that it has made and that the plaintiffs have accepted. The essential elements of that claim are the offer, the acceptance, and the failure to comply. The complaint includes those elements in paragraphs 19 through 21. The other allegations in the claims section of the complaint help to establish the plausibility of

4 An *offer of judgment* is a formal settlement offer whereby a defendant offers to permit the court to enter judgment against it in a certain amount or on certain terms. If the plaintiff rejects the offer of judgment and then loses at trial, or receives less at trial than the defendant has offered, the plaintiff is responsible for the costs of litigation after that date.

the plaintiffs' claim. The substance of the claim would not be different had the plaintiffs' attorney included only paragraphs 19 through 21 in the claims section, but the additional allegations satisfy the requirement of *Iqbal* that the plaintiffs allege facts that plausibly establish every essential element of the claim.

The plaintiff's attorney should organize the allegations in support of each claim in a way that will allow a complete recitation of every allegation necessary to satisfy the stricter requirements of Rule 8(a) while still being as concise as possible. While the best organization will often be chronological, an attorney can sometimes convey more information in an economical fashion by setting out the facts by category. Don't be afraid to choose the organization that allows you to lay out the facts in a way that is both clear and persuasive.

In the second sample complaint at the end of this chapter, the drafting attorney has used a list format, instead of chronology, in several places. The complaint alleges employment discrimination; in paragraphs 12, 16, and 18 of the complaint, the lists allow a direct comparison of the plaintiff to other employees. The lists also allow a more efficient and coherent presentation of the information they include. A chronological presentation of the same allegations would have scattered the items in the list throughout the allegations, making it harder for the reader to grasp important factual relationships.

As noted above, when listing the facts that each claim is based on, you should limit each paragraph to one discrete fact. One reason for this technique is anticipation of the defendant's reaction. Typically, in the "answer" to the complaint, the defendant will respond to each paragraph in one of three ways: by admitting the allegations, by denying the allegations, or by stating that the defendant "is without information or belief" that will allow it to admit or deny the allegations in that paragraph. If a paragraph contains multiple allegations, the defendant may deny the whole paragraph (or claim lack of information and belief) if the defendant can deny even one of those allegations. Accordingly, effective advocates strive to isolate each allegation in its own paragraph. Limiting each paragraph to one fact forces the defendant to admit as many of the allegations as possible and thus serves to identify the real areas of controversy in the case.

If many of the allegations in support of a claim come directly from a separate document, such as a contract or a lease, the plaintiff's attorney may choose to attach the document to the complaint, and then simply refer to the portions of the document that support the claim, rather than extensively quoting or paraphrasing the document. The references should be as specific as possible to make it easier for the court and its personnel to find the needed information.

Thus, if paragraphs are numbered, cite to the paragraph; if lines are numbered, cite to the page and the line.

5 If the plaintiff is asserting more than one claim, the specific allegations relating to the first claim will likely include a number of facts that also support other claims. When the allegations in support of the first claim are complete, the attorney may move to subsequent claims, incorporating allegations from the first claim by reference and adding only those allegations that are unique to the subsequent claim. Often, the first paragraph of a subsequent claim will say something like "Plaintiff incorporates by reference the allegations contained in paragraphs 16-20." Do not worry if your later allegations inadvertently repeat facts that you have already alleged; the purpose of the incorporation by reference is to ensure that all relevant facts are legally pled in the appropriate sections of the complaint.

5 Sample Complaint 2 at the end of this chapter illustrates this convention.

12.1.6. The Demand for Relief

Rule 8(a)'s final explicit requirement is a demand for relief, which may include alternative demands or demands for different types of relief. The demand for relief may also be called the "prayer" or "prayer for relief." Here, we will call it the *demand for relief*.

"Relief" is the term attorneys use to refer to any favorable outcome afforded by the law. Relief, thus, includes money, compelled action or inaction, or declarations that certain matters are or are not legally established. Compensatory damages are the most common form of relief demanded in a complaint, but a plaintiff may also demand statutory damages, punitive damages, and other forms of money damages. As an alternative or in addition to money damages, a plaintiff may demand injunctive relief or declaratory relief.

6 Regardless of the form of relief demanded, the attorney who drafts the complaint must have a basis for the demand. The factual allegations in the complaint must support the demand by demonstrating that the plaintiff has a plausible claim to the relief sought. In addition, the attorney must ascertain that the governing law makes available the form of relief demanded. If a governing statute clearly provides for statutory damages only, the complaint should not include a demand for compensatory damages. Similarly, if the plaintiff wants to seek punitive damages in the demand, the relevant statute or common law rules must allow for punitive damages, and the complaint must allege facts that meet the requirements for awarding punitive damages. So, if the relevant legal standard requires "ridiculous and egregious harms" in order to award punitive damages, the complaint must allege facts that show that defendant's behavior caused ridiculous and egregious harms to the plaintiff.

6 A careful writer connects the facts to the legal conclusions, e.g., "The facts alleged in paragraphs 24-26 show that the defendant has inflicted ridiculous and egregious harms on the plaintiff."

7 As in all things, big data may have helpful information. When deciding on the amount to demand, many attorneys consult websites that provide estimates of what amount of money is appropriate for certain kinds of lawsuits. We won't link to one here, because we don't want to endorse one. In general, never rely on just one source; compare the results from several and consider them in light of your knowledge about your case, the credibility of your witnesses, and the local culture of your jurisdiction.

7 Framing the demand for relief involves a certain amount of strategy on the part of the attorney. The amount and form of relief demanded will often establish the ceiling for what the plaintiff may receive, either in settlement or in litigation. So, the demand should be the best-case scenario under the governing law but not more. A demand that far exceeds what the facts would support or what the law allows will often cause the defendant and the court to view the complaint dismissively.

12.1.7. Local Rules and Special Situations

The complaint-drafting considerations included in this chapter include the major components of a typical civil complaint. They are not exhaustive, however. You should be aware of two important sources of additional requirements relating to complaints: (1) rules of procedure other than Rule 8(a) and its state parallels, and (2) the rules of the court in which you intend to file your complaint.

Rule 8(a) provides the requirements for a typical civil complaint. Other rules add specific requirements for special types of complaints. For example, Rule 9(b) of the Federal Rules of Civil Procedure adds specific requirements for claims of fraud or mistake in federal civil actions. Rule 9(h) adds specific requirements for admiralty and maritime claims. Rule 5.1 of the Federal Rules of Civil Procedure adds specific requirements for a complaint in which the constitutionality of a statute is challenged. Rule 23 sets forth specific additional requirements for class action complaints. These are just some of the special requirements addressed by procedural rules other than Rule 8(a).

Before filing a complaint, you should also consult the rules of the jurisdiction in which you intend to file it. As you know, these rules are called, either formally or informally, the "local rules." Consulting local rules is much easier now that they are generally available online, on the website of the court or of a particular judge.

Local rules do not often alter the requirements of the federal or state rules of civil procedure. They do supplement the generally applicable rules, however, and sometimes they add idiosyncratic requirements that relate to matters not addressed in the federal or state rules of civil procedure. Some jurisdictions have local rules governing the type and size of fonts used in documents filed there, for example. Local rules governing electronic filing, which is now available or mandatory in most courts, will have special relevance to an attorney who is about to initiate a case. A careful attorney will pay special attention to local rules before filing a complaint in any court, but especially before filing in a court in which that attorney has not practiced recently.

12.2. THE ANSWER

Much as Rule 8(a) never uses the word "complaint," Rule 8(b) does not include the word "answer." Instead, it refers to admissions, denials, and defenses. Its provisions govern an answer to a plaintiff's complaint and also answers to counterclaims, cross-claims, and third-party claims. It requires a party who is the defendant as to any claim to respond specifically to all allegations that make up any claim against it and to assert most defenses that it may have against liability for those claims.

This chapter will explain those requirements in a bit more detail. A sample answer follows the second sample complaint at the end of this chapter.

12.2.1. Admissions and Denials

The heart of Rule 8(b) is its requirement that a party who is the defendant as to any claim admit or deny the allegations that make up the claim. Rule 8(b)(3) permits various types of denials. The first is a general denial. If a defendant asserts a general denial, it is denying every allegation of the complaint, including jurisdictional allegations. A defendant who cannot in good faith deny all allegations has two additional options. It may respond to each numbered paragraph of the claim individually, admitting the allegations in the paragraph, denying the allegations in the paragraph, or denying part of the allegations in the paragraph while admitting the rest. In the alternative, the defendant may deny all allegations in the claim generally except for those that it specifically admits. Any allegation that a defendant fails to deny, except for allegations relating to damages, is deemed to have been admitted.

Rule 8(b) warns repeatedly that a defendant may deny an allegation only *in good faith*. In other words, a defendant must have a basis for a denial and may not simply deny an allegation because it does not know whether the allegation is true (or does not want it to be true). In fact, Rule 8(b) offers a defendant an alternative to denial for allegations about which it has an insufficient basis to respond. Rule 8(b)(5) allows a defendant to state that it "lacks knowledge or information sufficient to form a belief about the truth of an allegation." That statement has the same legal effect as a denial, but it allows a defendant to maintain good faith when it cannot deny the allegation on the basis of its current knowledge.

12.2.2. Defenses

Defendants assert two kinds of defenses in answers: affirmative defenses and denials. Rule 8(b) includes a list of affirmative defenses that a defendant must include in its answer or lose them forever. An affirmative defense is different from a denial. A denial is a defendant's way of saying, "I didn't do it." An affirmative defense says something like, "I may have done it, but that doesn't make me liable." A familiar affirmative defense to the criminal charge of murder, for example, is "self-defense." This affirmative defense admits that the defendant killed someone but alleges that the killing was justified by the victim's actions. The list of affirmative defenses in Rule 8(b) does not include all defenses, but if one of the listed defenses may be applicable to your client or the claim against it, you must assert it in the answer or assume the substantial risk of waiving it forever. So, take due care in considering whether each affirmative defense may apply.

12.3. A WORD ABOUT RULE 11

You may have heard your professors talk about avoiding Rule 11 violations without understanding what the professors mean. Rule 11 of the Federal Rules of Civil Procedure authorizes courts to sanction, or punish, attorneys who do not act honestly when submitting documents to a court. Of course, your professional and personal integrity and the integrity of your clients provide strong incentives to be honest when you draft complaints and answers. If you concoct allegations with no basis in the facts as you understand them, or you deny allegations with knowledge of their truth, your fabrication will eventually be apparent to your opponent and, likely, the court. You may never be able to recover your reputation for honesty and good faith. It is perhaps surprising to law students how small legal communities can be. Even in relatively large cities, the number of lawyers practicing in a given area of law is relatively small. Courts and opposing counsel will remember those attorneys who try to misrepresent the facts or the law.

The rules governing litigation in the federal and state court systems provide an additional incentive, however. Rule 11, which has parallels in every state, requires that the filing attorney sign every submission to the court. So, as the attorney filing a complaint or an answer, you will sign the last page. Your signature, even if electronic or typewritten, is a representation to the court that you have made a reasonable inquiry into the facts and the law and that the filing is well-supported by both. You violate Rule 11 if your pleading includes allegations that are not supported by information that is known to you at the time of filing. Rule 11 provides for sanctions, including monetary penalties, and those sanctions can be quite severe.

Under the federal rule and the rules of most of the states, the court need not wait to investigate until your opponent asks for sanctions. The court can issue a "show cause" order, which is an order requiring you to show that you have not violated Rule 11's requirements. The court's order, when it relates to a complaint, amounts to a requirement that the attorney identify the information that supported the allegations in question and was known to the attorney when the complaint was filed. No attorney wants to be in the position of having to admit to the court that an allegation or a denial was unsupported by then-known facts, *i.*e., that it was fabricated. The assertion that the attorney hoped that discovery would uncover information that would support the allegation will be little comfort to the attorney and worse, will carry little weight with the court.

12.4. CONCLUSION

This chapter is done, but your reading is not. Two sample complaints and a partial sample answer follow. By reading these samples—and the accompanying annotations—carefully, you will gain a more complete understanding of the architecture of complaints and answers.

SAMPLE COMPLAINT 1

8

IN THE UNITED STATES DISTRICT COURT
FOR THE SOUTHERN DISTRICT OF OHIO
WESTERN DIVISION

9

Brian Hartman, a minor child,   :

79 Hurley Drive   :   Case No.

Bonaventure, Ohio 45454,   :

and   :

Laurie and Stephen Hartman, on behalf   :

   of themselves and their minor child,   :

10

79 Hurley Drive   :   Complaint

Bonaventure, Ohio 45454,   :

        Plaintiffs,   :

v.   :

Bonaventure Local Village School District, :

10103 County Road 17   :

Bonaventure, Ohio 45454,   :

        Defendant.   :

Preliminary Statement

1.   This is a complaint by private citizens, a minor child and his parents, against a public entity that violated the minor child's civil rights. The minor child

11

and his parents seek declaratory and monetary relief for the institutional defen-

---

8 The caption begins with the name of the court. The particular formatting of party names, document names, and the like may vary according to local practice.

9 The case number is left blank in the complaint for the court to fill in. In all motions and other documents in the case, the attorney must include the case number that the court assigns to the case.

10 Again, consult local rules when filing a complaint. In many courts, if counsel seeks a jury trial, the complaint's caption must indicate that request.

11 Notice how the plaintiffs refer to the defendant. To avoid the possible positive connotations of "school district," plaintiffs use the phrase "institutional defendant" to advance their theme of "little guy against the big bureaucracy."

dant's actions in depriving the minor child of the free and appropriate public education to which he is entitled under federal law and which the public entity agreed to provide.

2. The minor child and his parents have adhered to every requirement of the governing statute, the Individuals with Disabilities Education Act ("IDEA"), despite significant opposition from the institutional defendant. The institutional defendant, nevertheless, has refused to comply with the law and with its own agreement to provide the minor child with a free and appropriate public education. Accordingly, the minor child and his parents are forced to bring this action to compel the institutional defendant to do what the law already requires of it and what it has already agreed to do.

12

13

Jurisdiction and Venue

3. This Court has jurisdiction over the Defendant, which is located in the Southern District of Ohio.

4. This Court has jurisdiction over the subject matter of the Plaintiffs' claims under 28 U.S.C. § 1331, which provides that the United States district courts shall have original jurisdiction over all civil actions arising under the laws of the United States. This civil action arises under the IDEA, 20 U.S.C. § 1400 et seq., a law of the United States.

14

12 The preliminary statement need not include numerous citations. This one includes an appropriate reference to the statute by name rather than by statute number.

13 Notice how the writer advances the theme: the plaintiffs have followed the law, but the defendants have not. The plaintiffs do not want to sue the school district but are being forced to, because the school district has gone back on its word and refuses to follow the law.

14 The IDEA is a well-known federal statute, but using the statute number reassures the reader that it is a federal law, i.e., a "law of the United States," for jurisdictional purposes.

5.   This Court is a proper venue for this action under 28 U.S.C. § 1391(b)(1) because the Defendant is situated in this judicial district.

The Parties

6.   Plaintiffs Brian Hartman, Laurie Hartman, and Stephen Hartman are residents of Bonaventure, Ohio, which is in the Southern District of Ohio.

7.   Plaintiff Brian Hartman is a minor child with a disability within the meaning of the IDEA, 20 U.S.C. § 1402(3)(A).

8.   Plaintiffs Laurie Hartman and Stephen Hartman are the parents of Plaintiff Brian Hartman and bring this action on his behalf.

9.   Defendant is a local educational agency as defined by the IDEA, 20 U.S.C. § 1402(19), and, accordingly, is obligated to provide a free and appropriate public education consisting of specialized education and related programs and services designed to meet the unique needs of Plaintiff Brian Hartman, a child with a disability who resides within Defendant's school district. Defendant is subject to the requirements of the IDEA, 20 U.S.C. § 1400, *et seq.,* and the implementing state and federal laws and regulations, and it must serve its students in conformity with those laws and regulations.

The Plaintiffs' Claim

10.   Plaintiff Brian Hartman, an eighth-grade student, has resided within the Defendant district since he began kindergarten.

---

15 This description of the defendant includes argumentative language, for a complaint is a persuasive document: you are trying to persuade the reader that the law applies to the facts in a way that benefits your client. Here, the writer describes the parties in a way that highlights the legal obligations that accompany the defendant's status as a school district.

11. Plaintiff Brian Hartman is mildly autistic, and employees of the Defendant determined that Brian Hartman was disabled as defined by the IDEA and eligible for special education services. The Defendant's employees made this determination when Brian Hartman was in first grade.

12. At no time since Brian Hartman was in first grade has the Defendant provided Plaintiff Brian Hartman with an Individualized Education Plan ("IEP") as required by the IDEA, 20 U.S.C. § 1402(14), in spite of annual requests by Plaintiffs Laurie Hartman and Stephen Hartman.

13. In September 2009, when Plaintiff Brian Hartman entered sixth grade, the Defendant district reevaluated Plaintiff Brian Hartman and again determined that he was eligible for special education services because of his autism. Plaintiffs Laurie Hartman and Stephen Hartman again requested an IEP, and the Defendant asked its learning specialist, Diane Fulton, to meet with the Plaintiffs and a social worker the Plaintiffs had hired. The purpose of this meeting was to develop an IEP.

14. At the conclusion of a series of meetings in September and October of 2009 between the Plaintiffs, their social worker, and Diane Fulton, Diane Fulton proposed an IEP that included a teaching assistant who would accompany Brian Hartman to four academic classes each day and meet with him during two study halls to review the material covered in those four classes. Diane Fulton estimated the cost of the teaching assistant to be $40,000 per academic year.

15. After Diane Fulton submitted her proposed IEP to her employer, the Defendant district, the Defendant district unilaterally changed its finding that Plain-

16

---

16 Note the juxtaposition of the cost of the IEP and the defendant's decision to change Brian Hartman's disability designation. The writer hopes that the reader will conclude that the decision was based on cost, not on sound educational theory.

tiff Brian Hartman was eligible for special education services. The Defendant wrote a letter to Plaintiffs Laurie Hartman and Stephen Hartman in which it indicated that Plaintiff Brian Hartman had been academically successful without an IEP from kindergarten through fifth grade and that his success was an indication that he was not disabled.

16. In 2010, Plaintiffs Laurie Hartman and Stephen Hartman again requested an IEP for Plaintiff Brian Hartman. When the Defendant did not respond to their request, Plaintiffs Laurie Hartman and Stephen Hartman removed Plaintiff Brian Hartman from Bonaventure Local Village School District and placed him in a residential school for students with autism at a cost of $50,000 per year. Plaintiffs Laurie Hartman and Brian Hartman paid for the placement from their own funds for the 2010-11 school year.

17. In August 2011, Plaintiffs Laurie Hartman and Stephen Hartman again asked for an IEP for Plaintiff Brian Hartman for the 2011-12 academic year. The Defendant did not respond to the request, and Plaintiffs Laurie Hartman and Stephen Hartman again placed Plaintiff Brian Hartman in a residential school for students with autism at their own expense. For the first half of the 2011-12 academic year, Plaintiffs Laurie Hartman and Stephen Hartman have paid $25,000 in tuition.

17. The IDEA permits a parent of a child with a disability to place the child in a private school unilaterally when the local school district has failed to provide a free and appropriate public education as required by the IDEA, 20 U.S.C. § 1412. The parent may then seek reimbursement for the tuition for the unilateral placement.

---

17 Throughout, the plaintiff cites to the specific statutory provisions that relate to specific allegations. This type of specificity helps the judge (and the judge's clerk) to assess the validity of the claims.

18. In July 2011, Plaintiffs Laurie Hartman and Stephen Hartman initiated an administrative due process hearing against the Defendant district. The Plaintiffs alleged that the Defendant had failed to comply with the substantive and procedural requirements of the IDEA. Plaintiffs Laurie Hartman and Stephen Hartman requested a determination that Plaintiff Brian Hartman was a child with a disability and eligible for special education services, including a free and appropriate public education and an IEP. Plaintiffs Laurie Hartman and Stephen Hartman also asked for a determination that they are eligible for reimbursement for tuition for the unilateral placement.

19. The administrative hearing concluded on September 17, 2011. Before a decision was issued, the Defendant made an offer of settlement under 20 U.S.C. § 1415(i)(3)(D) and an offer of judgment under Rule 68 of the Federal Rules of Civil Procedure. The Defendant offered an admission that Plaintiff Brian Hartman is eligible for special education services under the IDEA, reimbursement of tuition paid to the private residential school by Plaintiffs Laurie Hartman and Stephen Hartman, an IEP instating the teaching assistant recommendation made by learning specialist Diane Fulton in 2009, and attorney's fees.

20. On October, 2011, Plaintiffs accepted the offer of settlement and the offer of judgment.

21. To date, the Defendant district has refused to make payment to reimburse Plaintiffs Laurie Hartman and Stephen Hartman for education expenses arising from their unilateral placement of Brian Hartman or to take other actions required by the offer of settlement and the offer of judgment.

18 Many federal statutes require plaintiffs to take certain actions—such as seeking an administrative solution—before they can file a federal lawsuit. This allegation reassures the judge that the plaintiffs have met this administrative requirement.

19 Most complaints do not need constant repetition of plaintiff names. Here, however, some actions were taken by all of the plaintiffs, while most were taken either by the child plaintiff or the parent plaintiffs. Thus, the writer must identify which plaintiffs have taken which actions.

Demand for Relief

For those reasons, Plaintiffs Laurie Hartman and Stephen Hartman, for themselves and on behalf of Plaintiff Brian Hartman, demand judgment against Defendant Bonaventure Local Village School District as follows:

20

1. Declaratory judgment that Plaintiff Brian Hartman is entitled to an IEP, including a teaching assistant who will accompany Brian Hartman to four academic classes each day and meet with him during two study halls to review the material covered in these four classes beginning immediately and continuing until Brian Hartman graduates from high school or until the parties agree to an alternative IEP;

2. Monetary relief in the amount of $75,000 for private school tuition paid by Plaintiffs Laurie Hartman and Stephen Hartman;

3. Attorney's fees and costs incurred by Plaintiffs in the administrative hearing and this litigation; and

21

4. Other relief as appropriate.

_____
Monte G. Smith
Attorney for the Plaintiffs
1234 Fifth Street
Belleville, OH 43234
614-555-1212

22

Atty. I.D. 123-456-789

---

20 Notice that the first paragraph in the Demand for Relief is paragraph 1.

21 Most complaints include this phrase to ensure that the court can give relief that the plaintiff did not specifically ask for.

22 Consult local rules about signature block requirements. Some rules may require an attorney number or some other type of professional identification. While your signature verifies that you are vouching for the validity of the facts alleged in the complaint, some courts may require a separate statement in which you formally assert the validity of the alleged facts.

IN THE UNITED STATES DISTRICT COURT
FOR THE SOUTHERN DISTRICT OF OHIO
WESTERN DIVISION

Dr. Joan Cranmer,	:	
583 Clarendon Street	:	Case No. C-2-12-038
Valley, West Virginia 26110,	:	
	:	
Plaintiff,	:	Complaint and Jury Demand
	:	
v.	:	
	:	
Potsdam State University,	:	
101 South Water Street	:	
Potsdam, Ohio 44172,	:	
	:	
and	:	
	:	
Emilio Gutierrez,	:	
101 South Water Street	:	
Potsdam, Ohio 44172,	:	
Defendants.	:	

23

Preliminary Statement

1.   This is a civil rights action arising from Potsdam State University's decision to deny Dr. Joan Cranmer's application for promotion and tenure based upon the impermissible consideration of her gender. Dr. Cranmer brings this action pursuant to Title VII of the Civil Rights Act of 1964 as amended by the Civil Rights Act of 1991, 42 U.S.C. § 2000, *et seq.*

2.   Dr. Cranmer seeks an injunction requiring the Defendants to award her promotion and tenure, as well as compensatory damages for the economic and

---

23 Note the specific demand for a jury trial.

noneconomic injuries she has suffered as a result of the Defendants' unlawful consideration of delays in academic publication occasioned solely as a result of Dr. Cranmer's taking lawful leave in order to bear and care for children. This leave is a necessity for female professors who wish to have children but is not a necessity for their male colleagues.

[24]

Jurisdiction and Venue

3.   This Court has jurisdiction over the Defendants, who are residents of the Southern District of Ohio.

4.   This Court has jurisdiction over the subject matter of the Plaintiff's claims under 28 U.S.C. § 1331, which provides that the United States district courts shall have original jurisdiction over all civil actions arising under the laws of the United States. This civil action arises under Title VII, a federal statute. This court also has jurisdiction over the subject matter of Plaintiff's claims under 28 U.S.C. § 1332 on the basis of diversity because the Plaintiff is a citizen of West Virginia while neither defendant is a citizen of West Virginia.

5.   This Court is a proper venue for this action under 28 U.S.C. § 1391(b) because the Defendants are situated in this judicial district, the citizenship of the parties is diverse, and the Plaintiff's claim arises under the laws of the United States.

The Parties

6.   Plaintiff, Dr. Joan Cranmer, is a professor of History at Potsdam State University. Dr. Cranmer has taught continuously at Potsdam State Universi-

---

[24] Again, part of the plaintiff's theme is that the plaintiff was complying with relevant law.

ty since 2001 except for two semesters of leave, Autumn Semester of 2006 and Spring Semester of 2011, during each of which she gave birth. Dr. Cranmer met all requirements for promotion to Full Professor at Potsdam State University except for publication of two scholarly works of superior merit within ten years of hiring. Dr. Cranmer's second scholarly work was published in October 2001, ten years and one month after her hiring, having been delayed by the birth of Dr. Cranmer's second child.

7.   Dr. Cranmer resides in Valley, West Virginia.

8.   Defendant Potsdam State University is a state-supported institution of higher education located in Potsdam, Ohio, within the Southern District of Ohio. Potsdam State University is an "employer," as that term is defined by Title VII. Potsdam State University has established an unwritten policy relating to the timing requirements for obtaining tenure in the Department of History that permits the treatment of maternity leave as different from any other kind of leave, medical or otherwise. That policy has resulted in discrimination against female faculty members in the Department of History, including Dr. Cranmer.

9.   Defendant Emilio Gutierrez is Chair of the Department of History at Potsdam State University and a resident of Potsdam, Ohio in the Southern District of Ohio. Dr. Gutierrez is personally responsible for the adoption of the unwritten policy outlined in paragraph 8 above and is sued in his individual capacity.

---

25 Again, notice that the complaint uses the description of the parties to articulate certain damning details about the defendant.

Plaintiff's Claim

First Cause of Action: Sex Discrimination in Violation of Title VII

(42 U.S.C. § 2000e)

26
10. On November 7, 2011, Dr. Cranmer filed a charge of discrimination with the Equal Opportunity Employment Commission ("EEOC") on the basis of the Defendants' illegal actions as outlined in this Complaint.

11. On January 6, 2012, the EEOC issued a Notice of Right to Sue to Dr. Cranmer.

12. Dr. Cranmer received her Ph.D. in History from the University of Cincinnati in 2001. Her academic credentials were rated 9 out of 10 by the tenured faculty of Potsdam State University when she applied for an appointment as an Assistant Professor of History in 2001. The following members of the faculty of

27
the Department of History have been promoted to Full Professor while Defendant Gutierrez has been Chair of the Department: Jonathan Moor (academic credentials rating 8.5 of 10); Dwight Williamson (academic credentials rating 7.5 of 10); Donald Uhrich (academic credentials rating 8 of 10); and Robert Dovenbarger (academic credentials rating 8 of 10). The following members of the faculty of the Department of History have been denied promotion to Full Professor while Defendant Gutierrez has been Chair of the Department: Ellen Brose (academic credentials rating 9 of 10); Mary Ellen Ruhl (academic credentials rating 9.5 of 10); Joan Cranmer (academic credentials rating 9 of 10).

26 These paragraphs show that the plaintiff has met the administrative and procedural requirements that allow her to file a suit under Title VII.

27 By juxtaposing these details—lower-ranking men were promoted, while higher-ranking women were not promoted—the writer hopes to convince the reader that the University has a persistent pattern of discrimination against women.

13. To be eligible for promotion to Full Professor at Potsdam State University in Arts and Sciences, History, or Philosophy, a member of the faculty must publish at least two scholarly works of superior merit within ten years of hiring. A "scholarly work of superior merit" is defined as an "article in an academic journal, which must be peer-reviewed, in which scholarship relating to the faculty member's particular academic discipline is published, and which is judged by at least three of five eminent scholars in that academic discipline from whom the University solicits opinions to be of superior merit."

14. To be eligible for promotion to Full Professor at Potsdam State University, a member of the faculty in any department must have earned teaching review scores of at least 7 out of 10 in four of the five years preceding the application for promotion.

15. Dr. Cranmer published her first scholarly work in an academic journal in March 2004. Potsdam State University solicited opinions from five eminent scholars in the field of history; five out of five of these scholars judged the article to be of superior merit. Dr. Cranmer published her second scholarly work in an academic journal in October 2011. Potsdam State University solicited opinions from five eminent scholars in the field of history; five out of five of these scholars judged the article to be of superior merit. **28**

16. Four faculty members in the Department of History have been promoted to Full Professor while Defendant Gutierrez has been Chair of the Department: Jonathan Moor ("superior merit" votes 3 of 5; 4 of 5); Dwight Williamson ("supe-

28 The writer uses this unusual phrasing to match the parenthetical merit votes recounted in the next paragraph.

rior merit" votes 4 of 5; 4 of 5); Donald Uhrich ("superior merit" votes 5 of 5; 3 of 5); and Robert Dovenbarger ("superior merit" votes 4 of 5; 4 of 5). Three members of the faculty of the Department of History have been denied promotion to Full Professor while Defendant Gutierrez has been Chair of the Department: Ellen Brose ("superior merit" votes 4 of 5; 5 of 5); Mary Ellen Ruhl ("superior merit" votes 5 of 5; 5 of 5); Joan Cranmer ("superior merit" votes 5 of 5; 5 of 5).

17. In the five academic years leading up to her application for promotion to Full Professor, Dr. Cranmer received the following teaching review scores (out of a possible 10): 9.5, 10, 10, 9.5, 10.

18. Four faculty members in the Department of History have been promoted to Full Professor while Defendant Gutierrez has been Chair of the Department: Jonathan Moor (teaching review scores 8, 7, 8.5, 8, 8)); Dwight Williamson (teaching review scores 9, 9, 9, 9.5, 9.5); Donald Uhrich (teaching review scores 6, 8, 8.5, 8.5, 8.5); and Robert Dovenbarger (teaching review scores 9, 9.5, 10, 9, 9). Three members of the faculty of the Department of History have been denied promotion to Full Professor while Defendant Gutierrez has been Chair of the Department: Ellen Brose (teaching review scores 9, 9, 9, 9.5, 9.5); Mary Ellen Ruhl (teaching review scores 10, 10, 9, 9.5, 10); Joan Cranmer (teaching review scores 9.5, 10, 10, 9.5, 10).

19. Dr. Cranmer applied for promotion to Full Professor when she submitted her second scholarly work for publication. Her teaching review scores and "superior merit" votes establish that she is well qualified for promotion. Her qualifications exceed those of every member of the History faculty who has been promoted to Full Professor since Defendant Gutierrez become Chair of the department.

20. Dr. Cranmer was denied promotion to Full Professor because her second scholarly work was considered untimely, having been published ten years and one month after she was hired by Potsdam State University.

21. Defendant Gutierrez instructed tenured members of the History Department who were voting on Dr. Cranmer's application for promotion to Full Professor that they should not exclude the two semesters of maternity leave taken by Dr. Cranmer from the period during which Dr. Cranmer was to have published two scholarly works of superior merit.

22. The unwritten policy of Potsdam State University from at least the time of Dr. Cranmer's hiring has been that periods of medical leave are excluded from the timing requirements for promotion. Dr. Gutierrez has adhered to that policy in the case of at least one application for promotion. Robert Dovenbarger had taken medical leave of one academic year after undergoing a heart transplant. His second scholarly work was published ten years and seven months after his hiring by Potsdam State University. Robert Dovenbarger was promoted to Full Professor, nevertheless.

23. Other departments within Potsdam State University exclude periods of maternity leave, as well as medical leave, from the timing requirements associated with promotion. At least two members of Potsdam State University's faculty have been promoted after publishing scholarly works that would have been considered untimely had periods of maternity leave not been excluded.

24. Defendants have not identified a basis for the denial of Dr. Cranmer's application for tenure except for the delay in the publication of her second scholarly work. That delay was occasioned by her second maternity leave. Only women are

eligible for maternity leave. Defendant Gutierrez's interpretation of the policy regarding exclusion of periods of leave burdens only female members of the faculty.

29   25. Defendants' actions in denying Dr. Cranmer tenure constituted discrimination in the terms and conditions of her employment on the basis of her gender in violation of Title VII.

Defendants' Answer to Complaint

Second Cause of Action: Pregnancy Discrimination in Violation of Title VII

(42 U.S.C. § 2000e(k))

30   26. Plaintiff hereby incorporates by reference paragraphs 10 through 25 as set forth above.

     27. Defendants' actions in denying Dr. Cranmer tenure constituted discrimination in the terms and conditions of her employment on the basis of pregnancy and maternity in violation of Title VII.

Demand for Relief

Wherefore, Plaintiff Dr. Joan Cranmer demands judgment against Defendants Potsdam State University and Emilio Gutierrez as follows:

     1.   Declaratory relief establishing that Defendants' actions violated Title VII's prohibitions against discrimination on the basis of gender;

     2.   A permanent injunction awarding Dr. Joan Cranmer promotion to Full Professor;

---

29 Here, the writer articulates the precise legal violation. The previous paragraphs lay out the facts that establish that this allegation is "plausible" under the *Iqbal* standard.

30 This convention allows the plaintiff to repeat a series of allegations without restating them. It is a common complaint-drafting technique.

3.   Compensatory damages in an amount to be determined at trial for any economic injuries, including loss of salary and benefits suffered by Dr. Joan Cranmer as a proximate result of Defendants' discriminatory actions;

4.   Compensatory damages in an amount to be determined at trial for any noneconomic damages, including damages for emotional pain and suffering and harm to professional reputation suffered by Dr. Joan Cranmer as a proximate result of Defendants' discriminatory actions;

5.   An award of Dr. Cranmer's attorney fees and costs.

6.   Other relief as permitted by law.

_____

Mary Beth Beazley
Attorney for the Plaintiff
432 First Street
Valley, West Virginia
518-555-1212
Attorney Number 987-5432-1

SAMPLE ANSWER

IN THE UNITED STATES DISTRICT COURT
FOR THE SOUTHERN DISTRICT OF OHIO
WESTERN DIVISION

Dr. Joan Cranmer,	:	
583 Clarendon Street	:	Case No. C-2-12-038
Valley, West Virginia 26110,	:	
	:	
Plaintiff,	:	
	:	
v. :		
	:	
Potsdam State University,	:	
101 South Water Street	:	
Potsdam, Ohio 44172,	:	
	:	
and :		
	:	
Emilio Gutierrez,	:	
101 South Water Street	:	
Potsdam, Ohio 44172,	:	
	:	
Defendants.	:	

Defendants Potsdam State University and Emilio Gutierrez ("Defendants"),

for their answer to the Complaint, state as follows:

First Defense

1.   This paragraph is a characterization of this action to which no response

is required except to the extent that Defendants deny the suggestion that the

31 Defendants are not required to label an answer to plaintiff's specific allegations as a defense, but many defense attorneys do so to signal that the primary defense is the denial of any combination of allegations that would lead to liability. Defendants may also assert so-called affirmative defenses; these defenses argue that a defendant is not liable even if plaintiff's allegations are true. Affirmative defenses would follow the admissions and denials as to the plaintiff's specific allegations. In the employment discrimination context, a common affirmative defense is that the plaintiff's complaint was not timely filed, so the defendant is not liable even if all of the allegations are true.

denial of Plaintiff's application for promotion and tenure was based upon the impermissible consideration of her gender.

2.   This paragraph is a characterization of this action to which no response is required except to the extent that Defendants deny the suggestion that the denial of Plaintiff's application for promotion and tenure was based upon their consideration of delays in academic publication occasioned solely as a result of Dr. Cranmer's taking lawful leave in order to bear and care for children.

Jurisdiction and Venue

3.   Defendants admit that this Court has jurisdiction over them and that they are residents of the Southern District of Ohio.

4.   Defendants admit that his Court has jurisdiction over the subject matter of the Plaintiff's claims under 28 U.S.C. §§ 1331 and 1332, which speak for themselves.

5.   Defendants consent to this judicial district as a venue for this action.

The Parties

6.   Defendants admit the allegations in paragraph 6 except to the extent that they deny that the delay in the publication of Plaintiff's second scholarly work was occasioned solely by the birth of her second child. [32]

7.   Defendants admit the allegation of paragraph 7.

---

[32] Had the defendants failed to qualify their admission as to the allegations in this paragraph, they would likely be precluded from later attempting to demonstrate that Plaintiff brought her woes upon herself by procrastinating or otherwise failing to give the necessary attention to her publication obligations. In other words, they would be "stuck" with the admission that the publication delay was the result, solely, of pregnancy and childbirth-related delays.

8.   Defendants admit that Potsdam State University is a state-supported institution of higher education located in Potsdam, Ohio, in the Southern District of Ohio. Defendants further admit that Potsdam State University is an "employer," as that term is defined by Title VII. Defendants deny all other allegations in paragraph 8.

9.   Defendants admit that Emilio Gutierrez is Chair of the Department of History at Potsdam State University and a resident of Potsdam, Ohio, in the Southern District of Ohio. Defendants specifically deny the existence of an unwritten policy as alleged in paragraph 8 of the Complaint and, therefore, also deny that Emilio Gutierrez could have been responsible, in his official, personal, or individual capacity, for the adoption of that policy.

Plaintiff's Claim

First Cause of Action: Sex Discrimination in Violation of Title VII

(42 U.S.C. § 2000e)

10.   Defendants admit the allegation in paragraph 10.

11.   Defendants admit the allegation in paragraph 11.

12.   Defendants admit the allegations in paragraph 12.

13.   Defendants admit the allegation in paragraph 13.

14.   Defendants admit the allegation in paragraph 14.

15.   Defendants admit the allegation in paragraph 15.

16.   Defendants admit the allegation in paragraph 16.

17.   Defendants admit the allegation in paragraph 17.

18.   Defendants admit the allegation in paragraph 18.

33 The allegations in paragraph 12 are quite specific and, on their face, appear to be damning. This very general denial allows the defendants to avoid repeating them in their answer.

19. Defendants admit that Plaintiff applied for promotion to Full Professor when she submitted her second scholarly work for publication. Defendants deny the other allegations in paragraph 19 and specifically deny that teaching review scores and "superior merit" votes are the only bases employed by Potsdam State University for determining whether a faculty member is qualified for promotion. Defendants further specifically deny that Plaintiff's qualifications exceeded those of every member of the History faculty at Potsdam State University who was promoted to Full Professor while Defendant Gutierrez was Chair of the department.

20. Defendants admit the allegation in paragraph 20.

21. Defendants admit the allegation in paragraph 21.

22. Defendants deny the existence of a policy of Potsdam State University that periods of medical leave are excluded from the timing requirements for promotion. Defendants admit that Potsdam State University excluded a one-year period from the timing requirement for the promotion of Robert Dovenbarger because Dr. Dovenbarger was on full disability status during that period and not considered an employee of the Potsdam State University, in contrast to Plaintiff, who remained a compensated employee of Potsdam State University throughout the time period outlined in paragraph 21 of the Complaint. Defendants admit that Robert Dovenbarger was promoted to Full Professor.

23. Defendants deny that Potsdam State University has excluded a period of maternity leave from the timing requirements for promotion for any faculty member who has remained a compensated employee during maternity leave.

24. Defendants deny that they have failed to identify a basis for the denial of Dr. Cranmer's application for tenure. The denial was based on the untimeliness of the publication of her second scholarly work. Defendants further deny that the

34 publication policy burdens female members of the faculty, who are eligible for parental leave periods that are excluded from the timing requirements.

25. The allegation in paragraph 25 of the Complaint is a legal conclusion to **35** which no response is required. Defendants deny that their action in denying Dr. Cranmer tenure constituted discrimination in the terms and conditions of her employment on the basis of her gender in violation of Title VII.

Second Cause of Action: Pregnancy Discrimination in Violation of Title VII

(42 U.S.C. § 2000e(k))

36 **36** 26. Defendants hereby incorporate paragraphs 10 through 25 as set forth above by reference.

27. The allegation in paragraph 27 of the Complaint is a legal conclusion to which no response is required. Defendants deny that their actions in denying Dr. Cranmer tenure constituted discrimination in the terms and conditions of her employment on the basis of pregnancy and maternity in violation of Title VII.

Monte Smith
Attorney for Defendants
19 Twentieth Avenue
Potsdam, OH
472-555-3838
Attorney Number 14307-65

34 Here, the writer suggests the primary basis for the defense that the plaintiff chose to remain compensated during her leaves and was, therefore, not entitled to have the leave periods excluded from the publication timing requirements.

35 Note that the writer both asserts that no response is required because the paragraph states a legal conclusion and not a factual allegation and includes a denial in an abundance of caution. The writer includes that same dual response in paragraph 27.

36 This convention allows the defendants to repeat a series of admissions and denials without restating them. It is a common answer-drafting technique, but a writer should examine the incorporated paragraphs to ensure that differences in the plaintiff's allegations do not require a difference in the answer.

CHAPTER THIRTEEN

Persuasive Correspondence: Writing Demand Letters

As you may know, one way that an attorney advocates on behalf of a client is by sending out a *demand letter*. A demand letter is a formalized request, or demand, that is submitted to a client's opponent or the opponent's counsel. The letter demands that the opponent take a particular action; often, that action is the payment of money to the client, but the request might be non-monetary. For example, you may request that the opponent comply with a contract or stop violating a copyright (demand letters of this type are often known as "cease and desist" letters). The letter may lay out consequences that will occur if the opponent does not comply with the demand—e.g., a lawsuit—but not all demand letters specify consequences. Often, the demand letter is the first step in some sort of negotiation process between parties.

Demand letters may be sent at any point in time. Unlike a complaint, an answer, or a motion, for example, demand letters do not occupy a particular location on the litigation timeline. A demand letter is often sent in lieu of litigation: the opponent is given the opportunity to avoid litigation by paying money to the client or taking some other requested action. If litigation begins, there are a few times during the litigation at which it might be appropriate to send out a demand letter. This is not to say that demand letters are sent out lightly, or that they are sent out multiple times regarding the same matter (it would be unusual, but not unheard of, to send out more than one demand letter on the same matter).

A demand letter may be appropriate if a letter can show the opponent that taking the action you demand will be easier or better than the alternative that will or may result if the opponent does not take the action you demand. A pre-litigation letter, for example, might show the opponent how paying the demand is easier than facing the uncertainties of litigation. During litigation, a letter might be sent leading up to certain points of particular expense or uncertainty—for example, prior to extensive and expensive discovery, prior to the actual commencement of an expensive trial, or prior to an uncertain and possibly expensive jury verdict.

Some lawyers may believe that it is appropriate to send out a demand letter without conducting much research—perhaps on the theory that they may as well "take a shot," and that getting some money without spending much might provide a benefit for the client with minimal expense. Most experts advise, however, that the best demand letters are sent after conducting thorough research.

First, conducting adequate research allows you, the writer, to accurately articulate the strengths of the client's case, and the weaknesses of the opponent's case, as needed. Second, adequate research allows you to avoid misrepresenting the client's case, which may cause your opponent to take your demand less seriously and can also have legal consequences for your client in some circumstances.[1]

Even after you have decided that a demand letter is appropriate, you have several other strategic decisions to make. For example, you need to decide whether the letter should come from the client or from you, the attorney; you need to decide whether to address the letter to the opponent[2] directly or to the opponent's attorney; and you need to decide on the best timing for the letter.[3] In addition, you must decide what the tone of the letter will be. In rare situations, the letter can be written in a "take no prisoners" tone. Usually, how-

---

1. For example, in intellectual property cases, overstating the breadth of a copyright may, in certain circumstances, constitute a copyright violation. PATRICK J. FLINN, ASPEN PUBLISHERS HANDBOOK OF INTELLECTUAL PROPERTY CLAIMS & REMEDIES, § 4.03 (Aspen 2011).

2. Note that if the opponent is already represented by counsel, ethical obligations require you to send the letter to the attorney, even if you address the letter to the opponent.

3. Bret Rappaport, *A Shot Across the Bow: How to Write an Effective Demand Letter*, 5 J. ALWD 32 (2008) (noting that strategizing as to the time of the week or day may allow counsel to capitalize on the psychological mood of the opponent or his or her counsel).

ever, it is more effective for you to presume that your client does not want to burn all bridges in the relationship with the opponent. Accordingly, a more effective demand letter will be written in a professional tone, with the goal of convincing the reader that meeting the demand—or meeting with you and your client in order to negotiate—is in the best interests of all parties to the controversy.

13.1. PLANNING THE LETTER

Before you sit down to write the demand letter, you must first conduct factual research to be certain that you understand all relevant facts that can be obtained without formal discovery. As in all litigation, you should conduct due diligence to be as certain as you can that your client has not significantly misrepresented the controversy. Second, you must conduct legal research to identify the strengths and weaknesses of the client's case, including any defenses your opponent might reasonably raise. Third, you should try to identify, to the extent possible, reasons that the opponent might have for meeting your demand. Typically, the most obvious reason is to save money. Litigation is expensive, and if there is a reasonable chance that your client would be victorious in a lawsuit, it is probably much less expensive for the opponent to reach a settlement with your client.

Your opponent may have other reasons for meeting your demand, however. Doing so will allow the opponent to avoid the hassle and inconvenience of a trial; even if a trial is not contemplated, meeting your demand may help the opponent to avoid the possibility of unpleasant publicity. This benefit may be particularly relevant if your opponent is an institutional or corporate entity. In this situation, be sure to consult publicly available documents or websites as part of your factual or legal research; to the extent that you can find statements of the entity's goals (e.g., being a good corporate citizen or serving the people of a particular city or state), you can use those statements to help convince the opponent that meeting your demand is in its best interest.[4]

---

4. *See, e.g.*, Adam J. Blank & Patrick J. Kennedy, *Dynamic Demand Letters*, 45 TRIAL 28 (2009).

13.2. WRITING THE LETTER

Broadly stated, effective demand letters often contain the following six elements, although they may not always appear in this order:

- the purpose of the letter;
- the demand itself;
- the articulation of the problem, including any known evidence of culpability and of harm to the client;
- the benefits of meeting the demand;
- the possible or likely consequences of failure to meet the demand; and
- the deadline for meeting the demand.

13.2.1. The Purpose of the Letter

Your letter should not be coy. Tell the reader up front that you are writing to make a demand. If this letter is being sent before litigation has begun, state that you are making a demand based on the harm that your client has suffered or is suffering due to the opponent's action or inaction. If you are writing after litigation has begun, state that the timing is designed to allow the parties to avoid expenses that are likely to be incurred in the near future or in advance of some other imminent development in the litigation.

13.2.2. The Demand Itself

1 For example, the author may state early in the letter that "the purpose of this letter is to demand that you immediately cease and desist from infringing a patent held by my client." Later in the letter, the author can set out the details of the patent and the alleged infringement.

1 Commonly, the demand will appear at one of two locations: the first paragraph or the last paragraph. If the demand appears at the end of the letter, the first paragraph should announce that the demand is coming. (For example, "Finally, this letter will make a settlement demand.") If the primary purpose of the letter is to demand that a party cease and desist, the letter's author should state explicitly, early in the letter, that the author's client is asking the recipient or the recipient's client to cease and desist from the injurious behavior.

13.2.3. The Articulation of the Problem, Including Any Known Evidence of Culpability and of Harm to the Client

This piece is the meat of the letter. Tell the story of how the client was harmed or is being harmed. Include references to or quotations from any evidence you may have that establishes culpability, or describe information or documents you would offer into evidence when you know these are available. Be sure to include specifics that establish the harm to the client, including already-incurred medical expenses, the cost of any lost opportunities, pain and suffering, and the like. Your goal in this section of the letter is for the opponent to understand (a) what happened, (b) that you will be able to prove that the opponent is at fault for what happened, and (c) that you will be able to prove the harm—financial and otherwise—that your client has suffered.

The facts you include may depend on the status of the claim; if litigation has begun, the complaint will presumably contain all needed information about the nature of the claims and the alleged injuries to your client. Nevertheless, you may repeat some details if doing so will help the opponent to understand the validity of your demand. Think carefully about the facts you have amassed and about your audience. It is appropriate to "milk" some points to garner sympathy (or to make vivid how sympathetic your client will appear to a jury or court), but, as with all rhetorical techniques, be careful not to go too far.

A demand letter is different from a memo or a brief, in which you are likely to spend significant time citing and describing various statutes and cases. Before writing a demand letter, of course, you should become thoroughly familiar with the governing law, but you should not include a huge amount of detail. Instead, summarize the legal requirements, giving only the detail required for the opponent to understand his or her culpability. If a statute governs the situation, you may list it, but it is probably not fruitful to cite to cases in a demand letter. (For example, you might say, "As you may know, Code § 11111.04 requires that business owners keep their sidewalks free of ice and snow . . . " or, "As you may know, the legal standards governing employment relations require that government employers respect the free speech rights of their employees in most situations.").

As noted above, conducting legal research is important because doing so will allow you to identify possible defenses, and to anticipate those that your opponent may offer. An effective demand letter need not address every possible defense, but it should address defenses that the opponent is likely to raise. (For example, "Admittedly, the statute does not allow for recovery if the victim was teasing the dog at the time of the attack. As you know, of course, there was no teasing in this situation; Ms. Kish was reaching down to pat Muggs on the head when he bit her. Courts have refused to characterize this type of behavior as 'teasing.'").

Be certain to include any details that show the opponent's culpability, or any facts that will help the opponent to realize that he or she is at fault. (For example, "Contrary to best practices of your field, which can be found at www.ourbestpractices.fake, your employees have. . . .") If your opponent has made any admissions in writing—or if your client or potential witnesses have heard admissions that they will testify about in any trial—you may quote them or refer to them.

When articulating the harms your client has suffered, be thorough in your research and in your presentation. You do not want to make a demand that later turns out to be inadequate to cover ongoing medical expenses, for example. You (or your investigator) should talk to your client's medical provider about any future harm to your client that could result from physical injuries, stress, or other problems. When presenting these facts to your opponent, make clear that you will have proof to back up any claims, should the case go to (or continue on to) trial. (For example, "As my client's doctor will testify, this type of injury makes it likely that she will require a knee replacement within the next 10-20 years, before she is even 50 years old. Further, having a knee replacement at such a young age makes it likely that she will have to undergo a second knee replacement.")

13.2.4. The Benefits of Meeting the Demand

Many attorneys do not make statements about benefits explicitly, preferring to let the details of the potential expense do the talking. Also, if your opponent is already represented by counsel, counsel will be well aware of the costs of litigation. Of course, you may be concerned that your opponent's counsel will be motivated to avoid a settlement because a settlement means that the counsel's paycheck will be much smaller. In that situation, you might consider spending a little more time laying out the expenses of litigation (beyond the judgment itself) to be certain that the opponent is aware of these expenses. (For example, "As you know, the costs of preparing numerous witnesses, finding and paying fees of experts, and the hourly attorney fees for a week-long trial, are all likely to add significantly to the cost of litigation beyond the cost of the judgment that we will seek.")

13.2.5. The Possible or Likely Consequences of Failure to Meet the Demand

Your articulation of the problem and of the client's harms may be short, or it may cover several paragraphs. At some point, however, you should total all of the possible damages for which you seek recovery and provide the total amount of damages that you will seek. If you have already filed a complaint, this amount may have been mentioned already; of course, if further research has revealed other possible causes of action, your new amount may be higher than the amount mentioned there. In any event, be sure to feature the number prominently, as it represents the client's best incentive to settle. You should also note, of course, any intangible reasons for settlement, such as time lost to trial and possible harm to the opponent's reputation. If you are sending the demand letter in advance of the complaint, for example, the opponent may be motivated to settle so that a complaint—which is a public record—will never be filed.

A word about psychology here. Particularly if you are sending a letter before you have filed a lawsuit, the worst consequences for your opponent—the costs of a judgment against it—may be far in the future and are therefore likely to seem abstract. Research shows that human beings are more likely to be concerned about small, concrete pains in the present than about large, abstract pains that may occur in the future. People also tend to be optimistic and to think, for example, that it is preferable to avoid the immediate pain of a settlement now, believing optimistically that they will also be able to avoid the distant pain of a judgment against them later. Accordingly, when considering the consequences of a failure to meet your demand, try to identify and articulate as many immediate "pains" as you can.

These pains may include, for example, the pain of negative publicity or of complex and expensive discovery that will begin immediately. You may be more likely to achieve a settlement if you can make your opponent realize that it must worry not only about pains in the future, but also those in the present. Thus, in addition to describing the amount of money that may be lost in the distant future, try to identify a negative consequence that will happen immediately after the demand deadline passes, and be explicit. You might say, for example, "If you do not meet our demand, we have prepared a discovery request that will be delivered immediately and that will seek. . . ." The attorney may be more motivated to avoid dealing with your definite, unavoidable discovery request next week than to avoid an indefinite, but possibly avoidable million-dollar verdict several months hence.

13.2.6. The Deadline

Tell your opponent a date certain by which you expect an answer. Some demand letters are sent in anticipation of mediation, which many courts now require. In that situation, you can make reference to the anticipated mediation as a deadline. For example, "We expect to hear your answer at or before our mediation scheduled for February 10." If there is no scheduled meeting date on the calendar, provide a reasonable "deadline" yourself. We put the word in quotation marks because you, of course, have no real authority to impose a deadline. Nevertheless, by stating when you expect an answer, you give both sides a target. Your opponent has a date by which an answer is expected, and you have a date by which to begin follow-up. If you have threatened to file a complaint if your demand is not met, you must follow through on that threat.

By now, you may be wondering whether email is an appropriate medium for communicating demands. The short answer is "it depends." The longer answer is that the letter and the date of its receipt may have legal significance; therefore, an actual letter may be the wiser choice. For some types of claims, the fact that a defendant was aware of a potential breach or other potentially illegal behavior may impact a knowledge or notice element or the measure of damages. While an electronic record of receipt may be appropriate, in some cases it may be better to have a certified (snail) mail receipt. Local practice may guide you here.

13.3. CONCLUSION

Once again, the chapter is over, but your reading is not. A sample demand letter illustrating these principles follows.

SAMPLE DEMAND LETTER

VIA F-MAIL

Amy Dunn, Esq.
Dunn & Perek, LLC
4560 Hickory Road
Rockville, ST 01000

Re: *Jeannette L. Doyle, M.D., Inc. v.*
Allegiance Group Collections, Inc.
<u>Our File No. 46556</u>

Dear Amy:

I send this letter in anticipation of our mediation scheduled for November 15, 2020. This letter has three purposes. First, this letter provides an overview regarding the strengths of our claims against Allegiance Group. Second, this letter outlines the damages we will seek if this case goes to trial and, finally, this letter contains our settlement demand.

We are confident that we will establish liability against Allegiance in this case. As you know, our Complaint raises two causes of action: (1) breach of an agency relationship, and (2) breach of contract. The agency relationship between Allegiance and Dr. Doyle required Allegiance to use its "best efforts" and "best endeavors" to handle Dr. Doyle's medical billing. We will provide testimony at trial, both through fact and expert witnesses, that the first eight months of Allegiance's handling of Dr. Doyle's medical billing (from July of 2016 to February of 2017) was in breach of this agency arrangement. Despite making representations

2 F-Mail = "Fictional Mail."

3 By noting that the parties have a mediation scheduled for November 15, the writer gives an implicit deadline for the demand.

4 This paragraph articulates the letter's purpose and informs the reader that the demand will appear late in the letter ("finally"). Some letters include the demand in the first paragraph; if the demand is not there, the letter should inform the reader, as this letter does, that a demand is coming.

5 This sentence articulates the legal standard that governs this dispute. Note that it does not cite to a statute or a case. This paragraph articulates the problem, but it uses less detail because a complaint has already been filed.

that its collection of accounts receivable would go up by 30%, Allegiance in fact decreased Dr. Doyle's collection of accounts receivable. Mr. Entrikin has admitted that Allegiance, even at the time of entering into the arrangement with Dr. Doyle, was "making it a priority" to terminate medical practices. Further, Allegiance made knowing misrepresentations (readily acknowledged by Mr. Entrikin) about Allegiance's ability to increase Dr. Doyle's collection of accounts receivable. These statements also contradict the representations found on Allegiance's website, including its statement that "all of our clients can count on us; they are our highest priority." In addition, we are aware of many other facts that strongly support our claim and that we will present to the jury at trial.

Further, we will also seek damages at trial for the last five months of Allegiance's handling of Dr. Doyle's medical billing. In 2016, Allegiance made it a priority to stop servicing medical practices. As a result, Allegiance was apparently reducing the attention it paid to the collection of Dr. Doyle's accounts receivable and, eventually, this disregard resulted in a dramatic decline in Dr. Doyle's income. Any discussion that third-party payers' practices caused this decline is meritless; the testimony at trial will show that Dr. Doyle's subsequent billing service returned the percentage of accounts receivable back to its customary rate with no change in Dr. Doyle's handling of write-offs.

---

6 Identifying admissions of the opponent can be particularly useful.

7 The writer notes company statements from its website that are apparently inconsistent with the company's behavior in this case.

8 This paragraph contains further evidence of harm to the client.

9 Here, the writer anticipates defenses and undercuts them.

The evidence will also show that in lieu of demonstrating "good faith," "best efforts," and "best endeavors" to collect Dr. Doyle's accounts receivable, Allegiance only "skimmed the cream" off the collectibles. That is, Mr. Entrikin made it clear that when accounts became difficult to collect, Allegiance would encourage its employees to spend time collecting on more lucrative accounts. Failing to collect this "tough money" cut Dr. Doyle's profit margin, which is dramatically affected by swings of only a few percentage points. Again, this behavior shows that Allegiance was acting in its own best interests and <u>not</u> the interests of Dr. Doyle.

Additionally, we have retained David Knight of Knight & Moses to review Dr. Doyle's damages. Mr. Knight will render an opinion that Dr. Doyle incurred damages of approximately $135,000 as a result of Allegiance's failings during these two periods. We will provide our figures to you at the mediation.

Finally, if this litigation continues, we will amend our Complaint to raise claims under this state's Deceptive Trade Practices Act (in particular, a violation of § 13.02(C)(4)) to recover our attorneys' fees pursuant to § 15.03(F). The evidence supports such a claim based on the misrepresentation in the April 24, 2016 letter, which Mr. Entrikin himself readily concedes. Finally, we believe that we may have a claim for fraud, for which we would seek punitive damages in excess of $225,000. In sum, we would seek damages in excess of $400,000 if we are forced to try this case.

---

10 This paragraph provides more details about the opponent's culpability. The writer connects the requirements of the law, articulated above (good faith, best efforts, and best endeavors) with the facts (skimming the cream).

11 This paragraph refers to the evidence of harm, including the existence of specific records that will be used to establish financial harm.

12 In this paragraph, the writer identifies an immediate "pain": a new cause of action could be filed, presumably requiring immediate discovery.

13

    We are confident in our case; however, we recognize that everyone's interests may best be served by a timely settlement. Therefore, we make a settlement de-

14

mand of $200,000 for a full, final, and complete settlement of this matter.

Very truly yours,

Terrence Panice

TP:mgs
bcc: Dr. Jeannette L. Doyle

---

13 Here, the writer alludes to the fact that settling might be in the client's best interest. This point is strategically situated between the damages that will be sought — $400,000 — and the settlement demand — $200,000. The juxtaposition and chronology of these numbers makes one benefit of settling abundantly clear.

14 Here the writer makes the explicit settlement demand. Even if he had made the demand up front, it would be appropriate to repeat it here.

CHAPTER FOURTEEN

Logos, Pathos, Ethos, Typos: Writing and Designing a Reader-Friendly Document

We're guessing that when you first read the title to this chapter, you immediately thought, "One of these things is not like the other." As we noted in Chapter One, logos, pathos, and ethos are the three types of classic rhetoric, or persuasion. Legal writers use logos, or logic, to persuade by articulating the analytical truth of their arguments. They use pathos, or emotion, to persuade by evoking the sympathy of their readers for the plight of their clients. They use ethos, or character, to persuade by presenting themselves—as legal writers—in a way that inspires trust in their readers. You recognized, of course, that "typos" is not part of the classical rhetorician's toolkit. We think it should be, in a way. Not that we want to promote typos; what we want is to use the concept of typos as a reminder that the way that writers design, write, and present their documents has a strong impact on logos, pathos, and, especially, ethos. When a document is well-designed, it welcomes the reader and makes it easy for the reader to navigate within the document. When it is well-written, it saves the reader's mental energy and promotes comprehension. When it does not have typographical errors or grammatical mistakes, it frees the reader from distraction: the reader doesn't have to look past the errors to try to figure out what the writer must have meant. All of these features lead the reader to trust the writer and encourage the reader to continue reading, creating more opportunities for the reader to be persuaded by the document's substance and by the arguments that appeal to logos and pathos.

This chapter will first address document design issues, including issues that have many nuances in this transitional era between hard copy and digital documents. Next, it will address techniques for writing sentences more effectively. Finally, it will describe methods for proofreading final drafts.

14.1. DOCUMENT DESIGN FOR THE TWENTY-FIRST-CENTURY READER

Have you ever turned to a new page on a handout you were reading and found that there were *no* paragraph breaks? Or faced a solid wall of text that you were supposed to push your way through? We say "supposed" to push your way through because we're guessing that you took a break right then, or maybe even abandoned the handout for good. Try to remember that wall-of-text feeling, because that problem was caused by poor design, and you want to design your own documents so that your readers don't ever feel that way.

It's well beyond the scope of this book to tell you everything you need to know about document design, but there are a few principles that we want to share. The first, which is implicit in the previous paragraph, is this:

Readers need white space.

When we don't see enough white space on a page or a screen, it makes it hard to breathe, mentally: we don't get any breaks to process the information we take in, and if we're just looking for a specific point, we don't know where to begin looking. And that brings us to our second point:

Readers need to be able to navigate within and between documents.

There are a few ways that readers need to navigate within and even between documents. First, when they reach a page, either in hard copy or electronically, readers need to be able to tell where to start reading. At the end of a line, they need to navigate to the next line. At the end of a word, they have to navigate to the next word, and yes, at the end of each letter they have to navigate to the next letter. Fortunately, as we will explain, it's relatively easy for most writers to facilitate this kind of navigation.

Legal readers and digital readers have a few more navigational needs. As we've discussed, when they are reading legal documents, lawyers (and judges) are less likely to be linear readers and more likely to be active readers. They have an agenda. While they may read certain segments in a linear fashion, they will almost certainly have moments where they need to find a certain point, a certain issue, or a certain authority. Likewise, they may not be spending much time with that document; they may be moving from one document to another, or perhaps focusing on one document while they consult many other documents to verify or clarify information. Active readers need more finding tools than linear readers do. Some of them are the template items, the reader signals that we talked about in Chapter Nine. But thanks to the digital age, you have to do more than just include those signals in your document; you have to make sure that those signals are easy to find and easy to use.

In this section of the chapter, we will talk about how to provide adequate white space and how to make your documents easy for all kinds of readers to navigate. We will spend a little time focusing on digital readers, because our current methods of information delivery don't always take into account the special needs that digital readers have. The good news is that methods that help digital readers also help hard copy readers.

The information revolution has had a huge impact on lawyers and legal practice. We can now access information almost anywhere, and at almost any time, thanks not only to smartphones, laptops, and tablets, but also to computer research databases and wireless access to those databases. Further, once we have access to the information, we can use a variety of search mechanisms to find words or statute numbers that we are interested in.

But easy access comes with costs as well as benefits, and scientists are learning that digital readers do not read or comprehend information as effectively as readers of hard copy documents.[1] At first glance, this result seems surprising. After all, judges and clerks

---

1. *See, e.g.,* Anne Mangen, Bente R. Walgermo & Kolbjorn Bronnick, *Reading Linear Texts on Paper Versus Computer Screen: Effects on Reading Comprehension*, 58 Int'l J. Educ. Research 61-68 (2013). "Subjects who read the texts

read both digital and paper documents by deciphering the same 26 letters, by using their eyes to read those letters, and by moving their eyes from left to right across the lines of text. But it turns out that the medium in which we encounter the written word has an effect on how well we comprehend the information that we read.[2]

First, judges and clerks—like all readers—are reading with more than just their eyes. If they are reading a hard copy brief, they are likely holding it in their hands; their hands give them a physical awareness of the heft of the document, and of where they are within it—the beginning, middle, or end. They have this awareness without making any conscious effort, without even glancing around for a page number. In other words, they encounter the information physically as well as visually, and they maintain a subconscious image of the complete document. Even as they focus on one page, one sentence, or one word, they subconsciously imagine the physical context of the words they are reading, often retaining both the location within the document and the location on the page or pair of pages.[3] Because they have this spatial concept of how the pieces of information fit into the document, they can more easily grasp both large and small-scale organization.

When people read digital documents, in contrast, it is more difficult for them to conceptualize the parts they are not reading. They know that an electronic brief does not exist inside the computer as a physical stack of pages. Even if their electronic device simulates the sound of pages turning as they read, they never perceive the physical movement from the beginning of the document to the end: physically, they perceive every page identically. Comprehension suffers even more if they must scroll through the document—a common occurrence—because even that identical physical context is impermanent, as the words rise and fall on the screen.[4]

---

on paper performed significantly better [on reading comprehension tests] than subjects who read the texts on the computer screen." *Id.* at 65.

2. Further, the package that gives us those accessible documents—whether it is a desktop, a laptop, a tablet, or an iPhone—also brings with it a host of distractions that can affect our ability to read and retain the information that we read.

3. *See* Mangen et al., *supra* note 1, at 65-66 ("Evidence suggests that readers often recall where in a text some particular piece of information appeared (*e.g.*, toward the upper right corner or at the bottom of the page). . . . [T]he fixity of text printed on paper supports reader's construction of the spatial representation of the text by providing unequivocal and fixed spatial cues for text memory and recall.") (Citations omitted.)

4. *See* Mangen et al., *supra* note 1, at 65 ("Scrolling is known to hamper the process of reading, by imposing a spatial instability which may negatively affect

Accordingly, when reading digital documents, readers and users must work harder to understand the content and organization of the information in the brief. This requirement creates a problem, of course: we can't be sure that our readers will do the extra work. So, what should we do? Because digital documents are here to stay, we must use writing and presentation techniques that compensate for some of the hard copy benefits that are lost in digital documents.[5] First, we must provide adequate white space on the physical and digital page. Second, we must organize and present our text to make all kinds of navigation easy for our readers.

14.1.1. Providing Adequate White Space

You may not be in charge of deciding what margins and type-faces you should use in the documents that you submit to courts; as we have noted in our many discussions of local rules, most courts are pretty specific about what they want. Many courts are asking for larger fonts; the science shows that using bigger letters makes writing easier to read, both by reducing the number of characters per line and by reducing the density of the text. Unfortunately, most courts are wedded to one-inch margins all around, despite recent findings that readers benefit from larger margins, particularly on the outer margin of bound documents. (You may notice that the textbooks you read typically have larger outer margins.)

While you may not get to decide your margin size, you can decide the number of paragraph breaks you will include on every page. If your reader will be reading your document in hard copy, you should make it your goal to include at least two paragraph breaks per page. If your reader will be reading onscreen, you should consider including even more paragraph breaks, because many readers read on a screen that is shorter than the typical 11-inch piece of paper. If you are sending a message via email, strive to keep your paragraphs even shorter.

1 You should also be aware of white space when creating tables, roadmaps, and other offset text. The best technique is to indent your text from both the left and the right as needed. For tables, use the right indent to make sure that your text does not bleed over into the

1 In MS Word, this feature is on the Home menu on the toolbar in the "paragraph" window.

---

the reader's mental representation of the text and, by implication, comprehension.") (Citations omitted.)

5. *See, e.g.,* Robert Dubose, *Writing Appellate Briefs for Tablet Readers,* APPELLATE ISSUES (Spring 2012), *available at* http://www.americanbar.org/content/dam/aba/publications/appellate_issues/2012sprng_ai.authcheckdam.pdf (last accessed October 23, 2020).

2 "Double-indent" means to indent from the left and the right; it does not mean to indent twice from the left.

3 The space between lines is often called "leading" (rhymes with *sledding*), because printing press typesetters used strips of lead to separate the lines of text.

right-hand column, where you find the page numbers in tables of authority. For offset lists (as in a significant roadmap) or other offset text (as in long quotations), be sure to indent from the left and the right. **2**

3 Finally, you need to consider the amount of white space between lines. Most courts require double-spacing, but if you are writing to an audience other than a court, or if the court has not specified line spacing, consider alternatives. Typography experts like Matthew Butterick recommend line spacing that is closer to single-spacing than to double-spacing.[6]

By providing appropriate white space in your document, you present your arguments in a professional, inviting way, and you make your reader more likely to start reading and to continue reading.

14.1.2. Promoting Reader Navigation

4 The template items are headings, roadmap paragraphs, topic sentences, and connection-conclusions. *See* Chapter Nine.

4 As noted above, both active and linear readers need to navigate within your document and between your document and other documents. You can promote this navigation in at least three ways: (a) by left-justifying your text and formatting headings appropriately; (b) by numbering headings and using other template items effectively; and (c) by inserting bookmarks so that digital readers have a "guide on the side" while they read.

a. Navigation from Letter to Letter, from Word to Word, and from Line to Line

As we noted above, when we read, we must navigate from letter to letter, then word to word, and then line to line. Your word processor takes care of the letter-to-letter movement when you use proportionally spaced type, which compensates for differences in the width of letters. Take care, however, *not* to use all-caps type, and to single-space any multiple-lined headings within your document (even if double-spacing is mandated for the rest of the document).

You can promote letter-to-letter navigation by not using all-caps text. All-caps text interferes with letter-to-letter navigation because of the way we read. To greatly simplify reading theory, we move through text by alternating between movements (saccades) and rests for comprehension (fixations). As we saccade through the text, we use our direct vision to see only about five letters of text

---

6. Controlling the line spacing is relatively easy. Consult Butterick's Practical Typography website for more information: https://practicaltypography.com/line-spacing.html.

clearly, through the fovea, or center of our retina. Our peripheral vision sees other letters, but the images are blurred. Mixed-case text promotes easier navigation because our blurred peripheral vision can more easily discern lower-case letters (because they have more shape variation) and use them to build words. Unfortunately, many courts publish sample briefs that contain all-caps headings. Unless the court rules specify that you must use all caps, however, use ordinary capitalization: capitalize the first letter of the sentence and the first letters of proper nouns only. **5**

You can promote word-to-word navigation and line-to-line navigation by the way you *justify* and *align* your text. *Justifying* text is a concept that means aligning it along a margin or centering it. Most word processing systems have four possible justifications: centered text, left-justified text, right-justified text, and full-justified text.

Centered text is text that is placed on the line in such a way that the words are equidistant from both the left and right-hand margins. This means that each line of text starts in a different spot on the line, depending on the length of that line. This variation makes it harder for readers to navigate because when the eye sweeps left to find the next line, it will begin at a different place than the line before did. Centered text should never be used for any text other than short headings.

Bad Example (Centered Heading)

2.1. The Petitioner's efforts to escape its contractual waivers of immunity for copyright infringement highlight the need for blanket abrogation of state immunity.

Instead of centering your headings, align them one tab over from the number for the heading:

Better Example (Left Justified, Aligned Heading)

2.1. The Petitioner's efforts to escape its contractual waivers of immunity for copyright infringement highlight the need for blanket abrogation of state immunity.

This use of alignment highlights the number of the heading (which is a useful finding tool, as noted below) and makes it easy for the reader to navigate from line to line within the heading.

Left-justified text is the easiest to navigate, because the reader knows where each line will begin, and the spaces between the words are always the same.

Right-justified text is text that is aligned along the right margin. As with centered text, right-justified text makes line-to-line naviga-

5 Consult the ALWD or Bluebook Citation guides about when to capitalize words like plaintiff, defendant, and the like. Do not imitate book title capitalization methods. First, a CREXAC section is not a book (we hope). Second, book title capitalization can seem random to readers, who may waste time and energy subconsciously trying to discern a pattern.

tion difficult because each line starts in a different location. Right-justified text is generally used for artistic effect; outside of tables of contents or authorities, it is rarely used in legal writing.

6 *Kerning* refers to the spaces between letters; word-spacing software adjusts the spaces between words.

6 Full-justified text is aligned along both margins, as the text in this book is. Some writers like to set their word processing programs to full justification because full-justified text has a neater appearance. That's fine, if you're just going for a neat appearance. To go for *readability*, however, you should use left-justified text unless you are a professional publisher with access to sophisticated word-spacing and kerning software. Full-justified text does not affect line-to-line navigation, but it often makes word-to-word navigation more difficult. Full-justified text usually results in random spacing between words. When the space between each word and the next varies, reading feels out of rhythm, the way your steps feel out of rhythm if you have to walk on randomly spaced stepping-stones.

As you read this section, you may be thinking that we're making a lot of fuss over minute differences in reading time. And you're right that each of the problems we note here might cost a reader mere seconds in an extra saccade or fixation. Remember, though, how many thousands of lines of text your reader reads in a day or a week. Every time you make that reading process easier, you allow the reader to spend more energy on your substance and less energy on figuring out what you are saying.

b. Navigation Within and Between Documents

To promote navigation for all readers, you need to provide effective roadmaps, headings, and other reader signals. These are the elements of the document's *template*, which we addressed in Chapter Nine. For active readers, and especially for digital readers, you should format the information in those reader signals to maximize the reader's ability to find the signals, and to make those signals useful.

Enumerated headings are probably the most important reader signals in briefs to a court. As you know from your own behavior as a reader, you may go forward and backward within a document as you search for particular information. From your experience as a digital researcher, you know that digital readers may skip around in a document or move from document to document. When digital readers click on hyperlinks, they are essentially beamed up to a new document and have to figure out where they are. Both the substance and the numbering method of your documents can help readers know where they are and what they are reading about. First, traditional roman alphabet labels may not be helpful:

Heading Label that Is Less Effective for Active Readers and Digital Readers

B. Finding that a fish is a "tangible object" under the anti-shredding provision does not create an absurd result.

By using "B" as a label, the writer tells the reader only that this heading leads the second subpart of some argument within the document. The label does not reveal, however, whether that "B" is a subpart of argument "I," argument "II," or even argument "IX." By using scientific numbering,[7] the writer can signal the argument's approximate location:

Heading Label that Is More Effective for Active Readers and Digital Readers

3.2. Finding that a fish is a "tangible object" under the anti-shredding provision does not create an absurd result.

Unlike the label on the previous example, this label tells the reader that this argument is the second subpart within the third section of the argument as a whole. This kind of numbering can be especially useful in digital documents, when readers might use word searches that could jump them from page 1 to page 21. Seeing "3.2" in the heading gives them a good location cue.

In addition to effective enumeration, of course, you should use effective substantive headings, following the guidelines in Chapter Nine. Make sure you use language that will signal both the issue under discussion and your position on the issue. Likewise, use bold-faced type, which will allow users to see your headings as they scroll or scan through your document.

The other elements of the template can also help active readers. Your topic sentences and roadmap paragraphs can provide both context and finding tools for digital readers. Eye-tracking research shows that readers scan the first parts of pages and paragraphs to look for information that is useful to them.[8] You should therefore exploit those locations.

---

7. Daniel Sockwell, *Writing for the iPad Judge*, Colum. Bus. L. Rev. Online (Jan. 14, 2014), available at https://cblr.columbia.edu/writing-a-brief-for-the-ipad-judge/ (last accessed June 27, 2018).

8. *See, e.g.,* Geoffrey B. Duggan & Stephen J. Payne, *Skim Reading by Satisficing: Evidence from Eye Tracking*, Proceedings of the SIGCHI Conference on Human Factors in Computing Systems 1141-50, at 1146, 1147 (2011) (agreeing with a conclusion about eye-tracking studies showing that "skimmers begin every paragraph and continue reading until the rate of information gain drops below a threshold whereupon they skip to the beginning of the next paragraph,"

As you know from your own research behaviors, readers often use search terms to lead them to the most significant part of documents. Be sure to use phrases-that-pay appropriately, and to do so in a way that promotes searching and finding. Further, because new headings may draw a digital reader's focus in the same way that the top of a new page does, be sure to place context cues in these high-focus locations. For example, by using phrases-that-pay and other key language in your headings and topic sentences, as well as at the beginning of each new section, you can make it easier for the digital reader to understand how the different pieces of your argument fit together.

c. Inserting Bookmarks to Create a "Guide on the Side"

Finally, be thoughtful in how you choose and use your software. Our specific recommendations as to software are limited; by the time you read this book, new software, or updates to old software, might make our advice obsolete. When choosing software, however, be mindful of both court rules and the devices that judges and clerks use to read their briefs. If possible, use software that creates fixed pages; likewise, look for software that sends structural signals to your reader.[9]

7 As we write this text, the most recent update of MS Word creates this guide on the side, BUT the text does not "wrap," so the reader cannot see complete headings. PDF documents create a more complete guide on the side, BUT you must manually mark each bookmark. We hope software formatting continues to improve.

7 Currently, using .pdf format allows you to bookmark headings and element titles (e.g., Statement of the Case, Summary of the Argument). By creating bookmarks, you allow your reader to display a table of contents down the left-hand side of the screen. Scientific studies of readers show that this type of guide on the side provides useful context for readers and helps them to grasp a document's large-scale organization. Further, because each heading in the outline is a hyperlink, it allows readers to navigate easily between and among the various sections of the document.

It is tempting to take advantage of all of the bells and whistles that your software offers, but be mindful of the impact of your decisions. Inserting hyperlinks to cited cases within your argument can be useful, for example, but those links can also take the reader away from your document and into another document. If that document also has links, the reader may soon be many documents away from your well-crafted argument. If you believe that the court would benefit from the links, it may be better to include them in a table of

---

and explaining research results showing that "lines towards the top of the page were more likely to be fixated upon than lines towards the bottom of the page").

9. *See, e.g.,* Dubose, *supra* note 5 at 12 (making recommendations about highlighting structure for digital readers).

authorities or an appendix rather than in the body of the argument itself. If the court requires the links in text (as some courts do), see if you can format them so they look like the rest of your text, and so are less tempting for the reader to click on.

14.2. SENTENCING GUIDELINES (NOT THAT KIND)

Part one of this chapter was about easing navigation to promote legibility, that is, the ability to find and discern individual letters, words, and sentences. This section is about promoting *readability*: the ability to understand what those words mean. A complete discussion of effective sentence structure is beyond the scope of this book,[10] but we think it's worth spending some time on a few principles for effective writing that we refer to as *sentencing guidelines*. Of course, these are not guidelines about how long a sentence someone will serve in prison; they *are* meant to help your readers not feel like they have been sentenced to read your document as a punishment.

These guidelines are based on a couple of familiar principles: context and connection. Just as readers need context for documents, they need context for their sentences, and they look for that context in certain predictable locations in each sentence. Likewise, readers are constantly looking to make connections, to see relationships between and among the concepts in each sentence, paragraph, and page. If you write your sentences effectively, those connections will be accurate, and the readers will understand your meaning the first time through. If you have not written your sentences effectively, your readers will still try to make those connections, but they may make the wrong connections and so misunderstand your argument. Worse, if your readers become frustrated at having to work through your meaning, they may abandon the document.

With those thoughts in mind, here are our sentencing guidelines. Some of these guidelines are accepted principles of effective expository writing, others are principles of effective legal writing, and still others are warnings against mistakes that we see our students make—and that we don't want to see you make.

---

10. We recommend two books that do provide more complete discussions of effective sentence structure: ANNE ENQUIST, LAUREL CURRIE OATES & JEREMY FRANCIS, JUST WRITING (5th ed., Aspen 2017); JOSEPH WILLIAMS & JOSEPH BIZUP, STYLE: LESSONS IN CLARITY AND GRACE (12th ed., Pearson 2016).

14.2.1. Prefer Explicit Subjects and Verbs, and Keep Them Close to Each Other When Possible

Just as readers pay more attention to information at beginnings and endings of documents and sections, they place subconscious emphasis on the information in the verb position of a sentence. They also subconsciously look for the verb's actor—that is, the noun that is "doing" the action of the verb. You can control what information is in the subject position and the verb position and where (or whether) you include information about the verb's actor.[11] How you arrange that information will affect how efficiently and accurately your reader comprehends your message. As you know, you can present the same information in a variety of ways. To take a simple example:

The defendant stabbed the plaintiff.

The plaintiff was stabbed by the defendant.

The plaintiff was the victim of a stabbing.

A stabbing occurred.

An injury occurred.

All of these sentences could be used to describe a stabbing. In some of the sentences, the reader can instantly understand the complete story. In some others, however, the reader has to work harder to get that information; in still others, even when working hard, the reader can get only a vague idea of what has happened.

Thus, the way you use the parts of speech, and the way you arrange the information within a sentence, can each have a big impact on how quickly the reader understands the message. Information arrangement can sometimes have an impact on how the reader feels about the message as well. Take a look at these two versions of a sentence that might appear in a letter from a law school to its students:

This August, we will increase your tuition by $5,000 per year.

This August will see a tuition increase of $5,000 per year.

The first sentence is more likely to make the student angry at the law school administration. The subject-verb connection allows the reader to understand instantly that the law school is responsible for the tuition increase. The second sentence is a more typical example

---

11. *See, e.g.,* Williams & Bizup, *supra* note 10, at Lesson 3.

of how to deliver bad news. No one takes responsibility for the tuition increase; it seems to come from the outside. "Increase" is used as a noun, while it is a verb in the first sentence. Thus, the clarity that is helpful when easy understanding is beneficial ("the defendant stabbed the plaintiff") has quite a different impact on those rare occasions when the writer wants to blunt the impact of the message ("we will increase your tuition").

14.2.2. Avoid Needless Nominalizations and Needless Uses of Passive Voice

There are two methods you can use to make it more likely that you will write sentences with concrete subject-verb connections: (a) avoid needless nominalizations, and (b) avoid needless use of the passive voice. We'll take a moment to define our terms before we continue. A *nominalization* is, quite simply, a verb that has been turned into a noun. *Passive voice* describes the relationship between the verb and the subject of that verb. We'll explain each in turn.

a. Avoid Needless Nominalizations

When you *nominalize* a verb, you don't violate any rules of grammar, but you do slow down the reader's comprehension of the information in that word. Speakers of English understand verbs more quickly than any other part of speech, so when you want to speed comprehension, make sure that your verbs are carrying the crucial information in your sentence.

For example, the word *decision* is a nominalization of the verb *decide*. When you move *decide* from the verb position into the noun position, you lessen the impact of that verb:

We decided to raise your tuition.

We made a decision that a tuition increase is necessary.

Below, we have included two versions of an excerpt from a brief that argues that a state agency violated the First Amendment rights of a church when it said that the church was not eligible for a government program. Notice how nominalizations in one illustration and concrete subjects and verbs in the other affect the reader's comprehension:

The Missouri Department of Natural Resources' refusal to give grant money to The Child Learning Center strictly because it is owned by a religious organization, Trinity Lutheran Church, is a violation of the Free Exercise Clause guarantees in the First Amendment through the Fourteenth Amendment.

The Missouri Department of Natural Resources refused to give grant money to The Child Learning Center strictly because the Center is owned by Trinity Lutheran Church, a religious organization. This refusal violated the Center's Free Exercise rights guaranteed in the First Amendment through the Fourteenth Amendment.

8 As Anne Enquist advises, if you have a hard time finding the verbs, change the *tense* of the sentence. The words you change are the verbs. For example: "I love legal writing" is in the present tense. To change that sentence to past tense, write, "I loved legal writing." The word you changed, *love*, is the verb. (We hope that present tense is still appropriate.)

8 You can often find nominalizations by looking for words that end in "ence," "ment," or "ion." In the alternative, review your sentences (particularly overlong sentences) and circle just the verbs. When you find sentences in which all of the verbs are weak words without a lot of concrete meaning—e.g., was, is (or other *to be* verbs), had, made, occurred, existed, etc.—look for verbs that are "hidden" in nominalizations in that sentence.

When deciding whether or how to change nominalizations back into verbs, ask yourself whether you want to put more emphasis on the information that you nominalized. The answer may not always be yes. Sometimes, as in the tuition letter example above, you may want to deemphasize certain negative information. Unless you have a rhetorical reason to blunt certain information, however, you should generally avoid nominalizations. Thus, when revising your writing, identify your hidden verbs, find the actor that is "verbing" (i.e., doing the action of that verb), and create a stronger, more easily comprehensible sentence.

When looking for nominalizations, you might find a sentence like this:

The use of the funds in this grant is not about the promotion of any faith or faiths.

The only verb in this sentence is the word *is*. It's true that *use* and *grant* can be verbs, but they are serving as nouns in this sentence. Once you identify the hidden verbs *use, grant,* and *promotion,* you can work on making the sentence clearer:

[Someone] did not use the funds [that someone] granted [to someone] to promote any faith or faiths.

As you see, revising to avoid nominalizations provides a hidden benefit: You may realize when information is missing from the sentence. Thus, your next step might be to include some of the missing information. On the other hand, you may decide to leave some of the nominalizations as is:

The Church would not use this grant to promote any faith or faiths.

This revision indicates that the writer did not want to emphasize the source of the money but may have been willing to highlight what the church would or would not do with the funds.

Knowing how nominalizations can affect your writing can help you to make your points more explicitly when clarity is your goal and to blunt your message when it is appropriate to do so.

b. Don't Overuse Passive Voice

Most writers know about "tense" as it relates to verbs; they consciously decide, for example, whether to write in present tense or past tense. Many, however, are unfamiliar with the concept of "voice." No matter what its tense, a verb can be cast in active or passive voice. Voice relates not to the tense of the verb, but to whether the verb's actor is in the subject position of the sentence or clause. If the verb's actor is in the subject position, the verb is said to be cast in "active voice"; if the verb's actor is not in the subject position, the verb is said to be cast in "passive voice."

Almost every time a verb is cast in passive voice, the subject of the sentence is receiving the action of the verb rather than doing the action of the verb. Thus, in most cases, the subject of an active voice sentence or clause is "verbing"; the subject of a passive voice sentence or clause is "being verbed." Think of the subject passively receiving the action of the verb to help you remember the meaning of "passive voice":

The court decided the case.
(Active voice; the subject [court] is verbing [deciding].)

The case was decided by the court.
(Passive voice; the subject [case] is being verbed [being decided].)

Passive and active voice verbs, like nominalizations, are grammatically correct. Because readers understand active voice verbs more quickly, however, you should use active voice unless you have a specific reason to use passive voice. Passive voice is preferred on occasion:

1. if you don't know who the actor is or you want to hide or deemphasize the actor ("a decision was made to raise your tuition" hides the decision maker);

2. when you want to emphasize the object of the verb rather than the subject ("she was hit by a car" emphasizes the victim of the accident); or

3. when using passive voice allows you to enhance connections and readability by letting you put familiar information early in the sentence (e.g., "The court decided the free speech case two hours after the oral argument. The decision was rushed because the plaintiff's parade was scheduled the next day." Here, the use of passive voice in the second sentence allows the writer to put the familiar concept "decision" early in the sentence).

As we have noted, readers are constantly looking for context. For this reason, they will pay particular attention to information at the beginning of a sentence, seeking to understand how that sentence fits into what they are reading about. Look at these examples of similar information included in passive voice and active voice sentences. Try to decide which sentence might be better given various rhetorical situations:

A.1 The officers would undoubtedly have been distracted by the contraband cell phones, and the cell phones would have interfered with the officers' ability to maintain direct observation of the inmates on the bus.

A.2 The contraband cell phones would have undoubtedly distracted the officers and would have interfered with the officers' ability to maintain direct observation of the inmates on the bus.

B.1 Accordingly, the rule of lenity should be applied after a court has applied traditional statutory interpretation canons to a criminal statute and has determined that the statute is still ambiguous as to whether it encompasses the criminal conduct at issue.

B.2 Accordingly, a court should apply the rule of lenity only after it has applied traditional statutory interpretation canons to a criminal statute and has determined that the statute is still ambiguous as to whether it encompasses the criminal conduct at issue.

C.1 In August 2009, with both Williams and Chapin losing money in their respective businesses, negotiations were begun, with the apparent goal of a merger between the companies.

> **C.2** In August 2009, with both of their businesses losing money, Williams and Chapin began to negotiate a merger.

In sentence A.1, the beginning of the sentence focuses on *the officers*, while in sentence A.2, it focuses on *the contraband cell phones*. If the paragraph were about the various mistakes of the officers, sentence A.1 would be better, even though it is written in passive voice. If the focus of the paragraph were the various problems caused by contraband cell phones, sentence A.2 could be more effective.

The point of this section is not to say that you must eliminate all nominalizations and all uses of passive voice; rather, the point is that you should use nominalizations and passive voice only when you have a good reason to do so. When there is no reason to use them, use more direct, easier-to-understand subjects and verbs.

14.2.3. Keep Subjects Close to Verbs, Verbs Close to Objects, and Modifying Phrases Close to What They Modify

As we have noted, readers seek connection as well as context. When they see a verb, readers want to know who or what is verbing. When the verb takes an object, readers want to see that object as soon as possible. When words are close to each other, readers will assign meaning to that closeness. Frequently, writers cause confusion by misplacing information about time, place, or manner:

> The investor alleges that Fresh Foods executives made false and misleading statements about its business operations and failed to disclose that it was overcharging customers in a timely fashion.

This sentence gives readers the impression that there's something significant about overcharging customers in a timely fashion. The writer, however, meant to connect the time concept to the failure to disclose. Here is a possible revision:

> The investor alleges that Fresh Foods executives made false and misleading statements about its business operations and failed to disclose in a timely fashion that it was overcharging customers.

The following sentence, adapted from a sentence in a newspaper article, creates a horrifying image of goings on at the Museum of Natural History:

Rudolph Cole, a physical anthropologist, and Jamestown archaeologist Thomas Adams unveiled a reconstruction from the remains of "Jane," a 17th-century teenager from Jamestown who researchers believe may have been the victim of cannibalism at the National Museum of Natural History in Washington.

Thus, when editing your writing, pay particular attention to placement of time, place, and manner information and make sure that it is placed where it belongs. When in doubt, placing that information at the front of the sentence may be your best bet:

At the National Museum of Natural History in Washington, Rudolph Cole, a physical anthropologist, and Jamestown archaeologist Thomas Adams unveiled a reconstruction from the remains of "Jane," a 17th-century teenager from Jamestown who researchers believe may have been the victim of cannibalism.

14.2.4. Be Precise in Describing What Statutes and Rules Require and Forbid

Far too often, student legal writers get overly focused on the requirements of the relevant statutes or common law rules, and they forget that their requirements exist only in a specific context. We frequently read sentences like this in student writing:

Imprecise Description of Legal Requirement

The third element of Title VII retaliation states that the employer must take adverse action after the employee engages in a protected activity.

As you know, rules may permit behavior, require it, or forbid it. Without even looking at the statute or the case law, however, we are confident that the statute does not require employers to do any such thing. Rather, the rule requires that an employee must *prove* that behavior *in order to establish* that element of the test, as this revision makes clear:

More Precise Description of Legal Requirement

For Mr. Wendl to establish the third element of a Title VII retaliation claim, he must prove that his employer took an adverse action against him after Mr. Wendl had engaged in a protected activity.

Likewise, please don't ever write that a criminal statute requires a person to kill someone with malice aforethought. No statute requires murder, so please don't provoke anyone's malice by saying it does.

14.2.5. Enhance Clarity by (a) Moving Any Lists to the End of the Sentence, and (b) Enumerating the List or Using Word Signals to Help the Reader See the List

Because readers are looking for context early in the sentence, that is not a good place to put a list or other complicated information. Williams and Bizup advise that when you have complicated information to communicate, the reader can handle it better at the end of the sentence:

Less Effective Presentation of a List

Reassigning a worker to a less desirable shift, refusing to allow him to participate in training activities, and selectively enforcing discipline can all constitute adverse actions under Title VII.

By using enumeration and moving the list to the end of the sentence, the writer can begin the sentence with information that puts the list into its proper context:

More Effective Presentation of a List

Courts analyzing Title VII have found that employers have acted adversely to their employees when the employers have (1) reassigned workers to a less desirable shift, (2) refused to allow workers to participate in training activities, and (3) selectively enforced disciplinary policies against them.

14.2.6. Beware the Overusing of Gerunds

A verb that is turned into an "-ing" noun is known as a *gerund*. For example, if you wanted to talk about what happens when courts analyze a statute, you could talk about *when courts analyze a statute*, or *the analysis of a statute*, or *the analyzing of a statute*. In these three examples, only the first has a subject-verb combination; the other two are a noun (*the analysis*) and a gerund (*the analyzing*). It's rare that a gerund is the best way to express information. Almost always, you will help reader comprehension by using a noun or, even better, a subject-verb combination. The title of this subsection, for example, would be better as "Don't Overuse Gerunds."

Note the difference in readability between these two sentences:

> The plaintiff has produced evidence indicating that the defendant took an adverse employment action against her following her sexual harassment reports and her filing of criminal charges against Defendant's employee.

> The plaintiff's evidence indicates that the defendant took an adverse employment action against her after she submitted sexual harassment reports to her supervisor and filed criminal charges against Defendant's employee.

Of course, this list does not cover all possible problems with sentence structure, but we hope it helps you to find and fix common problems that interfere with reader comprehension.

14.3. AT LAST, TYPOS

Fairly or unfairly, many readers see mechanical mistakes as a sign of overall incompetence; too many typographical errors may lead the judge to mistrust the validity of the legal analysis. Justice Ginsburg has observed that if a brief is "sloppy" in regard to mechanics, "the judge may suspect its reliability in other respects as well."[12] Failure to take care with polishing may even cost you money. In a case that received wide publicity (including a story in the *New York Times*), an attorney whose courtroom work was praised had his fees for his written work cut in half—from $300 to $150 per hour—due in large part to sloppy proofreading.[13] When he was interviewed about the case, the federal judge who decided on the award of attorneys' fees commented that "no matter how good you are in front of the jury, most of your reputation's going to be built on what you write."[14]

If you are thinking that you can hire someone to edit your writing for you, you should know that it will probably be a while before

---

12. Ruth Bader Ginsburg, *Remarks on Appellate Advocacy*, 50 S.C. L. Rev. 567, 568 (1999).

13. *DeVore v. City of Philadelphia*, 2004 U.S. Dist. Lexis 3635, at *6 (E.D. Pa. Feb. 20, 2004). The court noted that counsel's lack of care "caused the court, and I am sure, defense counsel, to expend an inordinate amount of time deciphering the arguments." *Id.* at *6-7.

14. *All Things Considered, Magistrate Judge Jacob P. Hart Discusses His Fight to Get Lawyers to Clean Up Their Written Work* (Nat'l Pub. Radio broadcast, Mar. 4, 2004).

you can afford an assistant who can do this level of polishing. You must take responsibility for polishing the mechanics of your legal documents, because your document reflects on your client and on your competence. **9**

Polishing is hard for the same reason that revision is hard. Most people don't really see their writing when they review it. Instead, they see the document that they meant to write; their short-term memory interferes with their ability to see typographical errors or other problems. For that reason, this chapter identifies some objective methods for polishing that will help you to break up that relationship between your short-term memory and your document and help you to catch mistakes in both your writing and your analysis.

The best way to proofread effectively is to put your writing away for a while. If you've ever gone back and read a document that you wrote last year, or even last month, you've probably noticed several mistakes or style problems that you missed when you wrote it. If you are trying to polish a document that you wrote this morning, your short-term memory makes it hard for you to see your mistakes. It knows what you wanted to say, and it tends to gloss over the mistakes.[15] Therefore, if you can get a draft done a week before your deadline **10**, *don't* reread it and edit it every day. Instead, wait three days and do a thorough edit, and then wait three more days and do a final edit.[16] Even a little time can make some difference. In a crunch, that might mean taking a 15-minute walk and then coming back to edit.

A second effective polishing technique is to start in the middle when reviewing your work. Most writing teachers find that mechanical mistakes and other weaknesses show up more often in the second half of the document than in the first half. That's because many writers get bored with editing or polishing as they get closer to the end of the document; many give up before finishing the job. Even conscientious editors should give fresh eyes to different parts of the document at different times.

Generally, it is ineffective to proofread by reading the entire document very slowly once or twice, trying to catch every type of error.

9 Admittedly, when Mary Beth was a 21-year-old English major, she worked summers as a secretary for engineers. She would routinely rewrite their letters and then throw away their handwritten drafts so they couldn't call her on it. She is now shocked by her behavior.

10 Whenever we suggest this to our students, they laugh. We know why.

---

15. Of course, getting a friend or colleague to review the document can also be helpful because that person will not have the information in his or her short-term memory. In an academic setting, you should not use this method unless you have *specific* permission from your teacher. In a professional setting, asking a friend to review your work is fine; finding someone who has the time to help you is the hard part.

16. *See also* Judge Stephen J. Dwyer, Leonard J. Feldman & Ryan P. McBride, *How to Write, Edit, and Review Persuasive Briefs: Seven Guidelines from One Judge and Two Lawyers*, 31 Seattle U. L. Rev. 417, 425 (2008).

Instead, you should read the document through several times on the computer and several times in hard copy form. Make surgical strikes, focusing on only one or two aspects of the document at a time. For example, you can review the document once just looking at citation form, another time just looking at topic sentences, and so on. This chapter discusses proofreading techniques for both the digital and hard copy versions of the document.

14.3.1. Methods to Use on the Computer

You can do some proofreading while your document is still in digital form. First, you may want to enlarge the font size while you proofread. Enlarging the font (say, to 20- or 22-point) can have two benefits. First, you can focus more easily because you will have a smaller number of words on the screen at a time. Second, it will be easier to distance yourself from the text because the font change will significantly change the way the document looks.

Proofreading on a screen also allows you to use your computer software's "find and replace" function to your advantage. Although your eyes get tired, the computer never misses on a search, if you are searching precisely.

a. Pronoun Search

Use the "find and replace" function to search for *he, she, it, they*, and so on. Stop when you hit a pronoun and scrutinize it to make sure that the reader will have *no doubt* about the noun you are referring to (the antecedent). If there is any doubt, just repeat the noun. Also, make sure that you have not mistakenly used *they* in place of *it*. For example, a court or corporation should be referred to in the singular as *it*. Generally, don't use singular *they* to refer to individual generic persons; of course, if a person uses *they* as their pronoun, you should follow suit. When using singular *they*, however, be aware of possible ambiguity. Just as the word *you* may be confusing because it can be used as both a singular and a plural, singular *they* may cause the reader to re-read. Edit your writing with this concern in mind; when confusion is possible, repeat the noun rather than use singular *they*.

b. Apostrophe Search

If you tend to use too many apostrophes, use the "find" function to search for *s'* or *'s* so that you can scrutinize whether you've used each apostrophe correctly. If you use too few apostrophes, your task is a little harder. You could use the find function to find words that end in *s* by searching for *s[space]* or *s.[space]*. Once you are zeroed in on the potential problem words, consult grammar guidelines to see if you are using apostrophes correctly.

c. Quotation Mark Search

The rule in American English is that periods and commas *always* go inside quotation marks, even if you are quoting only one word or one letter:

Wrong Example

Judge Wald has noted that finding errors in a brief makes her "go back to square one in evaluating the counsel".

Correct Example

Judge Wald has noted that finding errors in a brief makes her "go back to square one in evaluating the counsel."

Wrong Example

The word "ace", which refers to both tennis and poker, begins with the letter "a".

Correct Example

The word "ace," which refers to both tennis and poker, begins with the letter "a."

To find errors of this type, use the "find" function to search for quotation marks, and check your punctuation. Also, check to make sure that all quotation marks come in pairs. Too often, when writers block and copy quotations, they place an opening quotation mark, then copy the language into the text, and neglect to insert the closing quotation mark. This mistake is the punctuation equivalent of leaving the refrigerator door open, and it is very annoying to readers. Be sure to proofread specifically for this problem.

d. Citation Search

[11] To review your citations, search *[begin underline]* or *[begin italics]* or even *v.* to help you find citations and scrutinize them in isolation. Three types of errors are particularly common: (1) incorrect volume or page numbers, (2) misspelled party names, and (3) missing pinpoint page numbers. Presume that every citation (other than one in the table of authorities) should have a pinpoint. Even if you are citing only to a general principle from the case, find a page on which that general principle appears, and use it as the pinpoint.

[11] Not all software allows you to search for codes. WordPerfect software does.

While you are looking at your citations, take a look at your long-form citations and make sure that you have included the appropriate court abbreviation in the parenthetical. If you are not sure what court the case comes from, check the caption of the opinion. Note, for example, that F. Supp. 3d publishes only district court decisions, so any opinion printed in an edition of F. Supp. 3d cannot be a circuit court decision.

e. Spell-Check

Run the spell-check early and often, but keep a few things in mind. First, keep your hand away from the mouse, or your finger off the button, so that you don't hit "replace" or "skip" by mistake. Second, don't hit "skip" as soon as you see a party name or a case name; make sure that you've spelled each one properly and consistently.

Third, after completing spell-check, use the "find and replace" function to search for typos that the spell-check function won't catch. In every document, look for *statue* for *statute*, *untied* for *united*, *form* for *from* (and vice versa), *reasonable* for *reasonably* (and vice versa), and *probable* for *probably* (and vice versa). You might consider setting your quick-correct feature to change *pubic* to *public* to avoid that potentially embarrassing error. If your document is about *probable cause* or *reasonable doubt*, it is even more important to do this kind of search. We have read several briefs in which students claim that there was no "probably cause" for the defendant's arrest, or that the defense could not establish "reasonably doubt." Because both forms of certain problem words could appear in the text, search for each form separately and make sure each use is proper.

In addition, you might use your software's quick-correct function to create a shortcut for any word or phrase that you tend to misspell, or that is particularly likely to crop up in this document. For example, you might program "rd/" to convert to "reasonable doubt" to ensure you don't make the reasonable/reasonably error. If you will sometimes need to type "reasonably doubt," you could create another shortcut, such as "ryd/."

As you can see, the "find and replace" function can help you to proofread on the computer in many different ways. You may be able to figure out other ways to make the computer's tireless brain work for you.

14.3.2. Methods to Use on the Hard Copy

Plan to print out a hard copy more than once before you must file the document. Because your brain works differently when you are looking at a computer screen than when you are looking at a hard copy, you will undoubtedly find errors on the hard copy that you missed when reading the document on the computer.

a. Check Paragraph Length

You may have created some overlong paragraphs as you revised; they will be evident on the hard copy. Remember that there are two reasons to create a paragraph break: substance and graphics. Even if you have not moved on to a new subject, the reader may need the brief visual rest that a paragraph break provides. A good default is to look for at least two paragraph breaks per page (more is fine). If you have only one paragraph break, you must find a place to create a new paragraph. Note that if you create an artificial paragraph break in this way, you may need to add a topic sentence to ensure that the reader can instantly understand how the paragraph is relevant to the point under discussion. The paragraph search is one hard copy technique that you can also use on the computer, especially if you have a big screen. Show multiple pages at once to get a good picture of your paragraph length.

b. Check Sentence Length

If you have a problem with overlong sentences, edit for them by looking for periods. Take a pencil and make a slash mark at every period; you can do this without even reading the text. When you're done, review the slash marks. If you see several sentences in a row that are over four lines long, review them and try to shorten at least one. One good way to shorten long sentences is to look for verbs. If you have three verbs in one sentence, try giving each verb a subject and its own sentence. If you see several sentences that are only one line long—and you're not using short sentences for occasional, dramatic effect—try to combine a couple of the short sentences.[17]

c. Review the Verbs

As we have noted, readers subconsciously pay more attention to information in the verb position. Thus, go through your document and circle all of your verbs, trying not to read the sentences. You should scrutinize all vague verbs, including *is*, *are*, *was*, *were*, *made*, *involved*, *existed*, *concerned*, *had*, and the like. Unless you are using them purposefully—e.g., to deemphasize information, or because you are using passive voice to avoid an unusually long subject—you should look for the better verb hidden in the sentence and revise accordingly.

---

17. *See* Mary Barnard Ray & Jill J. Ramsfield, Legal Writing: Getting It Right and Getting It Written 371-72 (4th ed., Thomson/West 2005).

d. Review the Signals to the Reader

The best way to review signals to the reader is to review the template items. Look at the first paragraph (or two) of each heading section for needed legal backstory and roadmap. Look at the last paragraph of each heading section for a concluding statement connecting the analysis to the point being covered within that CREXAC unit of discourse. Scan the first sentence of each paragraph to see how often your paragraphs begin with main points and include the phrases-that-pay. Scan through the document to make sure there are enough headings. If you go more than three or four pages without a new heading, scrutinize that section. Can you break that section down into two subsections? Have you gone onto a new point without labeling it with a heading? Similarly, review each roadmap and mini-roadmap, and then compare it to your headings. The roadmap should predict precisely the headings that follow.

e. Do a Ruler-Read, Read the Document Backwards, or Both

12 One of Mary Beth's moot court teams once submitted a brief with the word *certiorari* misspelled on the cover. During three weeks of practice arguments, every judge mentioned the typo and how annoying it was, and the students had to nod politely and thank them for noticing. Proofread your cover pages, and note that MS Word's spell-check does not read words in all-caps.

12 After you have taken these steps, read a hard copy aloud (as slowly as you can) backwards and forwards *with a ruler under each line as you read it.* Using the ruler helps to separate you from your text, breaking up that cozy relationship between your short-term memory and your document. When doing this ruler-read, include all extraneous materials, like cover pages and tables; these sections often get short shrift when it comes to proofreading.

In addition, you might try reading the document backwards. Many writers have a hard time reading from beginning to end because they get caught up in the substance of the document and forget to proofread. Start at the end and proofread one paragraph at a time to separate yourself from the substance as you read.

f. Repeat Any or All of the Above as Needed

If you keep finding new mistakes when using these techniques, you need to keep proofreading. Do not submit the final version of the document until you can read it through and find *no* mistakes.

14.3.3. Proofreading Your Revisions

Word processors have greatly improved the quality of written documents, but they are also responsible for a new type of editing error. In the past, when a writer revised a document, someone had to type the whole thing over again, and so it was fairly easy to substitute the new words and to leave the old words out. Now, with the constant editing that word processors allow, it is not uncommon to see both old and new versions of a phrase within a document: The writer typed the new phrase and forgot to delete the old one. Furthermore, writers who carelessly use the "find and replace" function frequently find sentences like this in their writing:

Bad Example

On Saturday, the Mr. Kish returned home.

The best way to avoid these types of errors is, once again, to focus your proofreading on different problems at different times. After each round of edits, scrutinize the words, lines, or paragraphs in which edits occurred (in hard copy, if you can afford the toner). Read those sections in isolation, so that you don't get caught up in the meaning of the words. In addition, *never* use the "replace all" function; doing so causes mistakes like the one shown above because it's difficult to envision all of the contexts in which a word or phrase might appear. Instead, look at each use of the word or phrase you are replacing to avoid mistakes.

14.4. THE LAST THING TO DO WITH THE DOCUMENT

This section is really about the second-to-the-last thing to do with the document. The last thing you should do is file it, send it, or turn it in to your teacher. But one last proofreading method you can use is to read it aloud, out of order. Either start in the middle, start on the last page and then read the second-to-the-last page, and so on, or mix up the pages and read them in a random order. Whichever method you use, your goal is to pay attention to individual words and sentences rather than to get swept away by your no doubt fascinating discussion of the law.

14.5. CONCLUSION

When you are reading something difficult on a computer, what do you do when you get frustrated? Our guess is that you are at least tempted to abandon the document and click on something more fun. Your readers feel those same temptations when they get frustrated. You can reduce reader frustration in at least three ways:

(1) design your document to make it more attractive;

(2) organize and present your information in a way that makes it easy for all readers to navigate and find meaningful context; and

(3) review your writing carefully to improve the readability of your sentences and paragraphs and eliminate distracting errors.

In practice, you will often need to write and file documents in a hurry, without time to polish and proofread in a leisurely way. Take the time now to develop an effective review process in which you pay attention to document design, sentence structure, and polishing. When you submit documents that demonstrate professionalism in both content and presentation, you enhance your credibility and increase your opportunities for success in law practice.

Everything Else

Legal writing professors love it when their alums write back and say things like, "My first week on my new job, they asked me to write a demand letter, and I knew just what to do thanks to your class!" We love to hear that our courses made our students feel confident about the demands of practice. Unfortunately, no legal writing course can cover every kind of document you will be asked to write as a lawyer. Nevertheless, this chapter is meant to help you to feel confident when you face the inevitable request for a document you have never written before, or maybe never even seen. While you might not know "just what to do," you can learn a protocol—a set of tasks that should help you to figure out how to get started—that will give you confidence that you will produce a useful document.

As you may have noticed by now (we hope), readers of legal writing have certain needs and expectations when they approach all types of legal writing. (In this chapter, we will refer only to "needs" to cover both needs and expectations.) In broad strokes, all readers need context, they need valid substance, they need to be able to comprehend the document easily, and they need to navigate effectively around the document so they can find crucial information and ignore information that they don't need.

This chapter lays out a seven-step protocol for you to follow when you need to write an unfamiliar document:

    (1) get one or more samples
    (2) before you review the sample, identify your goals for the document
    (3) annotate the samples
    (4) review the annotations with your reader in mind
    (5) consult with a mentor, if possible
    (6) write the document
    (7) review the draft, with reader needs in mind

15.1. GET ONE OR MORE SAMPLES, AND COURT RULES IF APPROPRIATE

You have no doubt noticed and appreciated the way this book and your professor have provided you with samples, and that's our first bit of advice. If a supervisor asks you to produce an unfamiliar document, it's absolutely okay to ask for a sample. If you are on your own and need to produce one, it's also absolutely okay to turn to legal databases or the internet to find one. In fact, if you can, you should get multiple samples. Further, during that first conversation about the document, schedule a follow-up appointment to discuss your progress, allowing time to complete steps two and three below.

If this document will be submitted to a court, check the rules of procedure and the court's local rules to see what requirements the court imposes for the document. If the court you are submitting to does not include requirements (or those requirements are unhelpfully general), consult the websites of similar courts for more guidance.

15.2. BEFORE YOU REVIEW THE SAMPLE, IDENTIFY YOUR GOALS FOR THE DOCUMENT

Here's the catch—don't just start imitating the sample immediately. Review the sample(s) with a few things in mind. Broadly stated, a lawyer's typical goal is to "win" for the client, but you should narrow your focus to your goals and the reader's needs when you consider what to include. Is this a letter in which you need to convince someone to do something? Is this a document in which your main goal is memorializing information? That is, is it creating an evidence trail to prove that something existed or something happened?

As part of this analysis, consider your audience. Is this a judge with a general docket, who may not have deep familiarity with these legal issues or your client's facts? Is it a client, who knows the facts but doesn't understand how the law works? Is it an opposing counsel, whose goals may be the opposite of yours?

Understanding your goals and the needs of your reader will help you to evaluate the samples you look at more effectively.

15.3. ANNOTATE THE SAMPLE, FOCUSING ON TYPICAL READER NEEDS

1 As a first step, review the document heading by heading and paragraph by paragraph, noting what is happening in each one. When doing so, be sure to answer "what is happening" at an appropriate level of abstraction. For example, let's presume you need to write a reasoned opinion letter to a client about a covenant not to compete. The sample you are reviewing is a reasoned opinion letter about how to dissolve a corporate relationship. Your annotations should not focus on the tasks necessary to dissolve a corporate relationship. Your goal is to identify the categories of information that appear in the letter.

1 Of course, some paragraphs may have more than one thing going on. Don't stop annotating a paragraph just because you've found one goal for the paragraph.

Focus on at least two categories of information when reviewing the document. First, what categories of substance do you see? Is the paragraph articulating a rule? Is it making a demand? Is it laying out facts? Second, look for context and for navigational signals. What reader signals does the writer send, with headings, topic sentences, or short paragraphs? If the document does not use headings, try to note where the document switches gears, and identify the kinds of headings that might be appropriate.

Try to be as specific as possible when annotating the document. For example, don't just write "relevant cases," and leave it at that. Look more closely. Is the writer providing detailed discussion of the cases, or just articulating rules or legal conclusions and citing to authority? Is the writer discussing the law generally without citing to any authority? Is the writer addressing both sides of the issues, only the winning side, or only the client's side? Is the writer providing hypothetical examples? What methods does the writer use to give the reader confidence in the substance?

Try putting yourself in the role of the supposed reader of this document. Does it give you all of the information that you think you would need? Notice when you feel lost or confused, or when you don't understand why certain information is or is not included.

Finally, if at all possible, review multiple samples. Doing so will allow you to notice what categories of information appear in all of the samples, and what categories come and go depending on reader needs or changes in the types of issues being addressed. If you are lucky enough to review strong and weak samples, you might be able to identify which categories of information are absolutely necessary, and which methods of providing information are unhelpful or confusing. Empathy for the reader is one of your most useful tools as a writer. By putting yourself in the role of unfamiliar reader, you can use your knowledge of legal writing and of the law to identify what needs to be included in the best documents of this type.

15.4.　EVALUATE THE ANNOTATIONS IN LIGHT OF YOUR CURRENT NEEDS

Once you have finished annotating the document, evaluate your annotations with your reader's needs in mind. Pay particular attention to ways in which you might want to depart from the specifics in the sample. If you were reviewing a sample exam, for instance, you might read analysis where there was no discussion of exceptions to a rule. But that one sample shouldn't tell you that exam answers should never include exceptions. The writer might not have included exceptions because that professor directed students to ignore irrelevant exceptions or to ignore all exceptions. On the other hand, maybe that particular rule did not have exceptions.

In other words, ask yourself if your document might need you to include information or reader signals that were not in the samples, either because there are wrinkles in your case that did not exist in the sample, or because the writer of that sample didn't understand reader needs the way you do. Likewise, it might be appropriate to omit certain aspects of the sample document if your case does not have the same wrinkles that existed in the sample case. When in doubt, consider treating any irrelevant facets of the sample as a "tell" issue. In the exam scenario, for instance, you might decide to include a sentence that says, "there are two exceptions to this rule, but neither is relevant here. *See Smith v. Beazley*, 101 P.3d 101, 110 (Nev. 2022) (discussing exceptions for frogs and toads)." Consider what the reader needs and expects, and what your case demands.

And of course, go beyond substantive concerns. Do the samples provide sufficient context? Could you add an introduction, recitals, or some other section that would do so? Would a reader be able to navigate the document? Can or should you add headings? If the sample included headings, are they substantive enough? Should they be more argumentative? If there is a particularly crucial piece of information that you want the reader to find, could you add a section, or use another method to highlight that information? If the document contains significant amounts of boilerplate, can you isolate or otherwise highlight the unique information to make it easier for a busy reader to find?

Be sure to consider document design when evaluating navigation concerns. Does the document use alignment and white space to make crucial information easy to find and irrelevant information easy to ignore? For example, as noted in Chapter Three, conventions require that a motion memo articulate the standard of review for that motion; labeling it with an explicit heading allows the reader to skip that information unless it is needed.

15.5. CONSULT WITH A MENTOR IF POSSIBLE

By now, you should have sketched out a tentative general outline (based on your annotations), and a specific outline (based on the needs of your case). If you have a mentor to talk to (especially the mentor who assigned the project), take a few minutes to get input on your outline and tentative plans for the document. If possible, ask if you can review the completed document with your mentor.

15.6. WRITE THE DOCUMENT

In this step, write the document. There's not much more to say here, but we recommend including sidebars noting any questions that you have while writing. These questions will help focus your revision and any conversation with your mentor.

15.7. REVIEW THE DOCUMENT

Review the document with the reader's needs in mind. Does the document provide appropriate substance? Does the writing follow the guidelines in Chapters Nine and Fourteen to promote easy comprehension? Where have you provided context? Does the context accurately foreshadow the content? Do the headings and document design allow for easy navigation within the document? Does the document follow the formal or informal rules of the relevant court? If possible, consult with your mentor again at this stage to get feedback.

15.8. CONCLUSION

Well, that's it. You can write anything now with the confidence that your writing will help your clients to achieve their goals. Congratulations!